LEGISLATIVE LIAISON

AMERICAN POLITICS RESEARCH SERIES

LEGISLATIVE LIAISON

Executive Leadership in Congress

ABRAHAM HOLTZMAN

NORTH CAROLINA STATE UNIVERSITY

RAND McNALLY & COMPANY • Chicago

AMERICAN POLITICS RESEARCH SERIES

Aaron Wildavsky, Series Editor

STEINER, *Social Insecurity: The Politics of Welfare*

DYE, *Politics, Economics, and the Public: Policy Outcomes in the American States*

SCHLESINGER, *Ambition and Politics: Political Careers in the United States*

BARBER, JAMES DAVID, *Power in Committees: An Experiment in the Governmental Process*

FRANCIS, *Legislative Issues in the Fifty States: A Comparative Analysis*

SHARKANSKY, *Spending in the American States*

KEECH, *The Impact of Negro Voting: The Role of the Vote in the Quest for Equality*

CRECINE, *Governmental Problem-Solving: A Computer Simulation of Municipal Budgeting*

DAVIS AND WEINBAUM, *Metropolitan Decision Processes: An Analysis of Case Studies*

ALFORD, *Bureaucracy and Participation: Political Cultures in Four Wisconsin Cities*

JACOB, *Debtors in Court: The Consumption of Government Services*

LIPSKY, *Protest in City Politics: Rent Strikes, Housing, and the Power of the Poor*

DEVINE, *The Attentive Public: Polyarchical Democracy*

HOLTZMAN, *Legislative Liaison: Executive Leadership in the Congress*

BARBER, JAMES ALDEN, JR., *Social Mobility and Voting Behavior*

To
Adam, Seth, Joshua, and Sylvia
for their patience, understanding, and assistance

PREFACE

THIS BOOK is a study in leadership which focuses upon one set of actors—legislative liaison agents—associated with the executive leaders of the national government and responsible for implementing their programs in the Congress. Since the research was undertaken in 1962–63 and the liaison agents were members of the Kennedy Administration, the study pertains principally to that administration. An effort was also made to contact White House and departmental liaison agents in the Eisenhower and Truman Administrations so that the data and conclusions might be relevant to executive leadership and executive-legislative relations regardless of administration. Legislative liaison in eight of the ten departments of the Kennedy Administration was studied. Post Office and Judiciary were omitted, since neither had an extensive program of legislation before the Congress in 1962–63 and the officers conducting legislative liaison for these departments also carried other major responsibilities.

An assumption underlying the research is that the executive branch of the national government may profitably be viewed as a political system with its own leaders and members, its own rules and behavior, its own boundaries and needs. The executive system must be seen, moreover, as being composed of two principal sets of actors—the politically responsible leaders, together with their associates and staff, and the career administrators or the bureaucracy. Congress may also be conceptualized as a separate system. The liaison officers of the executive departments and the White House are one set of linkages between these two systems.

The study concentrates upon one level of the executive system, one aspect of executive leadership, and one set of relations between the executive and legislative systems. Other important aspects of executive-legislative relations exist and deserve to be studied; they are not, however, the concern of this book.

The liaison agents are considered also within the context of the interest group–lobbyist approach to the Congress. An attempt is made to fit the findings of this study into the more general theory and data and to contribute to conclusions already reached in this area.

Methodologically this study is based almost entirely upon interview data obtained personally by the author. Through the cooperation of key actors in the executive and legislative systems, interviews were obtained with all the liaison agents, their executive leaders and associates, bureaucrats, legislators and staffs, and the lobbyists who dealt with these individuals. Unfortunately, there was little in the way of documentation with which to examine the interrelation of these actors. Moreover, an observer's role was not appropriate. When legislators and executive agents interact on policy or process, an observer who is a stranger to one of the parties is clearly an unwelcome restraint upon confidential relations. This I learned very quickly.

The interview technique has its limitations, but once proper rapport has been established between interviewer and interviewee, this method is capable of producing extremely valuable data. A disadvantage is that most of the data were given off the record and could not be attributed publicly to the source. Consequently, the major body of data in this book is not identified with any recognizable individual or department. The researcher must always be careful about relying unduly upon the assessments and interpretations of any respondent. One corrective is to interview in depth enough actors of the same type and to interview those who are involved in transactions with the principals under study. All the liaison officers in the White House and in the eight departments as well as three agencies were interviewed, as were members of their staffs. Interviews were also conducted with other executive actors in the departments, lobbyists for groups outside the national government, and liaison agents from previous administrations.

A final word about methodology: I followed the practice of taking extensive notes during each interview and reviewing them immediately thereafter to ensure their completeness. None of the respondents objected or seemed inhibited by this approach. The quotations used in the text, therefore, are as reasonably accurate as possible.

The Social Science Research Council generously supported this project, freeing me from teaching responsibilities during 1962–63. It is impossible to express adequately my thanks to the many Washingtonians who aided me; indeed, most insisted that they remain anonymous. A few must be afforded public recognition, for without their cooperation from the beginning, the doors of the executive system would never have been opened to me: Congressman Richard Bolling, Henry Hall Wilson, Lawrence F. O'Brien, Kenneth M. Birkhead, and Wilbur J. Cohen. All the liaison officers in the Kennedy Administration were most cooperative, speaking very frankly on extremely sensitive subjects and arranging their schedules so that each could be interviewed in depth over a number of sessions. And they willingly called others in order to secure me the proper entrée. Bryce N. Harlow proved exceptionally helpful in discussing legislative liaison during the Eisenhower Administration and in providing entrée to Republican congressmen and former legislative liaison agents.

I owe a note of thanks to Professor Aaron Wildavsky, my editor, and to Lawrence J. Malley and Mrs. Lolly Schwartz of Rand McNally for their assistance with the manuscript. Dr. John J. Corson afforded me the opportunity to participate in a conference on legislative liaison in the Johnson Administration sponsored by the Woodrow Wilson School of Public and International Affairs at Princeton University in 1965. Professors Lewis A. Dexter and Richard F. Fenno, Jr., permitted me to examine data from their own interviews with legislative and executive actors. Richard L. Engstrom permitted me to read his research paper on the liaison office in the Commerce Department, and Professor David M. Olson his paper on the Kennedy Administration's liaison with Congress. And my close friends and department chairmen Professors Preston W. Edsall and William J. Block made the necessary administrative arrangements to facilitate the research and writing. Mrs. Sally Parrish and Mrs. Alois Chalmers performed admirably as the principal typists.

This book would never have been written but for the encouragement and editorial assistance of my wife. Her interest, criticism, and hard work undergird the entire study. She and many others have contributed to this study, but I alone am responsible for any faults or errors it may contain.

ABRAHAM HOLTZMAN

CONTENTS

LIST OF TABLES

I want to be especially sure that each of you selects a top man to serve as your legislative liaison. Next to the Cabinet officer himself, I consider this the most important position in the department.

—*President Lyndon B. Johnson*
to the members of his Cabinet,
November 19, 1964

CHAPTER I

Strengthening the Executive
for Congressional Relations

A NEW SET of political actors has emerged in the national government: the legislative liaison or congressional relations officers of the executive system. As executive actors their purpose is to facilitate the operation of the administration within the Congress. At a minimum this involves the traditional liaison roles of maintaining good relations and communications with the Congress. At the maximum, however, their function is to help secure or inhibit congressional action that the White House and the departments deem vital to their self-interest. In this respect they are executive lobbyists responsible for aiding their political superiors to achieve their goals within the legislative system.

Lobbying on the part of the executive is not new. Presidents, departmental secretaries, and bureau heads have traditionally had a major stake in influencing the legislative climate and congressional behavior. What is new and of particular significance is (*a*) the increasing importance and recognition afforded legislative liaison as a special aspect of executive leadership and (*b*) the shifting of responsibility for liaison from a diffuse and diverse set of actors to a particular set of actors. Unlike those who formerly undertook liaison roles, the new actors operate at the highest political levels of the departments and the White House, and their primary concern is with the Congress. At the same time they provide their leaders with an effective means for exercising greater control over policy and relations with Congress as these pertain to their parts of the executive system.

The sharp differentiation in roles and actors has occurred in a relatively short and recent period of time; so recent, in fact, that one of the noteworthy characteristics of the Kennedy Administration, 1961–63, was the expansion and refinement of the legislative liaison network as a key element in executive relations with the Congress.

Undergirding this study of legislative liaison agents is the premise that the national executive may properly be conceptualized as a distinct political system with its own boundaries, leaders, etc. While the emphasis is primarily upon the dynamics of executive leadership, in a broader sense the subject of this study is also the relationship between two interdependent and often conflicting systems—the executive and the legislative.

As executive agents engaged in crossing the boundaries between the two systems, legislative liaison officers afford the social scientist an excellent vantage point for assessing important facets of intersystem relationships involving administration and Congress. The primary importance of these liaison officers is, of course, their contribution to the effectiveness of the politically responsible executive leaders in their dealings with the Congress. Consequently, attention is devoted initially to the emergence of legislative liaison agents as special actors in the executive system.

TRADITIONAL EXECUTIVE-LEGISLATIVE RELATIONS: THE BUREAU AS THE NEXUS OF POWER

The distinguishing characteristic of traditional executive-legislative relations was the pivotal role of the bureaucracy rather than that of the political leaders who were responsible for the executive departments. In the 1920s only the military departments and the Veterans' Bureau had established at their top level anything approaching a full-scale staff concerned with congressional liaison.[1] As for the remainder of the departments and agencies, it was the bureaus that generally assumed responsibility for the development and promotion of legislation. This practice, often encouraged by members of the legislative system, fostered a dispersion of executive energy, emphasized the special interests of administrative units rather than those of the departments, and catered to Congress' desire to keep a political finger in the executive pie.

A Hoover Commission task force in 1949 pointed up this paradox in which the politically responsible department secretary was in effect supplanted by his own bureau chiefs in his relations with the Congress. Bureau chiefs, concluded the Task Force on Departmental Management,

[1] See Richard E. Neustadt, "Presidential Clearance of Legislation" (unpublished Ph.D. dissertation, Columbia University, 1950), p. 309.

had built closer connections with the legislative committees than had department heads.[2] In a supplemental report, "Departmental Management in Practice," Dr. John D. Millett, a member of the task force, spelled out a more damning indictment.[3]

The department head, Millett asserted, was not traditionally the official and controlling point of contact between the legislative and administrative units. Consequently, his authority tended to be undermined and reduced by the direct relationship between bureau chiefs and congressional committees. Department heads suffered, moreover, from a lack of continuing political support from Congress. Not only did they often encounter more hostility than support in Congress, but some departments found it impossible to present a department-wide program or point of view that would attract congressional favor. A crucial factor here, argued Millett, was the absence of organized interest-group support for the departmental point of view. This in itself deprived the departmental leadership of extensive support in the Congress, which it needed for the advancement of its proposals.

An identical set of conclusions was drawn by an insider in the administration at the time. From the perspective of his experience in the Bureau of the Budget and in the White House, Richard E. Neustadt concluded in 1950 that departmental leaders simply did not meet the standards necessary for effective campaigning on behalf of major legislative proposals.[4] The bureaus, he explained, maintained supplemental channels of their own with Congress. These channels were usually older and often better established than those of the departments, and they sometimes overshadowed those of the departments. In "holding company" (confederate-type) departments, individual bureau chiefs were more likely to meet the requisite standards for political action in the Congress. They also tended to engage in productive campaigning more frequently than could usually be done at the departmental level. Neustadt found the principal exception to this practice to exist in the State Department, and then only under very special circumstances.

As late as 1955, when special departmental legislative liaison had become somewhat more widespread, J. Leiper Freeman's study *The Political Process: Executive Bureau–Legislative Committee Relations* found in bureau relations the key locus of executive influence and policy decisions in the Congress.[5] Freeman did note that "increasingly, at-

---

[2] The Commission on Organization of the Executive Branch of the Government, *Task Force Report on Departmental Management* (Washington, D.C.: U.S. Government Printing Office, January 1949), pt. 1.

[3] *Ibid.*, pt. 2, pp. 34–35.

[4] Neustadt, *op. cit.*, pp. 318–23.

[5] J. Leiper Freeman, *The Political Process: Executive Bureau–Legislative Committee Relations* (New York: Random House, 1955).

tempts of bureau heads to influence committee members are being routinized through provision in the departmental organizational structure for specialists in legislative liaison."[6] But, as he evaluated this liaison operation, it was primarily important as a communications device on day-to-day matters, and it was most effective in dealing with the extensive number of routine requests that came to Congress and which members referred to the executive for explanation and expeditious handling.

Freeman published his monograph in the third year of the first Eisenhower Administration. An examination of the *U.S. Government Organization Manual* for 1955 reveals that three of the ten departments had special legislative liaison staffs operating at the departmental level: Defense, State, and Health, Education, and Welfare (HEW). The *Manual* also disclosed that the executive assistant to the Postmaster General had been given the additional responsibility of maintaining liaison between the Postmaster General and Congress. In Commerce, as of 1954, the deputy general counsel had been designated the liaison officer for the department. Hence by 1955 two additional departments had officially recognized the importance of legislative liaison at the secretarial level. But responsibility for this function was delegated to staff officers who held other primary duties. Indeed, the same was actually true for Defense, where a new Assistant Secretary of Defense was responsible for public affairs as well as legislation. During 1955 a special officer for legislative liaison was also appointed for the first time in the office of the Secretary of Agriculture, a change that failed to show up in any issue of the *Manual*.[7]

By the third year of the Kennedy Administration, 1963, each of the ten departments had assigned a departmental-level priority to legislative liaison. And in all but two, Post Office and Justice, these staffs were concerned solely with congressional relations on a full-time basis.

INITIAL STEPS IN STRENGTHENING EXECUTIVE RELATIONSHIPS WITH CONGRESS

The creation of special departmental legislative liaison staffs preceded both the Kennedy and the Eisenhower Administrations. So, too, do the politico-historical roots of this new staff concept. The shift of

[6] *Ibid.,* p. 63.
[7] See Carl R. Sapp, "Legislative Reporting in the United States Department of Agriculture" (unpublished master's thesis, American University, 1962), p. 4. In 1955 the department denied to the Congress that it had a congressional liaison unit. It was afraid to do so, a key bureaucrat who asked to remain anonymous asserted in 1961. He had been closely associated with Agriculture's legislative liaison agents during the Eisenhower Administration.

initiative from the Congress to the President and the tremendous growth and political importance of the national bureaucracy have been explored elsewhere.[8] What is called for at this point is the highlighting of some of the critical steps in the changing relationship between the Congress and the presidency and the modifications occurring in the executive approach to the legislative system. Specifically, legislative liaison must be recognized as a developmental step in the strengthening of the presidency and the political leadership of the executive system as a whole.

While Woodrow Wilson helped reestablish the image of strong presidential leadership in Congress, it was the Budget and Accounting Act of 1921 that marked a decisive change in executive-legislative relations. This act formally shifted the initiative for developing the fiscal and legislative program of the national government from the legislature to the presidency. Henceforth, Congress operated basically within the confines of a plan conceived and proposed by the chief executive. Secondly, the President was provided with a special staff to carry out this function. Created in 1921 and shifted in 1939 to the Executive Office of the President, the Bureau of the Budget developed into the President's largest and most influential staff agency.

An integrated budget, which was presented to Congress as the President's own, inevitably required greater White House control over the departments, and this in turn brought the bureaus under greater supervision and control by the secretaries of the departments. Since departmental budgetary proposals had to be justified to the Budget Bureau of the President, bureau proposals had to be considered and evaluated from a departmental point of view. Special staffs, authorized initially by the Budget and Accounting Act of 1921, emerged at the secretarial level to cope with this task. In addition to operating as a central agency, the Budget Bureau served also as the President's principal tool for improving management throughout the executive. Budgetary planning and management control from the Office of the President introduced pressures upon the political superiors of the departments for the greater coordination and control of their departments.

In the substantive area of legislation, the initiative also passed in-

[8] See, for example, Neustadt, *op. cit.;* Paul H. Appleby, *Big Democracy* (New York: Knopf, 1945); Wilfred E. Binkley, *The Man in the White House: His Powers and Duties,* rev. ed. (New York: Harper & Row, 1964), chaps. 7 and 8; Lawrence H. Chamberlain, *The President, Congress, and Legislation* (New York: Columbia University Press, 1946); Edward C. Corwin, *The President, Office and Powers, 1787–1957* (New York: New York University Press, 1957), chap. 7; Clinton L. Rossiter, *The American Presidency,* 2nd ed. (New York: Harcourt, Brace & World, 1960); David B. Truman, *The Congressional Party: A Case Study* (New York: Wiley, 1959), pp. 1–10, 317–19; Peter Woll, *American Bureaucracy,* 1st ed. (New York: Norton, 1963).

creasingly to the chief executive, and not without the cooperation and compliance of the Congress. At least three factors especially relevant to the emergence of special legislative liaison actors were influential in effecting this process: (*a*) the development of a central legislative clearance and coordinating staff in the Executive Office of the President and its link with the new concept of a presidential legislative program; (*b*) the tremendous expansion and complexity of legislation, which imposed a considerable burden upon the ability of Congress to cope with its primary responsibility; and (*c*) the promotional activities of the new governmental agencies, created initially by the Roosevelt Administration and expanded as a result of the war and postwar crises.[9]

The Bureau of the Budget and Legislative Clearance

The role played by the Budget Bureau in the clearance of administration bills, agency proposals, and departmental reports to Congress moved the Bureau into a strategic position between the executive departments and Congress. Consequently departmental leaders were placed under increasing political pressure from the White House. Responsible for advancing their departments' legislative program within the context of the President's, they were confronted in their own bailiwicks with well-established, traditional bureau-congressional relations, which were not necessarily receptive to White House or departmental priorities. The secretaries of the departments found it imperative, therefore, to establish their own staffs, first for legislative programming (the conceptualization and development of legislative proposals) and finally for legislative liaison.

Only in 1939, when the Budget Bureau was transferred from the Treasury to the Executive Office of the President, did the substantive side of legislation begin to receive the staff attention previously devoted to expenditure policies.[10] By presidential order the bureau was given the specific duty to "assist the President by clearing and coordinating departmental advice on proposed legislation, and by making recommendations as to presidential action on legislative enactments in accordance with past practice."[11] During the war years the responsibility for legislative clearance was divided among the White House staff, the Budget Bureau, and the Office of War Mobilization and Reconversion.

[9] Of course, the personality, program, and tactics of F.D.R. were also of primary importance.

[10] See testimony by Roger W. Jones, Assistant Director for Legislative Reference, Bureau of the Budget, in U.S. House of Representatives, Select Committee on Lobbying Activities, *Hearings on Legislative Activities of Executive Agencies*, 81st Cong., 2nd sess. (Washington, D.C.: U.S. Government Printing Office, 1950), pt. 10, p. 8.

[11] *Ibid.,* p. 8.

Under President Harry S. Truman the entire operation was pulled back into the Bureau of the Budget.

In 1947 executive coordination and clearance of legislation acquired a new dimension. At the request of the President, the Budget Bureau assumed responsibility for what was formally called "the President's legislative program."[12] According to Roger W. Jones, under whose leadership the Bureau's Division of Legislative Reference carved out a creative role in this new area, this action was precipitated by the passage of the Employment Act of 1946.[13] With its enactment the President now delivered three major messages to Congress at the beginning of each session: the state-of-the-union message, the budget message, and an economic report. Consequently, the legislative proposals desired by the departments had to be coordinated with the program of the President so that the administration could present a unified approach to the Congress and the country. Departments and agencies were required to submit to the Bureau of the Budget all drafts of legislation which they themselves originated, all reports they made on legislation as requested by the committees and by individual congressmen, and even, on very important matters, copies of formal statements of testimony, so that the bureau could determine their relationship to the President's program.

Expansion and Complexity of Legislation: Congress Turns to the Executive

Congress itself turned increasingly to the executive for assistance in the face of the volume, complexity, and range of legislation confronting it. The Employment Act of 1946 constituted another shift of power and initiative to the executive, a culmination of the New Deal and wartime trends. As Roger W. Jones gently reminded members of a congressional investigating committee who questioned the propriety of the increased executive role in legislation, it was the Congress that was calling more and more upon executive agencies for assistance. In the Seventy-ninth, Eightieth, and Eighty-first Congresses, he pointed out, "We have seen many, many cases, *and an increasing number of cases,* in which a committee of the Congress has asked for specific drafting help from the executive agencies."[14] Congressional committees had even asked execu-

---

[12] *Ibid.,* p. 9.

[13] *Ibid.*

[14] *Ibid.,* p. 15 [italics added]. See also Sapp, *op. cit.,* pp. 18–19. "In earlier generations the Congress was sensitive about receiving legislative language from the executive departments. There was a feeling that the legislative drafting should be done by congressional staffs rather than by the executive agencies. In recent years there has been more of a tendency for the executive agencies to submit language with their recommendations. In some cases the departments have received congressional criticisms for not doing so."

tive agencies on many occasions to appoint "someone who is really more than a technical adviser on matters before them." And in other cases, Congress had requested that agencies open offices for formal liaison in the legislative office buildings "to which members could go for information, advice or help in terms of a member's attitude toward a measure, whether he wants to support it or oppose it."[15] These contacts were with the departments and agencies, it should be noted, not through the Bureau of the Budget.

Congress turned increasingly to the departments, moreover, for their comments upon legislative proposals before the committees. In fact, the legislative party leadership also availed itself of the new central executive coordinating machinery in the Bureau of the Budget. Neustadt wrote that in the Eighty-first Congress the Senate Majority Policy Committee as well as the House leadership turned to the Bureau of the Budget for direct reports on the administration's position regarding pending legislation.[16] And the House Rules Committee made it a practice of checking directly with the Bureau on bills that came before it.

Promotional Activities by Executive Agencies

At a time when individual members and the entire legislative system became increasingly dependent upon the executive for technical aid and political guidance on legislation, administrative agencies became more aggressive in advancing their proposals in Congress. Neustadt underlined the "increasing initiative in legislation on the part of the expanding promotional agencies" in his study of legislative clearance and the Bureau of the Budget in 1950.[17]

A key staff member of the House Appropriations Committee, looking back in 1963 upon the growth of executive lobbying since he first came to Congress in the 1920s, noted a significant change in the nature of executive contacts with the House.[18] Initially, as he recalled it, the Pensions Office and then the Civil Service Commission set up contact offices in the House Office Building, but merely to answer inquiries regarding claims and jobs. Congressmen wanted this service so as to respond more helpfully and promptly to the increasing number of inquiries from constituents. However, these contact offices had nothing to

[15] *Hearings on Legislative Activities of Executive Agencies*, p. 16.
[16] Neustadt, *op. cit.*, p. 122. See also Richard E. Neustadt, "Presidency and Legislation: The Growth of Central Clearance," *American Political Science Review*, 48 (September 1954): 661–62.
[17] Neustadt, "Presidential Clearance of Legislation," p. 309.
[18] Interview with author in 1963.

do with legislation; they did not push for the success or failure of legislative proposals.

During World War II the services also placed their liaison offices on the Hill, as did the War Production Board and other agencies. And in the postwar period a shift occurred, he observed. "They [the executive] had a lot of people who saw a chance to promote the interests of their departments; they were doing favors and maybe the congressmen could help them. So we observed a move from contact work to a major lobbying establishment."

From this staff member's perspective, the executive had capitalized upon the increasing services and favors it afforded House members as a consequence of the increased role of government in general and the executive in particular. The executive had transformed a more or less routine information-contact relationship into an executive lobbying operation. Within the context of the budget-appropriations process, this staff man could recall when departmental legislative liaison officers first began to intrude into the special relations that his committee had established with departmental budget officers and bureau heads.

LEGISLATIVE LIAISON: THIRD STEP IN STRENGTHENING EXECUTIVE RELATIONS WITH THE CONGRESS

Legislative liaison emerged in the executive system as the third step in the reshaping of the political leadership at the departmental level and at the level of the White House vis-à-vis the Congress. The initial move in this direction had been the establishment of budgetary controls at the departmental level under the impact of the Budget and Accounting Act and in response to the guidance of the Budget Bureau in the Office of the President. Acceptance of the concept of legislative programming at the White House and the secretarial levels and the strengthening of the office of the general counsel or solicitor within the departments represented a second step. It was, in fact, from within the general counsel's office that legislative liaison subsequently developed in a number of departments as a separate responsibility of leadership requiring a special staff.

Legislative Clearance and the Office of the General Counsel: Half Step Toward Special Legislative Liaison

Neustadt has pointed out that "the development of legislative clearance within departments has followed and paralleled the development of departmental budgeting."[19] He referred to the growth of a central presi-

---

[19] Neustadt, "Presidential Clearance of Legislation," p. 308.

dential clearance process as having had the same effect as a set of external pressures on the departments for increased leadership and control on the part of the secretaries.

When the departments first undertook to control their legislative programs, it was almost inevitable that the office of the solicitor or general counsel would prove to be the focal point for this effort. The legal staff was more skilled in drafting legislation than any other at the secretarial level. It was also responsible for determining legislative intent. Furthermore, these lawyers frequently worked with individual congressmen and their committees to ensure that the technical language appropriately fitted the political compromises and arrangements that were agreed upon.

Since legislative programming was assigned to the legal assistant to the departmental secretary, he was also given responsibility for legislative liaison when this concept began to win acceptance as properly residing under the secretary's jurisdiction. Additional internal and external forces coincided to reinforce this trend. Some department heads refused to establish special staffs of the stature and competence necessary to carry out the delicate job of legislative liaison. The fear that this might weaken their relations with the Congress was the underlying reason for their inaction. Neustadt pointed out that two successive secretaries of one of the largest departments had refused to create a high-level legislative liaison staff because "to do so would place in the hands of staff the relationships and trading stock on which the Secretary had to base his personal initiative and role in the process of policy and program-making."[20]

Of equal if not greater importance in channeling legislative liaison to the legal officer of the departments was the special role of the counsel in the White House. Legislative programming developed initially during President Truman's administration. Both Clark M. Clifford and Charles S. Murphy, who served as counsels to the President, played a major part in White House relations with Congress regarding legislation. In 1949 President Truman did appoint, for the first time in the history of the White House, two staff members to serve solely as legislative assistants. But in view of the personal role that Truman assumed in undertaking much of his own liaison with the Congress, the stature of the counsel to the President, and the rather low-level political status and experience of the legislative assistants, the latter never acquired the significance in the Truman White House that characterized their successors in the Eisenhower and Kennedy Administrations.

[20] *Ibid.,* p. 322.

With a few notable exceptions—State, Agriculture, HEW—legislative liaison initially developed, therefore, out of the offices of the departments' general counsels or solicitors. In 1963 the last of the executive departments finally transferred legislative liaison from the general counsel's office. Commerce had since 1954 designated its deputy general counsel to act as the department's congressional liaison officer. However, in 1963 the Secretary of Commerce decided to employ a special staff assistant with no other responsibility than that of legislative liaison. During the Eisenhower Administration the Department of Interior, which had also never established a separate liaison operation, entrusted legislative liaison to its solicitor's office. Only in 1962 was a special assistant to the Secretary, with a staff of his own, assigned to concentrate solely on congressional relations.

In the Housing and Home Finance Agency (HHFA), however, the agency in the national executive most closely approximating a department, the general counsel in 1963 continued to act for the administrator as his chief deputy on legislation and relations with Congress. While this agency had a congressional relations officer, he was never permitted to assume major responsibility for legislation or to serve as the administrator's close adviser and representative on important matters of legislative strategy and tactics.

The First Hoover Commission Endorses Legislative Liaison

Acceptance of the concept of legislative liaison as a unique aspect of executive leadership was encouraged by the recommendations of the first Hoover Commission.[21] In its final report as well as in the reports of a number of its task forces, the Hoover Commission not only endorsed legislative liaison as a responsibility of the secretaries of the departments, but sought to institutionalize its operations. In view of the stature of its membership and the high-level bipartisan political support it received, the Hoover Commission's recommendations can be credited with accelerating the acceptance and extension of legislative liaison that had already appeared at the secretarial staff level in a few of the departments before 1949.

Three Hoover Commission task forces presented different approaches to legislative liaison with the same end in view—strengthening

[21] Two years earlier Senator Estes Kefauver (D., Tenn.) had proposed establishing liaison officers at a near Cabinet rank, possibly as assistant secretaries in the departments and as deputy administrators for congressional relations in the major agencies (Estes Kefauver and Jack Levin, *A Twentieth-Century Congress* [New York: Duell, Sloan & Pierce, 1947], p. 150). Recommended also was the quartering of liaison officers from all departments and major agencies on Capitol Hill (*ibid.,* p. 149).

the political and administrative leadership positions of the department heads. The important Task Force on Departmental Management deemed it necessary to include a proposal on departmental legislative liaison, which, however, was phrased in rather general terms: "Departmental management must give increased attention to legislative liaison."[22] The authors pointed out that department heads were major links of communication between the chief executive and the Congress. It was they who had to present and defend the details of the President's program before Congress. They had to concern themselves with legislative liaison, since Congress conceived of one of its major roles as inquiring into the conduct of their departments. And the legislators served also as channels through which public criticism of executive agencies was brought to the attention of their administrators.

The *Task Force Report on National Security Organization* strongly endorsed control by the Secretary of Defense over the military departments. To this end the task force concluded that the secretary needed in his own office, under his own authority and direction, organizational units to unify policies on legislative matters throughout the military.[23] The method by which this control was to be exercised was to be left to his discretion.

The *Task Force Report on Foreign Affairs* revealed that the significance of legislative liaison for executive leadership had been grasped fully for the first time.[24] In addition to establishing good communications in order to prevent misunderstandings between the department and Congress, and to keep Congress aware of what was involved in foreign policy, proper legislative liaison was conceived of as including the delicate job of affecting the considerations and decisions of legislators.

As distinct from the rest of the executive, State had a long tradition of legislative liaison at the department-head level. At various times in the past, responsibility had been entrusted by the secretary to different aides—an assistant secretary, the head of the Consular Service, the counselor of the department, and in the 1940s to an Assistant Secretary for Congressional Relations. At the time of the Hoover report, however, and since 1947, legislative liaison had been assigned to a senior career officer with other high-level responsibilities of a critical nature. This arrangement had engendered extreme criticism both in and out of Congress at

[22] *Task Force Report on Departmental Management,* pt. 1, p. 15.

[23] The Commission on Organization of the Executive Branch of the Government, *Task Force Report on National Security Organization* (Washington, D.C.: U.S. Government Printing Office, January 1949), pp. 13–14.

[24] The Commission on Organization of the Executive Branch of the Government, *Task Force Report on Foreign Affairs* (Washington, D.C.: U.S. Government Printing Office, January 1949), pp. 32, 125–34.

the very time when State's relations with Congress had deteriorated precipitously.

The task force reporting on the organization of the government for the conduct of foreign affairs started with a more sweeping assumption than had the others in relating the position of the State Department to the Congress: "No problem confronting the United States in its foreign relations today is more crucial than the relationship between the Congress and the Executive Branch."[25] In order for the department to cope successfully with this problem, the task force assigned the highest priority to the establishment of proper legislative liaison and its institutionalization at the highest staff level in the secretary's office. The closest relationship was called for between legislative liaison and the making of public policy.

The comments in the *Task Force Report on Foreign Affairs* regarding legislative liaison are especially relevant in view of the subsequent recommendations advanced by the Hoover Commission as well as the then current practice in the national executive. First of all, the task force appears to have accepted the thesis that legislative liaison was not a part-time duty that could be shunted off on existing staff. Recommendation 16 called for a coordinated program of congressional liaison under the supervision of an assistant secretary who had no other obligations. Equally significant was the task force's acceptance of the premise that legislative liaison was essentially political rather than bureaucratic in nature. State's public relations activities, which had just been raised in importance to the level of an assistant secretaryship in 1946, were frankly conceded to be aimed at exerting public pressure on Congress. Legislative liaison therefore had to be elevated to equal rank and coordinated with the public relations unit to improve State's position vis-à-vis Congress. It was further suggested that legislative liaison should preferably not be conducted by permanent career officers. The political world was basically alien to their experience, and many of them considered it highly undesirable to engage in politics. In other words, legislative liaison was essentially a nonbureaucratic responsibility, which should be assigned to a political type.

It is apparent from its own recommendations, however, that the Hoover Commission never fully grasped or accepted either the potential of legislative liaison or the political implications as embodied in the thinking of the Task Force on Foreign Affairs. An Assistant Secretary for Congressional Relations was proposed for the State Department,[26]

[25] *Ibid.*, p. 125.
[26] A study of the operations of this officer and his liaison office during the Eisenhower Administration was presented by James A. Robinson, *Congress and Foreign*

and the strengthening of the Office of the Secretary of Defense was recommended. With regard to the other departments, the Hoover Commission adopted the more limited approach of its Task Force on Departmental Management.

A congressional liaison officer was recommended as a necessary staff assistant for the head of each of the executive departments.[27] Instead of placing the liaison officer in an intimate relationship with the secretary and giving him equal importance with his other immediate staff assistants, the Hoover Commission's proposal placed him at least one level removed from the secretary and under the supervision of an administrative assistant secretary. This administrative assistant secretary should preferably be appointed, contended the Hoover Commission, to head up and coordinate staff officers with administrative duties. This was a far cry from the essentially political approach toward legislative liaison accepted by the Task Force on Foreign Affairs.

Political reality has a way of imposing its own dictates upon well-ordered administrative arrangements. Once the Hoover Commission had recommended the establishment of congressional liaison officers in all of the departments and major agencies, legislative liaison acquired a status of its own and a legitimacy that could no longer be denied. The inherently political nature of legislative liaison predominated in the end over the much more circumscribed thinking of the Hoover Commission. Not one of the departments adopted the general legislative liaison organizational pattern proposed by the Hoover Commission. The special congressional liaison officers who finally emerged were attached directly to the secretaries, as was the case in the Kennedy Administration, or placed under a political assistant secretary, which occurred in the Labor Department during a part of the Eisenhower Administration.

Development of Legislative Liaison in the White House

The full extension of the concept of institutionalizing legislative liaison at the highest political level in all the departments must be attributed to the organization of a special legislative liaison unit in the White House and the increasing importance assigned to it. Specific White House recognition and implementation of the legislative liaison function had the same impact upon departmental thinking and organization as

---

Policy-Making: A Study in Legislative Influence and Initiative, rev. ed. (Homewood, Ill.: Dorsey Press, 1967), chaps. 4 and 5.

[27] The Commission on Organization of the Executive Branch of the Government, *General Management of the Executive Branch: A Report to the Congress* (Washington, D.C.: U.S. Government Printing Office, February 1949), p. 38.

had the Bureau of the Budget earlier with regard to budgeting and legislative programming. Departmental secretaries discovered that they and their staff assistants had to deal with this special unit in the White House with regard to the fate of their legislation in the Congress and in response to White House decisions about legislative priorities, strategies, and tactics.

Prior to the establishment of a special White House liaison staff, responsibility for liaison with Congress was neither clearly defined nor assigned within the Office of the President. In fact, two former senior members of the Executive Office of the President contend that before 1939 the chief liaison officer for the President was actually a member of the departmental political executive. John R. Steelman and H. Dewayne Kreager have written that up to that time, whoever filled the post of Under Secretary of Interior "filled the full-time role of the President's chief liaison officer with the Congress."[28] Nevertheless, under Franklin D. Roosevelt various departmental secretaries and presidential staff aides did assume the initiative for pieces of legislation as they were assigned to them by the President or as the secretaries and aides themselves took an interest in the passage of specific bills. This was true even under Truman, although the counsel to the President played a greater role in legislation. Commencing in 1949, two special staff aides to the President were designated legislative assistants responsible for liaison with the Congress.

In the late 1940s Neustadt had conceived of the Budget Bureau's Legislative Reference Division as undertaking an active role in all aspects of liaison. As he visualized it, legislative programming, which was the responsibility of this division, encompassed not only the development and shaping of proposed legislation, but also legislative liaison in the most creative sense—helping to make the necessary political adjustments to bills so as to enable them to win a majority vote and passage.[29] Sometimes, in fact, the officers of the Legislative Reference Division played this role; more often they were part of a team chaired by a White House representative. Despite the rather bold political role envisaged by Neustadt for the Legislative Reference Division, it was never fully realized. Instead the White House developed its own liaison organization, which was successively upgraded in importance under the Eisenhower and Kennedy Administrations.

Under the leadership of President Dwight D. Eisenhower, who was strongly disposed to a well-ordered organizational apparatus and to the

---

[28] John R. Steelman and H. Dewayne Kreager, "The Executive Office as Administrative Coordinator," *Law and Contemporary Problems,* 21 (Autumn 1956): 697.
[29] Neustadt, "Presidential Clearance of Legislation," pp. 144–48 *passim.*

staff concept, these informal and ad hoc arrangements were finally abandoned. For the first time a President of the United States publicly set up a congressional liaison unit with its own staff.[30] General Wilton B. Persons, a close friend of the President and a man with considerable experience in Congress as a former legislative liaison agent for the Army, was made Eisenhower's chief liaison agent for Congress. However, Sherman Adams, the functioning "assistant president," overshadowed everyone else within the White House staff. Bryce N. Harlow, who had served as one of Person's two immediate assistants, subsequently became the principal liaison agent when his predecessor moved up to fill Sherman Adams' position. A small number of assistants were assigned to the President's lobbyist in Congress.

With the advent of the Kennedy Administration, legislative liaison in the White House was elevated even higher in political importance. A close political intimate of the President, who had played a major role in Kennedy's campaigns to win the nomination and election, was designated Special Assistant for Congressional Relations and Personnel. Lawrence F. O'Brien held equal rank with the most important members of the White House staff, a position and status never before delegated to congressional liaison officers, not even under Eisenhower. Furthermore, O'Brien was provided with an enlarged staff of assistants to ensure that proper liaison was conducted with both the House and Senate as well as with the departments.

As the legislative liaison officers in the White House became one set of key staff aides to the chief executive, legislative liaison in the departments moved up accordingly. The White House unit in the Kennedy Administration sought to integrate the work of the departmental liaison units in developing an administration approach on items high on its list of legislative priorities. Within the departments legislative liaison officers became necessary and vital actors in their own departments' congressional relations. As integral elements in an expanded lobbying team, they represented a decided strengthening of the national executive in its relations with the Congress.

AN OVERVIEW

The activity of the liaison officers must be viewed as essentially a strengthening of the national political executive in its dealings with the

---

[30] Interview with Bryce N. Harlow, June 1963. See also Neil MacNeil, *Forge of Democracy: The House of Representatives* (New York: McKay, 1963), pp. 36, 254–55; MacNeil has mistakenly stated that Harlow was Eisenhower's chief lobbyist with Congress for eight years.

Congress. In order to understand more precisely how and why they operate, it is necessary first to examine the *sets of roles* available to them. Three groups of actors help define these roles: executive superiors and associates of the liaison officers, the legislators and their assistants, and the liaison agents themselves. Each of the following three chapters therefore focuses upon legislative liaison roles from the perspective of a different group of political actors. It is the departmental rather than the White House liaison agents who are the primary subjects under investigation.

In carrying out their roles, the legislative liaison agents engage in behavior that reflects their perceptions of the two systems in which they work, the resources available to them, and their particular relations with key executive and legislative actors. Chapters V through VIII examine these perceptions and behavior patterns with special reference to the problems, opportunities, and strategies of the departmental liaison officers in both systems. The special position of the White House liaison unit and its relationship with departmental staffs in affording an administration more integrated leadership vis-à-vis the Congress are developed separately. A concluding chapter assesses liaison officers within the broader context of executive leadership and political party as they pertain to executive-legislative relations. It also examines the differences and similarities between executive and other lobbyists who seek to influence the Congress, and considers the liaison agents in terms of certain problems inherent in the American democratic polity.

CHAPTER II

The Executive System Defines
Legislative Liaison Roles

LEGISLATIVE LIAISON AGENTS are essentially representatives of the executive system as well as actors within it. While the nature of their work requires them to concentrate upon and interact with members of the congressional system, it is in terms of their own system that their significance is largely defined. How legislative liaison is viewed by their fellow executive actors therefore largely determines these agents' scope of action and their value to the executive system. In effect, what is contended here is that the roles, functions, and significance of these special agents are shaped initially by the expectations of their immediate superiors and associates. The present chapter is based upon interviews with three sets of executive actors other than the liaison agents themselves: heads of departments and undersecretaries together with their personal assistants, assistant secretaries and other second-level political leaders, and assistants to the President who carried out legislative liaison from the White House. Since departmental liaison agents are responsible to these three groups of executive actors, bureau heads were for the most part not sampled.

LIAISON ROLES AS DEFINED BY CABINET MEMBERS, UNDERSECRETARIES, AND THEIR ASSISTANTS[1]

Three general views regarding departmental-congressional relations, which have significant implications for legislative liaison roles, emerged

[1] Interviews were conducted with a secretary from the Truman Administration and with four secretaries, three undersecretaries, and five personal or executive assistants to these senior leaders in the Departments of Agriculture, HEW, Interior, Labor, State, and Treasury in the Kennedy Administration.

as paramount in the thinking of senior political leaders. First, these leaders unanimously agreed and strongly asserted that within the department the secretary was almost invariably the most significant actor in dealing with the Congress and advancing the department's legislation. He was not merely the captain of the department, declared one secretary, but an integral part of the administration, and he was responsible for its legislative program. From the point of view of the department and the administration, "his personal capacities and relations on the Hill constitute the most important imperative" in congressional relations. A distinction was drawn by this secretary, and confirmed by others, between the effectiveness of the department head and all the other department actors in dealing with the legislative system. In another department the executive assistant to the secretary emphasized the primacy of the secretary in congressional relations in the following manner: "Only the secretary has the prestige to really cultivate the chairmen and other members, to have them in for lunch and supper at his home, to talk with them on the merits of our legislation, to hear objections and work out or approve compromises that are acceptable." The secretaries were characterized also as having better access to the majority party leadership in the Congress and to the White House than others in the department, and more influence with them. As a result, the nature of leadership exerted by the department head in congressional relations constitutes a very important variable affecting the roles of the legislative liaison officer.

Coexistent with this emphasis upon the secretary's primacy was a parallel view that *everyone* at the political leadership level was responsible for congressional relations. In the thinking of senior departmental political leaders, the liaison agent emerged as merely one among a number of actors properly interrelating with the Congress. "Legislative liaison is the responsibility of everyone in the secretary's office," pointed out Secretary of Agriculture Orville L. Freeman. "It is too important and there is too much to do to delegate it to any one person," contended Treasury Under Secretary Henry H. Fowler. "We must all shoulder the responsibility. We must be self-starters and not wait solely on the legislative liaison agent for action." A former Secretary of Labor, who had exerted vigorous leadership in dealing with Congress, noted that he had not confined his congressional relations to his liaison agent. He had assigned to one of his assistant secretaries responsibility for the department's minimum wage bill and he had used a group from within the bureaucracy to campaign for improved unemployment compensation legislation. "We all lobby," explained the executive assistant to the secretary in a fourth department. "The assistant secretaries and the secretary are very important in working with the Congress, and they are aided in these efforts by their own staffs." In the face of these attitudes, it is evident that all legislative liaison officers confront the problem of establishing appropriate relations with other executive actors who interrelate with Congress.

A third general perception expressed by the senior departmental political leaders was that legislative liaison agents had little or nothing to do with the appropriations committees of the Congress. "He has no roles to play there," stated one undersecretary. "It is a different and recognized procedure; there are not the same problems and needs as there are with authorization legislation." A former secretary who regretted this separation observed: "It is almost inevitable that the two are separate—that it is the administrative officers who get involved in appropriations." Although such career officers were also responsible to the secretary, for some reason this bifurcation evidently disturbed this former secretary: "I felt, as secretary, a little isolated from the appropriations process. If I had remained in office, my inclination was to move the legislative liaison agent more closely into the appropriations process."[2] The executive assistant to another secretary responded affirmatively when questioned as to the propriety of the legislative liaison officer's having a voice in this area, but he maintained that such involvement should be restricted to the executive system. His departmental agent sat in on budget review sessions and contributed advice, based upon his knowledge of the Congress, that helped change the department's approach to the appropriations committees. However, he did not interact directly with the members or staffs of these committees; this was primarily the responsibility of a career bureaucrat—the budget officer—as it was in other departments.

Within the parameters of the aforementioned conceptualization of departmental-legislative relations, however, liaison officers were viewed by their senior political leaders as carrying on important and essential functions. They were expected to perform a variety of roles vital to the conduct and success of the department and its political leadership. From the comments of these leaders it was evident that their liaison agents were expected to operate in two political systems, and indeed their roles, one set oriented toward the executive system and the other toward Congress, reflected these two foci. Neither set of roles was independent of the other; rather, they fed into each other, permitting the legislative liaison officers to operate more effectively in both.

[2] According to sources on the two Appropriations Committees in the Congress, a Secretary of Labor as well as the Secretary of Defense in the Kennedy Administration were rebuffed by these committees when they sought to move appropriations liaison closer to their special legislative liaison officers.

Executive-Oriented Roles

(A) ADVISER TO THE SECRETARY. With the exception of HEW, where the special legislative liaison officer was relegated to a secondary position because of the presence of an Assistant Secretary for Legislation and the preeminence of this individual during the Kennedy Administration, each legislative liaison officer in the departments studied was expected to act as an adviser to his secretary on congressional relations.[3] The liaison officer was not supposed to act as the department head's primary adviser on the substance of legislation, but rather as his principal adviser on congressional relations and the legislative process. It was fully recognized by senior departmental leaders, however, that the latter two areas clearly affected the substance of bills.

The following conceptualizations of the adviser role were expressed by Secretary of Agriculture Freeman and by former Secretary of Labor Arthur J. Goldberg:

He is my key adviser regarding Congress—what is happening in Congress and congressional relations, and what we should do about them. In policy meetings I expect him to recommend changes, if necessary, in proposed legislation and in our approaches in the Congress based upon his assessment of how such proposals and approaches would be received. [Freeman]

Legislation and congressional relations were among my primary concerns. I needed a specialist to give me the feel of what was going on and the problems we would encounter and were meeting. The Hill is a special institution, and a secretary is too busy with other tasks, many unrelated to Congress. Even if he is competent and aggressive himself regarding Congress, he does not have the time or complete specialization to do the day-to-day job. He needs someone to rely upon. [Goldberg]

A senior State Department official, who worked closely with Secretary Dean Rusk, noted that the latter looked to his Assistant Secretary for Congressional Relations for aid and advice, but purely on political matters: how to do it, whom to see, what the prospects were, what had to be done to get votes. Assistant Secretary Frederick G. Dutton did not participate in all the decisions on the policy proposals. When he did, however, his responsibility was to address himself not to what policy should be, but to congressional relations as they affected the acceptance of departmental policy. Similarly, the executive assistant to the secretary in a large domestic department pointed out that the liaison agent acted as an adviser to the secretary and to the other political

[3] In the one major agency that most closely approximated a department, HHFA, the general counsel also assumed primary responsibility for congressional relations, whereas the legislative liaison officer was relegated to minor service and informational roles with the Congress.

leaders. "His advice is called upon many times regarding members of the committees and the situation on the Hill." On policy his views were not governing, but "one reason he is in on important meetings is that he can anticipate things. In fact, he's in a position to stop fires before they even start by suggesting to us what we should or should not do."

(B) COORDINATOR. In the larger departments the role of coordinator emerged as one of great importance in the eyes of the secretaries, the undersecretaries, and their personal aides.[4] The resources of these departments were extensive and their legislative programs ambitious. A number of individuals at all levels dealt with the legislators. At the same time the secretary in each department demanded that his leadership shape the legislative relations of the department and that his and the administration's programs be supported. Someone, it was recognized within the political leadership, had to pull all this activity together so as to integrate it into a common departmental approach to the Congress.

"Traditionally ours has been a loose confederation," declared one secretary, "and the department tends even today to divide into different segments, each by and for itself." His department was now much more unified, and "in no small measure, this is due to the sensitivity of our legislative relations and to the fact that we have an integrated operation." In this respect the liaison agent was "absolutely vital to me as secretary." By serving as the focal point for coordinating departmental relations with Congress, this staff assistant had greatly helped the secretary overcome the traditional lack of unity within the department. Therefore the secretary attached great value to having the liaison agent participate in his policy and daily staff meetings, inform him regarding departmental activities in the Congress and advise him on appropriate action, and assume responsibility for integrating all actions concerned with Congress. But even with "the best legislative liaison assistant" in the executive system, there were times, acknowledged the secretary, when his department resembled a sieve more than an integrated, unified whole.

The executive assistant to the secretary in another confederate department frankly declared that his department was not fully coordinated and that many bureau chiefs often did not help the secretary's liaison agent. He was cognizant of the many difficulties confronting the liaison agent: "We are a confederation of warring bureaus. There are so many different and competing interests in the department."[5] Nevertheless, he as-

---

[4] To a much lesser extent, this was also the case in the smaller departments, although not in Treasury.

[5] An interview with a former undersecretary in this department, who had also served as its legislative counsel during the Eisenhower Administration, elicited the same assessment: "We had to control legislation across the board, on important and unimportant bills, otherwise the bureaus tried to run to the Hill on their own."

serted, a primary obligation of a liaison agent to his secretary was "to work as a coordinator of all the department's activities in the Congress."

A deputy undersecretary added another dimension to the role of coordinator. The liaison agent must know when and where to insert into the legislative equation each particular member of the department. By knowing with which policy areas and with which legislators each actor within the departmental leadership could best deal, the liaison agent was able to marshal the department's personnel resources so that they exerted the maximum possible influence for the department. "He should act as the fingerman, the guy who decides who needs to be seen and who sees whom," was the assessment of the executive assistant to another secretary.

(C) SERVICE EXPEDITER FOR CONGRESS. A third subset of roles develops out of a recognition by senior political leaders that (1) legislators make many demands upon the departments for information, administrative changes or rulings, personnel and policy decisions, and assistance of all types; (2) the size, anonymity, complexity, and procedures of their own bureaucracies often pose problems for congressmen when they wish to deal with the departments; and (3) satisfying congressmen pays off in good congressional relations. Legislators who are not discontented do not muddy up the waters for the executive. Moreover, favors performed for legislators build up credit upon which executive actors may subsequently draw.

A primary responsibility of legislative liaison agents, therefore, is to assist congressional actors in contacting and dealing with the executive system. Although the degree of emphasis they placed on this role varied, all the respondents referred to what may be designated as a service expediter role. One of his liaison agent's jobs, noted a secretary, was to ensure that requests from congressmen were expedited quickly, effectively, and "in terms of the interests of the department as well as the congressman." The liaison officer was to act as a service agency *for* the Congress on legislative and administrative problems, contended an undersecretary in another department. Congressmen were characterized as extremely sensitive about such matters; they became irritated when their requests and complaints were not followed through in the executive. It was the liaison agent's task to monitor the bureaucracy, to make certain it responded, and in a manner both understood and found useful by the legislator. Moreover, it was the liaison agent's responsibility to keep congressmen informed regarding departmental activities that affected their congressional districts: "Anything to allow the congressman to take credit with the folks back home so that they see his importance to them."

(D) INSIDE SPOKESMAN OR LEGISLATIVE ADVOCATE. At least two

senior political leaders and their immediate staff assistants postulated a complementary role that may be referred to as the inside spokesman or legislative advocate. It relates closely to the adviser role and has strong service overtones, but must be distinguished from both.

In two departments the role of inside spokesman for Congress was emphasized. To one undersecretary a unique attribute of the department's legislative liaison agent was his acting, at times, as a spokesman *for* the Congress *within* the department. As a result the senior officers comprehended better the legislative frame of reference in which they operated. An official close to the Secretary of State developed a similar theme based upon what he asserted was a problem peculiar to his department: the Assistant Secretary for Congressional Relations had to represent the Congress to the department, because the department was infected with xenophobia toward the legislature. Most Foreign Service officers, he argued, were extremely insensitive to domestic American politics. They had no special feel for or interest in such politics, and they refused to consider that the domestic policies that interested congressmen related legitimately to any policy considerations in the department. Not only was it incumbent upon the liaison officer as inside spokesman to alert the secretary to congressional moods and opinions, but it was incumbent upon him to fight the bureaucracy and others as well, "forcing them to compromise and come to terms with those they considered their enemies."

Congressionally Oriented Roles

The responses of senior executive leaders revealed that they envisaged their liaison officers as playing active roles within the legislative system as well as within the executive. Such roles were designed to help the political leaders in the administration bridge the gap between the two systems. Each of the three role orientations that emerged from this analysis—spokesman for the secretary, intelligence agent, lobbyist—interrelates with and facilitates the performance of the others.

(A) SPOKESMAN FOR THE SECRETARY. As spokesman for the secretary, the liaison officer was expected to make the department's position known on key proposals as well as to negotiate for the department. "He is a projection of the department and the secretary on the Hill, responsible for working with key committee members and staff on our proposals," emphasized one superior. But, it was asserted, he could never perform adequately in the Congress unless he was recognized as speaking in the name of the secretary. "He does speak for me, and they [the legislators] are fully cognizant of this fact," explained the secretary of a large department in the Kennedy Administration. "This is vital to his acceptance —his operation in the Congress—and it is vital to me."

In his role as spokesman the liaison officer was seen as removing a tremendous burden of day-to-day work from the secretary's shoulders. Moreover, he was able to handle difficult problems as they arose on the Hill and to resolve them so that they left no bad feelings. Departmental political leaders are extremely sensitive to the feelings of congressmen. They are aware that ruffled feelings often vent themselves in legislative behavior detrimental to the department. "He's there on the Hill and can react quickly to attacks upon me and the department. He is my spokesman. I wouldn't have it otherwise," emphasized a Democratic department head.

A different aspect of the spokesman role was advanced by an undersecretary. He and his secretary operated under constraints in dealing with Congress. Their departmental positions often precluded their contacting legislators, making mandatory the employment of a lower level assistant who could speak for them. "We can't go up and ask Congress what's the trouble. Why? Well, it would invite too many demands upon us." Demands made upon a liaison agent can be more readily rejected or adjusted by the department; if made directly upon the secretary or undersecretary, they involve a direct confrontation between the highest leadership of the department and the legislators, often escalating the importance of the item at issue. The legislative liaison officer acts, in effect, as a buffer between the senior departmental leaders and the legislators by reducing the political demands made upon his superiors, assuming some of the onus for negative decisions by them, and saving them for more meaningful interactions with legislators on more significant issues. The buffer aspect of this role in dealing with the complaints and demands of congressmen was underscored by other executive leaders. It obviously interrelates with the service expediter role that the liaison agent plays within his own department.

A somewhat different emphasis was placed upon the spokesman role by an undersecretary of a large confederate department in the Eisenhower Administration. "We needed one such man who was allowed to speak in the Congress at all times for the secretary as an informal secretary. This can't be done by the undersecretary—he has his own load in the department and *his own political identity*." As for the assistant secretaries, their day-to-day load was much too heavy: "They can't carry all the legislation." One of his premises—that a senior political leader in a department may have a political identity distinct from that of the secretary—was confirmed, in part, by the remarks of a Kennedy departmental leader. Commenting upon his department's legislative liaison agent, a

Democratic undersecretary noted that: "The secretary and X [the liaison agent] were more loyal to the administration than I was. I was inclined to be more independent and to lose gracefully when I felt the administration was wrong." Since the liaison agent identified with and always followed the direction of the secretary, he helped compensate for the undersecretary's somewhat different political posture and style.[6]

(B) INTELLIGENCE AGENT. The gathering and assessing of information about individual legislators and committees were considered essential to the liaison officer's making a contribution to the executive system. In effect, he must play the role of an intelligence agent. This is as vital to his role of adviser to his secretary as it is to his role of coordinator for his fellow executive actors. Without data on congressional interests, intentions, and actions, legislative liaison agents cannot operate effectively in any of their roles. Both their superiors and the latter's assistants designated the intelligence agent role as a *sine qua non* for departmental legislative liaison agents.

"Good intelligence," explained the secretary of a large department, "is absolutely vital in dealing with the Congress. We have to know what is happening, what is the thinking of the congressmen." Such data alerted him sufficiently so that he was prepared to deal with legislators before they called upon him. Executive leaders also considered intelligence crucial to the resolution of difficult problems as they developed on the Hill, to quick and effective reaction to attacks by legislators, to the anticipation of legislative action on executive bills, and to the executive assumption of initiative in Congress.

In emphasizing the importance of day-to-day intelligence with respect to the Congress, the secretary of a small department spoke of his liaison agent in the following terms: "He's got to get the scuttlebutt and the feel of timing on problems and legislation, flesh out the difficulties, and stay on top of them." A personal assistant to the secretary in a very large department was even more emphatic:

Intelligence is the vital function. It is vital for us to know what is going on, where there is a lack of communications, and what the rumors are. This can all get away from you, and very fast. Congressional relations is the frailest process; the most minute things are often the most important.

Executive actors viewed Congress as a highly complex system with which they had to deal and upon which they were dependent. The Congress could at any time pose a threat to them and their departments. Since they need congressional goodwill, cooperation, and votes for au-

---

[6] In only one department did a liaison officer indicate that he resisted lobbying for administration legislation as aggressively as his secretary had desired. See chap. 9.

thorization and appropriations legislation, it is imperative that senior executive actors possess proper intelligence about individual legislators and their subsystems. Executive actors must know as accurately as possible the thinking and actions of legislators, their intentions and what they are doing about them, which groups and individuals are lining up for and against the executive's proposals, and whether the time is appropriate—in terms of legislative mood—for executive intervention, advance, retreat, or compromise. The very number of legislators involved, the fluidity of the legislative climate, and the sensitive nature of much of the desired data present special problems, particularly for leaders outside the legislative system. While senior political executives themselves engage in direct relations with legislators, they carry other departmental burdens and responsibilities. They must consequently have reliable, expert assistance in obtaining and evaluating the necessary data on Congress, preferably a source responsible to them and operating out of their own system.[7] The legislative liaison officers meet this need.

(C) LOBBYIST FOR THE DEPARTMENT. It is noteworthy that senior departmental leaders and their assistants specifically distinguished between the lobbying and the intelligence responsibilities of legislative liaison agents. That they differentiated between the two and assigned a high priority to lobbying is a significant index to another set of liaison roles oriented toward the legislative system. When department chiefs referred to their liaison agents as lobbyists, what exactly did they mean? Did the term mean the same to all the department heads and their assistants? If not, what were the differences?

Different leaders emphasized different elements when they referred to lobbying, and there was some sharp division among them as to the type of lobbying in which the liaison agents should properly engage. As a lobbyist the liaison agent was expected to expedite the legislative process for the department's programs by communicating the department's position on its bills, helping to ascertain points for compromise and trading (although others were supposed to carry them through), obtaining votes, and selling substantive legislation. In its most extended version, the role of lobbyist called for him to be a seller of bills and designer of compromises as well as a processor, all within the area of policy decisions made by senior departmental actors. Most of the senior political leaders

---

[7] It should be noted, and will be discussed in chap. 8, that the party leaders of the legislative system have their own intelligence networks. Although the two networks interact and cooperate when both the legislative and executive leaders represent the same political party, each set of leaders prefer an intelligence operation directly responsible to itself. As is characteristic of the various executive establishments that maintain their own networks against external enemies, the executive and legislative intelligence agents are not always confident of the methods or results of the others.

27

and their immediate assistants in the departments did not expect their legislative liaison officers to exploit the outer limits of the lobbyist role, although a few did expect it.

The most forceful expression regarding the lobbyist role came from a former Secretary of State in a previous Democratic administration. Although State has since shifted considerably away from this conceptualization, it is worth citing as the type of broad, aggressive lobbying activities that an ambitious secretary envisages for his liaison agent. In his eyes, the role of the Assistant Secretary for Congressional Relations was inherently that of lobbyist. The department had to obtain from Congress authorizations and funds for its programs and administration. Moreover, Congress was always trying to infiltrate the department. This action had to be blunted or the proper accommodations designed. It was the assistant secretary's responsibility to "infiltrate the committees so that we are in on the drafting of bills—so that we help their members and staff write the bills." He had to work with and try to influence the congressional process, concentrate upon the key movers as well as those legislators who would subsequently occupy such positions, and help organize the outside interest groups behind the department's positions. According to this secretary, not only should the Assistant Secretary for Congressional Relations assume an active lobbyist role, but he should be the one responsible for managing and selling the department's proposals in the Congress.

While department heads and their personal assistants in the Kennedy Administration accepted much in this profile of the lobbyist role, their conceptualization of the role was more circumscribed. The legislative liaison agent did not testify before congressional committees; this responsibility belonged to the secretary, the undersecretary or undersecretaries and assistant secretaries, and the bureau heads. Even where the lobbyist role of the liaison agent was defined, as it was in the smaller departments, as doing everything to affect congressional attitudes and actions that the secretary and undersecretary did,[8] testifying before committees was excluded. Only the Assistant Secretary for Legislation in HEW testified on substance; his job, however, differed radically from that of the other departmental liaison officers in that he functioned as a principal originator and developer of legislation as well as the chief legislative liaison agent for HEW. Its Congressional Liaison Officer was, in fact, subordinate to him.

Limitations were implicit in the positive definitions of the lobbyist role subscribed to by senior departmental leaders in the Kennedy Admin-

[8] The only distinction that was made referred to the *extent* to which the senior officers participated, not the kind or quality of such involvement.

istration. They expected that liaison agents would at times engage in the substantive selling of their legislative program, but this was peripheral to their main preoccupation. An undersecretary in a small department observed that, while his liaison agent was an integral part of the departmental team that endeavored to educate and persuade legislators, actual leadership in selling substance inhered in the secretary and undersecretary. The liaison officer was permitted to handle certain minor pieces of legislation by himself, but he did not act as the field general for major legislation. The secretary of a large confederate department depicted his liaison agent as an extremely valuable member of a special departmental team, a team that the secretary held responsible for securing congressional approval of legislation. While his liaison agent did deal with congressmen occasionally regarding the substance of legislation, he was not included in this lobbying team as an expert on the details. This was left to others. In one of the smaller departments, however, both the secretary and his personal assistant stressed the importance of the legislative liaison officer's being involved in major substantive aspects of legislation as well as in the politics of the legislative process.

The distinction drawn by departmental leaders between a lobbying role on substance and on the political process merits further consideration. Most see the liaison agents as primarily concerned with the political process and only incidentally with substance. Political lobbying was defined by the senior executive leaders as including the search for points of compromise in legislation and the probing of congressmen or their staffs for the possibilities of arranging legislative accommodations. It also involved attempts at fashioning deals by which the department traded the special services and adjustments at its disposal for votes or favorable legislative attitudes. Political lobbying encompassed also the search for and direct solicitation of votes. Sometimes the difference between politics and the selling of substance was spelled out in the phrase "helping move the legislation along." "There are hundreds of things we push which require day-to-day work to get them through," explained the deputy undersecretary of a large confederate department. "The legislative liaison officer is responsible for expediting the legislative process for us."

The distinction between substantive selling and political lobbying becomes, at times, very fine indeed. And it is clearly one that liaison agents are expected to ignore. With few exceptions, however, others in the executive system were considered by departmental leaders to be more competent than the liaison agents in dealing with the substantive features of legislation.

(D) ADMINISTRATION AGENT. The expectations of these senior leaders postulated a fourth role for the liaison officer, that of administration agent. They recognized that while their liaison officers were serving as their departments' representatives, such agents might also be drafted by the White House legislative liaison office to be an extension of the President's direct lobbying apparatus. All the top departmental leaders and their assistants who were interviewed considered themselves part of the administration's team. They assumed that their liaison officers, as a matter of course, would cooperate with the White House.

LIAISON ROLES AS DEFINED BY SECONDARY POLITICAL LEADERS IN THE DEPARTMENTS

While legislative liaison agents are adjuncts to the department heads, they must work with and through assistant secretaries, general counsels, and agency heads if they are to function effectively in the roles expected of them by the departmental secretaries and undersecretaries. The second layer of the political executive is responsible for supervising and controlling the operations of the various units of the departments.[9] Its members tend to be primarily presidential appointees, unlike the liaison agents, who with two exceptions were appointees of the secretaries. Not only do assistant secretaries and agency heads carry administrative responsibilities in their departments, but they testify before congressional committees and lobby individual members.

From a secretary's point of view, it is these secondary leaders rather than the liaison agents who are the more significant substantive political spokesmen for the department. As his subordinate colleagues, they cannot avoid reflecting his conceptions of legislative liaison. At the same time, assistant secretaries and other secondary political leaders are often recruited from within Congress itself, or have been intimately involved with it in some capacity, either from within the executive or from outside the national government. Hence they may bring to their jobs their own well-defined conceptions of proper executive-legislative relations. The role expectations of the secondary political executives are bound to affect the definition of roles and the behavior of the liaison agents.

Three diverse sources of information permit conclusions to be drawn regarding the expectations of these secondary executive leaders: (1) a published study of executive actors who served during the Eisenhower Administration, (2) direct interviews that I conducted with leaders at

[9] See Dean E. Mann and Jameson W. Doig, *The Assistant Secretaries: Problems and Processes of Appointment* (Washington, D.C.: Brookings Institution, 1965). These authors rank the assistant secretaries at the second level of leadership, but they also include the undersecretaries in the second level. I have assigned the undersecretaries to the first rank of departmental leadership.

this level in the Kennedy Administration, and (3) a set of intradepartmental memoranda submitted by the secondary leadership in one department during the Kennedy Administration.

Expectations of Secondary Leaders in the Eisenhower Administration: The Brookings Institution Round Table

In 1958 a group of bureau chiefs and secondary-level executive leaders, participating in a Brookings Institution round table regarding their positions and problems, devoted some consideration to legislative liaison.[10] It should be noted from the outset that the orientation of most of the participants toward legislative liaison agents was negative. They were, observed Marver H. Bernstein, "impressed more with the liabilities than the benefits flowing from the work of the legislative liaison staff."[11] A number complained that liaison agents generated more legislative proposals than departmental leaders could advocate in a congressional session. Moreover, the feeling was expressed that legislative liaison staffs seldom relieved the senior leaders of the burden of executive communications with Congress.

Positive statements about liaison agents were rare. According to one member, legislative liaison agents were valuable as buffers in smoothing out conflict between particular congressmen and the executive. Two referred to their obtaining vital information from the Congress and one to the importance of their presenting the department's views to congressional committees. Liaison officers were pictured primarily, however, *as providing a useful mechanical apparatus for the processing of legislative documents.* Liaison agents did not help them sell legislation or even help to get it passed. One in the group went so far as to assert that legislative liaison agents failed to understand their own departments' bills.

It is necessary to be very cautious in extrapolating role expectations from the Brookings Institution study. Does one conclude from the general tone and critical comments by these secondary- and tertiary-level leaders in the Republican administration that they expected the legislative liaison agents to do more than process documents? This is suggested, at least, by the conclusion of a number of the round-table participants, as well as of the political scientist who wrote up the study, that most of the liaison jobs had not been well filled. Apparently these actors had had expectations that their liaison agents had not fulfilled.

[10] Marver H. Bernstein, *The Job of the Federal Executive* (Washington, D.C.: Brookings Institution, 1958), pp. 114–16. It should be noted that one undersecretary was a participant.
[11] *Ibid.*, p. 114.

Expectations of Secondary Leaders in the Kennedy Administration

A well-defined, positive conception of the liaison agents' roles and functions emerged from interviews with secondary political leaders in the departments of the Kennedy Administration.[12] Except for those in one major agency, the Housing and Home Finance Agency (HHFA), the Kennedy leaders contrasted very sharply in their attitudes toward liaison agents with those of the Eisenhower executives reported by Bernstein. Not a single secondary executive leader in the Kennedy Administration complained that his congressional relations officer burdened him with an excessive amount of legislation. The Assistant Secretary for Legislation in HEW, who was in effect the principal liaison agent for the department, was an exception in that he did assume responsibility for the development of legislation, but this was expected of his office and especially of the individual occupying it at the time. It was, in fact, incomprehensible to the Democratic secondary leadership that anyone at their level in the Eisenhower Administration would voice concern about liaison agents' generating legislation; this was simply not their responsibility. Nor was a single complaint registered that liaison agents failed to relieve departmental leaders of the burden of communicating with Congress; just the reverse was the case.

Among the Kennedy Administration's secondary leaders, only the general counsel of HHFA considered the legislative liaison officer to be primarily a processor of information and services for Congress.[13] HHFA was at the time the only agency comparable to a department whose official legal officer assumed major responsibility for dealing with Congress. Even the roles of HEW's Congressional Liaison Officer, who was subordinate to an assistant secretary for legislation rather than to the secretary, carried a significance greater than the roles of her counterpart in HHFA.[14] In addition to processing legislative requests to the department and relaying

[12] Interviews were conducted with two general counsels, six assistant secretaries, a number of their immediate deputies and assistants, and some of their associates of almost comparable political orientation and responsibility in the Departments of Agriculture, Commerce, Defense, HEW, Labor, and Treasury. Interviewed also was the general counsel of HHFA, an independent agency responsible for a significant part of the Kennedy Administration's legislative program.

[13] His previous liaison agent had, in fact, resigned because of this extremely restricted definition.

[14] Upon the resignation of the person filling the post of Congressional Liaison Officer in HEW, the more mundane servicing of congressmen was conducted by the clerical staff in the office, but the other responsibilities of the liaison agent were completely absorbed into the office of the Assistant Secretary for Legislation. For a while the position of congressional relations officer remained vacant. When a replacement was selected during the Johnson Administration, he was not assigned the major nonservice responsibilities of his predecessor.

its announcements to the congressmen, she was expected to engage in intelligence work in the Congress and to act as an ally with key legislators on the House Education and Labor Committee, as well as the Rules Committee, in order to help expedite the department's legislation.

The secondary political leaders expected to share in the job of dealing with the Congress, and all of them became involved at times in significant ways. However, they did not devote more than a small portion of their time to congressional relations, and all asserted that primary responsibility for congressional relations properly belonged to the liaison agents. An assistant secretary for a small department expressed their attitude in these terms:

All the top leaders in the department concern themselves with legislation. But we can't do it all. The congressional relations officer covers all the legislation for the department while the rest of us are interested in specific pieces of legislation; we have other things to do. He plays a coordinating role with the secretary and undersecretary to maintain a smooth working operation.

Should the position of special liaison officer be abolished, contended an assistant secretary in a large department, "the rest of us would have to spend an awful lot more time at it [legislative relations]." Their own approach to the Congress would as a result be more chaotic and less effective.

The implications of the coordinator role extend beyond the political leadership centered around the secretary. In a previous administration, noted an assistant secretary, the agencies of the department had worked directly with individual congressmen and committees, both on policy and on a technical level. Consequently, "they tended to go off on their own." The agency people now recognized that they could be more effective by working with and through the secretary's assistant for congressional relations than by operating independently of the department head. Moreover, they had also discovered that, with his fingers on all facets of the department's congressional relations, the liaison agent was in a better position to enhance the secretary's ability to supervise and centralize congressional relations throughout the department.

The manner in which assistant secretaries and their colleagues perceived Congress related directly to the liaison officers' roles as intelligence agents and troubleshooters. Congress was seen as uncertain, highly fluid, and emotional. It was difficult, they asserted, for executive leaders to find out what was going on. Yet it was vital for them to have this information if they were to maintain perspective and balance in dealing with Congress. This made it imperative for legislative liaison officers constantly to assess the mood, expectations, and actions of legislators, and to relay their findings to the secretary, the undersecretary, and the assistant secretaries. Explained one assistant secretary:

We depend upon him. You can't abolish the office of congressional relations officer. He keeps us posted on the thinking up there regarding our legislation. Sure, he isn't the chief negotiator with Congress on substance, but he serves as a control or warning function so we can react in terms of proper relationships with congressmen.

With the proper intelligence, political policy leaders of the executive or their allies can be brought into the legislative process at crucial places and times. The assistant secretaries cited numerous examples of the usefulness of such data, one of which aptly illustrates this function. Treasury's liaison agent had concluded at one point that the California delegation was becoming increasingly nervous on the Kennedy tax bill of 1962; its members were wavering on one particular provision because of a deluge of letters from their constituents. Realizing that they needed technical as well as political reassurance if they were to stay in line on this provision, he arranged a successful meeting between the delegation and his senior departmental political officers. "It makes a big difference in the behavior of legislators," explained another assistant secretary, "if the congressional relations officer is able to set it up so that a secretary or an interest group or another senator is sent to talk with a particular senator."

In contrast with the Eisenhower leaders' complaint that legislative liaison agents did not sell or even understand legislation and were of little or no help in securing its adoption, the secondary leaders in the Kennedy Administration strongly endorsed the work of their agents. While these Democratic leaders agreed that they and their political superiors, not the liaison agents, were the principal substantive spokesmen for the departments, they expressed the belief that their liaison agents should also deal with the Congress on the substance of legislation.

Within one independent agency and one department in the Kennedy Administration, however, a restrictive interpretation of legislative liaison roles did prevail among secondary executive leaders. In HHFA, it went so far as to freeze out the congressional relations officer from virtually any meaningful role. Its general counsel insisted that responsibility for congressional relations and legislation could not be delegated.

A somewhat less rigid view prevailed among a mixed group of leaders in a large confederate department.[15] In response to a request from

[15] In this group were two special assistants to the secretary and the latter's deputy, two assistant secretaries, two administrators of agencies, and an assistant director of a bureau. Since the general counsel also forwarded a memorandum that endorsed the report of a final committee of four in the group, the views of nine executive leaders, political (at the senior and secondary levels) and bureaucratic, were represented.

their undersecretary, they had submitted memoranda on the advisability of having a special officer on the secretary's staff for liaison rather than letting it continue as one of the responsibilities of the department's general counsel. The memoranda were strikingly similar in their limited conceptualization of the roles of this special liaison officer. All concurred in the need for an actor concerned solely with the department's legislative liaison and responsible immediately to the secretary. They agreed that his central role should be that of coordinator. It was this role that was most frequently envisaged and deemed significant. The only other role in which at least three of the memoranda concurred was that of service expediter for Congress. Only one memorandum envisaged the liaison officer as engaging in "head counting" (intelligence agent), and one suggested that he would facilitate the passage of legislation (lobbyist). Two did refer to his cooperating with the White House liaison personnel, but solely in terms of tapping their information and securing their assistance. It should be noted that compared with the other departments, this one was not consistently involved in a demanding program of new legislation or the reauthorization of controversial programs.

Within the rest of the departments, however, actors at the second level of political leadership were in agreement that their congressional relations officers should undertake a wide variety of positive roles, including effecting the passage of legislation. In two of the smaller departments the legislative liaison officers were expected to play major roles in explaining, selling, and lobbying when their departments' bills were being considered. They were assigned full responsibility for certain legislation—under the secretary's direction, of course—but their general responsibility cut across all legislative areas. The assistant secretaries expected that in filling such roles their liaison agents would be able to take complex issues and translate them into terms comprehensible to the legislators. It was also their responsibility to help search for compromises and to resolve problems with congressmen so as "to enable us to get around obstacles that we all are aware of." If necessary, they were to ascertain which groups in the congressmen's constituencies objected to the departments' bills so that "we in the executive can get together with them and work out the problems, if possible, and have them feed this back to the congressmen."

In the larger departments substantive selling was considered much more the province of the other members of the political leadership. The congressional relations officer, nevertheless, was still seen as an aide and a collaborator with his principals in such endeavors, although more as a processor than as a substantive advocate. In Defense, for example, direct lobbying was primarily the job of the assistant secretaries; the liaison agent's job, as one of them pointed out, was to "goose the others to sell

35

the program in the Congress." This department's liaison agent was viewed primarily as an intelligence agent collecting data on the members of the Armed Services Committees, as an adviser to the secretary, and as a coordinator for working the key departmental leaders into Congress.

SECONDARY EXECUTIVE ACTORS DEFINE ROLES BROADLY: A CASE STUDY. A set of interviews conducted within one large department with a special group of secondary-level actors particularly concerned with Congress affords a detailed picture of the full range of roles expected of a liaison agent. Three political-level actors—the department's general counsel, a senior economist, and the deputy administrator of an agency— together with the liaison agent were utilized by the secretary as a team in dealing with certain controversial types of legislation.[16] The economist and the deputy administrator were not strictly secondary-level political leaders, but political appointees who operated within the inner circle of the secretary's advisers and who dissociated themselves from the bureaucracy.

As advisers to and co-workers with the secretary, all three executive actors saw their liaison officer as filling roles similar to their own secretary's. This was stated forcefully by the deputy administrator and confirmed by the others: "X [the liaison agent] is very close to the secretary; he helps guide him the right way. In fact, without him, the secretary would not be able to do the good job that he is accomplishing in Congress." Not only did their fellow team member participate in all staff conferences of the department head, but he had ready access to the secretary whenever he deemed it necessary. Both the secretary and the undersecretary frequently called upon him for advice. The liaison agent read and commented upon the mail sent by congressmen to the secretary as well as his correspondence with the Congress; he prepared drafts for most of the secretary's correspondence and also signed most of it. Consequently, he was in a strategic position to watch for and catch the little things that might have slipped through, but which were very important in dealing with Congress. The liaison officer handled almost all the secretary's political problems originating on the Hill and those stemming from the secretary's own initiative in dealing with Congress.

"We, too, do legislative liaison," declared the other members of the team. "We work with the chairman, with the subcommittees, and with others. We work out compromises and political problems." Each of them considered the liaison agent an integral member of his team: he engaged in the same tasks as they, but more in terms of pulling things together for

---

[16] None of these interviews was utilized in developing the preceding discussions of secondary leaders.

the team and for the department. The economist expressed the viewpoint of the substantive expert: "We have special information and skills. Our job is to lay out the argument in conference, in caucus, and in their offices. X gets us to the right person at the right time." More often than his colleagues on the team, he could sense when things were going wrong, added the deputy administrator. And he knew which man at the top executive level to introduce into the congressional system to correct and smooth things over with its members. When the liaison agent had felt, for example, that the Oregon congressmen were "not right" on the department's position, he had requested one of his teammates to go with him to shore up the delegation. "He discovered a serious problem with the chairman of our principal committee, and he asked me to go down with him. We hammered out something agreeable to the chairman and ourselves at the chairman's office that night."

The department's general counsel stressed another aspect of coordination: "Everything relative to the agencies in the department is supposed to coordinate through the secretary's office—and X plays a crucial role here." From the point of view of his political leaders and associates, the liaison agent provided an effective mechanism whereby the secretary could exercise control over the powerful agencies within the department. In fact, the deputy administrator contended that one of the agent's greatest services to the secretary was conducting liaison between the secretary and his agency heads. He spent considerable time with agency and subagency heads, learning their problems, discovering how best to aid them, winning their confidence, and helping the secretary keep on top of agency plans and actions that had implications for congressional relations. In this manner he was building them into a more general departmental team under the leadership of the secretary and the undersecretary.

Intelligence was also judged to be an important, integral part of the legislative liaison agent's job. To intervene successfully in the legislative process, his teammates required accurate information about the personalities, attitudes, expectations, problems, and actions of members of the committees vital to their department. Some of this they knew themselves, but they were too busy with their executive-oriented tasks to feel confident that they were on top of these legislative data. The liaison agent was supposed to provide this information. They relied upon him for guidance on the timing of their intervention as well as for discerning soft spots in the department's position in the Congress. He was expected to help them determine when, where, and with whom the department might have to compromise: "At times he has to be able to tell us how far we must go in this respect and when we can't gain anything more." This meant a constant concern on his part with cultivating congressmen, especially those on substantive committees with which the department was most intimately related.

Their liaison agent, one team member pointed out, had learned from talking with a key congressman that a conference committee dealing with an important bill of theirs was deadlocked and almost certain to break up. "With this information, we unraveled the problem, got a meeting with the House committee chairman, the subcommittee chairman, and ourselves, and we averted a catastrophe." It was the liaison agent's responsibility also to assess the general mood of the House. "The others and I are not competent to do this. We don't know how an issue is going to be presented, whether an apparent technicality is the key vote or not, whether it's worth risking a major battle on it." Or, as the deputy administrator observed, "It's not just data or opinions on particular congressmen that we need, but the feel regarding the Congress."

They expected the liaison agent to explain legislation, to persuade legislators and their staffs, and to write speeches for legislative actors. "Of course, he lobbies with the rest of us, but we spend more time on the substance of the legislation." His role as troubleshooter, ascertaining and analyzing troublesome situations and resolving them by himself if possible, was especially stressed.

He was referred to by his three colleagues (as well as by others) as the department's chief "head counter." It was the liaison agent's responsibility to provide them and the secretary with an accurate assessment of the voting intentions of legislators. Asserted the general counsel of the department: "Head counting is damned important. It has to be done to get our program through. Any broad, across-the-board program is so controversial that it takes a lot of planning, cajoling, and pushing to get it through." The deputy administrator added: "Congress has little motivating power on its own; the nature of the legislative process is inertia. The executive must therefore always be pushing, and X [the liaison agent] is one of the leading pushers." Did the liaison agent personally swing votes for the department? Yes, sometimes, although many elements entered into a legislator's voting decision. Occasionally the liaison officer was successful on the basis of merit or friendship; more often success was won by logrolling—votes exchanged for departmental adjustments in patronage, legislation, and administrative decisions. "A congressman lets you know. If you can get him an adjustment on something, he can come along."

Of all the possible roles that the liaison agent played, that of service expediter for legislators was afforded the least recognition. Two did not even allude to it, while the third team member failed to assign it importance. However, in response to a direct question they acknowledged that the liaison officer did service the congressmen in response to their requests and complaints.

Most of the first- and second-level political actors in the departments distinguished between the roles that liaison agents played in legislative processes and the roles they played in legislative substance, although almost all conceded that one basically affected the other. The liaison agent's team members concurred. He affected policy decisions "to the extent that he is often asked, 'What will they [the congressmen] accept?' " An example was cited: Considerable debate had occurred within the department on whether to abandon a major legislative provision before they were forced to lose it on the House floor. It was the liaison officer's judgment that the department had votes to spare in favor of the provision. Although the department had prepared a substitute provision for the majority leader to introduce, "we stayed with our original provision, and won."

Two roles that carried the legislative liaison agent outside the department and the Congress were suggested by his colleagues on the team. They considered the White House to be another one of his constituencies, as well as an invaluable ally in advancing the department's bills. Others in the department talked with the President and with his substantive aides, but the congressional relations officer interrelated with the special legislative liaison staff of the White House. Furthermore, he conducted liaison with many of the department's associated interest groups. While other actors in the department also dealt with its clientele groups, the congressional relations officer was held responsible for working in the secretary's name to line up their support for the department's program and to join with them in planning strategy and tactics. It was acknowledged that his value to the department was enhanced by his contacts with influential interest groups outside the usual clientele.

Two aspects of legislative liaison were mentioned that either had been excluded from the jurisdiction of these agents by other executive actors or had never been specified. These were appropriations and patronage. The general counsel alone noted that his department's congressional relations officer became involved in appropriations politics, although not so much as in basic legislation. And another on the team reported that the liaison agent also handled patronage for the secretary.

To sum up, in the words of the senior member of the team: "His job is to establish the most effective working relationship between the department and the Congress and between the department and the White House to the mutual benefit of the department and the administration from the point of view of legislation." Within this broad mandate, the legislative liaison agent in this department was encouraged to exploit the complete range of roles available to actors at his level in the executive system.

ROLE EXPECTATIONS EXPRESSED BY
WHITE HOUSE LIAISON ACTORS

Departmental political leaders expected that their congressional relations officers would cooperate with the White House legislative liaison staff for the self-interest and legislation of the department as well as of the administration. Consequently, White House legislative liaison agents were also queried about the roles in which departmental liaison agents should engage. A fuller treatment of the White House liaison operation itself, and the relationships between these two sets of liaison agents, is deferred to a subsequent chapter.

From the point of view of the Kennedy White House liaison staff,[17] departmental liaison officers were players on the administration's team. "Our entire approach, regardless of department or bill, is that this is a Kennedy proposal," asserted the Assistant to the President for Congressional Relations. "We therefore expect the departments to support and to be involved in campaigns for each other's bills." As team players, departmental liaison agents were to exchange information on congressional intelligence with the White House staff, to cooperate in the solicitation of congressional support, to help on strategy and tactics, and to follow the leadership of the White House actors.

Departmental legislative liaison officers were conceived of as focusing primarily upon their committees rather than upon the entire House or Senate. White House actors cited the role of intelligence agent most often; not merely the accumulation of intelligence, but its assessment: "They should know the temper of Congress, have a feel for the situation." Departmental agents were expected to cultivate congressional goodwill: "They should nourish relations with the committee members, establish good relations with them." The service expediter role within the department was frequently specified in this context, for the White House liaison staff visualized such relations, in large measure, as "doing things for congressmen," who would reciprocate with votes, attendance, other types of cooperation or merely goodwill. Service was also stressed in relation to White House needs. Departmental congressional relations officers were expected to know their own departments well so as to be able to accommodate the White House actors when they passed along congressional requests they had received themselves. The White House

[17] Interviews were conducted with Lawrence F. O'Brien, Henry Hall Wilson, Jr., Mike N. Manatos, Richard K. Donahue, Charles U. Daly, and Claude Desautels.

actors expected that departmental liaison agents would not let them down, that they would be able to get results, if only because the prestige and influence of the White House were at stake.

Interestingly enough, one senior aide to the President's chief assistant for congressional relations contended that departmental liaison agents should sometimes say no to White House requests. If they did not turn him down every so often, he felt that they were not upholding the integrity of their departments and the administration of their programs. To respond in the negative too frequently, however, led to a loss of confidence in the department's congressional relations officer and to the White House agent's finding other channels into the department.

White House liaison officers wanted their departmental counterparts to pursue all the roles envisaged for them by their departmental superiors and associates. Reflecting the hardheaded approach of the White House to winning, the President's liaison staff stressed two additional aspects of liaison, only one of which had been cited by departmental leaders. These may be conceptualized as mobilizing the outside constituencies. The White House staff expected departmental congressional relations officers to help organize and utilize the lobbyists and interest groups that were closely allied with the departments. The second set of expectations extended to the constituencies of the legislators. As one White House liaison officer expressed it: "They [departmental liaison agents] should be able to engage in the energetic currying of the constituency of the congressional district." More frequently, however, this type of lobbying was recognized as a responsibility of the White House liaison officer, rather than the departmental officer.

Two members of the Eisenhower White House liaison team were also interviewed.[18] Their expectations regarding departmental legislative liaison officers roughly paralled those of the Kennedy White House. They pointed to the same primary legislative focus for departmental liaison agents—their substantive committees. They stressed much more such roles as coordinator of departmental political resources, spokesman for and adviser to the secretary, intelligence agent, service expediter, and troubleshooter, and they placed much less emphasis upon departmental agents' being integral parts of the White House or administration team or acting as lobbyists to the fullest extent envisaged by Kennedy Administration leaders. At the same time the Republican White House agents concurred with their Democratic counterparts that departmental liaison officers were essential to the secretaries in exerting leadership within their own departments and within Congress.

[18] Bryce N. Harlow and Edward A. McCabe.

CHAPTER III

The Legislative System
Defines Liaison Roles

RESPONSIBLE as the legislative liaison agents are to the executive system, their functions are basically defined in terms of their knowledge of and operation in the Congress. True, the executive system has its own imperatives, which define the roles and significance of its liaison agents. However, as their principal area of concentration, the Congress cannot avoid affecting the opportunities as well as the styles of these actors.

The freedom of legislative liaison agents to maneuver within the Congress stems, therefore, in good part from the attitudes, actions, and desires of the legislative actors themselves. If congressmen accept executive participation in the legislative process as legitimate, even desirable, then the climate is such that the executive agents can operate within very permissive parameters. On the other hand, should members object strongly to executive intervention, the range of such permissible behavior will be curtailed sharply. Moreover, the very involvement of legislative liaison agents in congressional activities may become an additional irritant in a relationship that is inherently abrasive anyway. The willingness of congressional actors to permit the boundaries of their system to be penetrated by agents for the executive political leadership becomes critical to the roles that liaison officers may play.

THE LEGISLATIVE SYSTEM AND EXECUTIVE LOBBYISTS:
FOUR HYPOTHESES

The increasingly sophisticated study of Congress affords the political scientist a number of generalizations which may serve as the basis for hypotheses regarding the interaction between legislative and executive actors. Four such hypotheses, which relate to liaison roles as viewed from the perspective of the legislator and his system, are considered here.

HYPOTHESIS I: BUILT-IN ANTAGONISMS
LEAD CONGRESS TO LIMIT LIAISON ROLES

One of the more traditional concepts concerning legislative-executive relations is that of built-in frustration. In essence the built-in frustration theory rests upon the existence of two systems that have different responsibilities but overlapping powers. This relationship is established by the Constitution with its separation of powers and checks and balances. Each system has an inherent and often conflicting voice in the affairs of the other. Indeed, their very pulsebeats are different. The executive is characterized by great centralization, specialization, and professionalism; its pace tends to be one of dispatch; its outlook is international as well as national. The tempo of Congress is much slower, deliberative often to the point of an incapacity for action. The Congress has an institutional and a historical sense of its own importance, in which is incorporated an attitude of independence from and suspicion of the executive. Politically, the national legislature is responsive to local interests and regional arrangements; organizationally, it is characterized by a fragmentation of leadership. Different constituencies, different responsibilities, different *Weltanschauungen* lead inevitably to misunderstandings and conflict.

Two respected political scientists, Joseph P. Harris and Rowland Egger, have capsuled this relationship in these terms:

Two great energy systems, each with powers of aggression and defense, each active in areas which vitally involve the interests of the other, and neither able to operate without some degree of concurrence from the other unavoidably become involved in a contest as to which shall receive the superior accommodation at any particular time. When to the sources of conflict instinct in the structure of the government are added those which derive from the political system that has grown up around the Constitution a normally adversary relationship between the President and the Congress is . . . inevitable.[1]

The suspicion and hostility inherent in a frustration-conflict relationship should, it is hypothesized, *impose very severe limitations upon roles available to the legislative liaison agents of the executive.* Antagonism on the part of congressmen toward these agents should be even more intensified, since the liaison post was created, in part, to cut

[1] Joseph P. Harris and Rowland Egger, *The President and Congress* (New York: McGraw-Hill, 1963), p. 43.

43

across traditional patterns of cooperation between bureau chiefs and particular members as well as committees of the Congress. It was anticipated that legislative liaison would be regarded as an unwarranted intrusion by the executive into the legislative system and as a direct threat to congressional intervention and control over key parts of the executive system.

Officially, Congress has rejected the legitimacy of executive lobbying. Several statutes form a body of regulatory and prohibitory legislation relating to the improper use of appropriated funds by the executive for the purpose of influencing Congress.[2] In 1913 a statute was passed which applied to all executive departments and agencies. Congress (5 U.S. Code 54) prohibited the use of money appropriated by any act for the compensation of publicity experts unless it had been specifically appropriated for that purpose. Specific limitations against lobbying with federal funds have also been inserted by Congress in appropriations bills. In 1950, for example, the appropriations acts of the Departments of Agriculture and Interior carried such restrictions. Public Law 87-741, a miscellaneous agencies' appropriations act, adopted in 1962, forbade the use of appropriated funds for propaganda purposes to support or defeat legislation pending before the Congress.

The most sweeping prohibitive congressional action, and one with which all legislative liaison agents are familiar, is found in 18 U.S. Code, Section 1913:

Lobbying with Appropriated Moneys

No part of the money appropriated by any enactment of Congress shall, in the absence of express authorization by Congress, be used directly or indirectly to pay for any personal service, advertisement, telegram, telephone, letter, printed or written matter, or other device, intended or designed to influence in any manner a Member of Congress, to favor or oppose, by vote or otherwise, any legislation or appropriation by Congress, whether before or after the introduction of any bill or resolution proposing such legislation or appropriation; but this shall not prevent officers or employees of the United States or of its departments or agencies from communicating to Members of Congress on the request of any Member or to Congress, *through the proper official channels,* requests for legislation or appropriations which they deem necessary for the efficient conduct of the public business.

Whoever, being an officer or employee of the United States or of any department or agency thereof, violates or attempts to violate this section, shall be fined not more than $500 or imprisoned not more than one year, or both;

---

[2] U.S. House of Representatives, Select Committee on Lobbying Activities, *Hearings on Legislative Activities of Executive Agencies,* 81st Cong., 2nd sess. (Washington, D.C.: U.S. Government Printing Office, 1950), pt. 10, pp. 1–2, 31ff.

and after notice and hearing by the superior officer vested with the power of removing him, shall be removed from office or employment. . . .[3]

Explicit as it is, the prohibition embodied in this statute fades quickly in the face of the key escape clause. This clause authorizes the executive, on its own initiative presumably, to communicate with members of Congress through the "proper official channels" regarding requests for legislation and appropriations that the executive deems necessary. As interpreted by the chairman of the House Select Committee on Lobbying Activities in 1950, this law recognized the necessity for the executive branch to be able to make its views known to Congress on all matters on which it had responsibilities, duties, and opinions.[4] Executive agencies, he affirmed, had a definite requirement to express their views to Congress, to request legislation, to draft bills, to make suggestions; they had the right to seek to "influence, encourage, promote or retard legislation" through *proper official channels.*

At the same time, the propriety of having executive officers respond to inquiries from individual members and committees was also protected. Members of the legislative system may not have wanted to be lobbied by the executive, but they did not want any interference with their own access to information and advice. This exception can and does nullify, in effect, the thrust of the statute. Since legislative liaison agents are responsible for advancing the cause of the departmental executives and the White House in Congress, the occasion to respond to a legislator's inquiry can afford them a wide range of opportunities. An active, imaginative liaison agent cultivates, even stimulates, questions from legislators so that their inquiries become entrées for legitimate advocacy of the executive point of view.

"Like Prohibition," remarked one member of the House of Representatives in regard to this statute, "it is observed by all parties in the breach rather than in practice." And yet, regardless of the fact that both congressmen and liaison agents pay only lip service to the law, liaison agents feel that it imposes a degree of restraint upon their behavior. As we shall see later, this has affected the style of liaison agents. All of those I interviewed were clearly aware of the criminal code as it pertained to their lobbying activities among congressmen. They commented that they made certain always to remain clearly within the letter of the law. "Of course," they explained, "we violate it [the spirit of the law] every day."

The initial hypothesis, while apparently confirmed by congressional action in limiting executive-legislative relations, in fact is partially re-

[3] *Ibid.*, p. 61 [italics added].
[4] *Ibid.*, p. 1.

pudiated by the language of the statute defining this relationship. The prohibition against executive lobbying of Congress with appropriated funds and without congressional consent constitutes merely one facet of an ambivalent attitude toward the executive. It is clear from this formal expression of congressional sentiment that, although Congress repudiates executive lobbying, its members want aid and advice from the executive, and executive initiative in its own behalf is considered legitimate if conducted through the "proper official channels."

Loopholes exist, therefore, created by Congress for its own purposes, which provide the legal opportunities for liaison agents to play a number of roles. Aside from an information-response function, the nature of these roles and the degree of congressional acceptance of such roles cannot be ascertained by recourse to the legal statute alone. The statute does not specify what congressmen want or why, how they view executive action in the legislature, or what specific roles they consider permissible for legislative liaison agents to pursue. The legal, public posture of Congress must be tested against the private behavioral patterns and attitudes of the members of the legislative system.

HYPOTHESIS II: CONGRESSIONAL NORMS AND NEEDS FACILITATE LOBBYING ROLES

Another set of generalizations which leads to a different hypothesis regarding liaison roles emerges from research on the relationship between interest groups and legislators. A legislator is constantly in need of relevant information. He is faced with a continuous series of decisions to be made and about which, generally, he has only imperfect knowledge. Any decision he makes is potentially harmful to his standing within the legislature, his party, and his constituency. Groups that provide relevant information are therefore especially valuable to him in minimizing the political costs involved in making decisions.

David B. Truman has made this a key point in *The Governmental Process:* "One important factor among the informal determinants of access is created by the legislator-politician's need of information and the ability of the group to supply it."[5] The legislator is portrayed as needing both technical knowledge regarding the content of policy issues and political knowledge regarding the strength of competing forces and the consequences of alternative decisions.

In their study of four state legislatures, the authors of *The Legislative System* conclude that "the general picture which emerges . . . shows

---

[5] David B. Truman, *The Governmental Process* (New York: Wiley, 1951), p. 333.

legislators preferring pressure groups to serve as indicators of sentiment in significant elements of the population and, perhaps even more preferably, as supplementary staff sources which legislators can call on as needed."[6] John C. Wahlke and his associates maintain that pressure groups are most welcomed by state legislators when they present information that helps legislators work out compromises and adjustments among groups, rather than when the lobbyists confine themselves to the mere assertion of their interests. And Lester W. Milbrath, in *The Washington Lobbyists,* contends that one of the real services furnished by lobbyists, for which no substitute exists, is the clash of viewpoints.[7] As spokesmen for organized groups who enable decision-makers to hear opposing points of view, lobbyists carry out an essential representational function.

Lewis A. Dexter, who questioned congressmen regarding lobbying relative to the extensions of the Reciprocal Trade Agreements Act, came to the conclusion that "vigorous representation of a partisan interest turns out to be per se legitimate."[8] It is legitimate in the eyes of the congressmen, he asserted, provided it is devoid of any threat. In fact, a number of congressmen complained that they were insufficiently contacted by lobbying organizations; they wanted and needed more information! "To many congressmen," reported Dexter, "the interest organization is a source of information about the attitudes of significant groups in his public, a source of research data and speech material, and an unofficial propaganda ally to help him put his own case forward."[9]

From this body of research regarding private lobbyists we can advance a hypothesis about the relations between members of the congressional system and liaison agents for the executive. *To the extent that executive agents are seen as furnishing congressmen with services, information, and a representation of interests that facilitate legislative roles and coincide with legislative norms, their function will be considered a legitimate one. The roles they play in the legislative system will in turn be permissive; indeed, they will have the latitude to play a number of roles.*

---

[6] John C. Wahlke, Heinz Eulau, William Buchanan, and Le Roy C. Ferguson, *The Legislative System, Explorations in Legislative Behavior* (New York: Wiley, 1962), p. 338.
[7] Lester W. Milbrath, *The Washington Lobbyists* (Chicago: Rand McNally, 1963), pp. 313–14.
[8] Raymond A. Bauer, Ithiel de Sola Pool, and Lewis A. Dexter, *American Business and Public Policy: The Politics of Foreign Trade* (New York: Atherton Press, 1963), p. 434.
[9] *Ibid.,* pp. 440–41.

As part of this study, interviews were conducted with a sample of members of Congress and their staffs.[10] In addition to being asked about their relations with departmental and White House legislative liaison agents, they were queried as to the legitimacy of executive lobbying in general, and of the liaison agents in particular. The basic assumption underlying this line of inquiry was that the roles available to the legislative liaison agents would be determined, in large part, by the members in the legislative system with whom they must interact.

The responses clustered almost entirely around two major types of affirmation regarding the propriety and value of executive lobbying through special legislative liaison agents. One stressed its value to the President and the departments; the other emphasized its service to members of the Congress. Each was made up of a number of components that reflected the congressmen's varying conceptions of executive involvement in the legislature, their own needs, and the significance they attributed to both.

Lobbying in Congress Is an Essential Aspect of the Presidency and the Executive

(A) THE EXECUTIVE OFFERS A LEGISLATIVE PROGRAM. That the executive must have a program and must promote it was one major theme. It was stated most emphatically by an urban midwestern Democrat who consistently aided the administration: "They [the White House and the departments] have a right to try to get their bills passed; after all, the President is the chief legislator." A New York Democrat, who had opposed the administration on a number of key issues and who had publicly criticized undesirable lobbying by the executive, insisted nevertheless that "legitimate lobbying has its merits." It was legitimate for

---

[10] Semistructured interviews were conducted with fifty-nine House members, the assistants to seven other House members, and staff assistants on six House committees. A purposive rather than a random sample was employed. Members were sought whose committee jurisdiction covered the executive departments studied and whose positions or inclinations were likely to bring them into contact with the legislative liaison agents. This type of sample produced, therefore, a disproportionally greater number of Democrats than Republicans and a high percentage of those occupying leadership positions. Within this latter category were five committee chairmen, a large number of subcommittee chairmen, the Democratic majority leader and whip, and a former Republican floor leader.

Some of the relevant House committees were surveyed in greater depth than were others, in particular: Agriculture, Appropriations, Education and Labor, Foreign Affairs, Interior, and Ways and Means. A smaller number of legislative actors were interviewed from the committees on Armed Services, Foreign and Interstate Commerce, Rules, and Science and Astronautics.

Fifteen senators were also interviewed, as were the assistants to sixteen additional senators.

the executive not only to present its views factually and to provide information, but also "to ask congressmen to listen to its views. The executive has to present a program, and it is legitimate where the whip system tells of danger points for the executive to talk to a congressman and present facts which they would believe will influence the congressman's decision." And a southern Democrat who was a party leader in the House observed: "Theoretically, in a pure separation of powers, the executive should not be lobbyists. But certainly in this century, the executive has to have a program and has to promote the passage of it."

Even among those who in any way deplored the presence or exercise of executive leadership in legislation, some conceded the importance of lobbying for the executive. A conservative southern senator's administrative assistant, who had served as a staff assistant in the House, acknowledged that: "I don't like it when they try to dig support out from us. But from the executive point of view, they have the responsibility to move legislation!" And a rural southern Democrat acquiesced reluctantly to the operation of executive liaison agents: "Of course it's legitimate. Almost all the legislation that has a chance originates in the executive. Unfortunately this is the case today; the executive preempts the field. The executive has to lobby."

(B) THE SECRETARY OF A DEPARTMENT IS POLITICALLY RESPONSIBLE FOR HIS PROGRAM. Congressmen recognize that the secretary of an executive department is a political leader who has a tremendous job to do and is entitled to staff aid in negotiating with them. This thesis was advanced by a subcommittee chairman in the House Agriculture Committee: "The secretary can't do all the work by himself. So much is demanded of him—he has to administer his department and he is responsible for the passage of his legislative program. The special legislative liaison operation is both necessary and legitimate since the secretary is politically responsible."

A senior member of the Alabama delegation agreed that, since the secretary was politically responsible for his department's program, "it is perfectly all right for a direct representative of the secretary to lobby for him." This justification was also tied to the need for executive coordination in dealing with the legislative committee most important to a department's program by a senior northeastern Republican and a senior southern Democrat. The latter contended that:

The secretary needs to deal with us on the committee and with other congressmen, and he needs a coordinated program and course of action. Someone has to speak for the secretary and avoid contradiction. If this responsibility were divided among the operating heads, there would be no coordination within the department in its approach to us, and the department would suffer.

(C) THE EXECUTIVE NEEDS TO LOBBY BECAUSE OF THE NATURE OF THE CONGRESS AND THE LEGISLATIVE PROCESS. Congress operates through the Senate and the House of Representatives and a large number of committees and subcommittees. It is also characterized by a labyrinth of intangible relations among individual members. The complexities and difficulties inherent in the legislative process were stressed repeatedly by congressmen and their assistants in justifying executive lobbying. No one individual, it was argued, could effectively dent the surface of Congress. The only way for the policies of the President to get through Congress was by extensive executive lobbying. If the departmental leadership neglected to maintain its relationship with the Congress, it, too, would suffer. "Without strong links with House and Senate committees through its legislative liaison," explained a senior Texas Democrat, "the departmental executive would be at a distinct disadvantage. If I were in the Cabinet, I'd have the most capable man as my congressional relations officer."

The importance of fashioning coalitions in the legislative process was stressed by a liberal, middle-ranking member of the House Interstate and Foreign Commerce Committee: "No person or group can whiplash the Congress, but the executive lobbyists can be important in helping put together the coalition necessary to get bills passed." A similar point of view was expressed by the counsel to a subcommittee in the House:

If there were no legislative liaison, this would make it very difficult to get through a legislative program that is oriented to administration policy. Congressmen are primarily interested in problems in their own districts, and seldom is a piece of legislation suited for all congressional districts. It takes a central force to give cohesion to 435 members with widely different problems. There needs to be someone to fill the gap between executive policy and law-making—to translate executive policy into legislative force.

Congressmen are well aware that it is difficult for an outsider to keep fully abreast of what is transpiring within their own system. A ranking Republican on the Interior Committee of the House stressed that executive lobbyists were not only legitimate but absolutely vital. "Otherwise the executive operates in the dark here with regard to the bills it proposes. And that's damned risky." Congress does not spontaneously enact legislation, acknowledged these legislators. Unless the departments and the White House take an active part in shaping the legislation, the program that the executive leadership desired might be sidetracked or altered to conform to the values and ambitions of others.

(D) PROPER COMMUNICATIONS ARE NECESSARY IF THE EXECUTIVE IS TO OPERATE SUCCESSFULLY IN THE LEGISLATURE. In a more restrictive sense, legislative liaison is conceived of by legislators as part of a communications system vital to the executive. "The absence of communications is fatal in the executive-legislative process. Communications is extremely vital to their [executive] legislative program," explained one Interior subcommittee chairman in the House. To which a senior southern senator added:

They [the executive] can't afford to have a breakdown of their lines of communications; neither, in fact, can we. Otherwise neither would get much done. It is not inopportune for the executive to try to sell a case to me or any other legislator. It is vital for the executive to make their case.

Another senior southerner, a member of the Senate Agriculture Committee, indicated that senators expected and welcomed the White House legislative liaison men. The liaison officers knew the priorities. "We can't read through all their [executive] messages and know what their priorities are."

Congressional Self-Interest and Legislative Liaison Coincide

Congressional self-interest is an essential element in the general approval or acceptance accorded by legislators to executive lobbying. What is significant is that the individual congressman is personally cognizant of the importance of legislative liaison to himself or his staff. He perceives legislative liaison as aiding him in his various roles as a congressman. Self-interest, like presidential leadership, has multiple ramifications.

(A) LEGISLATIVE LIAISON PROVIDES ACCESS TO THE SECRETARY OF THE DEPARTMENT. Direct access to executive policy-makers is often as indispensable for the legislator as access to the legislator is for the liaison agent. "A department has many faces," explained a senior Democrat on the House Interstate and Foreign Commerce Committee. "It is a complicated piece of machinery and has many interests. How does a congressman deal with it all if he needs to deal effectively with those who make policy?" Since access to the secretary was important, noted a subcommittee chairman of the House Interior Committee, "good legislative liaison is an asset to a congressman." Committee members wanted to be kept informed on the thinking of the departmental secretary and at the same time to have a direct line to him. "Our job has so many facets," asserted a Texas Democrat on the House Agriculture Committee, "it is impossible for one man to do. Therefore, we must depend upon the executive for facts and for their integrity. It helps us greatly if the department's man can answer our questions and get to the secretary."

(B) LIAISON AGENTS PROVIDE LEGISLATORS WITH A NECESSARY POINT OF VIEW. A number of the studies cited have mentioned that state as well as national legislators have viewed lobbyists as fulfilling a proper and useful function in meeting the need of the legislators for more information upon which to base their decisions. A midwestern Democrat on the House Agriculture Committee responded in the same manner: "It is a necessary and legitimate role for them to help me. I need to get all sides of the question in the quickest way." In the process he pointed out:

It is legitimate for departmental and White House liaison agents to get full advantage out of a congressman, to find out where things are wrong. If they can do some selling on the side, well, that's an extra bonus. I have no objection to any kind of lobbyist as long as he identifies himself.

Similar views were echoed on the Senate side. The general counsel to one of the standing committees, a man of considerable influence and prestige within the Senate and among private lobbyists and liaison agents, observed:

They serve functions similar to other lobbyists. The senators don't object to executive people acting as lobbyists. The very persistent guy with the point of view is valuable and I want the interests to come in. How else am I going to find out how and where the legislation is going to affect them?

(C) LEGISLATIVE LIAISON AGENTS PROVIDE "LEGISLATIVE TYPES" IN THE CONGRESS WITH COLLABORATORS. The legislative liaison agents are also very useful to congressmen as collaborators. This was pointed up in the caustic comments of a committee chairman: "A large percentage of congressmen need executive liaison. These are not legislators; they have neither the time to study nor the inclination to do the work." Consequently, they relied upon the executive actors to compensate for their inadequacies. An urban, midwestern Democrat from another committee and his assistant, who concerned themselves with the fashioning of legislation and the politics of its passage, presented a different picture. "It is exactly the intelligent legislative types who depend upon the liaison agents," they contended. The congressman derisively rejected the notion that those members who were not "real" legislators needed legislative liaison agents the most. Just the reverse; it would be intolerable for "our types" without the existence of the liaison agents:

What are we supposed to do, sit up here isolated? We need to scheme and plot together. We need someone political, above the bureaucratic level. They are valuable to us for their perspective and contacts; they can discuss and point out the political implications of various provisions and amendments. If one is for the administration's program, and the objective is to get it or to come as close as possible, they are very useful to us.

The importance of having access to political as distinct from bureaucratic types from the executive departments was emphasized by a Republican on the Education and Labor Committee and another on the Agriculture Committee, both of whom were classified by their colleagues as "legislative types," i.e., those who devoted themselves to the fashioning of legislation and the politics of its passage. They needed and wanted to deal with those individuals who represented the secretary, understood their political problems, and could help them "factor into" legislation. A southerner on a third committee made virtually the same point: "A member needs to know what the departmental position is and how far it'll go toward his position. Legislators can't operate in a vacuum." And the chairman of one House committee boasted that he had been the one who had induced his major department to set up its legislative liaison staff. He and the others on the committee had concluded that they needed proper liaison in proposing and moving legislation.

(D) LEGISLATIVE LIAISON HELPS CONGRESSMEN MEET CONSTITUENT NEEDS. A dominant motif among legislative actors is that it is politic to respond promptly and helpfully to requests from their constituents. But frequently constituents seek information and favors that only the executive can provide. "Proper legislative liaison ought to be maintained to enable the legislative branch to meet the needs of its constituents," asserted a senior southerner on two House committees. The representative felt that the legislative liaison officers were valuable conduits for the conveyance of information from the Congress to the departments and back. This position was stated in personal terms by a northeastern Democrat on the Science and Astronautics Committee: "Legislative liaison helps expedite my requests to the departments and agencies and gives me information and material I need to explain to my people."

From a totally different point of view, a committee chairman underscored the importance of executive aid to congressmen. This chairman had scornfully rejected any executive influence upon himself, although he knew and worked with the liaison officer of the department most directly concerned with his committee. Most members of his committee, he charged, were not legislators but errand boys who solicited the executive on behalf of their constituents. To the extent that they made their interests known, they became vulnerable to maneuvering by the executive.

Summary: Legislative Norms and Needs Facilitate the Playing of Liaison Roles by Executive Actors

A dominant note, then, in current legislative-executive relations is the wholehearted acceptance of executive lobbying by members of Congress and their staffs. Congressmen consider it to be not merely a proper operation but a necessary and valuable one. In the face of this congruence, we can state conclusively that the hypothesis is confirmed: the operating norms of the legislative system facilitate a variety of fruitful roles for legislative liaison agents.

In transactional terms the roles available to legislative liaison agents are determined by the legislators' needs (their vulnerability) and perceptions (their value judgments) of the proper role of the political executive. The legislators also perceive these relationships within a particular situational context. The nature of the institutions and the political processes within the legislative and the executive sysems make executive intervention mandatory and therefore legitimate in the eyes of congressmen.

HYPOTHESIS III: CONGRESSIONAL SENIORITY ENHANCES THE ACCEPTANCE OF EXECUTIVE LOBBYISTS IN THE LEGISLATIVE SYSTEM

A third hypothesis emerges from the concept of seniority, which is probably the most important unofficial index of status and power held by members of Congress. *Acceptance of legislative liaison (or lobbying) as a proper executive role in the legislative system should,* it was expected, *increase with an increase in the seniority of the members of Congress.* This hypothesis is based upon the assumption that the members with the longest continuous service in a legislative body have greater opportunities than do others to play significant roles in the committee-legislative process. Consequently, they would have a heightened appreciation of the necessity and usefulness of executive intervention. In part, this hypothesis rests also upon the findings of Wahlke and his associates, who state that legislators who have had more years of service tend to be facilitators: they are more sympathetic to and possess more knowledge about pressure groups than legislators who have had less service.[11] Commitment to the legislative process is seen as increasing with service, and the world of the legislator is depicted as one of active, pervasive pressure groups. All things being equal, therefore, increased seniority in the Congress and in the committee subsystem might be expected to predispose legislators to respond more favorably to executive agents and their activities.

The congressmen queried in this study were ranked into three groups of descending order of seniority—high (seven terms or more),

[11] Wahlke *et al., op. cit.,* pp. 325–28.

medium (three to six terms), low (one to two terms).[12] They were sub-sequently divided into two categories: those who expressed approval of legislative liaison or executive lobbying and those who in any way indicated a negative attitude. Table III.1 reveals that the overwhelming majority of House members in all three rank orders of seniority endorsed executive lobbying and legislative liaison. Hence the hypothesis was not confirmed by the data. While Table III.1 also shows that disapproving attitudes were revealed by high rather than low representatives, the former group included a disproportionate number of members from the Appropriations Committee, a subsystem of the House that was atypical in its negative attitudes toward departmental agents.

An examination of the reasons cited in approving legislative liaison indicates that seniority bears a more meaningful relationship to executive lobbying than would appear from the data. With the exception of one medium-ranking congressman, only members with high seniority emphasized executive lobbying in terms of the departmental secretaries' political needs. These congressmen had obviously established the closest relationships with the departments that appeared before their committees, and they identified with the problems of the political heads of the departments. In fact, if we examine the responses of those few members who expressed any negative attitudes toward executive lobbying, over half of whom ranked in the high-seniority group, all but one actually approved of some kind of liaison, departmental and/or White House.

The most characteristic attitude among favorable congressmen in all three ranks, from freshmen through chairmen, was an assessment of executive lobbying and/or legislative liaison in terms of its service and value to themselves. Only by a very small margin were departmental needs stressed more by those in the high-seniority category than by those in the other categories. The self-interest of the legislators was clearly identified with the services that executive agents could provide.

Almost as many House members within each seniority rank emphasized the importance of the President as the chief legislator. This expectation by legislators that the President would lead the Congress has been cited in other studies. Donald R. Matthews has written that "this expecta-

---

[12] The sample did not accurately reflect the proportion of high, medium, and low congressmen in the House of Representatives. This was initially attempted. However, it became immediately apparent that while low-ranking congressmen held opinions about the propriety of executive intervention, they had little direct contact with or knowledge about the liaison agents. To ascertain the nature and types of involvement of such executive actors in the legislative system from the perspective of the congressmen, it was therefore necessary to rely much more extensively upon the more senior members.

TABLE III.1

Attitudes of House Members Regarding the Propriety of
Executive Lobbying by Liaison Agents, by Seniority

Congressmen Expressing Unqualified Approval[a]

Reasons for Approval	*Seniority*[b]		
	High *(N-23)*	*Medium* *(N-19)*	*Low* *(N-9)*
The President has a program	14	9	5
The departmental secretary is politically responsible	15	1	0
The nature of Congress	8	5	1
Valuable to congressmen	13	10	7

Congressmen Expressing Negative Attitudes[a]

Reasons for Disapproval	*Seniority*[b]		
	High *(N-6)*	*Medium* *(N-2)*	*Low* *(N-0)*
Breaks down our form of government	3	0	0
Interferes with legislative process	3	1	0
No right to tell us how to vote	1	1	0

[a] Some congressmen expressed a number of responses. The total number of reasons does not therefore necessarily coincide with the number of respondents.
[b] High: seven terms or more; medium: three to six terms; low: one to two terms.

tion, with all its ambiguities, is as widespread on Capitol Hill as anywhere else. . . . Few if any senators expressed opposition to presidential leadership as such."[13] From the comments of Democratic and Republican House members who participated in the 1959 Brookings Institution Round Table on Congress, Charles L. Clapp concludes that congressmen expect to hear from the administration on all important issues.[14] Complaints were voiced that they did not often know what this position was and that insufficient efforts were made by the administration to ensure support from its own party in Congress. If senators objected at all, Matthews remarked, "it

[13] Donald R. Matthews, *U.S. Senators and Their World* (Chapel Hill: University of North Carolina Press, 1960), p. 140.
[14] Charles L. Clapp, *The Congressman: His Work as He Sees It* (Washington, D.C.: Brookings Institution, 1963), pp. 153–54.

was to the direction, ineffectiveness, or lack of legislative leadership from the White House."[15]

Surprisingly few House members in the sample were in any way negative toward legislative liaison or executive lobbying: only eight who were entirely within the medium and high seniority ranks. And all but one accepted the legitimacy of the White House legislative liaison operation. He claimed that it was absolutely improper for the administration to lobby; it was a criminal violation of the laws of Congress, laws that should be strictly enforced. Among the eight, however, members differed markedly in both negative and positive comments regarding lobbying by departmental liaison agents. Two members rejected the legitimacy of departmental liaison agents operating before their committee (Appropriations), but explained that it was proper with other committees. In fact, one asserted: "If I were a secretary of a department, I would want someone [like that] to speak for me and to negotiate with committees and members of Congress."

Two others, the chairman and the ranking minority member on his committee, independently agreed that legislative liaison agents might be useful to their secretaries and to the younger members of the Congress. From their own point of view, it represented an unwarranted intrusion in the legislative process. And one other, in the medium seniority rank, maintained that it was legitimate if legislative liaison agents confined themselves to providing information when legislators requested it of them. Only one high- and one medium-seniority member actually thought the departmental liaison apparatus was undesirable and useless, and called for its total dismantling.

Fifteen senators, together with some of their assistants, were interviewed for this study, as were the staff assistants to sixteen other senators and the professional staffmen on six of the Senate standing committees.[16] The difference between this group and those in the House of Representatives was twofold. With the exception of two staff members of the Senate Appropriations Committee, not one of the senators or any of the other staff assistants indicated that executive lobbying or legislative liaison was inappropriate. However, more often than in the House, White House liaison was distinguished from that of the departments and accorded a higher degree of recognition and importance. And in the Senate much

---

[15] Matthews, *op. cit.*, p. 142.

[16] Administrative and legislative assistants to individual senators and staff members on the Senate committees were interviewed carefully and their responses incorporated into the findings. It is my belief, based in part on experience and concurred with by the legislative liaison agents, that on the whole the Senate employed a higher caliber of staff than the House, and that Senate staff members were much closer to their principals and more involved in the politics and substance of legislation.

greater emphasis was placed upon the aid that liaison agents furnished senators and their staffs rather than on the Chief Executive as chief legislator. But this latter concept is implicit, it might be argued, in the higher respect granted White House liaison.

HYPOTHESIS IV: CONGRESSIONAL PARTY AFFILIATIONS LEAD TO DIFFERENT ATTITUDES REGARDING EXECUTIVE LOBBYING

Does party affiliation affect congressional orientation toward executive lobbying? On the whole, during the last thirty years Republican congressmen have been more reluctant and Democrats more willing to vote for executive discretion in foreign affairs, in administrative reorganization, in the advancement of new proposals, and in the financing of governmental programs. The Republican party in general and many of its leaders and members in the Congress have tended to be more suspicious than Democrats toward the executive and more hostile toward the presidency.[17] On the basis of these conclusions, it was hypothesized that *party affiliation would make a significant difference in how members of Congress viewed the liaison agents of the executive.* Republicans, it was anticipated, would be much less prone than Democratic legislators to grant latitude toward the executive in lobbying Congress, especially at a time when the President was a Democrat.

This hypothesis is not borne out by the data. None of the four Republican senators who were interviewed opposed executive lobbying, although one voiced reservations about certain tactics employed by the Eisenhower and Kennedy White Houses. The four and the assistants to seven other Republican senators all agreed on the importance and usefulness of legis-

---

[17] In his analysis of the Republican party in 1952, Samuel Lubell refers to the Republican attitude toward the presidency as "perhaps the most basic of all the Republican contradictions–the G.O.P.'s fondness for a weak President" (*The Future of American Politics* [New York: Harper, 1952], p. 242). Malcolm Moos, himself an active Republican, accepts the thesis that the "decisive" Republicans in Congress are those who favor the congressional over the presidential form of government (*The Republicans: A History of Their Party* [New York: Random House, 1956], p. 518). A perusal of the *Congressional Quarterly Almanac*'s "Key Votes" for 1961–63 indicates that the majority of Republicans tended to oppose and the majority of Democrats to support efforts on the part of the President to enhance his initiative and discretion in public policy. Of course, the President's party in the Congress is nominally committed to backing his leadership, and more was involved in all of these votes than the mere question of presidential power. Nevertheless, the votes in 1954 on the Bricker Amendment, for example, at the time of a Republican President as well as a Republican Congress, disclose a very deep suspicion of the presidency among a majority of Republican senators. See *Congressional Quarterly Almanac, 1954,* vol. 10 (Washington, D.C.: Congressional Quarterly, Inc., 1955), p. 294.

lative liaison. Indeed, one of these assistants had previously worked as the congressional relations officer for HEW under Eisenhower, and one of the senators had served as Assistant Secretary for Congressional Relations in State under Secretary John Foster Dulles.

Among the eighteen Republicans interviewed in the House, admittedly a small sample, only four responded in accordance with the hypothesis. Although one condemned executive lobbying as a breakdown of our form of government—the separation of powers—he suggested that liaison might be useful to the departments as well as to the younger members of Congress. Another felt that administration lobbying was not only a criminal violation that should be stopped, but a violation of the integrity and independence of Congress. It was permissible, he argued, for the administration to *respond* to the legislators, but not to try to manipulate them. Service to congressmen was, of course, desirable.

The other two House Republicans who responded negatively disapproved of liaison agents' lobbying with their committee; but they approved of their operating before other committees. Since the negative comments of these two Republicans coincided with those of two senior Democrats on their committee, Appropriations, these individuals appear to reflect a committee response rather than a party response. And in view of the same attitude on the part of staff members of the House and Senate Appropriations Committees, a response strikingly different from that of the staffs of any of the other committees, the pattern would seem to be conclusive. This is the only case where the policy orientation of House members and staff seemed to affect their attitudes toward the liaison officials of the executive system. The House Appropriations Committee represents a subsystem distinctly different from the rest of the legislative system, as Richard F. Fenno, Jr., has so perceptively demonstrated.[18] From the responses of the staff aides, although not its legislators, the Senate Appropriations Committee has much in common with its House counterpart regarding the impropriety of legislative liaison actors' involvement in appropriation politics. This subject is deferred temporarily for treatment in another context in this chapter.

One exception to this pattern that characterized the House Appropriations Committee was a very junior Democratic congressman. He revealed a more positive approach to departmental legislative liaison, which may be explained, in part, by the fact that he was an active legislative type who had collaborated with legislative liaison agents while serving on

---

[18] See Richard F. Fenno, Jr., *The Power of the Purse: Appropriations Politics in the Congress* (Boston: Little, Brown, 1966).

other committees. And, in view of his very short service on the Appropriations Committee, it can be assumed that he had not yet been affected by the unofficial but very influential norms of this committee.

CONGRESSIONAL RESTRAINTS UPON EXECUTIVE LOBBYING

Even though the needs, desires, and norms of members of the congressional system facilitate a wide range of roles for liaison agents, the limitations in the legislative climate which narrow the boundaries of permissibility for executive lobbying must be further examined. One set of limitations, embodied in the 1919 law prohibiting executive lobbying, is formal and involves the use of drastic sanctions. But the more important restrictions placed by the legislature upon executive lobbying arise from other forces: the premium placed by congressmen upon their right to intervene in the executive system, the way in which members of the legislative system perceive themselves, the special norms and positions assumed by members of the Appropriations Committees. Although these are informal in nature and extralegal, they impose restraints upon the executive lobbyists and isolate them from entire segments of the legislative system.

The Difficulty of Imposing Formal Restrictions

The U.S. Code prohibits the use of appropriated funds to influence members of Congress to favor or oppose legislation or appropriations in any manner except through proper official channels. However, the limited extent to which the law has been invoked reveals both congressional reluctance to wield this weapon against executive lobbyists and the difficulty of applying it to concrete cases.

In the hearings on legislative activities of executive agencies conducted in 1950 by the House Select Committee on Lobbying Activities, the Assistant to the Comptroller General (in charge of legislative activities) stressed repeatedly the great difficulty involved in enforcing the formal prohibitions against executive lobbying.[19] Either the language of the law was inadequate, he suggested, or enforcement was actually in the hands of another branch of the executive, the Justice Department. When complaints had been lodged regarding the expenditures of federal funds to influence legislation, the Comptroller General could do no more than disallow a few telephone calls and telegrams in the postaudit.

It was almost impossible, contended the Assistant to the Comptroller General, to recognize the unlawful use of funds for lobbying activities

[19] *Hearings on Legislative Activities of Executive Agencies,* pp. 30–34.

from the documents submitted by the departments. A trip by a government official to the capital may have been undertaken to enlist the aid of specific congressmen for his department's legislation. But all such trips were labeled "official business." Campaigns throughout the country by department and agency heads to activate pressure upon members of the Congress were also very difficult to control. It was hard to draw the line between the dissemination of information as well as the contacting of groups whose interests coincided with those of the agencies, which actions often had specific legislative authority, and the same activities for the direct purpose of influencing legislation.

Nevertheless, when congressmen view lobbying by the executive as a direct threat to their special position and status, they can react forcefully. This is especially true when the transgressors are bureaucrats, but also when they are legislative liaison agents who are expendable assistants to their departmental secretaries. Once the confrontation is abstracted from the acceptable frame of reference—that of bargaining or service relations between executive and legislative actors—and is transformed into a question as to whether the former are more powerful than the latter, the legislators tolerate no resolution other than legislative supremacy.

A case in point was the conflict between the Customs Service and the House Appropriations Committee in the late 1940s.[20] The committee had granted the Customs Service an increase in its appropriations, but had refused its request for additional increases. Within twenty-four hours an extensive propaganda campaign was developed throughout the country to "force Congress to give the Customs Service the appropriations it requested." This campaign was traced directly to the head of the Customs Service. In response to congressional protests and pressure, he was relieved of his position by the Secretary of the Treasury.

Undoubtedly congressmen were irritated by propaganda spread by the Customs Service that this refusal to provide funds meant that customs inspectors would be discharged and that American ports would be open to smugglers and dope peddlers. What directly challenged the position of the Congress and enraged its members were the "open boasts by the officials that they would *compel* the Congress of the United States to give them the money requested whether they wanted to or not."[21] Congressmen saw the issue in the following terms: "whether the bureaucracy was more powerful than the representatives of the people, whether they could compel the Congress, through pressure and propaganda, to appropriate unnecessary funds."[22]

[20] *Ibid.*, pp. 22–23.
[21] *Ibid.*, p. 23 [italics added].
[22] *Ibid.*

In general, members of the legislative system differentiate between the heads of the departments and bureaucratic officials. Departmental secretaries are considered to be political leaders. Hence they are granted much more discretion in their dealings with Congress. Moreover, an attack upon a department head by opposition-party legislators tends to shift the conflict from one between Congress and the executive to one of partisan politics.

Congressional toleration of efforts by Cabinet members to influence the fate of legislation tends to be very liberal. It should be reiterated that departmental liaison officers are also viewed as political appointees of and advisers to the executive heads of the departments. Hence they share, although to a much more limited degree, in the discretion afforded their superiors to engage in political maneuvering with congressmen.

Some of the most flagrant violations of the antilobbying law by departmental secretaries have been accepted with a modicum of congressional protest. In the fall of 1962 the new Secretary of HEW, Anthony J. Celebrezze, undertook to throw the influence of his office behind the administration's College Aid Bill (H.R. 8900), which was in trouble in the House of Representatives. Accordingly, he sent a long telegram to each representative, urging him to support this legislation; "a three-foot lobbying effort," Congressman Peter Frelinghuysen, Jr. (R., N.J.), called it.[23] Only three congressmen, all Republicans, responded publicly to this action: one more in sorrow than in anger; another who announced that the cost for the telegrams totaled $13,000; and the third contended that the secretary had violated the law.[24]

Within the department the telegram was considered a major tactical error. Nevertheless, the secretary's relations with Congress were not seriously impaired. The secretary explained that he had not known his appeal was to be sent by telegram, and he announced that specific instructions had been issued to ensure that this procedure would not be repeated.[25] With that the incident seems to have lost any further political significance.

A year later, even less attention was paid in Congress to the somewhat similar behavior of two other cabinet officers. In August 1963 both the Secretary of Defense and the Secretary of State intervened directly in the fight on the Foreign Aid Bill by sending cosigned letters to House members urging its adoption. Only one member, a Republican, reacted hostilely. Congressman H. R. Gross (Iowa) demanded that the two sec-

[23] See *Congressional Record*, 87th Cong., 2nd sess., September 20, 1962, p. 20142.
[24] *Ibid.*, p. 20143.
[25] *New York Times*, September 21, 1962.

retaries be prosecuted for their letter.[26] He correctly pointed out that they had violated that part of the U.S. Code that forbids the use of appropriated funds to influence any member of Congress by letter to favor or oppose pending legislation. But, as the *New York Times* correspondent noted: "Nobody on either side of the aisle took the proposal seriously."[27]

The extent of legislative acceptance of executive lobbying by department heads is further illustrated by the reaction to Secretary of Agriculture Orville L. Freeman's efforts on behalf of the administration's agricultural program. On a number of occasions when administration-sponsored agricultural legislation was to be voted upon and the outcome was uncertain, the Secretary of Agriculture, together with his legislative liaison officer, lobbied in the halls of the Congress. Operating out of the Speaker's Office in the House, Freeman met with a number of congressmen in an attempt to secure their votes. Aside from some random grumbling by a few Republicans, the legislators appeared to have accepted this type of lobbying with equanimity. After all, a Republican congressman observed, Postmaster Arthur E. Summerfield had operated in a similar fashion during the Eisenhower Administration.

When, on the other hand, the Secretary of Agriculture and his staff undertook in the spring of 1963 to go directly to the farmers in behalf of a wheat referendum that the administration supported, congressional reaction was vociferous. Again it was only opposition-party legislators who criticized executive lobbying. The roar of anger from Republican members indicated that a raw partisan nerve had been touched. The referendum had become a bitter party battle—the administration and its coalition of agricultural interest groups in direct conflict with the opposition party and its interest-group allies.

In July of that year Senator Milward L. Simpson (R., Wyo.) introduced a bill, S. 1939, that would have made executive use of appropriated funds to influence the vote of any person in any referendum held in accordance with an act of Congress a crime subject to a $500 fine, a year in prison, and dismissal. "It is patent that Secretary Freeman and his De-

---

[26] *Congressional Record,* 88th Cong., 1st sess., August 20, 1963, pp. 15448–49. See also *New York Times,* August 21, 1963.

[27] *New York Times,* August 21, 1963. Without taking a position on the merits of the law prohibiting executive lobbying, Senator Norris Cotton (R., N.H.) suggested in 1967 that the Congress decide on whether to retain and enforce the law, relax its provisions and make them more practical, or abolish it outright. It was, he claimed, being honored only in the breach. See *Congressional Record,* 90th Cong., 1st sess., March 7, 1967, pp. S3276–77. For a more aggressive Republican statement, see Ancher Nelson, "Lobbying by the Administration," in *We Propose: A Modern Congress, Selected Proposals by the House Republican Task Force on Congressional Reform and Minority Staffing,* ed. Mary McInnis (New York: McGraw-Hill, 1966), pp. 143–59.

partment of Agriculture violated the law and used the appropriated funds illegally," he argued.[28] This bill was never considered. Again the legislative system glossed over a violation of the antilobbying law.

Formal Limitations Outside the Antilobbying Law

In its most extreme exercise of power, Congress has imposed financial limitations upon legislative liaison when it deems such activity inappropriate. A cost limitation was applied in 1958 to all legislative liaison activities of the military services.[29] This move was prompted in part by congressional reaction to excessive lobbying by the services and to bitter interservice rivalry. As the Defense Department's legislative liaison officer explained in 1961 before a House subcommittee on appropriations: "I understand that the reasons Congress felt there was a need to . . . [limit] these activities was primarily because the services were somewhat overzealous in their campaigning for 'pet projects.' "[30]

Perhaps a more significant factor influencing Congress to impose such a limitation was the sharp criticism of military legislative liaison voiced by President Eisenhower. In his message on the proposed reorganization of the Department of Defense on April 3, 1958, the Chief Executive sharply attacked interservice rivalries in the Congress and pinpointed legislative liaison as well as the public affairs activities of the military departments as the principal outlets for these rivalries.[31]

Informal Limitations: The Style of Executive Lobbying Must Not Be Crude

Congressmen do not like to be threatened.[32] Since the operation of liaison agents in the legislative system depends so much on their acceptance by the legislators, executive lobbyists cannot afford to resort to threats. This informal limitation applies much more to departmental liaison officers than it does to White House lobbyists.

---

[28] *Congressional Record,* 88th Cong., 1st sess., July 25, 1963, pp. 13386–87; *New York Times,* July 26, 1963.

[29] U.S. House of Representatives, Committee on Appropriations, *House Report No. 1830,* 85th Cong., 2nd sess., May 28, 1958, p. 19; and H.R. 12738, sec. 632, 85th Cong., 2nd sess.

[30] U.S. House of Representatives, Subcommittee of Committee on Appropriations, *Hearings on Department of Defense Appropriations for 1962,* 87th Cong., 1st sess. (Washington, D.C.: U.S. Government Printing Office, 1961), pt. 2, "Operations and Maintenance," p. 1022.

[31] See *Congressional Record*, 85th Cong., 2nd sess., April 3, 1958, pp. 6259–63. See especially p. 6263.

[32] See Bauer, Pool, and Dexter, *op. cit.,* p. 434.

The cry that executive lobbyists were twisting the legislators' arms and that this was improper was raised repeatedly during the Kennedy Administration. Rarely is arm-twisting defined in precise terms, but it implies the use of threats to deny a congressman certain requests or aid in connection with his personal legislation or appropriations for his district and state, or to deprive him and his constituency of existing programs or services. In 1962, for example, Republicans accused the administration of stimulating businessmen in their constituencies to pressure them to support a bill increasing the national debt limit; it was claimed that such businessmen had been warned that defense contracts would be reduced if the debt ceiling were not raised.[33] Other arm-twisting has involved the threat to withhold campaign funds and the stimulation of activity among political party leaders in constituencies or among interest groups to apply pressure on legislators.

The debate over one of the Kennedy Administration's agricultural bills of 1962[34] reveals different congressional reactions to two types of arm-twisting lobbying by the executive. Minority Leader Charles A. Halleck had read into the *Congressional Record* a press release by a New York Democrat to exemplify the massive arm-twisting to which the administration had resorted. Congressman Otis G. Pike (D., N. Y.), had written that "this week my arm aches from the twisting it has taken lately." Not only had he received phone calls on the bill from the administration, but a friendly representative from the Post Office Department had approached him. This visitor had not talked about the eight new applications for post offices in the congressman's district which were then pending; he had merely wanted to talk about the farm bill. "Now isn't it odd," the congressman wrote, "that the man who came to talk about the farm bill came from the Post Office Department and not the Department of Agriculture? Do you suppose it had anything to do with those pending post offices? The arm aches this week. . . ."[35]

When I interviewed him a year later, Congressman Pike made it perfectly clear that the Post Office representative had not overtly threatened any reprisal if he voted against the administration. What Pike objected to so strongly was the implicit threat. Why else was the Post Office representative sent? And he considered it an insult to his intelligence to be

---

[33] See *Congressional Record,* 87th Cong., 2nd sess., June 13, 1962, pp. 10408–10. The ranking Republican on the Ways and Means Committee, John W. Byrnes (Wisc.), charged that the administration was engaged in criminal conduct (*ibid.,* p. 10490).
[34] See *Congressional Record,* 87th Cong., 2nd sess., June 21, 1962, pp. 11342–43.
[35] *Ibid.,* p. 11342.

lobbied on an agriculture bill by a Post Office agent who, he charged, knew nothing about agriculture anyway.

Congressman Pike's press release, it should be noted, was publicized by the Republican floor leader in the midst of a sharp partisan battle over the administration's agriculture bill. During the debate another Democrat, Congressman Richard H. Ichord of Missouri, declared that, despite a visit from a Department of Defense representative who had come to his office to discuss the debt-limit bill, he had voted in opposition to the administration. He did not consider such activity arm-twisting, although his own district contained an army installation. Referring to Minority Leader Halleck, Congressman Ichord recommended that "if he can't stand a little arm-twisting in this game, he had better get out of it, because this is the rough game of politics."[36]

The administration's drive behind the debt-limit bill and the agriculture bill of 1962 engendered considerable criticism within the Congress on the type of lobbying employed. It was characterized as direct, aggressive, and often very crude. It was the crudeness of style on the part of some executive lobbyists, more than arm-twisting, that irritated so many congressmen.

Such charges of arm-twisting most probably represent a reflex action to an application of pressure or a manifestation of partisan politics rather than a rejection of executive intervention in the Congress. An influential legislative type in the House, in the high-seniority group (eight terms of office), made these perceptive remarks on the subject:

The congressional reaction to lobbying by the executive is one of constant bitching. The greater the amount of effort that is exerted by the executive, the louder the complaint and the greater the criticism. Congressmen are always dissatisfied with what they get and annoyed because they have to pay for it. If the bill is an easy win for the administration, little or no pressure is applied. If it is a tough fight, though, they apply great pressure.

And referring to complaints about the pressure that Secretary of the Interior Stewart L. Udall exerted in the Rules Committee fight of 1961, this legislator said:

The further they are behind, the tougher the pressure will get. The complaints that the opposition articulates are as phony as a three-dollar bill. We did the same in regard to pressure by [Postmaster General] Summerfield; we claimed that this was an unwarranted executive intrusion in the legislative process. It's part of the game, part of the American myth that the executive executes and the Congress legislates. These complaints can, however, occasionally be effec-

---

[36] *Ibid.,* p. 11343.

tive. They serve as pegs for people who want to oppose and who use the argument of executive intrusion as an effective excuse.

Even this congressman, a skilled, tough veteran of innumerable battles in the House of Representatives, conceded that executive lobbyists could be crude. The White House, he contended, lost out when it pressed the panic button on certain bills and turned some of the departmental types loose in the Congress. Here he was referring not to the established liaison units in the departments, but to the extra personnel that had been called upon to supplement executive lobbying efforts. "They have no finesse. They try to bully, and this is a dangerous tactic to employ upon a House member."[37]

The administrative assistant to a southern congressman informed me that his superior had almost changed his mind and voted against the bill to raise the ceiling on the debt limit in 1962 because of the pressure brought to bear upon him. Not only had the Treasury Department called him on the bill, but so had the Post Office. This, he felt, was totally unnecessary and "damned annoying." He was even more irritated when a uniformed officer from the Department of Defense came to his office to demonstrate how a military installation in his district might be hurt unless the debt limit were raised.

This administrative assistant aptly summarized one problem facing executive lobbyists: "Lobbying by legislative liaison officers, unless conducted by extremely skilled individuals, gets awfully obvious to the congressman, who tends to resent it." His congressman was all the more irritated with the lieutenant colonel who visited him because the officer knew nothing about the bill. From the congressman's point of view, the officer had obviously been handed the names of some legislators with instructions to "see this list." Whether this had occurred or not is irrelevant. What is significant is that congressmen dislike to be approached in this manner; no congressman likes to think of himself as a name on a bureaucrat's list.

The administrative assistant to an active subcommittee chairman in the House of Representatives was highly incensed at the crude attitude exhibited by a White House liaison agent toward the assistant's employer and toward congressmen in general. This White House representative, he contended, used devices more appropriate to "muscling delegates in a political convention" than to dealing with elected representatives of the people. In the Speaker's Lobby he had overheard the White House lobbyist say, "Anyone have a dime? I want to buy a congressman." This fa-

---

[37] See also Meg Greenfield, "Why Are You Calling Me, Son?," *Reporter*, 27 (August 16, 1962): 29–31.

cetious remark angered not only the administrative assistant, but also a number of congressmen who had overheard it. On two other occasions, White House lobbyists had actually cursed his representative in the presence of the administrative assistant and other witnesses. A departmental legislative liaison agent corroborated both of these stories.

Informal Limitations: Liaison Agents Must Respect Congressional Ties to the Bureaucracy

It is evident that congressmen wish to maintain their own channels into the bureaucracy and that they intend to protect the special mutually beneficial relationships that have been established. Should liaison officers appear to interfere with these lines of communications, Congress is prepared to apply pressure upon them to desist.

A case in point arose when the Assistant Secretary of State for Congressional Relations, Frederick G. Dutton, sought to coordinate all the relations between members of his department and members of the legislative system. On February 19, 1962, Dutton circulated in the department a memorandum regarding the establishment of a central file on congressional contacts by officers of the department and their immediate subordinates.[38] Its declared purpose was "to bring together and more fully utilize information individually obtained concerning members of the Congress." Cards were distributed for department personnel to complete and forward to Dutton's office concerning any meeting, telephone call, or social contact they might have had with congressmen or their staffs. Information was requested regarding informal meetings as well as official contacts. The congressional response was instantaneous and hostile.

As the assistant secretary explained later in a letter to Senator Thomas J. Dodd (D., Conn.), chairman of the Senate Judiciary Committee's Subcommittee on Internal Security, he had taken this step in order "to provide more adequate service by the Department for Members of Congress and to increase the Department's understanding of matters of current concern to individual Congressmen."[39] Informal requests for information directed to a particular office in the department were often relevant in other bureaus, and "better service could be provided by getting the inquiries centrally considered." As for information on the attitudes of congressmen regarding the trade bill and the U.N. bond legislation, which the cards called for, Dutton specified that these

[38] A copy of the memorandum is found in U.S. Senate, Committee on the Judiciary, Subcommittee to Investigate the Administration of the Internal Security Act . . . , *Hearings on State Department Security,* 87th Cong., 2nd sess. (Washington, D.C.: U.S. Government Printing Office, March 15, 1962), p. 430.
[39] *Ibid.,* p. 429.

data were desirable because both bills were likely to be considered that spring.

It is noteworthy that the Assistant Secretary for Congressional Relations carefully justified his action in terms of services provided by the department for Congress and of better executive understanding of matters that concerned individual legislators. These justifications coincided with congressional norms for legislative liaison by the executive.

Obviously other motives entered into this attempt to set up a central file. The collection of political intelligence is a major facet of a lobbyist's job. If the department better understood the problems and interests of each congressman, its lobbyists could more effectively focus upon them. Knowledge gleaned from contacts with congressmen on their attitudes toward the trade bill and the U.N. bond proposal would be vital to the department as well as to the White House, which had a special unit working on the trade bill. Intelligence data are also very critical in decisions that require correct timing, which in the Congress is a very delicate matter.

To some members of the legislative system, the memorandum seemed to be motivated by still other considerations. By permitting the assistant secretary to monitor all channels between congressmen and the department, the memorandum appeared to constitute an effort by the political executive to intervene between the Congress and individuals within the bureaucracy. Never explicitly articulated in the hearings that publicized Dutton's memorandum, this suspicion lay behind the questions raised by the counsel to the Internal Security Subcommittee when he queried a State Department employee: "I do not want to put you on the spot, but does that not impress you as rather an infringement of a man's privacy and his constitutional freedom of association?"[40]

Freedom to associate with congressmen and their staffs was never prohibited to State bureaucrats by the Dutton memorandum. However, the principal reason for the hearings was an attempt by members of the legislative system to pressure the State Department to retain an employee who had provided information to certain congressmen on a confidential basis. In the suspicious eyes of the subcommittee, the creation of the central file was part of an effort to ascertain and close off sources from within the department that were unofficially feeding material to the committee.

The Assistant Secretary of State for Congressional Relations canceled his memorandum immediately upon notice of congressional disapproval. In his letter of explanation to the chairman of the subcommittee, he wrote: "Prior to my memorandum being raised in the meeting of the subcommittee, I learned of the possible objection to it by a Member

---

[40] *Ibid.*, p. 430.

of the House, and since my purpose here is to strengthen the Department's relations with the Congress, not impose any difficulties, the procedure was discontinued . . . [as of] March 14."[41] The subcommittee hearings were held on March 15.

Liaison agents are extremely sensitive to the attitudes of congressmen and especially to charges of undue interference in the legislative prerogative. Executive lobbyists require a permissive climate in which to operate, since the members of the legislative system have it within their means to withhold or grant what the liaison agents and the executive need: political intelligence, cooperation in legislative campaigns, votes, etc.

In the case of State's memorandum, the line between acceptable and unacceptable action by an executive lobbyist had been breached. That it had occurred in an especially delicate area—the State Department, where congressional relations are at best tenuous and probably involve more legislative suspicion than in any other department—contributed, no doubt, to the committee's intervention and to the alacrity with which the assistant secretary withdrew his memorandum. However, legislative liaison officers in virtually all the departments sought to develop a central clearance of one sort or another on contacts between the Congress and their departments.

The Appropriations Committees: Legislative Liaison Agents Not Welcome

Although the legislative system as a whole is receptive to lobbying by liaison agents, one important subsystem is actively hostile. The antipathy toward departmental legislative liaison agents manifested by the House Appropriations Committee and by the staff members of the Senate committee excludes these executive agents from a most important center of power in the House and seriously handicaps them in dealing with another in the Senate. While the restraints placed upon the access by legislative liaison agents to the Appropriations Committees are informal, they are nevertheless effective. That the departmental liaison officers do intervene occasionally in appropriation politics was evident from interviews with these actors; but, they pointed out, they were only peripherally involved.[42] More often, departmental liaison officers called upon the White House lobbyists for help in overturning decisions of the Appropriations Committees.

[41] *Ibid.*, p. 429.
[42] Professor Milbrath errs in stating that one of the major concerns of the departmental legislative liaison staff is "to protect the appropriations for the department" (*op. cit.*, p. 10).

Why is it that both staff and members of the House Appropriations Committee resist any association with these executive agents in contrast with the cooperative, permissive attitude on the part of other committees? The heart of the matter is to be found in the special perception of its tasks that the House Appropriations Committee has evolved, in the special relations with and attitude toward the bureaucracy that Appropriations members and staff have established, and in the long practice, hallowed by tradition, of the Appropriations Committee's dealing with a particular set of officers from the departmental executive.

The study by Richard F. Fenno, Jr., on the House Appropriations Committee revealed that its members conceived of their tasks not only as different from those of all other standing committees, but as among the most important in the legislative system.[43] In the members' view, the Constitution endowed the committee with special obligations and prerogatives. Committee norms revolved around the notion that this committee had an overriding responsibility—to safeguard the treasury; to protect the taxpayer; to guard against the extravagance, waste, and irresponsibility that were endemic in the executive.

When committee members and staff were interviewed regarding their relations with and attitudes toward the legislative liaison agents,[44] it was apparent that Appropriations epitomized the tendency within Congress to insist upon its own special ties with the bureaucracy. The political executive was seen as a third force whose interests might be and often were antithetical to those of the Appropriations Committees as well as the bureaucracy.

The House committee members and staff members of both committees objected to legislative liaison agents' dealing with them on appropriations; they wanted to have nothing to do with these executive actors. "It is a policy in our committee," explained a high-seniority Republican serving on two Appropriations subcommittees, one to which Democrats and Republicans alike subscribed. His views on committee attitudes were confirmed by the Democratic chairman of one of these subcommittees.

The departmental secretaries who have attempted to use their legislative liaison personnel to coordinate or control departmental relations with these committees have been rebuffed. House Committee members consider these efforts an unwarranted and undesirable intrusion in their affairs. "Secretary McNamara wanted to shift control of DOD's relations with us

[43] See Fenno, *op. cit.,* chap. 3, "The House Committee I: Committee Expectations and Adaptations."
[44] Interviews were conducted by the author with four high-seniority members of the committee and one low-seniority member. Two staff members from the House committee and two from the Senate committee were also interviewed.

to his legislative liaison staff," asserted a member of the Military Affairs Subcommittee, "but we sent word that this was totally unacceptable." A member of the Subcommittee on HEW and Labor Appropriations pointed out that former Secretary of Labor Arthur J. Goldberg had also wanted to control relations with this subcommittee through his legislative liaison unit; but, the congressman explained, both he and the chairman had made their opposition very clear to the secretary. A senior staff assistant on the Senate Appropriations Committee also reported attempts by department heads to have legislative liaison actors "invade" the relations between the departments and the committee. "They are always repulsed, but there is a constant desire and pressure on the part of legislative liaison people to control relations with the committee."

When the reasons for this antipathy are analyzed, the crucial factor that emerges is that legislative liaison agents appear to violate the basic norms of the House Appropriations Committee, norms that are apparently subscribed to by staff members of the Senate committee. The remarks of a senior staff assistant to the House Appropriations Committee are particularly pertinent: "Legislative liaison is pushing for more money and for different programs that aren't on the books." On the other hand, the departmental budget officers with whom the committees have worked for decades "are supporting the budget; that is what the law says they should do." These sentiments express the primary norms of House Appropriations Committee members and staff: economy and resistance to executive extravagance with its requests for more funds and more spending programs.

Legislative liaison officers were also considered to represent the interests of political executive leaders in contrast with those of the committees. In distinguishing between legislative liaison agents and departmental budget officers, a senior staff assistant from the Senate Appropriations Committee commented about the latter: "They help us rather than peddle the wares of the department." Legislative liaison agents were considered biased in favor of the departmental secretary, who placed the interests of the political executive first, above those of the committee and the bureaucracy. A Republican member of the House Appropriations Committee was even more explicit in rejecting the appearance of legislative liaison agents before his committee: "Legislative liaison agents are special pleaders for the point of view of the department. We find that legislative liaison people oppose the reductions we make. They contact congressmen to reverse our positions." In effect, he continued, they were lobbyists for the secretary: "We try them out every so often but we always find that they cover up." They were established in the first place, he argued, upon the justification that they would help the departments respond to congressional requests. But "they don't share our interest in the making of independent judgments; they exist primarily to protect and advise their secretaries."

A third dimension in this antagonism relates to the second, but has wider implications: Liaison agents are seen as blocking the intervention of these committees into the executive system. House committee members felt that they could not operate as they should—in accordance with their norms—unless they had unlimited access to the interstices of the departments. "We want the facts and not the policy point of view," declared one of the House Appropriations Committee members, "so we want to protect the working divisions [in the departments] when this point of view is different from the secretary's." A member of the House Subcommittee on HEW and Labor Appropriations declared: "In each one of the bureaus, the individual handling the money knows all the dirt. He can give us more information and more useful information than could anyone in the secretary's office." Appropriations Committee members wanted bureaucrats to come to them and to be dependent upon them. This general attitude was summed up in its baldest terms in the following remarks by an Appropriations congressman:

We want and need all kinds of information and for the people from the departments to trust us, and we'll respect their confidence. You never want things set up so that the bureau heads in a department can hide behind some legislative liaison guy or assistant secretary responsible for legislation. *If it ever gets to that point, the Appropriations Committee won't be able to do its job.* We don't want a level between us and the department. Now the bureau chiefs will come to us and say, "We didn't want to do this but the department or the White House insists, so the Bureau of the Budget requires it."

An additional aspect of executive–Appropriations Committee relations that restricts legislative liaison agents is the long-term practice by these committees of dealing with special budget officers at the departmental level. Such officers were provided for over forty years ago by the Budget and Accounting Act of 1921, whereas full-scale legislative liaison staffs have only recently emerged in the secretaries' offices. Moreover, budget officers tend to be administrative career servants who occupy their positions for long periods, while liaison agents are political appointees and change with the administration.

As a consequence, when legislative liaison agents attempted to develop contacts with these committees, they discovered that the congressmen and their staffs had already established close, comfortable relations with the departmental budgetary staffs. "The budgetary people know what we want" and "They help us rather than peddle the wares of the departments" were the comments of senior staff members on the House and Senate committees. The House staff member added: *"Budget officers are not lobbyists,* although some do push when they can, and this is appropriate." Furthermore, budget officers are seen as supporting the budget. "We have our own liaison people from the department office," a congressman explained. "We have to have people we can trust." Apropos of one such budget officer, he commented: "He is loyal to us." With regard to another: "He will not mislead me on anything." Both were in his office several times a week, informing him about what had transpired in the department. "If they don't level with us," he explained, both Democrats and Republicans on the committee would unite in defense of the committee's right to full and honest information.

In 1961 a member of the State Department, who had been closely associated with its liaison officers in the past, lamented the lack of rapport between executive lobbyists and the appropriations subsystem of the Congress. "There wasn't any consultation between State and the Appropriations Committees," he disclosed. This was a real problem that "we ought to be able to deal with and don't know how." As far as he could recall, he knew of only one instance of general consultation with an Appropriations Committee. During the Eisenhower Administration, the Assistant Secretary for Congressional Relations had represented the undersecretary in explaining the department's position on a foreign policy issue to the House committee. Apropos of the meeting, this staff member noted:

You've never seen a more suspicious group of people. . . . Nobody had ever done this before. They didn't know why we were there. They were not accustomed to this kind of consultation. The atmosphere was frigid and their attitude was one of "What is it you fellows are trying to put over?"

The Congress is a tradition-oriented system, and its norms reflect this fact. It respects and prefers arrangements with the executive that are familiar, comfortable, and trustworthy. "Authorizations and appropriations," explained one Appropriations Committee staff member, "have always been handled by different people and the system has worked very well through the years." Appropriations Committee staff members can always rely upon departmental budget officers to answer their detailed inquiries on the budget and the department, and with a minimum of delay. The staff on the two committees maintained that legislative liaison agents did not have the facts or the know-how to meet the needs of their committees. It was contended, in effect, that legislative liaison agents were not Appropriations Committee types who reflected the norms and fulfilled the needs of these committees.

As forcefully as these conclusions have been advanced, they can be adopted only provisionally in the absence of more systematic interviewing among legislators on both committees.[45] All those committee staff members who were interviewed were in complete agreement, and they claimed to reflect the thinking of their staff associates. Only one among the five representatives on the House committee who were interviewed disagreed with his colleagues, and he was among the most junior members of the committee.

Two senators who were members of the Senate Appropriations Committee, a Democrat and a senior Republican, and an assistant to another Democratic member on that committee reflected a totally different approach to departmental liaison agents from that of their own committee staff and their House colleagues. The three reported that departmental and agency liaison agents sought their cooperation on appropriations and that they welcomed such efforts. They had no objection to being lobbied on appropriations bills, and they often collaborated with such executive agents.

Two factors that distinguish the Senate Appropriations Committee from its counterpart in the House may explain these differences in attitude among legislators. Except for a few who were on very minor committees and one who served on an important committee (Atomic Energy), the fifty House Appropriations Committee members served on this committee alone. In contrast, all the senators on the Appropriations Committee served also on other standing committees. Hence they and their personal staffs were accustomed to working with the secretaries and their personal representatives, liaison agents among them, whose departments came under the jurisdiction of their other major committee assignments. If these departments encountered trouble with their appropriations, they could rely upon sympathetic senators from their authorization committees who were at the same time members of the Appropriations Committee.

The second distinction between House and Senate Appropriations Committees was the different roles they assumed. The House committee dug deeper into details, played the role of economizer, and tended to cut executive proposals. The Senate committee played the role of an appeals board. It was less thorough in its examination of appropriations requests and tended to concentrate on areas where executive leaders requested the restoration of funds cut by the House. In this capacity, too, senators would be more likely to be approached by the legislative liaison

[45] Unfortunately Fenno's superb study of the two Appropriations Committees does not touch upon relations between their members and staff and the legislative liaison agents.

staffs with whose departments they were already familiar and with whom they had already cooperated in authorization politics.

Again, the number of senators on this committee and their personal assistants who were interviewed was too small to permit a conclusive assertion that the legislative liaison agents found a more permissive environment among Appropriations senators than among Appropriations representatives, or that the difference, if there actually was one, stemmed from the nature and composition of these two subsystems of the Congress. The evidence, however, justifies the tentative acceptance of such conclusions.

CHAPTER IV

Legislative Liaison Officers:
Their Roles and Career Backgrounds

IT IS APPARENT that a wide degree of consensus exists among legislators and executive leaders in their expectations regarding legislative liaison. This facilitates, indeed demands, the playing of certain roles by congressional relations officers who must interact with both groups. The thinking of those engaged in liaison work must reflect that of their executive superiors as well as that of the legislative actors. Roles are not totally predetermined by others, however, but are shaped also by the individuals who perform them.

This necessitates a concern with the role orientations of the legislative liaison officers themselves to ascertain whether these coincide with, supplement, or conflict with those of the legislators or executive leaders. It is also pertinent to approach their roles from the perspective of the recruitment pattern through which the liaison officers are brought into the executive system. Do their career backgrounds fit the roles assigned by their principals to this position?

LEGISLATIVE LIAISON OFFICERS
DEFINE THEIR OWN ROLES

"I have two sets of clients, Congress and the executive," was the comment of a number of departmental liaison officers in the Kennedy Administration. The two-client concept has important implications for their roles. For if expectations may be considered equivalent to signals, then liaison officers need to be sensitively attuned to both sets of clients. To do otherwise might severely restrict their access to and maneuverability within both systems, sharply depreciating their value to both sets of actors.

77

The primary loyalty of the liaison officers is, of course, to their executive superiors, whose expectations are afforded the highest precedence. Nevertheless, any difference in or conflict between the demands and attitudes of their two clients inevitably raises problems for these executive agents. Such problems are discussed in subsequent chapters.

Not surprisingly, the roles that legislative liaison officers envisaged for their positions coincided with those expected of them by executive leaders and congressmen. Furthermore, the liaison agents in the eight departments surveyed during the Kennedy Administration, as well as their counterparts in five of these departments from the Eisenhower Administration, were in general accord on a common set of roles. It should be noted, however, that not all conceived of themselves as being properly engaged in identical sets of roles and that distinct nuances appeared even in their conceptualization of common roles. Some of the liaison officers objected, moreover, to certain restraints that one or both sets of clients had imposed upon them. While grudgingly accepting such limitations, they deemed it necessary at times to play roles in areas ostensibly prohibited or foreclosed to them.

Adviser to the Secretary

The role of adviser to the secretary was accorded the highest priority by all the departmental liaison agents. It was their contention that they should be their department heads' principal advisers on Congress. And, with a few exceptions, because of very special circumstances in their departments, they believed themselves to be filling this role.

The heart of his job, his greatest value to the department, asserted an Assistant Secretary of State for Congressional Relations, lay in his serving as adviser to the secretary and other departmental officers on legislation and on their relations with the Congress. A liaison agent for a small department described his adviser role in terms that paralleled those of his counterparts:

I act as adviser to the secretary on legislation as well as on the politics of legislation. In the former capacity, it's my job to point out any problems that particular provisions might cause us in view of what I know about congressional attitudes, likes, and dislikes. In terms of the latter, it is to advise and help decide on the timing of our moves in the Congress, to brief the secretary on whom he is to see and what questions he can expect when he testifies, how he should deal with certain members and with problems that arise in Congress.

It was also his job, he maintained, to staff the secretary for internal administrative decisions and acts that had an impact upon the department's legislation.

Some of the liaison officers were personally responsible for preparing the testimony their secretaries gave before congressional committees, while others were more concerned with pulling together the supporting material and making certain that others in the department prepared the secretary properly. All felt that they were capable and should be called upon for advice on what was needed to ensure the passage of legislation.

As advisers to their secretaries, the liaison officers believed that they should exercise some influence upon the development of legislation before it was presented to the Congress. The tremendous demands imposed upon them by their other roles made this task difficult. One liaison officer remarked wistfully that he had accepted the position on the condition that he have a voice in the making of policy. Once on the job, however, he discovered that it was extremely difficult to involve himself in legislative development; he was simply too busy with the other aspects of his work. Nevertheless, the other departmenal liaison officers asserted that they did have some voice in the development of legislation.

In the event that they possessed special knowledge on substance, their views were properly considered. But principally their task was to ensure that the legislation, as it was drawn up, did not create unexpected political problems, and that senior departmental leaders were made aware of the ones they would have to face in the Congress. "I'm really only in on the development of legislation as guardian of political problems," stated a legislative liaison agent who was actively involved with Congress in both substance and process. "I'm supposed to be in on the policy formulation team. My views are important in areas where I know the substance and where there are problems of a political nature. I point out possible mistakes and clashes with Congress—then my views are listened to and discussed." Another indicated that he had served on the task force that had developed a particular piece of legislation; a third, that if he possessed special knowledge on substance, he would disclose it at a stage prior to the proposed legislation's being considered at the secretarial level. Otherwise, he had no voice on the substance of legislation, except as it affected the Hill and the bill's chances there.

Again, it is necessary to point out that the Assistant Secretary for Legislation in HEW during the Kennedy Administration was a special case. Since he was directly in charge of legislative development for the department, he had a major part in the substantive as well as the other aspects of legislation.

Spokesman for the Secretary

Liaison agents deemed it essential that they act as spokesmen for their department heads. Unless this was clearly understood in the Congress as well as in the departments, their status and their usefulness, they asserted, were gravely impaired. All the liaison officers recognized that others, senior departmental leaders, also spoke for the departments. The latter were pictured for the most part, though, as interacting with the Congress in specific subject areas and with a few designated legislators. With the exception of appropriations items, legislative liaison officers claimed that their own jurisdiction cut across all areas of legislation in the departments, that it involved them more frequently in the congressional system, and that they interacted with a greater number of legislators. Only one liaison officer insisted upon acting also as the single channel for all informal, nonpublic negotiations with the Congress. Conceding that in certain policy areas others negotiated at times for the department, on the whole, he noted, "I insist that the assistant secretaries and the undersecretary deal with the Congress through me." Appropriations he exempted.

As spokesmen for their secretaries, they carried out their roles informally and quietly; they rarely assumed a public posture. Before the public and the Congress, the principal departmental policy spokesmen were properly the secretary, undersecretary or undersecretaries, assistant secretaries, and agency or bureau heads. Aside from HEW's Assistant Secretary for Legislation, who testified in his own right, none of the legislative liaison agents suggested that they be permitted to testify before the committees dealing with their departments' legislation. On the other hand, a few appeared before appropriations subcommittees concerning the funding of their personal offices.

Coordinator

Some legislative liaison officers ranked the role of coordinator next in importance to that of adviser. From their point of view this role demanded their pulling together their departments' human resources for congressional relations and making certain that particular executive actors involved themselves in the Congress at the proper time and with the proper legislators. (Appropriations politics was excluded from this, as it was from almost all other roles.)

The liaison officers for the Secretary of Defense probably emphasized coordination more than the others. With three relatively independent military departments combined in Defense, it was little wonder that one of the liaison officers reported: "My most important job relative to the department is a coordinating one, so we'll pull together in putting our best legislative foot forward." His predecessor accented the importance of "providing close coordination among the three services so that they know what the secretary is going to do and how he is going to play ball." And both spoke of activating the DOD assistant secretaries in congressional relations. Liaison officers in the other departments, which did not approximate the divisions in Defense, also maintained that the role of coordinator was absolutely vital. Where, as in a subordinate agency in one department, it was evident that the liaison officer was not permitted to assume such a role, this constituted the basis for one of his major grievances.

Liaison agents also helped coordinate their departments' public approach to the committee hearing process in the Congress. Although a number claimed that they briefed only their own secretaries, others pointed out that on very controversial bills they coached departmental witnesses on the atmosphere to be anticipated in committees, the political styles and interests of the congressmen, and the questions to which they might be subjected. Only one noted that he had a voice in the selection of such witnesses.

Intelligence Agent

A number of liaison officers ranked the role of intelligence agent among the three most important to the success of their jobs. So, too, did officers in the few agencies within these departments that staffed their own legislative liaison shops. On the other hand, while all of the liaison agents engaged personally in intelligence work, some of the department-level officers categorized the gathering of intelligence data as primarily a responsibility of their office staffs.

HEW's atypical situation warrants a brief comment. Its congressional liaison officer was separate from but subordinate to the Assistant Secretary for Legislation, who himself preempted the important liaison roles, and whose personal staff also engaged in intelligence work. The assistant secretary viewed the Congressional Liaison Officer almost exclusively as an intelligence agent. The Congressional Liaison Officer, however, saw herself as also properly involved in other important roles. When her position became vacant, the assistant secretary's staff assumed full responsibility for intelligence work.

An important aspect of intelligence work is ascertaining the policy positions and the voting intentions of legislators as well as the political combinations among them which can prove significant for the departments' bills. "A lot of the job is knowing where you stand," pointed out one agent. "What do we have to do? What are the problems facing us in getting the legislation through? How hard do we have to work?" And running through all their interviews was the refrain: "We must engage in nose counting." If it merely enables executive leaders to be in a stronger position to resist the compromises they find distasteful, then a careful assessment of how noses are pointed becomes extremely important.

A corollary responsibility of the liaison officer as intelligence agent is to anticipate trouble not directly pertinent to legislation. "It's our job to smell out trouble and nip it in the bud ourselves, if possible," explained one liaison agent. "To keep abreast is to be forewarned" was the slogan of a liaison agent whose superiors were being subjected to congressional attacks and investigations. Or, as a third expressed it, their responsibility was to pinpoint trouble spots so that senior departmental leaders could prevent or resolve problems, thereby avoiding the development of antagonistic feelings among legislators.

Lobbyist

Allied with the spokesman role are others that demand of the liaison agents even greater involvement in the legislative process. These are encompassed under the role category of lobbyist and break down into two distinct subdivisions: political collaborator and advocate.

(A) POLITICAL COLLABORATOR. In the interests of their departments and the administration, liaison officers actively engaged in collaborative endeavors with the legislative leadership and with members of their congressional committees. As the liaison officers conceived it, this role called for them to work closely with the key committee members, especially the chairmen, in order to keep them informed about the thinking and actions of the political leadership of the departments, to seek their counsel, to cooperate with them in ensuring that a quorum appeared for committee hearings and markup sessions, to plan tactics and strategy, and to count noses together.

Departmental agents differed somewhat in defining their relations with the Democratic floor leaders in the Congress. All agreed, though, that the White House liaison staff played a more significant role with these leaders than they. In two departments liaison agents maintained that they should rely upon the White House staff to deal with the party leadership. Other departmental liaison agents, however, contended that it was also their responsibility to seek out these party leaders, and that the party leaders sought to utilize them as collaborators.

(B) ADVOCATE. Most of the liaison agents pictured themselves as active advocates. They explained the features and effects of their bills to the members of Congress and endeavored to sell them on the legislation. "Yes, I do negotiate with congressmen," declared the liaison agent for a large confederate department.

I do all or most of the work on a number of bills plus work out some of the agreements and concessions. I try to influence members on and off of the committees on our legislation and even on getting a vote from Rules. Of course, others in the department, the secretary and assistant secretaries, do this too.

An Assistant Secretary of State for Congressional Relations pointed out: "I don't engage in any hard sell, but I do justify the program. It is vital to explain personally to them |legislators| why the department reaches its conclusions." Neither he nor his staff, he hastened to add, were policy spokesmen to the extent that they could make or interpret foreign policy. Others within the department carried this responsibility; he helped bring these individuals to the Hill. A third liaison agent, in another large department, depicted himself as negotiating with key committees on routine matters of legislation and amendments while his secretary dealt with Congress on major policy matters. However, he noted that he, too, sometimes negotiated with the chairmen on policy.

The primary selling job was carried on by others in the department; with few exceptions, liaison officers pictured themselves as important but largely auxiliary actors in this endeavor. Even those who believed that they had sufficient discretion and authority to make compromises on substance in negotiating with legislators conceded that this was basically the province of their senior departmental leaders. Liaison officers who engaged in such activity made absolutely certain there was prior agreement at the top, and they checked back carefully with their superiors. The Assistant Secretary for Legislation in HEW, who enjoyed the widest latitude to act, indicated that he, too, cleared such activities in advance with his superiors in the department and in the White House.

Only one legislative liaison agent rejected the notion that he should properly engage in an advocate role. Among the other liaison officers the assistant for legislative liaison in Defense was the least involved in this role. In his view this was basically the responsibility of the assistant secretaries of the Department of Defense. With responsibility for congressional relations in HEW divided between a special liaison officer and an assistant secretary, the former felt that she participated only minimally in selling compared with liaison agents in other departments. Both this Democratic liaison officer in HEW and a former Republican liaison agent in another department maintained, however, that they should properly have been permitted to play a more responsible role as advocate for their departments. Both alluded to problems with their secretaries, problems that will be discussed in a subsequent chapter.

Administration Partisans

All the Kennedy departmental liaison agents depicted themselves as part of the administration team; i.e., they were also White House agents. It was their responsibility to feed congressional intelligence and other data into the White House as well as to cooperate with its liaison staff in behalf of legislation to which the White House had assigned a high priority. Nevertheless one liaison agent had serious reservations about adopting too partisan a role. He seemed to emphasize his responsibility to his department above his obligation to the White House. On the other hand, another liaison officer expressed a sense of higher loyalty to the White House than to the department: "My first loyalty is to the White House. I see myself as a representative of the President and his program." None of the others saw any conflict between their responsibilities. Their own departmental chiefs were leaders in the administration; therefore, when the White House asked for cooperation, these liaison agents gave it. "I have three bosses," pointed out a liaison agent for Defense. "These are the secretary, the White House, and the Congress."

Service Expediter

The tremendous range of legislative needs and demands, which only the executive system can satisfy, affords ample opportunity for liaison agents to undertake a service expediter role. All of the departmental and agency liaison officers categorized the role of service expediter as proper and necessary, for it was accepted as axiomatic that good service helped build good congressional relations. Conversely, to service their congressional clients inadequately was to place a strain upon their personal relations with legislators and to risk souring legislative attitudes toward their departments.

While most liaison agents recognized the significance of this role, very few assigned to it the importance of their other roles. However, with certain congressmen, whose goodwill and cooperation liaison agents very keenly desired, the service expediter role acquired a special significance.

Roles in the Appropriations Process

Legislative liaison agents acknowledged that they were not expected to play any roles in the appropriations process. They pointed out that this area was assigned to others in their departments. Nevertheless, they insisted upon the prerogative of intervening when their departments faced major crises in appropriations.

"I participate on a consultative basis on the politics of and problems in appropriations," noted one agent. Disclosed another: "I am not responsible for the appropriations process, and I only intervene when we are in trouble." Bureau heads in both departments confirmed the fact that, while these liaison agents had very little to do with appropriations, they were called in on a few difficult situations. "I did hear him giving advice on dealing with congressmen and the leadership on appropriations," asserted one bureaucrat, "but he has much less influence here than on substantive legislation, although he does have some."

In two departments legislative liaison agents contended that it was they who should properly be responsible for congressional relations dealing with appropriations as well as authorization politics. Their secretaries would thereby avoid any slippage likely to be incurred in coordinating the two separate units. Moreover, contacts with and intelligence from appropriations congressmen would contribute to the liaison agents' handling of authorization politics more effectively and vice versa. And with both aspects of congressional relations under their jurisdiction, they could deal more skillfully with attacks upon their secretaries or with investigations of their departments. In the words of one of these liaison agents: "I'd have a larger view of what goes on and could put the pieces together easier. This way I have to 'liaise' within my own department." Although a number of their counterparts in the other departments agreed that this division in responsibility complicated their jobs as coordinators, most felt that it imposed no undue handicap upon their secretaries or their own work.

Roles with Interest Groups

Legislative liaison agents did not concur on the need to assume a special role with interest groups. Cooperation with special clientele and other sympathetic interest groups in behalf of the departments' programs was considered an important, integral part of their jobs by the liaison agents in four departments. On the other hand, two legislative liaison officers could conceive of no proper or necessary role in working closely with outside groups. The liaison officers in two additional departments explained that others were assigned the role of working with friendly interest groups.

CAREER PATTERNS AND LIAISON ROLES

It is pertinent at this point to inquire into the relationship between the hiring of actors as legislative liaison officers and the roles identified with these positions. Do their career backgrounds reveal any systematic set of assumptions on the part of their superiors, the senior political leaders of the executive system? Are the criteria for hiring valid for the roles that liaison officers must play? When executive lobbyists are compared with those employed by private interest groups in Washington, D.C., are significant differences evident in their career patterns and consequently in the orientation that each group brings to its position?

The Hiring Process

One of my initial assumptions was that the White House would be the dominant partner in hiring departmental liaison agents. After all, department and White House leaders during the Kennedy Administration, as well as the departmental liaison officers themselves, envisaged the latter as instruments of the White House.

The part played by the White House in the selection of departmental liaison officers was, however, an ambivalent one. It was evident that the White House had some voice in their selection. However, President Kennedy's Special Assistant for Congressional Relations exercised little or no initiative in organizing the selection process or in consciously placing at the departmental level individuals upon whom he personally could rely as part of an administration team. Interestingly enough, the same ambivalent pattern held true during the Eisenhower Administration. But then, the liaison leadership in the Eisenhower White House did not insist, as did its Kennedy counterpart, upon departmental liaison officers' acting as partisan members of the administration team.

The selection process for departmental liaison officers duplicated that of the subcabinet echelons in the departments. As Dean E. Mann and Jameson W. Doig have demonstrated, the latter "is a highly decentralized and personalized process revolving around respective department and agency heads."[1] While the President and his staff remain relatively inactive in selecting subcabinet officials, the department heads rely largely upon their own circle of friends. On the whole, a secretary is afforded wide latitude in the choice of his subordinates. The White House has confined itself mostly to the setting of standards. In the one area in which the White House has consistently asserted itself, that of the political background of the candidates, those considered unreliable have encountered White House opposition and vetoes.

Only in the case of a few departments, and primarily where the appointment involved a subcabinet position rather than the position of staff assistant to a secretary, did the Kennedy White House assert its prerogative in designating the legislative liaison agent. The secretary in each of these departments may have had some voice, but the initiative lay with the White House; and as long as the department head did not insist upon a veto, the decision prevailed. In this manner State was provided with its initial Assistant Secretary for Congressional Relations. When the incumbent in State was transferred from his position, his replacement, Fred-

---

[1] Dean E. Mann and Jameson W. Doig, *The Assistant Secretaries: Problems and Processes of Appointment* (Washington, D.C.: Brookings Institution, 1965), p. 265.

erick G. Dutton, was moved into it directly from the White House staff.[2] Dutton informed me that he was approached by Secretary Dean Rusk with the concurrence of the President. But, in view of Roger Hilsman's recollection of the major changes in State's leadership at the time, discontent in the White House, particularly on the part of the President, appears to have led to these shifts.[3]

The White House also imposed its choice on HEW in 1961. The individual chosen to be Assistant Secretary for Legislation had been a key policy adviser on social security to John F. Kennedy in the 1960 presidential campaign. As for the selection of the Congressional Liaison Officer, it stemmed purely from internal Democratic party considerations. Both were White House appointments, the former at the highest political level there and the latter at a considerably lower echelon, but neither appointee was suggested by the secretary of HEW. When the Congressional Liaison Officer resigned in 1964, there was no effort for a time to fill the position. When someone was eventually selected, the decision was made this time within the department and not by the Johnson White House.

In the other six departments, the initiative for employing liaison officers came from the secretary, from within the ranks of his immediate associates, or even from the Hill. In Agriculture the position was filled by someone who came highly recommended from the Hill; a staff member to a Democratic senator had actually phoned the senior departmental leaders, calling their attention to him. On the other hand, the appointee knew the undersecretary very well and had known the secretary when the latter had been a governor. In Defense the first of Mr. McNamara's liaison assistants was well known to senior people in the department and in the White House; it was, however, the Deputy Secretary of Defense who, according to the liaison officer, knew him very well and asked him to serve. His own deputy, whom he personally had chosen, succeeded him.

[2] Perhaps the Kennedy White House assumed a greater responsibility for State (and foreign affairs) than for any other department. It would make sense, in view of the limited domestic constituency of State, the traditional role that the President plays as head of foreign affairs, the special leadership President Kennedy exerted in foreign affairs, and the personality and style of his Secretary of State. I was informed that the Johnson White House did have a major voice in the selection of the Assistant Secretary of State for Congressional Relations when that position fell vacant in 1964. Apparently the White House exercised a veto, and the President may actually have made the decision on the nominee. One of those considered, who was even favorably interviewed by the secretary, told me he was informed that the final decision and the standards that determined the choice had been those of the White House. On the other hand, in the Eisenhower Administration, Secretary John Foster Dulles brought in his own choices for that position.

[3] Roger Hilsman, *To Move a Nation* (Garden City, N.Y.: Doubleday, 1967), pp. 26–27, 34–39, 50–54.

The liaison agent in Treasury reported that the department secretary had acted on his own initiative; he had decided early in the game whom he wanted and had invited him down to the temporary White House in Palm Beach. This offer was, interestingly enough, initially rejected, only to be subsequently accepted after further solicitation by the secretary, who enlisted the help of the nominee's business associates to persuade him to take the job. In Interior and Commerce, the initiative for the decisions also lay solely within the departments, not with the White House. Each of the selected liaison agents was known previously by his secretary.

Initially, in the Department of Labor, an assistant secretary carried the responsibility for congressional relations along with his many other duties. When legislative liaison was spun off to a special post of its own, it went to an individual whom the secretary had known. The liaison agent thought that his appointment had been the secretary's decision, but he attributed his initial consideration for the job to his contacts with White House staffmen with whom he had been associated in the Senate. But since he had originally been nominated by this same secretary for an appointment in a related agency, his employment as departmental liaison officer may have been largely the secretary's own decision.

In two of the departments in the period of 1961–64, Defense and Treasury, vacancies in these positions were filled from within the liaison agents' own staffs; their deputies were elevated to the positions. The secretaries had the major hand in these promotions; if the White House exercised any influence, it was minor.

This recruitment pattern produced a set of political actors who, with only one exception, were responsible and loyal primarily to their secretaries. Hence they could be trusted to work within the secretaries' frame of reference and to speak and act for them without any qualifications. Only the Congressional Liaison Officer in HEW, whose appointment was determined exclusively by the Kennedy White House, never became a close associate of the first secretary or his successor. On the other hand, this Congressional Liaison Officer always felt that her primary loyalty and responsibility were first to the White House, and only thereafter to the secretary!

Had the White House insisted upon placing its nominees as personal assistants to the secretaries in order to create a tightly bound White House–oriented operation, this might have proved dysfunctional. In view of the intimate relationship that should exist between a department head and his personal assistants, especially in such a delicate area as congressional relations, such a course could have introduced discord and strain.

Career Patterns

The departmental liaison officers of the Kennedy Administration came to their positions with extensive experience in the legislative and executive systems of government, principally of the national government. It was clear from their interviews that they felt their executive superiors desired assistants who already had the experience and know-how in dealing with members of the Congress. A strong background of political party identification and activity also appeared to be important in the recruitment process.

(A) CONGRESSIONAL-EXECUTIVE EXPERIENCE. A perusal of the career patterns of the eleven full-time legislative liaison officers for the eight departments under study (see Table IV.1) reveals that six (approximately 55 percent) had been previously employed in the Congress. Two were former members of the House of Representatives; three were administrative assistants to congressmen; and one was on the staff of a committee. If the three with a record of having worked intimately with the Congress, although not officially as a part of it, are added, this group includes nine of the eleven liaison officers. Assistant Secretary Wilbur J. Cohen's (HEW) involvement with the Congress extended from his work on the initial Social Security Act in the 1930s to his acting as a consultant to Senator Robert S. Kerr (D., Okla.) in the late 1950s. Norman Paul (Defense) had been Deputy Director for Congressional Relations (FAO) and had undertaken legislative liaison work for the CIA; David E. McGiffert (Defense) had served as Deputy to the Assistant to the Secretary for Legislative Affairs (DOD). Moreover, two of these three had also interacted personally with congressmen and committees in their capacity as representatives of private interest groups.

The remaining two among the eleven had no record of working in or with the Congress before assuming their liaison positions. However, one of them, Assistant Secretary for Congressional Relations (State) Dutton, had served as special counsel to the Judiciary Committee in the California Senate and had acted as his governor's principal assistant for legislative relations. With the exception, therefore, of only one legislative liaison agent, the entire group was composed of actors who either had been legislators or staff assistants to legislators or had been responsible for working together with and/or lobbying members of legislative systems.

Table IV.1 reveals, however, that more individuals came to their liaison jobs with executive experience than with congressional experience. It is nonetheless misleading to assume from such data a greater reliance by their employers on executive than legislative experience. The execu-

TABLE IV.1

Previous Governmental Career Patterns of Legislative Liaison Officers
in Eight Departments of the Kennedy Administration

Name	*Department*	National				State	
		Congress		*Executive*			
		Staff	*Member*	*Political*	*Career*	*Legislature*	*Political Executive*
Akin, Mrs. Jim G.	HEW						
Barr, Joseph W.	Treasury		X				
Birkhead, Kenneth M.	Agriculture	X					
Cohen, Wilbur J.	HEW				X		
Dutton, Frederick G.	State		X			X	X
Hays, Brooks	State			X	X		
McConnell, Robert S.	Interior	X		X			
McGiffert, David E.	Defense			X	X		
Merrick, Samuel V.	Labor	X			X		
Paul, Norman S.	Defense			X	X		
Stillman, John S.	Commerce	X		X	X		X

tive experience of one was limited to legislative liaison work alone; he had been recruited into the executive to serve as an assistant to his departmental legislative liaison officer. Two had been working as assistants within other areas of the political executive, one for approximately one year, the other for two, when they were chosen for liaison work. However, they were specifically requested to assume liaison positions because of their previous legislative experience: one had been an administrative assistant in the House of Representatives for fourteen years, the other for two years. A fourth had served in the Kennedy White House for less than a year—his sole experience in the national executive—when he was requested to become Assistant Secretary of State for Congressional Relations. Only three had extensive careers in the bureaucracies of the national executive system, one of whom had worked in legislative liaison for two separate agencies. Brooks Hays had also served in the national bureaucracy, although for only a brief period in his youth. He had assumed responsibility for liaison at State after having held a position at the highest political policy level of the Tennessee Valley Authority. But he was chosen principally for his congressional experience: he had been a member of the House of Representatives for sixteen years, and a very popular one, too. Among the eleven liaison officers, three possessed no previous experience in the executive system at any level.

This pattern contrasts sharply with that of the Washington lobbyists for private interest groups. Whereas half of Lester W. Milbrath's sample of such lobbyists came to lobbying directly from jobs in the executive or the legislature, only 21 percent of these had ever served in any capacity on the Hill.[4] Not only did twice as many private lobbyists come to their jobs directly from the executive as from Congress, but, according to Milbrath, "The evidence is very clear—the executive branch is . . . the most important source for recruiting persons for lobbying positions."[5]

In terms of their career backgrounds, the legislative liaison agents represented extremely valuable assets for their senior political leaders in the executive. They contributed to that leadership what traditionally has been lacking in its second echelons—congressional experience. In the last two decades, a substantial number of assistant secretaries and undersecretaries have had some type of administrative experience in government prior to their appointments. But the experts contend that "too many . . . arrive . . . who are totally unfamiliar with their work as political executives. . . ."[6] After reviewing the selection of men for the second echelon

[4] Lester W. Milbrath, *The Washington Lobbyists* (Chicago: Rand McNally, 1963), chap. 4, "Recruitment of Lobbyists."
[5] *Ibid.,* p. 69.
[6] Mann and Doig, *op. cit.,* p. 266.

of the President's executive team, Mann and Doig conclude that: "The government is largely dependent on untrained people to fill its policy-making positions."[7]

Those who occupy the primary and secondary levels of political leadership in the executive system must interact with congressmen and involve themselves in the legislative process. In these efforts they require guidance and advice that can be provided by actors who fill legislative liaison positions. Even for those leaders who feel particularly competent in dealing with Congress, the cumulative experience represented in the career patterns of the new executive lobbyists proves advantageous. For with their special assistants already sensitized to the norms, processes, and problems of the legislative system, executive political leaders can afford to concentrate more on familiarizing themselves with their own jobs and carrying out their policy-making and administrative responsibilities.

As a group, private lobbyists do not constitute an important source of executive lobbyists. At first this seems inexplicable. Many Washington lobbyists for interest groups are experienced in working with both legislative and executive actors. I had initially assumed that the professional lobbyists in Washington would constitute a reservoir of talent from which executive leaders would draw their liaison officers. However, only two of the eleven departmental liaison agents had ever professionally lobbied from outside the national government,[8] one as an executive director of an interest group and subsequently as a lobbyist for another interest group, the other as a lawyer whose clients' affairs had brought him into contact with congressional committees. A third had testified on behalf of legislation when he was the principal (elected) spokesman of a professional group, but he insisted that he did not lobby for that group.

(B) STRONG POLITICAL PARTY AFFILIATION. In all probability, one major explanation for this failure to tap professional Washington lobbyists for legislative liaison positions lies in the differential involvement of these two sets of actors in political party activity. Milbrath has demonstrated that "persons with wide political party experience are seldom chosen as lobbyists."[9] A knowledge of political party activity, he concludes from his study, was not essential in order to comprehend the decision-making processes in the legislative or executive systems. More-

---

[7] *Ibid.,* p. 264.

[8] The same observation holds true at the level of the agencies. Of the two liaison agents in AID, the two in ARA, and the two in HHFA, only one was a professional private lobbyist. The first assistant to the administrator (HHFA) for congressional relations had lobbied for the American Municipal Association.

[9] Milbrath, *op. cit.,* p. 71.

over, a lobbyist who was closely identified with either of the major political parties confronted a serious problem: he was disadvantaged in dealing with members of the opposite party in the government.

A distinct party identification, on the other hand, was apparently exactly what the secretaries in the Kennedy departments preferred. Among the eleven departmental liaison agents, nine had been Democratic party activists: they had held appointive or elective positions. A tenth had been staff assistant to Democratic senators. Their records also revealed considerable campaign experience. Table IV. 2 indicates their varied and extensive involvement as party partisans.

In contrast with nonexecutive lobbyists, whose interest-group clients were composed of both Republicans and Democrats and whose leaders were almost invariably nonpartisan in their approach to the executive and legislative systems, liaison agents had a partisan set of bosses and represented a partisan constituency.[10] They served as staff assistants to department secretaries who were either outstanding Democratic party leaders or who, as cabinet members, were spokesmen for the Kennedy Administration. Since their own superior was the head of the national Democratic party, the departmental secretaries adopted the posture of the Democratic President. For their aides, whom they had to trust and to whom they turned for assistance and advice in advancing their programs under the auspices of the Democratic President, they relied upon those who were already identified with the Democratic party.

A strong party background was obviously essential, since departmental liaison agents had to work intimately with and secure the aid of the White House. The Special Assistant to the President for Congressional Relations, Lawrence F. O'Brien, was the epitome of the partisan type: he had long been active in Massachusetts Democratic politics; he had been an assistant to a Democratic congressman from Massachusetts; and he had helped manage John F. Kennedy's campaigns for the U.S. Senate and for his nomination and election to the presidency. Moreover, the majority of members in both branches of the Congress were Democrats, which meant also, therefore, the majority floor leaders, the committee chairmen, and a majority on each congressional committee. The mutuality of interests inherent in a common party affiliation afforded the secretaries and their assistants distinct advantages in cooperating and bargaining with Democratic congressional leaders and members on the administration's legislative program and the departments' proposals.

[10] With only a few exceptions, the departmental liaison officers in the Eisenhower Administration were Republicans who had held positions in their party or had been identified with Republican legislators.

TABLE IV.2

Prior Democratic Party Activity of Legislative Liaison Officers
in Eight Departments of the Kennedy Administration

Officer and Department	Offices or Activity in State-Local Parties	Offices or Activity in National Party	Congressional Party	Prior Identification with Democratic Executives in Washington
Akin, Mrs. Jim G. (HEW)	State party politics; managed congressional candidate's campaign	Headquarters staff member, Citizens for Kennedy-Johnson, 1960; Democratic National Finance Committee chairman for Texas		
Barr, Joseph W. (Treasury)	Candidate for Congress		Congressman	
Birkhead, Kenneth M. (Agriculture)	Manager for candidate for U.S. Senate; campaigned for several congressmen	Assistant director of public relations and finance director, Democratic National Committee	Assistant to director, U.S. Senate Democratic Campaign Committee; assistant to whip, U.S. Senate	
Cohen, Wilbur J. (HEW)	Adviser to governor; director of research for gubernatorial candidate	Chairman, Kennedy's Task Force on Health and Social Security, 1960 campaign	Adviser to congressmen	
Dutton, Frederick G. (State)	Executive assistant to governor of California; state chairman, Brown for Governor campaign	California chairman for Stevenson; deputy national chairman, Citizens for Kennedy-Johnson, 1960		Special Assistant to the President, Kennedy Administration

Name			
Hays, Brooks (State)	Campaigned for nomination and election to Congress	Delegate to Democratic National Conventions; member of Democratic National Committee	Congressman
McConnell, Robert S. (Interior)	County chairman		Administrative assistant to two congressmen (wife: secretary to director, House of Representatives Democratic Campaign Committee)
McGiffert, David E. (Defense)			Deputy to legislative liaison officer, Defense Department, Kennedy Administration
Merrick, Samuel V. (Labor)			Three years on staff of Senate committee
Paul, Norman S. (Defense)		Kennedy campaign coordinator, New York, 1960	
Stillman, John S. (Commerce)	Democratic-Liberal candidate for state office; candidate for Democratic nomination for Attorney General; county chairman; delegate to state conventions	Delegate to Democratic National Conventions; Kennedy campaign coordinator, New York, 1960	

To the private lobbyists in Milbrath's study partisan identification was dysfunctional; it isolated them from governmental officials in the other party. Whether the liaison officers' Democratic identification proved dysfunctional is postponed for consideration in another context. At this point it is sufficient to recognize that during the Kennedy Administration the political leaders of the executive system accepted partisanship as a positive element in its relationship with the Congress and were prepared to pay the price, if any.

(C) SUBSTANTIVE KNOWLEDGE. An additional major facet of the career backgrounds of liaison agents is the close correspondence between the subject areas of their previous careers and their present ones. It was only natural that department heads would be partial to political actors possessing some knowledge of their departments' substantive programs. That this aspect of their careers was decidedly functional in terms of the needs of the executive political leaders and of the congressional relations officers themselves is obvious. With possibly only two exceptions, and in these cases the appointments were dictated by White House considerations, the experience of the liaison officers and their departments' substantive concerns did coincide. Consequently most legislative liaison officers were not unfamiliar with the special language, problems, and general features of their departments when they started their assignments.

(D) MISCELLANEOUS. Minor background characteristics of congressional relations officers pertain to age, sex, and occupation. A relatively young group was employed in these positions during the Kennedy Administration. Nine were in their forties when they were selected, and one was still in his thirties. Only one, former Congressman Brooks Hays, was older; he was sixty-three. Milbrath's sample of Washington lobbyists indicates their age only at the time he interviewed them: almost three-quarters were between forty and sixty. By the end of 1963, when this study of legislative liaison agents was concluded, one had just turned fifty and the oldest individual had left the ranks of this group. On the whole, then, the executive lobbyists were a younger group than were the private Washington lobbyists.[11]

All but one of these departmental agents were men. The woman did have difficulties in her job; but, although a few congressmen expressed a sense of disquiet about a woman holding the post, her problems stemmed from reasons other than sex. Among the thirty or so professionals on the staffs of the liaison officers in all ten executive departments,

[11] The six who held liaison positions in the three agencies that were studied—AID, ARA, and HHFA—were also in their thirties and forties.

only three women were employed during this period, and these in the eight departments under study. One was a political patronage appointee imposed on the liaison officer by his department superiors. The second was an experienced party professional with extensive contacts among Democrats in both House and Senate. The third combined considerable substantive expertise with political party and legislative experience. In all probability a selectivity factor—a disposition among executive leaders and legislators to exclude women from consideration as serious political actors—operated against their being chosen for legislative liaison jobs. On the other hand, fewer women than men combined legislative experience with political party activity—two of the most important characteristics of the liaison agents. Whatever the reason, this pattern of employing men rather than women was apparent in the agencies that were studied as well as in the new departments established during the Johnson Administration. To the best of my knowledge, none of the departmental liaison agents during the Eisenhower Administration were women.

In view of the well-documented ubiquity of lawyers within the American political party and legislative systems, it is not surprising that seven of the eleven liaison officers were members of the legal profession.[12] None of them, however, came directly to their liaison positions from a purely legal position, although one was entirely involved in legal affairs when he was first employed as deputy to his legislative liaison agent. Among the four nonlawyer executive lobbyists, no other profession had more than one representative. One was a long-term bureaucrat and university professor; another was a banker-businessman (two of the lawyers had also been in business); a third can be described in no more apt terms than as a political operator. After earning an M.A. in history in his early twenties, he became executive director of a liberal political organization. Thereafter he engaged in political party, interest-group, and legislative employment. The one woman within the group classified herself as a housewife.

(E) POSTLIAISON CAREERS. Was the legislative liaison job a dead end politically? Or did it represent a steppingstone to the higher levels of political leadership? If the latter should be the case, the position would offer particularly attractive possibilities for enticing ambitious young politicos into the executive system. And it could increase the number of

---

[12] In the two departments not studied, Post Office and Justice, the liaison agent in the former was a journalist, in the latter a lawyer. Lawyers predominated within the professions represented among the Eisenhower departmental liaison agents. And the largest group among Milbrath's sample of private Washington lobbyists were also lawyers.

TABLE IV.3

Relation Between Legislative Liaison Officers' Departments
and Their Previous Careers

Department	Liaison Officer	Relevant Work Experience	Index of Relationship of Work Experience to Department
State	Hays	Member of House Foreign Affairs Committee	High
Treasury	Dutton	Secretary to the Cabinet	Low
	Barr	Member of House Banking and Currency Committee; banker and businessman	High
Agriculture	Birkhead	Assistant to U.S. senator who served on Agriculture and Appropriations Committees	Medium to high
Labor	Merrick	Staff assistant on Senate Labor and Public Welfare Committee; private labor relations consultant; 15 years with NLRB, 4 as special assistant to counsel	High
Commerce	Stillman	Deputy to Under Secretary of Commerce; member and chairman, New York State Bridge Authority; divisional counsel, National Production Authority; businessman	High
Defense	Paul	General Counsel's Office, ECA; Mutual Security Administration; Deputy Director for Congressional Relations, FOA; congressional relations and substantive work, CIA	Medium to high

TABLE IV.3 (continued)

Department	Liaison Officer	Relevant Work Experience	Index of Relationship of Work Experience to Department
	McGiffert	Deputy to Assistant to Secretary of Defense for Legislative Affairs; lawyer-lobbyist for private clients, with contacts with Joint Committee on Atomic Energy	Medium
Interior	McConnell	Special assistant to an assistant secretary in Department of Interior; 14 years as administrative assistant to 2 New Mexico congressmen who served on House Interior and Appropriations Committees; officer, Resettlement Administration	High
HEW	Cohen	Head of Kennedy's Task Force on Health and Social Security, 1960; consultant to U.S. senator on social security; professor of public welfare administration; long-time member of Federal Security Agency; departmental employee of HEW	High
	Akin	None	None

senior political actors competent to deal with the Congress. On the other hand, too rapid a turnover, even among those going up rather than out, could prove dysfunctional to the leaders of the executive system, for each new liaison agent must develop and cultivate a set of complex relationships with large numbers of actors in both systems.

In the brief period of the Kennedy Administration, 1961 through most of 1963, only one departmental liaison officer was moved out of his position and his department, while another was elevated to a subcabinet position. By 1966, during the Johnson Administration, four of the eleven had been promoted to higher leadership positions in the political executive, one held down a nominal job in the White House, three were no longer in the executive system, and three remained as assistants to their secretaries for legislative relations.

Among those advancing to more senior political policy positions were the Assistant Secretary for Legislation (HEW) and the Assistant to the Secretary for Congressional Relations (Treasury). Both were chosen to be undersecretaries of their departments.[13] In Defense the initial Assistant to the Secretary for Legislative Affairs was appointed Assistant Secretary of Defense for Manpower and his successor was designated Under Secretary of the Army. In all four cases, executive lobbyists were able to advance into the ranks of senior political leaders within their own departments.

State's first Assistant Secretary for Congressional Relations had been moved up very early to a minor position on the White House staff. There he was almost entirely engaged in public relations with groups outside the national government. His successor in State departed in 1964 to a senior position with the Democratic National Committee after which he reentered private law practice and state politics. Commerce's first congressional relations officer became the executive director of the American Veterans' Committee. And the initial congressional liaison officer in HEW resigned when she married a member of the House of Representatives.

Liaison agents at the agency level had a mixed record. The first congressional relations officer for HHFA resigned in frustration because of the limited roles afforded him by that agency's political leadership. He assumed a position with the U.S. Conference of Mayors. His immediate successor joined the Department of Commerce as Deputy Administrator for Regional Economic Development. The serious problems AID encountered in the Congress led to changes in its top political leadership, including the legislative liaison officers. Its initial liaison officer, who had

---

[13] In 1967 HEW Under Secretary Wilbur Cohen was named secretary.

been a staff assistant to a western Democratic senator, returned to his job with that senator. The second one, a former administrative assistant in the House of Representatives who subsequently worked in the field for AID, left the government to become a vice-president for Eastern Airlines. In the Area Redevelopment Administration, an agency within the Department of Commerce, the initial Special Assistant to the Administrator (for Congressional Affairs) moved to a more substantive job in another executive agency.

That three of the original eleven departmental liaison agents continued in their jobs throughout the major part of the Johnson Administration does not signify that they failed to impress their superiors as political operators. They would have been eliminated long ago had this been true. One, in fact, was acclaimed the most able liaison agent among all the departments by his secretary, most of his fellow liaison agents, the private lobbyists who worked with him, and the White House. And another, very respected within his own department and by most of the private lobbyists, was at one time under serious consideration for a higher appointment.

Most of the legislative liaison agents in the Kennedy Administration who left their positions remained political actors in the national executive or legislative systems. Since over one-third of those at the departmental level moved into higher leadership positions, it may be hypothesized that the roles they played, together with their experience and contacts, alerted their superiors to their qualification for higher leadership assignments. It must also be recognized that the second echelon of executive leadership in the departments is itself characterized by a relatively high turnover. The President and department heads constantly face the problem of recruiting capable persons. This pressing demand for political-executive talent in the departments affords many opportunities for advancement to ambitious, capable individuals who assume legislative liaison positions. To the extent that they move up to senior political positions responsible for policy and administration, the liaison officers enhance the overall competence of the executive system's political leadership in dealing with Congress.

CHAPTER V

Liaison Officers in the Executive System:
Problems, Opportunities, Strategies

LEGISLATIVE LIAISON AGENTS must first work out acceptable relational patterns within their own departments if they are to play meaningful roles in the Congress for their secretaries and the President. Indeed, their congressionally focused roles feed into those that are executive-oriented, and vice versa. The nature of their opportunities and problems and their responses to both have much in common. All liaison officers must deal with similar sets of executive actors who hold, in general, common assumptions regarding liaison roles. These executive actors must be mobilized and the departments' resources exploited behind a program of effective congressional relations and specific campaigns for bills. Consequently, the liaison agents confront a variety of independent and semi-independent actors in their own system on whom they are dependent for support and cooperation, but who carry other responsibilities and whose interests do not always coincide with those of the liaison agents.

Given the common nature of their responsibilities, tasks, and general problems, liaison agents—regardless of department—tend to develop similar strategies and tactics for dealing with their own systems. At the same time each department is unique. Within his departmental frame of reference a liaison officer must cope with the styles and desires of his own political leaders and career administrators. In the legislature, each department deals with special committees and with specific formal and informal leaders. The liaison agent encounters, therefore, a preexisting, special set of relations between members of his department and the legislative system to which he must accommodate himself. It is axiomatic, of course, that personality traits will also differentiate the liaison actors, that their behavior and style will be individually as well as institutionally determined. Postponed to a subsequent chapter is another executive variable—the White House and its superior claim to leadership in the executive system.

LIAISON AGENTS AND THEIR PRINCIPALS

Social science research does not abound in studies of the relations between agents and their principals and the impact of these relations upon the behavior of the agents and their ability to achieve their goals.[1] Rather, attention has been focused primarily upon the agent and his target or on the relations between two sets of principals in the administration and the Congress or on interest groups and official decision-making bodies. It may just be that these are the most significant, that the relationship between a principal and his agent is inconsequential in the mix of elements affecting the policy decisions and behavior of other actors with whom a principal and his agent interacts.

At the minimum, however, two considerations suggest the contrary. First, if political scientists are concerned with relations between systems or subsystems, with actors who cross boundary lines to help shape the course of another system—whether in international relations or between a state governor and his legislature or an interest group and an executive agency—then detailed attention must also focus upon the agents and their principals. Secondly, if one assumes, as I, that the increasing complexity within systems and the increasing interdependency among subsystems spur the differentiation of roles and functions among actors

[1] Only a few recent studies devote any attention to this area of inquiry. Lester W. Milbrath does touch upon it in *The Washington Lobbyists* (Chicago: Rand McNally, 1963), chap. 7, "Lobbyists as They Relate to Their Employers." However, the primary focus is on the various types of lobbyists according to their source of employment. Attention to the relations between businessmen and lobbyists for the associations to which they belong is limited to a few general remarks relative to the attitudes of each in Raymond A. Bauer, Ithiel de Sola Pool, and Lewis A. Dexter, *American Business and Public Policy: The Politics of Foreign Trade* (New York: Atherton Press, 1963), pp. 328–31. Businessmen were reported to downgrade the value of their associations' lobbyists; and the latter reciprocated, characterizing the businessmen as politically naïve. The impact of such relations on the lobbying of these agents is not explored. In discerning articles on the "Assistant to" in business and other administrative settings, Thomas L. Whisler devotes some attention to the significance of relations between leaders and agents. See Thomas L. Whisler, "The 'Assistant to' in Four Administrative Settings," *Administrative Science Quarterly*, 5 (September 1960): 181–216; "The 'Assistant to': The Man in Motley," *Journal of Business*, 29 (October 1956): 274–79. The problems of certain types of staff assistants in labor unions arising out of their relations with their principals is dealt with by Harold L. Wilensky, *Intellectuals in Labor Unions: Organizational Pressures on Professional Roles* (Glencoe, Ill.: Free Press, 1956).

concerned with leadership, then the relations between principals and their agents, who are responsible for assisting them in exercising leadership, is of the utmost significance. Evidence from the present study warrants the assertion that an important area of study in influence, power, and interpersonal relations remains neglected if we fail to push our investigations in both directions. Not merely must relations between principals or agents with targets be examined, but also relations between principals and agents themselves, and their effect on the goals and behavior of both in dealing with such targets.

The Secretary

(A) PRIMACY OF THE SECRETARY. The secretary's primacy in the political process was the initial premise voiced by all legislative liaison officers, whether they were staff assistants to the secretary or assistant secretaries. "The entire set of relations with the Congress is dependent upon the secretary," asserted a Democratic executive lobbyist in one of the largest domestic departments. "With different secretaries there may be considerably different relations with the Congress. The department cannot be viewed apart from the personality of the secretary." Apropos of his working effectively within the department as well as in the Congress, a Republican Assistant Secretary for Congressional Relations in State concluded: "This job [legislative liaison] depends entirely on the attitude and approach of the cabinet member; he is the boss."

As the department's political head, the secretary is responsible for its internal operation and its legislative program. He speaks for the department within the administration and to the public. In the Congress he is the department's most important actor, testifying publicly in its behalf and being recognized by the legislators as its leader. The most difficult decisions ultimately come to him for their resolution. His undersecretary and assistant secretaries also represent the department, but they act invariably under the policy determined by the secretary and in accordance with his wishes.

To no other factor do legislative liaison agents ascribe greater importance, in terms of shaping their behavior and influencing their effectiveness, than to their own immediate superiors, the departmental secretaries. A brief résumé of the principal roles that the liaison officers must play demonstrates the centrality of the departmental secretary in their universe. Within their own departments, the liaison agents are expected to act as advisers to their secretaries; serve as coordinators for them; provide channels to the secretaries for legislators and interest groups; represent, speak, and negotiate for their secretaries in the Congress; act as buffers for them; and obtain intelligence for them. An analysis of the most detailed description of a liaison agent's job—one made available by the incumbent in Agriculture in the Kennedy Administration —reveals, for example, that five of the nine items describing his duties refer directly to his responsibilities to his secretary. Hence the relations between the legislative liaison agent and the secretary are crucial to the former's functioning in both systems: in the legislature, to advance and defend the interests of the department as a whole and the secretary in particular, as well as the administration; in the executive, to assist the secretary in exercising political control over his department in his deal- ings with the Congress.

It is in the capacity of assistants, in all but two cases staff assistants, that liaison agents relate to their secretaries. In almost all instances it is the secretaries who have initiated the recruitment or promotion or who have had the final say in determining the occupant for this position. The titles of the liaison agents, ranging from Assistant to the Secretary for Legislative Affairs to Deputy to the Secretary for Congressional Re- lations, illuminate their dependency upon the department head. The secretary is the independent variable, the agent the dependent variable. Even when the exceptions in rank are noted—an Assistant Secretary for Legislation in HEW and an Assistant Secretary for Congressional Re- lations in State—these subcabinet officials are subordinate to their de- partment heads.

(B) THE SECRETARY SHOULD BE A SOPHISTICATED POLITICAL ACTOR IN DEALING WITH THE CONGRESS. Both Democratic and Repub- lican liaison agents agreed they could best operate in their roles in the Congress when the departmental secretary had the following character- istics: (1) He was sensitive to the political process, to the give and take, and to the need for compromise. He comprehended the complex opera- tion of Congress, and he understood the motives and stimuli that entered into the decision-making and behavior of its members. (2) The secre- tary was willing to engage in the politics of shaping legislative attitudes toward the department and the marshaling of support and votes for its objectives. (3) His involvement was personal and flexible. The secretary had to place himself at his liaison agent's disposal, as a resource to be used within the Congress. A secretary who conformed to these criteria was considered by the liaison officers to be a tremendous asset to them and their departments. To the extent that a department head deviated from this model, he handicapped the efforts of his special agent in the Congress.

The liaison agent for Agriculture in the Kennedy Administration gave his superior the highest rating: "My secretary is the most valuable man in the department with regard to the Congress. Our principal bills have a hard enough time as it is, but they would never have gotten anyplace but for his personal contacts and appearances on the Hill."[2] His secretary was both the chief and an integral part of the department's team for developing good legislative relations and for selling bills to the Congress. In addition, the secretary was willing to meet with legislators whenever his liaison agent asked him. This was especially important, contended the liaison officer, because his was a tough department with habitual discontent among its clientele and deep divisions among its associated interest groups. Moreover, its major legislative proposals encountered considerable partisan opposition.

A Republican Assistant Secretary for Congressional Relations (State) placed great emphasis upon the legislative sophistication of Secretary John Foster Dulles in simplifying his own job. "I was fortunate," he recalled. "Dulles had been a senator himself for a brief time, and even before that he'd had something to do with the Congress and foreign policy politics. He understood executive-legislative relations very well."

On the other hand, complaints by departmental legislative liaison officers from the Kennedy and Eisenhower Administrations underscored the difficulties imposed by secretaries who did not measure up to their criteria. At the extreme, secretarial attitudes may isolate the liaison officer from significant relations with the Congress. Only one agent, in the Eisenhower Administration, declared that his secretary had placed him in such a position: "My major problem was the secretary and his view of congressional relations." Congressional relations were accorded only secondary importance by this secretary, who preferred "to maintain the administrative over the congressional if the two conflicted." He did not particularly like congressional relations. "We tried to establish good relations between the secretary and the Hill, but most of our efforts did not work well." The secretary tired of lunching with key legislative actors, and he did not invite congressmen to the department for consultation except at the last minute, which only irritated them. Nor did he like the Republican leaders in the House of Representatives; he felt that "he could not win with those fellows anyway." To aggravate matters, the secretary preferred not to go to the Hill. "We would tell him time after time: 'You've got to go there. Congressmen love to show off with a cabinet member.' "

Some liaison agents within the Kennedy Administration also complained that congressional relations were complicated for them by their

[2] The assistant to this liaison agent, who was accorded more independence and responsibility than most such assistants, noted that, in contacting congressmen on legislation, she shifted those who wavered or were in the negative to her immediate boss or to the secretary, whom she characterized as "the best lobbyist in the department."

bosses' unrealistic attitudes. This was especially true in Defense and State. According to one Assistant for Legislative Affairs to the Secretary of Defense: "The secretary does not look at Congress as a political process."[3] This caused the department considerable trouble. Another of the secretary's failings was that he was an uncompromising person. "He does not make deals. If he doesn't get what he asks for, it's OK with him. I've advised him that this course of action arouses hostility on the Hill." Still other difficulties arose because his secretary "did not fully understand the Senate. The Senate is a closed club. Once they feel that one member is aggrieved, they stick together even if the executive is right." In State an officer responsible for liaison added another dimension to this complaint about the nonpolitical approach of secretaries: "The problem is to convince Secretary [Dean] Rusk that merit and argument are not enough. Personal and power relations are just as critical."

In a third, much smaller department, the secretary's assistant for legislative liaison also attributed many of his problems in the Congress to his department head. At fault was the secretary's style and also his lack of political experience. "He's not a politician, and doesn't savvy the business of the Hill. As a result he's apt to act in such a way as to cause me great trouble. His sense of timing isn't good and this does handicap me as a liaison man." By temperament and habit, he asserted, the secretary was not particularly suited to deal with the Congress: "He's a man of great precision and economy of words, and that doesn't fit into the pace of Congress. It's leisurely and involves a great deal of waste of time."

A comparison of the styles of two secretaries in a large department by an executive lobbyist who represented both in the Congress illustrates two extremes. "Secretary X is less willing and less interested in talking with congressmen himself. He doesn't envisage his role as the cajoling, manipulating role that Y does." Secretary X talked with congressmen, of course, "but he tends to avoid it whenever he can. He is more cautious than Y and feels he can wear out his welcome easily, that he has to be careful since every time he asks for a favor it's money in the bank and they will ask for it." This had not bothered Y, who took the position: "Of course, this is the game."

There was another significant difference in the styles of the two secretaries. Whereas Secretary X did not like to go to the Hill, compelling his agent to substitute for him, Secretary Y had gone all the time to

[3] The liaison agent who succeeded him agreed. "The secretary is not politically oriented and this does create problems in the Congress." There had been times when, had the secretary sat down with congressional actors "early in the game, it might have saved us a lot of trouble."

manipulate the legislative process, and his assistant frequently accompanied him. Secretary X did not like to be involved in legislation. He would not do anything unless he had to do it, the White House requested it, or his assistant pressured him sufficiently. Aside from testifying, he took no positive action in the process. "Secretary Y always asked me, 'Is there anything you want me to do? I want to do whatever you say. You're my legislative adviser. Whatever you think is important, I'll do.' " The styles of the two secretaries coincided with their diverse ambitions. Secretary X, who was cautious, sought little publicity and avoided controversy with the Congress on most issues. He hoped for an appointment to a permanent, nonpartisan position. The temperament as well as the ambitions of Y for higher elective office made him politically conscious. He was anxious for involvement in the making of controversial public policy and for attention from the press.

Obviously Secretary X did not conform to the model developed by the liaison officers in the Kennedy and Eisenhower Administrations. Instead of being a source of strength, he was a burden and a problem. And yet his agent claimed that by assuming more responsibility and by becoming even more active, he was able to compensate in part for his secretary's inadequacies. A former legislative liaison agent from another department in the Eisenhower Administration denied that there was much that a liaison officer could do under such circumstances. His secretary's political stance and relations with the Congress had seriously impaired his own effectiveness; he could not substitute for the department head or devise alternative strategies to offset his deficiencies. His Democratic counterpart in the same department, who also encountered difficulties with his own secretary, was nevertheless able to involve himself actively in relations with congressmen. While he agreed that he could not completely compensate for his secretary's weaknesses, he stressed that it was incumbent upon him as the liaison officer to build support for his department's legislation.

The differences in response of the two Democratic agents as distinct from that of the Republican agent warrant some explanation. Three hypotheses may be advanced, each of which complements the others. The first is that the political stance of the administration is the decisive factor in determining the initiative and involvement of departmental liaison agents, regardless of the degree of political adequacy of their secretaries. The Kennedy Administration was intensely concerned with moving an ambitious, positive program through the Congress. Aside from the Trade Expansion Act of 1962, which was primarily a White House operation, the major proposals came to Congress under the auspices of the separate departments as well as the White House. The White House insisted that the departments were an integral part of the administration team in the Congress. Hence the departmental liaison agents were pressed by the White House liaison staff as well as by their immediate superiors to help advance their legislation. Disengagement was frowned upon. Under such circumstances, the personalities and styles of the secretaries per se were subordinate to the demands of the administration.

The Republican liaison officer, on the other hand, described the Eisenhower White House as not greatly interested in advancing legislation in his department's primary field. Nor was the White House anxious to antagonize conservative Republicans on the substantive legislative committees or the Democratic House chairman, who "did not find anything acceptable that we in the department were peddling." When these circumstances coincided with a secretary who shunned an active role in congressional politics, the departmental legislative liaison officer was greatly restricted in the roles he could play.

A second hypothesis relates to the political nature of the agent rather than his principal. Agents with backgrounds of strong legislative partisan involvement are more likely than those with little or no comparable background to overcome the limitations of a secretary who recoils from aggressive congressional relations. The background of the particular Republican legislative liaison agent, in sharp contrast with that of the two Democrats, did not disclose prior legislative or political party experience. Moreover, he was confronted with a Congress controlled by Democrats. This suggests the third hypothesis: A Congress dominated by the same party as the executive in all probability facilitates intervention by legislative liaison actors; when the legislative system is dominated by the opposite party, the executive actors will operate more circumspectly. These three hypotheses help explain the differences in response of liaison agents, all of whom faced similar problems with their secretaries in dealing with Congress.

(C) THE IMPORTANCE OF A RELATIONSHIP OF CONFIDENCE AND CLOSENESS BETWEEN PRINCIPAL AND AGENT. To perform successfully as adviser to the secretary on congressional relations, the liaison agent must relate personally to his principal in specific ways. Essential elements in their relations are confidence and closeness.

As one agent trenchantly put it: "If the secretary has no confidence in him, the guy has nothing to do." Aside from a special case in HEW, none of the liaison agents in the eight Kennedy departments reported such an intolerable relationship. Nor did it apparently exist in the Eisenhower Administration.

Where a lack of closeness or confidence did manifest itself to *some degree,* owing to the personality of the secretary, his style, or his hesitancy to work with an assistant whom he had inherited, the liaison agent found it difficult to act as an adviser and to play some of his other roles. The principal himself was disadvantaged thereby, a point emphasized by a Republican whose department had changed leaders: "I did not have a close relationship with the new secretary. As a result he bumped into problems with the Congress because he did not get the proper advice. Finally, however, he started to call on me, and we worked things out and worked closely together."

During the period when Abraham Ribicoff was secretary in HEW, the Congressional Liaison Officer was extremely frustrated by her poor relations with him. She had been placed there by the White House and was not his personal designee. Moreover, the secretary's mode of operation was to work intimately with a few people only. On legislation and congressional relations he dealt almost exclusively with his own personal assistant and the Assistant Secretary for Legislation. He never permitted the Congressional Liaision Officer to work closely with him. She was inevitably downgraded in the department and circumscribed sharply in her congressionally oriented roles. She was handicapped even in trying to help advance the department's bills, because, she claimed, particular policies were being made without her knowledge. This relationship between the liaison agent and her secretary was so atypical in the Kennedy Administration, however, that it is not included in the analysis that follows, except where it is specifically mentioned.

A lack of closeness between the department head and his lobbyist may manifest itself in the secretary's unwillingness to clarify the degree of discretion and support that the agent commands. Even the most competent departmental lobbyist finds such ambiguity extremely frustrating. Such a relationship developed initially between a new secretary and his subordinate in a Kennedy department.

My new role is much less definite than it was with A [the previous secretary] when it was exactly clear what I could and could not do. I knew instinctively with A. B [the new secretary] expects you to do everything, but you're not quite sure how far to go because he doesn't spell it out. When the chips are down I go ahead, but not because of Secretary B. He makes me more cautious because he won't quite tell me to go ahead or not.

If his secretary had urged him to exercise his own judgment and promised to support him, he would have proceeded more confidently. As it was, however: "I have to be ever so much more careful in evaluating things now—whom to work with and how."

An adviser must have access to his principal. All the legislative liaison agents emphasized that they had to have immediate, direct contact with their secretaries, not indirect contact through intermediaries. Their relationship had to be one of easy and continuous interaction.

Their principals had to afford them the opportunity to offer advice when policy decisions were being made, not afterward.

None of the departmental liaison officers in the Kennedy Administration (except for the special case in HEW) encountered any trouble with the initial requirement. Two, in fact, had insisted upon this condition before accepting their positions. One of them pointed out that when he had first talked with the secretary about undertaking legislative liaison, it was under the jurisdiction of an assistant secretary. "The thought was I'd be under him, but I wouldn't buy this. The only way to be in charge of legislation for the secretary was to report directly to him, not to go through anyone else." When the same department was administered by Republicans, the legislative liaison agent reported initially to an assistant secretary and subsequently to the undersecretary and the secretary.

Aside from one liaison officer, none of the others experienced difficulties in conferring with their secretaries whenever they deemed it necessary. Their offices were in close physical proximity to their principals' —"right down the hall." Even the liaison agent who deliberately chose a suite of offices a floor below his secretary's ("I don't want my office near him; he's too busy and confusing") had immediate access to the secretary's private elevator. Not only were they constantly conversing with their secretaries over the telephone, but the liaison officers reported a very high frequency of personal contacts with them, meeting in their offices several times a day and attending their staff meetings.

Legislative liaison agents felt strongly about having a direct voice in determining policy that affected congressional relations. Only one or two expressed discontent about not being as fully involved as they believed they should be. "Am I privy to everything I should be?" mused an agent in a large department in the Kennedy Administration. "No, I'm not. The liaison agent ought to know exactly what is going on in the department, at the top level at least, at all times; he should be privy to all things. I don't get the feeling that the secretary calls me in on most." In contrast, a tough-minded, independent Assistant Secretary for Congressional Relations (State) in a previous Democratic administration had insisted upon the following condition when he was assigned to the job.

I had to be in on policy; it was a must. "Don't hold me responsible," I told the secretary and the others, "for foolishness on the Hill unless I'm in on all policy decisions affecting the Hill. You can't make policy decisions even God can't get through and then expect me to do it." As a result, I was in on all the policy decisions and I exercised important power—said "this will or won't go." Once I told the undersecretary, "I'll not push for it unless you change the language so that it can pass."

One of his successors in the same department during the Kennedy Administration remarked: "I have no problem in this respect. I am completely brought in on policy-making—at levels of informal discussion and when the legislation is put together. And I sound off in policy discussions."

The significance of the liaison agents' free and complete access to their principals may be more precisely delineated by contrasting two extreme cases in the Kennedy Administration. An exasperated liaison agent in one department expressed his frustration at the handicap imposed by what he considered a denial of proper access. His counterpart in a much larger department voiced his satisfaction with the full access accorded him by his secretary. Both were competent liaison agents and reported that they had their principals' confidence. Interviews with their secretaries and the latter's personal assistants confirmed these assessments.

The first agent noted that he did participate when policy was developed during the fall of the year. With respect to substantive issues on which he was knowledgeable, political problems that affected proposed legislation, and personal relations with individual legislators, his views were discussed and heeded. However, he encountered problems in maintaining close and continuous contact with his secretary. "I want to have him see A; urge him not to talk with Congressman B until he talks with me first; fill him in on the complexities of the situation; make certain he's staffed right on things he's doing within the department that have an impact on Congress." His previous secretary had pursued a policy of being constantly accessible to his staff.

I see Secretary Y only three or four times a week for any length of time, while I met with X seven or more times a week and more often for brief consultations. I can't stick my head in to Y. He doesn't like to be intruded upon and have the subject changed. But sometimes it just has to be done.

Moreover, his present secretary often departed from Washington, D.C., without consulting his liaison agent, "even though I may think it politically important that he delay temporarily." It wasn't part of his secretary's makeup, he asserted, to rely upon staff.

At times the new secretary convened meetings with only his subcabinet officials, and the liaison agent found himself excluded. The secretary complicated his agent's job and aggravated his own problems in the Congress.

As a result of all this, he does things with an impact—an important, complicating impact—upon our problems with the Congress without having the proper staff around him. I realize that staff magnifies its importance, but without staff there's no telling where he'll end up.

In contrast the legislative liaison officer in the other department complained humorously that his role as adviser left him little time to go to the Hill. The secretary was readily accessible and made great use of him. He portrayed himself as an intimate adviser to his principal, and on many issues. "I see him many times during the day—three times so far this morning." Paradoxically, he contended: "The secretary brings me in on more things than I care to do—anything applicable to policy that may affect the Hill or be of interest to the Hill." It was the liaison agent's practice to attend any secretarial-level meeting relating to policy in which he was interested. The secretary had established a departmental rule that his liaison man was to be included in whatever the latter felt was essential to his job. Consequently he examined the secretary's schedule every day and participated in what he deemed most important.

In discussions on policy, the secretary would always ask for his comments and/or objections.

I comment where it affects the Hill, but usually not on policy. Usually I have very little substantive knowledge on policy, but where I do, I make it known before it gets to the secretary's office. I do say at times: "Wait a week or a day, or give me some time to talk to the members of the subcommittee before we issue an administrative order."

Unless he had a voice at the top policy level on the timing of legislative or administrative policy decisions and on the effect of the substance of such decisions upon the Congress, he maintained, he could not properly assist his secretary, and his own job in the Congress would become needlessly complicated.

Interviews with leaders in this department confirmed the picture of a very close relationship between secretary and liaison officer. The fact that the latter was a long-time personal friend of the secretary as well as the undersecretary undoubtedly facilitated their easy, intimate relationship. The personality and style of the secretary should not be overlooked. He had prior political-executive experience. He worked well with his staff and respected its members; they in turn admired him tremendously. Similarly, the personality of the liaison agent and his expertise contributed to his relationship with the departmental leader. He was considered the most skilled and experienced of all the liaison agents in the Kennedy Administration. He was a congenial individual who possessed an excellent sense of humor and an ability to maintain a sense of balance in tight situations.

The relationship between principal and agent in this department and its value to the other executive leaders is epitomized in an anecdote that touches only indirectly upon Congress or legislation. As related by another member of the secretary's staff, the secretary had become so edgy and irritable during one period, being harried by the Congress and the press, that his staff began to worry about his health and about his effect upon the department and its congressional relations. The liaison agent solicited the aid of the secretary's wife and helped rearrange the secretary's agenda so that he was conveniently scheduled to spend some time in Florida. "He came back a new man, more effective than ever," noted a senior department official who was very close to both the secretary and the congressional relations officer. Commenting upon the latter's contributions to the department, he exclaimed: "How do you measure something like this? It was invaluable to the undersecretary, to the assistant secretary, and to me."

(D) THE SECRETARY MUST ENSURE THAT HIS AGENT IS RECOGNIZED AS HIS SPOKESMAN IN CONGRESSIONAL RELATIONS. Each liaison agent wants his secretary to demonstrate conclusively to others in the department and the Congress that he speaks for and represents the department head. Considering the roles that congressmen want the liaison officer to play—acting for and serving as a conduit to the secretary—it is absolutely essential for the agent's effective participation in the Congress that such a relationship be clearly established by his secretary. Otherwise, the liaison agent loses his ability to maneuver or negotiate from a position of strength, and legislators have no confidence in him. They may bypass him for that level in the department which will most expeditiously complete their communications circuits. Dependent as he is in his own department upon the other political leaders and the career personnel who must convey intelligence data about Congress, expedite legislative requests, share information on executive plans, and participate in common action regarding the Congress, the liaison officer must also be recognized by them as the secretary's spokesman if he is to secure their cooperation.

All the Democratic and Republican liaison agents at the secretarial level expressed confidence that this relationship had been firmly established by their principals. The dimension of importance they assigned to it emerged in the remarks of one Democratic assistant:

My value to the department stems, in large part, because I do represent the secretary and am able to speak for him in situations with regard to legislation. I'll talk with two or three congressmen. "Will this do? No? Then what about this?" This kind of conversation can only take place if they know you speak for your boss, if you have the discretion and confidence from your boss in your operations.

Conceding that his freedom to participate in policy meetings might irritate agency heads and assistant secretaries, another Democratic liaison officer asserted that it was nonetheless vital that he participate. Others in the departmental political leadership had to accept him as the secretary's man, not as a snooper, in order for him to operate effectively. His secretary, he explained, had announced such a policy in the department and confirmed it in his behavior toward him in front of others.

A former Republican Assistant Secretary for Congressional Relations (State) affirmed the importance of being known as the secretary's man. Perhaps the delicate position of the congressional relations officer's job in State, even at the high rank of an assistant secretary, accounts in part for his comments:

This job isn't worth a damn unless the secretary says to everyone: "This is my man as far as Congress is concerned." The only way anyone in this job can talk policy in the Senate is to have the absolute trust of the secretary. Dulles always kept me informed; he never made a contact with a congressman that he didn't tell me about. He told the department that as his representative I was not in the direct chain of command. I could go to any assistant secretary or undersecretary, and he insisted I report directly to him.

Other Senior Political Officers as Principals and Associates

Although a secretary is the head of a department, he shares his power and duties with a number of senior political officers: an undersecretary or undersecretaries, assistant secretaries, heads of subordinate agencies, and a general counsel. They, too, are appointed by the President and confirmed by the Senate, which action provides them with some sort of independent power position within the department. They assume responsibility for supervising and operating the various units of the department and for helping the secretary exercise control over the entire department. In these capacities they, too, testify before Congress on legislation and on administration. Legislators address themselves both informally and formally to these political subleaders with regard to bills under consideration, proposals for legislation, and a wide range of administrative rulings and decisions. In turn, these senior executive actors find they must initiate relations—seek support and goodwill, explain, collaborate—with the members of Congress.

Undersecretaries in some departments (HEW under Ribicoff's leadership is one example) had virtually no contact with the Congress. In Treasury, on the other hand, the undersecretary acted as the major political leader and coordinator for specific legislative campaigns, while the congressional relations officer served as a subordinate lobbyist in such endeavors. In still other departments (Agriculture, for example) the undersecretary played a role somewhere in between these extremes.

On the other hand, most of the assistant secretaries in each department were associated to some extent with the Congress.

In representing the secretary, the legislative liaison agent is responsible for the entire range of legislative and congressional relations within the department, appropriations excluded except in special emergencies. In contrast, assistant secretaries and administrators of agencies are primarily responsible for the bills and congressional relations affecting their special jurisdictions. Their involvement poses specific problems for a department's congressional relations officer in that a number of executive actors, more senior and more powerful within the department than he, also represent the department or parts of it. He must ensure that all speak, in effect, with one voice, or at least for the common good of the department as defined by the secretary. He has to prevent them from preempting or undercutting his own roles in congressional relations. And he needs to cope with the potential wastage of executive resources.

It is through his coordinator role that the liaison agent seeks to resolve these problems. It is a role that both he and his senior political leaders define as vital to the best interests of the department. And yet in each department the attitudes of the liaison agent and these senior officials determine the degree of cooperation that permits the agent to play this role successfully. Three types of relations were evident in the eight departments: two contrasted sharply and the third represented a series of variations of patterns that fell in between the extremes.

(A) MAXIMUM CONTROL BY THE LIAISON AGENT. In one department the liaison agent sought to maintain a pattern of maximum control over his department's relations with the Congress. Although it was a small department without any independent agencies, which itself reduced the problem of coordination, he was adamant that the leaders of the department relate to the Congress solely through him. The department was one, he claimed, in which free-wheeling relationships between senior officers and the Congress had long been traditional. Apparently he had made a special issue of it and had devoted considerable energy to ensuring that such relationships would be reduced to an absolute minimum or eliminated altogether.

"The secretary and the undersecretary agree that I should be the *single* channel between the department and the Congress," he declared. Neither the undersecretary nor the assistant secretaries carried on any relations of their own with the Congress, he claimed, and "when they try, I try to stop it." As for the solicitor of the department, he "deals with Congress through me almost a hundred percent of the time." When major bills required policy clearance within the department, the liaison agent did check with the solicitor, and he often brought along the latter or his representative when he went to the Congress. "After all, I'm in the exposed position of saying yes or no, of binding people, and I am not expert in everything." He did utilize others in the department for certain tasks, "but to have them all free-wheeling is bad." Even his first secretary, with whom he had been close and who was very competent in congressional relations, had sometimes interacted with congressmen without informing him. "Now," he reported, he was fully "athwart that traffic."

Interviews with his initial secretary and with others in the department indicate that the liaison agent undoubtedly encountered some difficulty in imposing this control over his senior political officers. Despite his close relationship with the liaison agent, the first department head had made an assistant secretary responsible for the politics of one area of legislation in the Congress. Something of a free-wheeler himself, the former secretary reported that in dealing with the legislature he had been prepared to utilize anyone who was politically sensitive, who understood the Congress, and who had special relations with its members. The liaison agent conceded that this substantive area was very complex, and one in which he had no expertise. Consequently, he reported, he had deferred to the assistant secretary, who was very conscientious about keeping him informed. One was left with the impression, however, that despite the liaison agent's ostensible acceptance of this situation, such an arrangement was in his opinion not the most desirable; rather it was to be regretted.

(B) MINIMUM CONTROL. The opposite style in working with senior political officers was pursued by a legislative liaison agent in a large confederate department. Only a minimal effort was made to impose personal control over the congressional relations of the many leaders in this department who were actively engaged in dealing with members of the Congress —the secretary, the undersecretary, all the assistant secretaries, the general counsel, and the administrators of the constituent agencies. A number of them possessed independent power bases with clientele groups or had close ties to powerful congressmen.

A hypothesis might be advanced that, under such ostensibly unfavorable circumstances, a departmental legislative liaison agent would encounter great difficulties in performing his role as coordinator; either he would have to exert a tremendous effort to retain any semblance of control or he would have to abjure any serious attempt to behave as the secretary's coordinator for the department. Such a liaison officer, we might expect, would manifest considerable frustration in his relations with other executive actors at the political leadership level. Nothing, however, could have been further from the truth. Not only did the officer who actually operated under these circumstances praise his senior associates and superiors for cooperating splendidly, but their cooperation, he contended, enhanced his ability to act as adviser to the secretary, lobbyist in the Congress, and coordinator for the department. His political superiors and associates emphasized in their interviews that he was essential to their own relations with the Congress, and therefore his cooperation and activity were vital to the best interests of the department.

This legislative liaison officer pictured himself as an integral member of the political team that represented the department in its dealings with the Congress. He spoke directly for the secretary and he served as a cooperating equal with the other political officers in their combined efforts to obtain legislation, defend the secretary and the department, and advance the department's interests both within and outside the Congress. From their point of view, the undersecretary, the assistant secretaries, the general counsel, and the most aggressive of the agency heads unequivocably labeled him an indispensable member of their team. Without him, they noted, neither they nor the secretary could operate as effectively in the Congress. Each asserted that he sought advice from and shared political information with the liaison agent. In effect, the latter acted as the key coordinator for all of them.

The liaison agent characterized his relations with them in the following manner:

They keep me fully informed. We sit in the secretary's meetings and work together as his team in dealing with the Congress. I rely upon them and they upon me and my staff; neither of us could do a good job without the other. We're working together so closely all the time—calling each other, sending memos back and forth, visiting legislators together, devising strategy and tactics, substituting for each other when the politics of the situation require it— that I have no problems with them and no problem in keeping control of what's going on.

From his point of view, therefore, there was no need for any effort to interpose himself, as was the case in the first department, between the senior political executive actors and the Congress. They knew what to do and how to do it, he explained, and they made very certain to consult with him whenever any problems or questions arose.

A similar picture was painted by the senior political leaders of the department, from the secretary on down. As spelled out by the secretary, a few of his people combined technical proficiency and excellent congressional relations experience in a legislative area of considerable significance for the department. Together with his legislative liaison agent, they comprised a specific team for this program. But his special agent worked with others in the department on additional sets of problems and programs. "He is not there as a technician on the program; they carry it forward. He is there to coordinate and integrate the work with Congress on policy and legislation. His direct responsibility is the total, overall departmental posture in relation with the Congress."

The deputy undersecretary, a former administrative assistant in the Senate, noted that the liaison officer also engaged in selling, but that the rest of them backstopped him since he wasn't enough of a substantive expert. "He's the most popular guy in the department. He knows exactly when and where to bring each assistant secretary or the secretary into the Congress and with what areas and interests each can most effectively deal. He's a wonderful unifying force." All who worked with this liaison officer attested to his valuable service to them and to their department.

One explanation for the strategies and styles of the two liaison agents just compared may be attributed to the size of their departments. An insistence upon maximum control may simply be more feasible in a smaller department than in a large confederate one. Whereas the first liaison agent made no reference to size, the second did cite the size of his department and its large number of senior political actors as constituting an element to consider. Too much importance must not be ascribed to size alone, however, since it is possible to reverse the argument. A large confederate department may impose a greater strain upon coordination, inducing its legislative liaison officer to attempt to exert more control over relations with the Congress. And the lesser number of political leaders in a small department as well as the more intimate contact between them and the liaison agent may permit a more relaxed style.

The extent to which a liaison agent plays a role on the substantive side of legislation may also help explain the difference in relations between the two liaison agents and their associates at the political leadership level. In the first department the liaison agent considered himself an expert in the policy area of its bills. In fact, he declared himself to be more of an expert than most of the others within the leadership. This explains, in large part, his insistence upon preempting the major role, subordinate, of course, to that of his secretary, in dealing with the Congress; other actors would only "foul up the work." In contrast, the legislative liaison agent in the second department made no pretense at being a policy expert. "I am really a people dealer" was his catchphrase. Since he felt that others in the department were more expert than he, they should play important roles of their own.

Still another factor affecting the relations between the senior leaders and the liaison agent in his role as coordinator is the confidence that the executive actors have in each other. In the second department the senior leaders had the highest confidence in their liaison agent, which he reciprocated; all of them emphasized this point. The members of this team regarded each other as equals who respected each other's competence and cooperated with and relied upon one another. In the first department, the liaison agent did not look upon most of his associates or seniors as equals. Commenting on the team pattern in the first department, he said: "It would be fine, I'd like it very much. But we can't do it with our people. We don't have that sort of talent around here." From the remarks of a knowledgeable assistant secretary within his own department, it was clear that the competence and talent of the liaison officer were also questioned.

The personality of a liaison agent may also shape the relational patterns he establishes with his senior political leaders. In the second department the liaison officer was an extremely relaxed, congenial individual, marvelously easy to deal with. All his associates commented upon these traits and upon his ability to remain at ease and approach all emergencies with a sense of humor. Although he worked exceptionally hard at his job, he seemed at all times the epitome of calmness and confidence. The liaison agent in the other department was also a very hard-working, able individual, but he seemed much less relaxed, somewhat on edge. He tended at times to become rather impatient and sarcastic, and he was not averse, apparently, to behaving in this manner with those who impressed him as fools or as naïve. These personal characteristics became quite clear during the lengthy interviews I had with the two of them. It is entirely possible that such personality traits were attributable to the relative degree of certainty and confidence each developed with his associates and superiors in his own department. This was not the conclusion, however, of other actors who were interviewed, several of whom had known one or both liaison agents when the latter had worked in the Congress.

(C) VARIATIONS BETWEEN THE EXTREMES. The relational patterns of liaison agents and political superiors fell between these two extremes in the remaining six departments that were studied. In one small department the only political leaders participating in congressional relations were the liaison officer, the secretary, the undersecretary, and one assistant secretary. A team concept somewhat analogous to that of the previously cited department was in operation. The liaison officer worked on substance, but was primarily responsible for process and politics, although in a subordinate capacity to the undersecretary, who was field general on certain important bills. At the same time minor pieces of legislation were delegated to the liaison agent to carry both substantively and politically. He had no complaints regarding his associates, and they looked upon him as an able, functioning member of the department's high command who acted somewhat as a coordinator for the secretary and undersecretary. So few prominent actors were involved, however, that coordination was actually a minor problem; it virtually took care of itself in this small, tightly knit group.

On the other hand, the liaison agent in a large confederate department complained that he was not obtaining the full cooperation he required from his senior leaders. Although this was causing him some concern, it was his contention that he was still able to exercise control over the politics of the department's bills in the Congress. His associates and senior leaders claimed that they conveyed to him political intelligence from their contacts with legislators, but it seemed evident from their remarks that not all the relevant data were being forwarded. And in a number of instances these leaders acted on their own with congressmen, without even consulting the liaison officer to obtain relevant information concerning these legislators or to ascertain whether their timing or methods were appropriate.

In HEW, another large confederate department, the assistant secretary responsible for legislation, who also dominated its congressional affairs, appeared to exercise effective control over the relations of senior political leaders with the Congress. Coordination presented no major difficulty because of the small number of actors involved. Aside from the secretary and this assistant secretary, the top leadership of the department was composed of an undersecretary and one other assistant secretary, neither of whom was active in the Congress. Moreover, the Assistant Secretary for Legislation was clearly the most competent in terms of substance and in his knowledge of and experience with the Congress. But even in this department some problems of coordination developed. For example, the secretary had assigned to one of his special assistants responsibility for legislation in a specific area and for relations with the appropriate committee. When the assistant secretary was queried about his relations with this special assistant to the secretary, he remarked wryly: "He plays it pretty close to his chest, but every so often he does come in to check with us."

LIAISON AGENTS AND THE BUREAUCRACY

One basis for the recommendation by the initial Hoover Commission that each departmental secretary be provided with a special congressional relations staff was the conclusion that the bureaus were more closely linked to the Congress than the departmental leadership. The bureaus were deemed to be more capable of launching and carrying through legislative campaigns. Implicit in this analysis was the thesis that the bureaus often operated within the Congress in pursuit of their own interests, which were not necessarily those of the departmental leaders or the administration. The assumption that departments were divided into different groups of actors—political executive actors and career executive actors—was also accepted by the second Hoover Commission.[4]

Cooperation and Conflict Between Political and Career Actors

Departmental liaison officers and their staffs were queried about their relations with the bureaucracy. It was hypothesized that the bureaucracy would emerge as a distinct and significant variable affecting the liaison officers' operations in both the executive and legislative systems, and that these political actors would have to develop appropriate behavior patterns to control, nullify, or utilize this variable. It was further hypothesized that the introduction of congressional liaison officers into the executive system to supplant or control bureau-legislative dealings, in the interest of departmental-level goals, would result in strained relations between political and career actors.

(A) LIAISON AGENTS VIEW THE BUREAUCRACY AS A DISTINCT SUBSYSTEM. Legislative liaison agents made a clear distinction between their own immediate associates and superiors and the bureaucracy in their departments. They considered themselves and their associates (including their superiors) as members of a distinct political leadership group. Since they represented the same general interests, if political executive actors did pose problems, such problems did not arise out of cross-purposes among them. Moreover, a number of these actors came from legislative and political backgrounds similar to those of the liaison agents.

The liaison agents perceived the bureaucracy as constituting a distinct subsystem of its own. Its actors had their own rules, loyalties, and interests, which might or might not coincide with their larger system, whose leaders were the political chiefs of the departments and, ultimately, the President. It was a subsystem, moreover, with perceptible boundaries, psychological as well as legal, which had to be penetrated by the liaison agents if they were to perform their roles successfully. At the same time it was a subsystem—more precisely a number of subsystems in each department—the activities of whose leading actors often paralleled those of the political executive actors in the Congress. Both sets of actors were

---

[4] The distinction between political and career executive actors is accepted also by the following students of the national executive system: Marver H. Bernstein, *The Job of the Federal Executive* (Washington, D.C.: Brookings Institution, 1958); Dean E. Mann and Jameson W. Doig, *The Assistant Secretaries: Problems and Processes of Appointment* (Washington, D.C.: Brookings Institution, 1965); John J. Corson and R. Shale Paul, *Men Near the Top: Filling Key Posts in the Federal Service* (Baltimore: Johns Hopkins Press, 1966).

dependent upon the Congress for authorization and appropriations legislation. Both were tied to the Congress through different levels of cooperative endeavors with its actors and through congressional devices for controlling the executive. In this context it was essential to the liaison officers that bureaucratic actors subordinate their ambitions and activities vis-à-vis the Congress to those of their political leaders. As political actors the liaison officers demanded that the bureaucratic system be placed at their disposition in dealing with the Congress and/or the White House. Hence the bureaucracy constituted an environmental constraint with which somehow they had to cope.

Despite the conflict implicit in these perceptions, the Kennedy legislative liaison agents *on the whole* judged the bureaucracy to be well behaved and properly subordinate to the political executive leaders. The liaison officers evidenced, however, a sense of latent tension and uncertainty regarding career personnel which surfaced quickly during their interviews. Although the relationship of the political actors with the bureaucratic actors was primarily one of cooperation and collaboration, the bureaucracy tended to be viewed with a mixture of suspicion as to its motives; contempt, in part, for its lack of political astuteness; fear for the political deals it could arrange with an all too cooperative Congress; frustration apropos of professional or bureaucratic norms that conflicted with congressional norms and interests to the detriment of the political executive; and resentment at its unwillingness to subordinate itself as a resource to the strategy and tactics of the liaison agents.

A word of caution is in order. In none of the eight departments were all these negative attitudes identified with any single liaison agent. On the other hand, none among the liaison agents or their staffs failed to reflect at least one of these attitudes, and some expressed many more. What has been projected up to this point, then, is a composite of the negative attitudes of the liaison agents, enough of which were held in common so that it may be said to characterize departmental liaison agents in general. Since the comments of liaison agents in five departments of the Eisenhower Administration coincided with those of the Kennedy Administration, we are obviously dealing with attitudes that these agents hold regardless of party. It may be hypothesized that political actors in subsequent administrations will manifest comparable attitudes toward their bureaucracies.

In general the relationship between political executive actors and career administrators constitutes an important subject, meriting greater attention than has been accorded it. What follows is an exploration of merely one facet of such a relationship, the principal portion of which focuses upon the attitudes and behavior of the liaison agents. The attitudes of the bureaucrats toward legislative liaison agents are only partially explored in this study.[5]

(B) COOPERATIVE AND COMPLEMENTARY BEHAVIOR. Liaison agents from both parties *wanted* the bureaucracy to play an active role with the Congress. They recognized that the bureaus had established working relations with legislators on committees crucial to the departments. As long as the efforts of the bureaucrats did not conflict with the legislative programs, strategies, or tactics of the political executives, the interests of a department were enhanced insofar as the self-interest of each of its parts was advanced.

Four confederate departments will be cited to illustrate this tolerant, indeed positive, support for active bureaucratic involvement with the Congress and cooperation between the two sets of executive actors. And both Republican and Democratic political executive actors will be quoted.

"We often released the bureaus to do their own work on the Hill," explained a political actor who had been responsible for legislative liaison during the Eisenhower Administration. "But my staff was expected to know what was going on." A more positive note was sounded by the Democratic liaison agent for that department: "I encourage them to go to the Hill and use their old contacts and continue their friendships, and of course to let us know what they are doing." He tried to acknowledge their good work by having the secretary call career personnel to express his appreciation. "My problem from the beginning," related another Democratic liaison agent, "was the coordination of intelligence and information. I want to know about their contacts with the Congress, not to stop them." Upon assuming their positions, both of these Democratic liaison agents had organized liaison networks within their departments. Personnel was selected for the networks by the bureau heads in the first department and by the liaison agent himself in the second department. These bureaucrats worked personally with the departmental liaison staffs when the latter required cooperation from their bureaus and agencies.

In the other two departments the responsible political actors expressed themselves somewhat differently from their colleagues. They felt that on the whole they were fully on top of their departments' relations with the Congress. "The bureaucracy does not get in the way of my ambitions," claimed one of the liaison officers. "Most of the agencies in the department do a lot of Hill work. As long as there's some kind of sense to it, it's OK with us." X agency he described as "a very good lobbying

---

[5] Bernstein, *op. cit.,* pp. 114–16, does offer some evidence of attitudes of career administrators toward the liaison officers during the Eisenhower Administration.

outfit" with whose leaders he enjoyed good relations. He consulted with them on their needs and on how to accomplish their objectives. "We know what they work on, and I hear things on the Hill and discuss them with their chief. They call me and ask what should be done." He contrasted his situation with some departments in which a sizable number of bureaucrats were on the Hill lobbying, and the liaison staff did not always know what the former were doing: "I'm lucky. Our people are active, yet they keep in close touch with me. And anyway, we don't have enough people to do the work ourselves, so it works out all right."

According to his counterpart in the other department, there were closer relations with key senators and congressmen down the line of the department which were more important than some of his own. He acknowledged that many strings stretched from the bureaucracy to the Hill. "My policy is not to interfere with them. They get a lot through on a professional basis. I don't have the staff or the time. And as a matter of principle in legislative relations, I don't believe in using my big chips when I don't have to." Responding to a question about the control he exercised over agency liaison, he added: "I can't control it all; there is too much going on within the department. The problem is to control what is important and what you can do something about."

By supporting within departmentally determined guidelines the legislative programs or appropriations that benefit them, the bureaucracy assumes a load that would otherwise have to be borne by the political leadership. Actors in bureaus and agencies possess specialized knowledge regarding their own administrative responsibilities. Equally if not more important, they have developed contacts with the appropriate legislators and committees to advance their own interests. It is questionable whether legislative liaison agents in large departments, even if they so desired, could successfully displace the bureaucracy in its traditional relations with the Congress; the legislators would most certainly object. However, to a large extent such relations are perceived by liaison agents as proceeding from a professional basis—from the technical proficiency of career administrators. And when politics is engaged in by subunits within the departments, it is often in behalf of goals either approved by or not conflicting with those of the senior political leaders. What the liaison agents do insist upon, at a minimum in such cases, is being kept informed regarding congressional relations. Liaison agents need to have their fingers on the pulse and range of their departments' interactions with the Congress.

(C) TENSION AND CONFLICT BETWEEN POLITICAL AND BUREAU-CRATIC ACTORS OVER POLICY, STRATEGY, AND TACTICS. That tension develops between liaison agents and bureaucrats is inevitable. This occurs at various levels of importance, the more serious revolving around policy differences. Career administrators are not always willing to confine them-selves to goals agreed upon by the political leadership, especially when their own recommendations have been overridden. Political leaders may not exert themselves in behalf of that part of their legislative program to which a particular career executive actor is committed. The political superiors may decide upon other priorities, or the White House may insist upon its own. When a career administrator undertakes to advance goals or strategies for his unit that conflict with those determined by the department, he is bound to clash with the activities and the ambitions of the departmental liaison agent. He may thwart the latter completely, or he may in the process cause him considerable trouble. Since productive congressional relations must be carefully nurtured and legislative majori-ties easily become unstuck, the introduction of any additional confusion greatly complicates the problems of the departmental liaison officers.

Except in the case of Defense, which will be referred to later, very few departmental liaison agents claimed that bureaucrats had lobbied for programs that did not have the approval of the senior political leadership. A Republican liaison officer from HEW charged that the Water Pollution Act of 1956 was not an administration measure but an agency-commit-tee creation. "They went around us. Their people cooperated with the committee members on the Hill." On other bills, he acknowledged: "We had lots of unsolicited and undesired help." A colleague from a different department in the Eisenhower Administration verified this charge. He had observed bureaucrats from HEW working the Hill in opposition to their secretary's position.

Democratic liaison agents from two of the four confederate depart-ments cited earlier, in the context of support for bureaucratic involvement in the Congress, noted a few such occurrences. The liaison agent who had remarked upon his luck in having bureaucrats cooperate with him could recall encountering only one or two cases of real trouble with agencies. In one instance, since it was clear to him that the key legislators were not prepared to support the agency's proposals, he had not intervened when the agency campaigned for a program that "was not within the wishes of the administration."

In the other department, however, the congressional relations staff bitterly condemned independent politics on the part of some of their bureaucrats. In particular they cited a senior departmental budget officer, a career official responsible for liaison with the appropriations commit-tees, who had sought on his own initiative to divert funds for a depart-mental program from the secretary's office to one of the agencies. He had made his own arrangements with an appropriations subcommittee on the "legislative intent" of another program—an important consideration for its subsequent administration—without clearing with the secretary's political advisers. And when a legislator had quietly pushed through a resolution in this same appropriations committee which could have proved extremely embarrassing to the department's political leaders, this career administrator had failed to alert them or their associates.

Apropos of their counterparts in appropriations liaison, invariably career administrators, none of the legislative liaison officers in the other seven departments ascribed to them any lack of cooperation or undercutting of their secretaries' positions. Any criticism stemmed primarily from their belief that these budget officers were not equipped, as were the legislative liaison agents, to work with interest groups and to stimulate the grass roots. A number of liaison officers commented unfavorably on an old-crony type of relationship that the budget officers had developed with the appropriations committees. Some of these political actors asserted that they should not have to liaise with others in the executive regarding appropriations in the Congress; this should be their own responsibility.

The limited number of complaints and cases cited by political executive actors appears to demonstrate that on the whole they do not find the bureaucracy espousing contrary policy positions in the Congress. Nevertheless, such is not the sum total of bureau-congressional relations. *At the level of attitudes, tactics, and strategy, liaison agents were adamant that their efforts in the Congress were often impeded by bureaucratic action or inaction.*

Career administrators were charged by a number of liaison officers with pursuing their parochial points of view at a time when the political leaders wanted to impress upon legislators the importance of their own programs. In effect, what was objected to was a failure on the part of bureaucrats to coordinate with and subordinate themselves to the legislative liaison agents. As representatives of their secretaries, responsible for helping them coordinate the departments' programs and relations with the Congress, the liaison agents were in a better position to know the priorities of the political leadership on policy, strategy, and tactics.

Examples offered by a Republican who headed up legislative liaison for one department and by a Democratic agent in another illustrate this conflict. The Republican had been the deputy general counsel responsible for supervising the department's legislative liaison; at the time no special actor had been assigned this responsibility. He asserted that one inherent problem in congressional relations was the tendency of bureaus and agencies to peddle their programs to the same legislators without regard for each other and in ignorance of broader administration strategy.

Take the case of this Democratic committee chairman in the Senate. It had been a particularly rough day for him. One of his important constituents had given him hell, and he'd had an awful row with another. That day five people from my department talked with him *before* I got there. They weren't working against us; in fact, what each was peddling was legitimate. But we had presidential priority. And if he was the key to the trade bill and we wanted to focus his attention on this item, they were certainly fuzzing everything up. When I got there he was livid with rage. "What the hell is going on?" he demanded. "Can't you see if you can make any order out of this?"

The problem of coordination among executive actors before congressmen are approached was an extremely important one, contended a Democratic liaison agent. The bureaus were often ignorant of the higher political strategy that dictated certain actions and not others.

Sometimes the departmental leaders make certain assumptions on legislation that's holed up in Rules, and we don't want the agencies to operate on the Hill for such legislation. On the other hand, if we tell the agencies that the department has given up on their legislation, which it has, they'll scream and go out to the country for support.

When a major departmental legislative proposal was given priority, the legislative agent directed the agency people not to ask any favors from committee members.

The agencies want to ask Congressman X for votes on ————, but I won't let them. We want him on ———— [the major legislation]. I don't want them asking favors of him; we're saving him for the big one. Many of our career people just don't have any idea of the political relationships among congressmen and the arrangements that are made with the House leadership. They could upset the whole applecart.

In terms of communications theory, political executive actors endeavor to keep open channels to important legislative actors for their own signals, which carry the highest departmental or administration priorities. At the same time bureaus and agencies are encouraged to advance their own interests within the context of departmental goals. The two conflict when bureau signals either overload the communications network. creating too much static, or confuse or anger the receivers. The circuits may be completed by bureaucratic signals that raise the costs and efforts required of political leaders or cause the receiver to lose interest in any further inputs from them into the network. Implicit in this analysis is an assumption by the legislative liaison agents that career executives lack a proper sense of timing, a key ingredient in legislative politics. They do not always grasp the complex political arrangements that characterize legislative systems, and they may operate upon assumptions that have been invalidated by subsequent strategic decisions of the political leadership. Such decisions may, in fact, be withheld from career administrators in order to preclude their taking their case to their special publics —clientele groups and friends in the Congress.

(D) CONFLICTS OVER THE BUREAUCRACY AS A RESOURCE. Another source of tension between legislative liaison officers and bureaucrats stems from a conception by the former that the bureaucracy is a resource, intrinsic to the department, which the political leadership may expend in behalf of its legislative campaigns or in smoothing over congressional relations. Liaison agents endeavor to create goodwill in the legislative system, to build up reserves of credit with legislators and their staffs upon which they may subsequently draw. Such efforts involve the granting of services and favors (about which more will be said in a subsequent chapter). In the process, liaison agents demonstrate to legislative actors that the latter may profitably turn to them for assistance from the departments and for common endeavors in the Congress. Since much of what congressmen want is operationally in the hands of career actors, the cooperation of the bureaucracy is essential to those responsible for department-congressional relations.

However, the bureaucracy may play its own political game and prove reluctant to participate in one directed by political actors. Its members may refuse to cooperate with the legislative liaison agents or they may hide behind the literal interpretation of rules. They may decline to move quickly when immediate action is deemed vital by actors representing political executive leaders, or they may phrase their responses so carefully as to afford liaison agents and legislators little substance upon which to act. Conversely, bureaucrats may panic and overrespond, or they may provide a frank opinion but not a particularly diplomatic one.

Under such circumstances the liaison agent, whose job is endless in its demands and delicate in its complexities, finds himself all too often frustrated by members of his department when he tries to carry out a number of his roles. In fact, he may end up battling parts of his own bureaucracy in order to prevent relations with the legislative system from deteriorating. "Often we have to fight them [the bureaus], to force them to give congressmen the proper answers. They hate to admit mistakes. We often have to urge the agency to take a second look at a request."

The political executive is much more willing to bend or waive the rules in order to accommodate the politician in the Congress; the bureaucrat is more prone to be suspicious of both sets of politicians and to react from an administrative or professional point of view. It is no surprise, therefore, to hear a Democratic departmental liaison officer say: "I have to keep good relations with the bureaucracy or they won't play ball with me," and then to add bitterly: "The civil service has its own politics. It's a third force. They know they'll be here when we've gone. I'd make anyone above GS Twelve non–civil service." A liaison staff member in another department charged: "They [the bureaucrats] hate us with a vengeance, though it varies with the agencies, of course. We work for the administration and are politically responsible. They are independent and are ongoing professional operators with their own clientele."

Two Democratic liaison agents from domestic departments reported difficulties with their bureaucracies in providing legislators with a valuable service: jobs for their constituents and friends. The nature of their complaints was completely different, reflecting the type of problems each encountered in mobilizing the resources of his own department. One liaison agent condemned the negative attitudes of his bureaucrats regarding congressional intervention for jobs:

The bureaucracy is simply not sympathetic to the Congress. I have a hard time to make them understand that if a congressman recommends someone for a job, he is not necessarily incapable. The bureaucracy tends to become a closed clique. We have trouble in making them understand that Congress should even be kept advised of changes in personnel.

Legislators were frequently pressured for jobs by their constituents and sometimes by their party organizations. In view of the fact that the department employed a large work force with well-paying positions distributed throughout the country, it was inevitable, he said, that congressmen would turn to his department.

The second liaison agent confronted different types of bureaucratic actors. These were more than eager to assist inquiring congressmen, he related. His dilemma arose from their preference for making personal deals directly with legislators and not permitting the department (the political executive) to take credit for such favors. Without such credit, he complained, he was being denied an important resource that could be used to bargain with legislators; the bureaus rather than the secretary's office were being strengthened in the Congress, and the secretary's office was unable to improve the posture of the total department in the Congress. Moreover, he charged, some bureaus even announced these personnel changes without affording him or the congressmen prior notice. "There's almost nothing that makes some congressmen hit the ceiling more than for a bureau to undercut them by not letting them let the guy know that the job is his and thereby take the credit." After one particularly sensitive incident, he had sent a sharp memorandum to all bureaus and personnel officers:

> One of the most sensitive areas of Congressional relations relates to the proper handling of personnel recommended by Members of Congress . . . for positions in the Department. Because, by the very nature of things, we will be able to place so very few of those recommended by Congressmen, it is important that we get full credit for those we do hire.
>
> Accordingly, no one is to notify a Member of Congress that a person will be hired except through my office. Furthermore, insofar as possible, if a Congressman has taken a particular interest in a certain person, the Congressman himself should be given the opportunity to advise the individual that he will be hired.[6]

Legislative liaison officers claimed also that career administrators were often inflexible as well as insensitive to the political needs of legislators when the latter approached the executive system for other types of assistance and for guidance. Unfortunately, contended the liaison agents, this ineptness could sour relations between the congressman or his staff and the department as a whole. "Sometimes they're completely blind to the needs of the Congress," exclaimed a liaison staffman after he had sidetracked a particularly inept bureaucratic response to a senator. Periodically he conducted spot checks of letters from the agencies to the Congress. In one case he discovered that a senator had requested material to refute the late Rachel Carson on the danger of insecticides. The responsible bureau had forwarded a routine reply form stating that it had insufficient funds and staff to do the job. By calling within the department, the liaison staff assistant learned that the head of an international committee on pesticides and chemicals was on its staff. When he phoned the senator's assistant to assure him that a suitable refutation would be forthcoming, the latter exploded in anger: "What is this? Have you forgotten what it's like up here? We're being bugged with mail on Carson's article. Get us something on the subject so that we can answer and damned quick."

Another senator had asked the department to express a policy position on his bill. One of the bureaus prepared a reply for the secretary's signature to the effect that the department's position was adverse to the legislator's bill. This, too, was discovered before it progressed to the secretary. Conducting his own investigation, the assistant concluded that the senator's bill contained good, bad, and neutral features. "Here the bureau would have had the department caught in committing itself by

[6] Memorandum in Department X, from its legislative liaison agent, April 22, 1963, "Subject: Relations with Congress Concerning Personnel Matters."

letter to the effect that the bill was adverse to the public interest when the bill has at least six good features." It was "politically more advisable," he explained, "to spell out the good features and say that we can go along with them at the same time that we present our negative comments."[7]

At least two control devices were employed by legislative liaison agents to monitor, make proper adjustments in, and take advantage of the relations between bureaus and the Congress. The formal rules of some departments—State and Commerce, for example—required all written correspondence to the Congress from the bureaucracy to pass through the office of the legislative liaison agents.[8] In State the Assistant Secretary for Congressional Relations signed all mail originating in the department, which afforded him the opportunity to review it and return to the bureucracy anything that needed revision. A few liaison officers also requested from their bureaucrats a daily report of incoming as well as outgoing congressional mail.

Legislative liaison agents pointed out that congressmen became extremely exasperated when their requests for information and assistance were not acknowledged or answered, or when an inordinate delay preceded a reply. Bureaucrats were disposed, they noted, to act upon such communications in the order in which they were received. A response to a member of a committee handling the department's bills might be delayed because communications from legislators of less significance to the department had preceded his. Routine developed a priority of its own, and administrative tasks might be given precedence over congressional mail. As a consequence legislative liaison agents and their staffs found that they had to supervise constantly the responses of the bureaucracy to verify that the appropriate answers were being forwarded and congressional correspondence moved with dispatch. "The understanding is that everyone drops everything when they get a call from our office," reported a liaison agent who had painstakingly developed a network of assistants at

---

[7] A 1962 study of "legislative reporting" in another department documents "a recent tendency" by the politicians in the secretariat to ameliorate and correct for a bureaucratic lack of "political sense" that can cause trouble for the department. See Carl R. Sapp, "Legislative Reporting in the United States Department of Agriculture" (unpublished master's dissertation, American University, 1962), p. 18.

[8] Invariably nonroutine congressional mail from the department's appropriations subcommittees is called to the attention of the Assistant Secretary for Administration, and replies to such congressional matters are cleared with this officer before mailing. As clarified in a memorandum by the liaison agent in Commerce to the bureaus, the Assistant Secretary for Administration was to be sent "correspondence relating to any budgetary matter in the Department, or any request for services or favors of a substantive nature which would improve our relationships with them." Memorandum, "Subject: Congressional Mail," from the Deputy to the Secretary for Congressional Relations, Department of Commerce, May 17, 1963.

the bureau-agency level. "I sold them on it. I know that when I was on the Hill we appreciated good service and got damned angry when we couldn't get a proper response from the department."

Outgoing letters provide the secretaries' assistants only one index of the scope of congressional recourse to their departments and of the relationship between the bureaucracy and legislative actors. Liaison agents also asked bureaus for memoranda of telephone conversations and of personal contacts of an official nature. Having glanced through files of such memoranda in a number of liaison offices, I can attest to the routine nature of much of this kind of contact. Nevertheless, this too can be valuable, said one liaison agent: "I know I can rely on them, especially for routine things. Most things are routine. What is important is to recognize that which looks routine but which will blow up later because the bureaucracy will carry out the rules literally." Data that alert the liaison agent to trouble, cue him in to the ambitions of a particular legislator at the moment, or call his attention to services rendered by the department that may be capitalized upon in approaching a legislator are obviously very useful.

Only one Democratic liaison agent encountered difficulty in persuading bureaucrats of the importance of providing such data. It was not that the bureau people were obstreperous, he explained; many simply did not want to be bothered. On the other hand, a liaison agent in the Eisenhower Administration, confronting a Democratic Congress and working with a bureaucracy that had been developed largely during the Roosevelt and Truman Administrations, charged that "we caught them [bureaucrats] deliberately not turning in their memos regarding their going to the Hill. And the orders were 'a memorandum to us from anyone who's going.' " Yet, in the identical department during the Kennedy Administration, the liaison agent reported that he could not keep up with the hundreds of memoranda advising him on bureaucratic-congressional contacts.

That legislative liaison agents may seek to expand their intelligence nets to obtain data from *informal* contacts between bureaucrats and legislative actors has been noted in a previous chapter. This becomes a more delicate matter than the simple monitoring of official relations, for it touches upon the sensitivity of legislators regarding their privileged contacts with bureaucrats. In the case of the State Department in the Kennedy Administration, where such intelligence efforts became too overt, congressmen reacted quickly to protect their contacts. Upon learning how State's Assistant Secretary for Congressional Relations had been burned on this issue, another departmental liaison agent immediately approached members of the committee staff that had raised the alarm to assure them that he imposed no such demands upon the bureaucrats in his department. No other departmental liaison officers in the Kennedy Administration insisted that bureaucrats inform them of their informal, off-duty relations with legislative actors. A Republican liaison agent reported that he had sought such information, and that, despite a Congress dominated by the opposite party, no issue had even been raised. Apparently he had not employed an official memorandum for his purpose, nor had anyone in his department leaked the news to the Congress.

Three Cases in Liaison Agent–Bureaucratic Relations

Three departments have been selected for special comment, none of which have figured in the examples cited earlier. In the first department, which will remain anonymous, the pattern represents an effort at tight control by the liaison agent over his bureaus' relations with the Congress. It is described also because it was one of the few departments in which career executives were interviewed regarding their relations with departmental liaison officers. The usual policy of deleting references to the names of departments will be waived for the other two. Each constitutes a unique case of relations among bureaucrats, legislative actors, and liaison agents.

(A) DEPARTMENT X: THE LIAISON AGENT ATTEMPTS TO EXERCISE TIGHT CONTROL OVER BUREAU-CONGRESSIONAL RELATIONS. The legislative liaison agent in this small department maintained that members of the bureaucracy were basically not competent to deal with the Congress.[9] Therefore, he felt, they should not be permitted to do favors for legislators on their own initiative, nor should they be permitted to go to the Hill except under close supervision. Such control over them was necessary, he argued, even though this made for considerable tension at times between the two types of executive actors.

The bureaucracy, he asserted, was so abysmally ignorant of congressional affairs that he had to spend valuable time and effort educating the department on how to deal with the Congress. Basically, its members did not understand the Congress, and as a result "they goof up or tend to feel outraged" at the political response of the legislators. In addition, they made administrative decisions that had an impact in congressional districts without taking into consideration the consequences for the legislative process. The timing of such decisions often proved embarrassing

---

[9] An identical position was taken independently by the former Republican liaison agent for this department: "The bureau heads think they can handle the political, but they can't always do so. The career guys simply cannot handle political matters on substance in dealing with congressmen."

for the department's political leaders in their dealings with the Congress, and the liaison agent had to work hard at putting out the fires started by bureau ineptness.

In his eyes, bureaucrats were overendowed with innocence. They were both overscared and underscared by things congressional. "Like innocents," they responded to congressional queries for information by supplying data that caused all sorts of trouble for the department. Some, moreover, could not resist acting as advisers to congressmen on legislation, offering advice that turned out at times to be detrimental to the department's overall interests. On the other hand, bureaucrats were impatient with and exhibited a kind of contempt for the constituent inquiries that were forwarded to the department by congressmen. Congressmen abhorred what they called bureaucratic gobbledygook, but few among the career officials knew how to furnish legislators with immediately usable responses that they could convey to their constituents. The liaison officer had to persuade his bureaucrats to employ intelligible English.

An assessment of this liaison agent was provided by a sophisticated bureau chief within the department. He was quick to credit the liaison agent with competence and ability, and he attested to the valuable aid that the latter had furnished him. The liaison agent was characterized as exerting strong leadership with regard to the Hill by insisting upon full coordination—he was to be kept informed by the bureau of all its contacts with the Congress and, when possible, to participate in them. But his performance was good, in the bureau chief's opinion: "I get all the help I need, and I'm interested in results." He was impressed with the liaison agent's wide acquaintanceship on the Hill, his perceptive analysis of legislators and their staffs, and his understanding of the department's programs.

Nevertheless, asserted the bureau chief, legislative liaison agents and bureau heads had different roles to play in relation to Congress. The bureau was concerned with its own substantive program. "We are interested principally in promoting our own program, getting it accepted and resolving problems, some of which are political." The legislative liaison agent represented a broader constituency, and he was much more concerned with the political point of view. "He relates to Congress in the broadest sense and is much more concerned with the political objectives of the administration than we are." The bureau was then carrying on a campaign in the Congress, in cooperation with its state affiliates, to negate efforts by private groups to cut its budget. "I consult with X [the liaison agent] and keep him informed, but we run this. I, too, make contacts with congressmen and senators."

What the bureau chief objected to was the tight coordination and control that the secretary's assistant was attempting to impose upon career administrators in the department. He opposed such a policy as unduly restricting his own efforts to advance the interests of his bureau in the Congress. For example, he sharply questioned the need for anyone from the liaison staff to participate in all the contacts he and his staff made with the Congress.

Someone from his staff goes up with me and sits like a lump on a log; he doesn't know enough to contribute. [Here he exempted the liaison agent himself.] It's better to have his staffman home than for us to bring someone along when the fellow doesn't know what's going on. He should depend more on his career people.

His major complaint concerned a new policy the liaison agent was trying to implement and which the bureau chief was resisting. It required clearance with the liaison officer before any bureau contacts with congressmen could be initiated. This policy was being justified on the basis of an incident in which, according to the liaison officer, the department had fared badly owing to a failure to clear with him in advance. Although the bureau chief disagreed with this interpretation, he recognized the possibility of undesirable developments for the department in the absence of prior clearance with its expert on Congress. But, he argued, it would be better if fewer inhibitions were imposed on himself and his staff, even if this resulted in occasional incidents. He was concerned that this policy would seriously handicap him in dealing effectively with the Congress. "I frequently pick up the phone and call. Or it works the other way. A congressman calls me, and I take advantage of the opportunity to offer two or three things I want to get across. This back and forth is a pretty free thing." It was not a question of secrecy, he continued, but "if I need prior clearance to discuss programs, this policy would seriously inhibit me as a bureau head."

Differences in approach between bureaucratic and liaison actors were manifested also in the critical remarks of a career administrator from another part of the department. Much lower in rank than the first, this bureaucrat was nevertheless an individual of expert knowledge who maintained excellent relations with one of the department's House committees and who had been used for a technical type of substantive liaison with its members. The secretary's liaison aide was characterized as involving himself heavily in substance and "not always to its advantage." He was charged with being overly political in his approach to the Congress, too prone to compromise substance in order to obtain votes. "I am aware," this bureau official said, "that the political realities can't be avoided or neglected. But sometimes the political can undermine what we're trying to do in the substance of the legislation." The liaison agent was also criticized for failing to consult properly with the substantive experts in the department. "He sometimes doesn't see the backhand effects of the compromises he agrees to. On their face, they don't look harmful. But occasionally when we get down to the working of the provisions, they are harmful."

That this bureaucrat ascribed to the liaison agent the motto "Let's not go up with a program unless we can win" reveals, in part, the difference in emphasis of career administrators and political leaders. Both are obviously concerned with substance and with winning, but the bureaucrats stress the nature of the program and its administration; the legislative liaison agents, the necessity of being able to market the commodity successfully in the Congress.

(B) THE DEPARTMENT OF DEFENSE: DEALING WITH THE BUREAUCRACY IS LIKE RIDING A TIGER. Incorporating within itself three separate departments, each with its own political subleadership and distinct bureaucracy, Defense is monstrously difficult for any secretary to control administratively and politically. Outdating the Department of Defense (DOD) and its secretary by over a century and a half, the Departments of the Army (formerly War) and the Navy have a long, established tradition of close and independent relations with the Congress. And the newly created Department of the Air Force has quickly emulated its sister services.

The service departments have traditionally been jealous of each other and have competed within both the executive system and the Congress. Moreover, they have not taken too readily to the imposition of a single, integrating political leader responsible solely to the President. More than any other cabinet officer, the Secretary of the Department of Defense (SOD) probably faces the greatest challenge from his bureaucracies in controlling and coordinating his multifaceted department internally as well as in its congressional relations. His assistant for legislative affairs shares with him the task of imposing integration upon the entire department in its relations with the Congress.

Although each of the service departments has a small set of political executives at its head and a larger group of civilian career administrators, they are primarily departments of the uniformed services. They represent a type of bureaucracy that differs considerably from the predominantly civilian bureaucracy in the other departments. Moreover, Defense is atypical for still another reason. The military departments have long conducted their own liaison with the Congress. One of the distinguishing characteristics of the Department of Defense is that each of the subordinate departments maintains a large legislative liaison staff of its own, composed of uniformed service personnel chosen from within its own ranks and headed by a field-grade officer. The Office of the Secretary of the Department of Defense, on the other hand, maintains a much smaller unit headed by a civilian political (noncareer) type, whose staff is approximately half civilian political personnel and half military, with officers from all the services.

According to the two DOD liaison officers who served during the Kennedy Administration, they and their secretary ruled uneasily over the three service departments. One of these congressional relations officers stated ruefully: "Legislative liaison in DOD is like riding a tiger. If he feels friendly, OK. If not, look out, you're in trouble." Each military department cooperated with the SOD in relation to the Congress when its interests coincided with his, but each attempted to play its own game when their interests conflicted. Control and coordination from the secretarial level were very difficult to impose, in large measure because key individuals in the Congress had long opposed such domination by the senior political executive within Defense. Hence, the SOD's legislative liaison agents faced the very delicate task of trying to protect their secretary and the latter's overall policies for his department in their dealings with the Armed Services Committees.

The DOD liaison agents did not consider the service departments' liaison staffs a source of trouble or conflict within the bureaucracy. For the most part they were deemed to be able men who did a good job and showed great integrity in dealing with the DOD liaison agents. "Our real problems are rarely if ever with the different legislative liaison staffs of the military, but with other guys in their departments." Only once had bad relations developed between the liaison chief of a service department and a liaison officer for the SOD in the Kennedy Administration; apparently it was strictly a personality difference rather than a policy conflict. However, it was pointed out, when a military department was in rebellion against the policies of the SOD, that service's legislative liaison staff withdrew from the usual cooperative arrangements with the DOD liaison officer. Under such circumstances, the latter could not rely upon the service's liaison staff as a resource for intelligence or as an aid in working with the Congress.

One problem confronting any Secretary of the Department of Defense and his liaison agent is that of holding his subordinate departments in tandem. Traditional jealousies and rivalries among the services place a great strain upon integration. The separate bureaucracies are not averse to extending the fight with each other beyond the executive system. "I expect," declared one DOD liaison agent, "two things from them [the services' legislative liaison staffs]: to do a good job with the legislation that is assigned them and not to undercut their sister military services." Neither of the two liaison assistants to the secretary (DOD) in the Kennedy Administration had serious complaints about any failure of the services' liaison staffs to meet either criteria. But they reported that intense rivalry among the services during the Eisenhower Administration had led to bitter competition within the Congress and to a congressional reaction that took the form of a reduction in appropriations for their liaison staffs. In attempting to have this limitation rescinded, the Assistant to the Secretary (DOD) for Legislative Affairs promised an appropriations subcommittee in 1961: "Let me assure you that Secretary McNamara has informed the military departments' secretaries and the service chiefs that this type of activity must be controlled."[10]

The competition during the Eisenhower Administration had been so intense that it proved impossible for the political leadership in the DOD to control. In his message on reorganizing the Department of Defense on April 3, 1958, the President himself was forced to take public cognizance of it and to act.[11] The legislative liaison as well as the public affairs sections of the services were the "principal outlets for such rivalries," the President announced. In order to minimize the possibility of one service advancing its interests at the expense of the other services or of the overall national and defense requirements, the President directed his secretary (DOD) to review the number and activities of the military departments' personnel engaged in legislative liaison and public affairs activities. The secretary was requested to strengthen DOD supervision over such activities and to move such personnel and activities as were necessary into his own office. The military services were compelled to cut back on their liaison staffs in the fiscal year 1959 and were permitted no increase in the fiscal year 1960.[12] Their liaison officers were

[10] U.S. House of Representatives, Subcommittee of the Committee on Appropriations, *Hearings on Department of Defense Appropriations for 1962*, 87th Cong., 1st sess. (Washington, D.C.: U.S. Government Printing Office, 1961), pt. 2, "Operation and Maintenance," p. 1022.

[11] National Archives and Records Service, *Public Papers of the Presidents of the United States: Dwight D. Eisenhower, 1958* (Washington, D.C.: U.S. Government Printing Office, 1959), pp. 274–90.

[12] In 1959 the Secretary of Defense issued directives to the three services and to his own Assistant for Legislative Affairs in which he defined legislative liaison as involving frequent direct and personal contacts with members of the Congress. Funds for fiscal year 1959 provided for a 17 percent reduction in legislative liaison for the Air Force, 21 percent for the Navy, and 18 percent for the Army, as well as a 41 percent increase for the Office of the Secretary of Defense to strengthen overall direction and coordination of legislative liaison. U.S. House of Representatives Subcommittee of the Committee on Appropriations, *Hearings on Department of Defense Appropriations for 1960*, 86th Cong., 1st sess. (Washington, D.C.: U.S. Government Printing Office, 1959), pt. 4, "Operation and Maintenance," pp. 1021, 1085.

no longer permitted to make unsolicited calls on the offices of individual senators and representatives relative to legislation.

In the Kennedy Administration the secretary (DOD) proved to be an exceptionally strong leader, but he too encountered problems in his efforts to dominate and determine the entire department's policy with regard to Congress. It was not merely a question of the three bureaucracies' refusing to subordinate themselves and intervening on their own in the legislative system. "The congressional leaders do not want a working, central departmental control mechanism over the three departments," observed one of Robert S. McNamara's liaison agents. "They are afraid it may be the beginning of the end of the separate services as well as a loss of their own control over the department." Secretary McNamara, he claimed, had arrived with the notion that the services would first present their recommendations within the department, and, if their differences with the secretary could not be resolved, they were all to go to the President, together or independently. "But once the final decision was made, all would fall in line. This just wasn't so, McNamara was shocked to learn."

According to this liaison officer, one set of problems arose for the Secretary of Defense because the services approached the Congress before he did. Even before the budget was presented to the Congress, the services would brief the committees' staffs and the chairmen on their own positions. When the secretary appeared before the committees he found himself at a great disadvantage. The extent to which the services had differed with the administration, and their opposition to the administration, had been divulged to the legislators. "This means that if he wants to really run the department, he runs right into the services and the committee chairmen."

When a service department was in conflict with the policy position of the secretary (DOD), the best his liaison agent could hope for was that the military officers would abstain from the fight in the Congress. "Take the RS Seventy issue. You can't expect the Air Force to move favorably or be with us since General X is opposing it. All we can hope is that they'll stay out of the Congress." But it was clear that the services did not stay out.

The rules of the game, noted a DOD liaison agent, were that the military was to articulate publicly the position agreed upon by the highest political leaders and not to offer their own opinions unless the committee members directly asked for them. One way to engage in end runs around the official department position was to arrange to have the right questions asked of them by the legislators and their staffs. In the course of a very controversial congressional investigation during the Kennedy Administration, in which the secretary (DOD) was intimately involved, one of the service departments "did not answer straight and tried to volunteer information." To undercut the secretary (DOD), disclosed the liaison officer, the service department had worked with the committee to draw up questions that would embarrass the secretary (DOD). "This we were aware of; it's the nature of the beast." What could be done about it? In the long run, he observed, some people get fired. With regard to certain issues—military pay bills—the liaison officer acknowledged that the services could not be excluded completely from the department's dealings with the Congress. "I don't try to do anything about their efforts, but if they go too far, I sit on them."

In terms of the *total* posture of the Department of Defense and its relations with the service departments in the Congress, the problem of the political leadership with the three bureaucracies was probably over-inflated, concluded a DOD liaison agent, but it still remained a serious one. However, problems of coordination and control from above were inevitable; and such problems would continue as long as the Defense Department remained institutionalized in the form of a separate secretary for defense and three military departments, each of the latter having special interests and expecting to represent them to the Congress, and as long as key congressmen encouraged such practices.

(C) THE DEPARTMENT OF STATE: THE BUREAUCRACY NEITHER UNDERSTANDS NOR LIKES THE CONGRESS. The bureaucracy in State presents a totally diverse set of problems for its legislative liaison agents to overcome in carrying out their roles vis-à-vis the Congress. Compared with those in the other seven departments studied, the liaison agent and his staff in State in 1962–63 devoted a disproportionate effort to improving relations with the Congress and to educating State's own bureaucracy. The liaison personnel at the secretarial level clearly felt that their department's congressional relations suffered from the negative attitudes and inadequacies of the program-oriented career people. This was equally discernible to other political actors in the department. A high-ranking noncareer official, who was close to Secretary Dean Rusk and dealt with the career officers, made the following comment about the problems of the Assistant Secretary for Congressional Relations:

Dutton has to fight more in his department than any of the other legislative liaison people. Their departments are politically oriented and sensitive, and they're more involved. Ours is not. So Dutton has an important role—that of fighting within his own department for some understanding and sensitivity toward Congress; it's damned important. Most of the Foreign Service officers are extremely insensitive to domestic American politics; they have no interest or feeling for it.

"I am a bridge between two different institutions with two different attitudes," explained Assistant Secretary Frederick G. Dutton. Among his primary jobs was that of changing the attitude of the department toward the Congress as well as the attitude of congressmen toward the department. As a result, he admitted, "I am a double agent, and in the department I am suspect as representing the congressional point of view. Of course I do overstate the congressional point of view in order to overcome the entrenched departmental point of view."

One feature of the department that blocked successful communications between executive and legislative actors was the propensity of State's bureaucrats to view politics as something contemptible. Moreover, they were suspicious of the Congress and distrusted the motives of its members. In the opinion of State's personnel, foreign policy was best left to the department; Congress intervened only to meddle irresponsibly. "Those preoccupied with foreign affairs," Dutton once wrote in a draft of an article, "are hesitant about subjecting sensitive international problems to the rough and tumble of the Hill . . . appalled by legislative statements and actions based upon an inadequate knowledge." In the published article that explored the antagonism between State and the Congress, he reported that departmental actors categorized congressional complaints about foreign policy in such terms as "uninformed," "opportunistic," and "special-interest motivated."[13] Many in State, he counseled, had to learn to accept the fact that "Congress has entered into the world as never before, and is there to stay."

The unwillingness of career administrators in the department to go to the Congress also handicapped the department. By meeting with legislators, argued Assistant Secretary Dutton, they would come to know them better and understand their point of view. At the same time, the legislators themselves would become acquainted with foreign policy experts. This might counteract the negative attitudes congressmen exhibited toward State. Even career officials who occupied assistant secretarial positions, he noted, were reluctant to go to the Hill, although he tried to activate them to do so. More effective congressional-departmental cooperation, he concluded, could be built on twenty to thirty people rather than simply on the secretary, a few senior political leaders, and the liaison officer and his staff.

In addition to his own personal proselyting to correct departmental attitudes, he had sought to institutionalize means for improved communications and understanding. Meetings were arranged between Foreign

---

[13] Frederick G. Dutton, " 'Cold War' Between the Hill and Foggy Bottom," *New York Times Magazine*, September 15, 1963, pp. 36, 94–95.

Service officers ("It is astonishing how lacking this elite group is in its perceptions of Congress and legislative problems") and legislative actors. One such session brought together several hundred Foreign Service officers with three senators—Bourke B. Hickenlooper (R., Iowa), Claiborne Pell (D., R.I.), and Hubert H. Humphrey (D., Minn.)—whose committee assignments included six major committees in addition to Foreign Relations. The three senators attempted to explain to the bureaucrats the perspective of the legislator and addressed themselves to what they thought was wrong with departmental-congressional relations.[14] A subsequent session was held between a small group of key staff assistants in the Congress and senior leaders in the department. Assistant Secretary Dutton also persuaded the department to incorporate in the training of its junior Foreign Service officers an apprenticeship in a congressman's office. He had fought for a four-week apprenticeship, but the senior Foreign Service officers had resisted and the period had been reduced to two weeks. In addition, he initiated a program whereby Foreign Service officers visited their own congressmen before going overseas.

The antagonism between Congress and State could never be completely eliminated, Dutton acknowledged. Basic differences between them made a considerable amount of friction inevitable. At the same time, "substantially more and better contacts are needed between these two distinct and sometimes remote groups, if the underlying attitudes and semantics that breed much of the difficulty are to be straightened out."[15]

A somewhat similar set of problems, but even more aggravated, confronted the legislative liaison apparatus in the Agency for International Development (AID) within State.[16] However, the initial and an important concern of one of its senior members had a different focus— the bureaucracy's negative attitudes toward its own legislative liaison shop and the impact of such attitudes upon the efforts of this staff. The bureaucracy, he contended, did not have a high opinion of its senior liaison agent, or, for that matter, of the entire legislative liaison operation. In the eyes of the career officials, the liaison officer and his chief

[14] Cabell Phillips commented upon this meeting in the *New York Times,* June 16, 1962.
[15] Dutton, *op. cit.,* p. 95.
[16] Although State's agencies, such as AID and the Disarmament Agency, possess their own legislative liaison shops, their liaison officers and staffs are political, non-career officers, not members of the operating bureaucracy, as is the case in the three service departments in Defense. Together with the political liaison staff of the Secretary of State, they share common problems in dealing with their own bureaucracies. At least AID and State do; no interviewing was conducted in the Disarmament Agency.

assistant had very little knowledge of the agency's program. "This attitude handicaps us," he lamented. "We are closed out by the program people, although we ought to influence the program to help shape it in accordance with the congressional view so it'll have a better chance to get passed."

Most career personnel in AID and in State rejected outside advice, feeling that Congress did not understand the AID program and should not tamper with it. Indeed, it was the bureaucratic belief that the Congress, the President, the American people, and the legislative liaison agents should not have any say in the program, he charged. This attitude hurt the agency, for the President and the Congress could not and would not permit the agency alone to shape its policies. It also imposed great difficulties upon the legislative liaison officer and his staff in their attempts to develop effective congressional relations.

To compound the problems for the legislative liaison staff, some important career people in AID refused to go to the Hill to talk with legislators. Regional administrators and top officials were reluctant to take even elementary steps to improve congressional relations. Either they disliked doing them or they considered them unimportant, he declared. And yet AID suffered from what was probably the worst congressional relations of any agency or department within the executive system. Efforts to remedy the situation within the agency had not proven too successful, he conceded.

Frozen out of a voice in shaping the program to enhance its chances on the Hill and contemptuously dismissed by their own career officers, the liaison staff had to resort at times to radical measures in order to exert some influence on the program that their agency carried to the Congress. Occasionally they reversed their focus and utilized the Congress as a means for influencing their own program people! "We write speeches here and get powerful members of the Congress to give them; and then our program people listen." To support or reinforce the liaison staff's position, they inserted into such speeches a few policy points on legislation that might have some influence with the agency itself.

AID's bureaucratic resistance to its own liaison staff in 1962–63 and its hostility to Congress epitomize one extreme in the relations between political executives and career executive actors. In such policy areas as defense and foreign affairs, the liaison agents confront special problems vis-à-vis their bureaucracies, although the nature of such problems is different in each area. It is clear, however, that all departmental liaison officers must to some extent concern themselves with their bureaucracies if the leadership of their political superiors is to be effectively implemented in the Congress.

CHAPTER VI

Liaison Officers Appraise
the Congress

As COMPLICATED as his relations are with fellow actors within his department, the liaison officer must still develop another pattern of relations with actors in the legislative system. His value to his executive superiors and associates is premised almost entirely upon his expertise and familiarity with a system that differs from their own and which is not their primary focus and responsibility. Not only are they extremely dependent upon the Congress, but they must endeavor to lead it in directions that they choose, an undertaking requiring from them and their assistants for legislative liaison the most sensitive and sophisticated understanding of the legislative system.

As the specialist in congressional relations for his senior political leaders, the liaison agent must fill a number of roles that bring him intimately in contact with the Hill. One aspect of his involvement, serving as a unit of the White House team, is deferred to a subsequent chapter. However, much of what follows is relevant to the role of White House agent or administration team player.

An underlying assumption in this study is that the manner in which a particular actor perceives his environment will greatly affect his behavior toward others within that environment. That it does not totally determine this behavior is clear from the data that has been presented. The priorities, perceptions, and demands of key actors within the executive lobbyist's own system also condition his behavior patterns. Nonetheless, his own perceptions largely define the environment for him. To the extent that he perceives restraints, challenges, or opportunities in this environment, he will shape his strategy and tactics accordingly.

It would have proved useful to initiate a consideration of such perceptions on the part of liaison officers by placing it within the broader context of theory and data based upon lobbyists in general. Research in this aspect of private lobbyist–legislator relations is not as barren as it is regarding the relations of lobbyists within their own system. However, there still is a regrettable lack of attention to the private lobbyists' perceptions of legislative systems and to the effect of such perceptions upon their strategies and tactics for interacting with legislative actors.

Some recent studies that touch upon the lobbyist–legislator relationship have tended to portray the relationship solely from the legislators' point of view.[1] Other writers have recorded their own perceptions of the roles and relative effectiveness of lobbyists in terms of the authors' understanding of the dynamics of the legislative system.[2] Even Lester W. Milbrath's study, which focuses primarily upon the Washington, D.C., lobbyists themselves, is incomplete for our purposes.[3] References will be made to valuable comparable data in his book on the perceptions of the Congress by such lobbyists, but on the whole *The Washington Lobbyists* only begins to probe the dimensions of this matter. James A. Robinson does touch briefly and specifically upon State's liaison agents' perceptions in his *Congress and Foreign Policy-Making,* but he is concerned primarily with their assumption that congressmen will respond favorably to the department if it handles their requests properly.[4] This will be dealt with in the following chapter.

A caveat must be entered regarding the data that will be presented about the attitude of departmental lobbyists toward the Congress. It is evident that their perceptions of the legislative system were conditioned by the particular relations existing between their own departments and the Congress. After all, they were departmental officers concerned primarily with the legislation and congressional relations of their own parts of the executive system. Hence they focused upon the special subsystems of the Congress relevant to their departments. To the extent that a department had its own problems and that certain legislative actors loomed

[1] See, for example, John C. Wahlke, Heinz Eulau, William Buchanan, and Le Roy C. Ferguson, *The Legislative System: Explorations in Legislative Behavior* (New York: Wiley, 1962), chap. 14, "The Legislator and the Interests: Pressure-Group Roles." For a different type of study see Donald R. Matthews, *United States Senators and Their World* (Chapel Hill: University of North Carolina Press, 1960), chap. 8, "Senators and Lobbyists."

[2] See Raymond A. Bauer, Ithiel de Sola Pool, and Lewis A. Dexter, *American Business and Public Policy: The Politics of Foreign Trade* (New York: Atherton Press, 1963), pt. 4, "The Pressure Groups." See also William Buchanan, *Legislative Partisanship: The Deviant Case of California* (Berkeley: University of California Press, 1963).

[3] Lester W. Milbrath, *The Washington Lobbyists* (Chicago: Rand McNally, 1963).

[4] James A. Robinson, *Congress and Foreign Policy-Making: A Study in Legislative Influence and Initiative,* rev. ed. (Homewood, Ill.: Dorsey Press, 1967), pp. 162–65; see also pp. 185–90.

larger in importance to it than to another department, these factors helped define the way a liaison officer perceived the *system as a whole*. Even as a subordinate member of the White House operation in the Congress, the departmental lobbyist confined himself principally to his normal pattern of interaction with the Congress, i.e., that determined by his departmental responsibilities.

At the same time he was tempted to generalize about the legislative system as a whole; in part because, as has been noted earlier, he either had been a member of that system or had worked intimately with it from outside its boundaries; in part because the liaison officer was compelled to interact with increasingly wider circles of legislative actors if his department's legislation was to progress successfully toward enactment. In the end, he dealt with the whole of the Congress, not just its parts.

Let us examine first those common elements that departmental legislative liaison agents ascribed to the legislative system, keeping in mind that these lobbyists stressed different attributes at different times, according to their unique set of departmental relations with the Congress. Examples of special relations between departments and Congress that may affect differentially the approach and behavior of departmental lobbyists will also be considered.

THE LEGISLATIVE ENVIRONMENT IS AN UNCERTAIN ONE[5]

Uncertainty and irrationality were considered by departmental lobbyists in the Kennedy Administration to comprise one set of fundamental characteristics of the legislative system. The two were mentioned often enough to reveal that this aspect of the legislative system caused them serious concern, a concern that impelled them to devote considerable time and effort to compensate for it.

Some qualifications must be introduced, since they claimed that their assessment was valid for the Congress as a whole. While the liaison agents ascribed both uncertainty and irrationality to the Congress, their examples expressed, in effect, a reaction to their work in the House of Representatives, rather than the Senate. In fact, when they were sub-

[5] Richard F. Fenno, Jr., has shown that bureaucratic leaders, including departmental budget officers, are also concerned with uncertainty in their dealings with the congressional appropriations committees. See Richard F. Fenno, Jr., *The Power of the Purse: Appropriations Politics in the Congress* (Boston: Little, Brown, 1966), pp. 291–314. Fenno's treatment of this perception of uncertainty relates to one special set of committees and is developed almost entirely in terms of the behavior of agency actors in reducing this uncertainty with these committees. The behavior of the legislative liaison agents in reducing uncertainty in their relations with the Congress is one item covered in subsequent chapters focusing upon strategies and tactics.

sequently pressed on whether they were overgeneralizing about the Congress, they conceded that most of their problems arose in the House. But they insisted that uncertainty and irrationality were pertinent to the Senate as well, although to a much lesser extent, and that their successors in subsequent administrations would undoubtedly assess the Congress in identical terms.[6]

It is possible that their conclusions are valid only for the House, or at least sufficiently so to delineate a substantive difference between the House and the Senate in this regard, rather than a valid conceptualization about the Congress. Or their assessment may actually have reflected another variable: the party balance in the Congress. The Senate had a very comfortable Democratic majority in 1961–63 (in 1961 and 1962 there were 65 Democrats, 35 Republicans; in 1963, 67 Democrats, 33 Republicans). A much closer division existed in the House of Representatives (in 1961 there were 263 Democrats, 174 Republicans; in 1962, 256 Democrats, 178 Republicans; in 1963, 258 Democrats, 177 Republicans). This afforded the southern Democrats in the House a tremendous advantage: if they cooperated, the administration's legislation was assured of passage; if they did not, it was in serious trouble. The narrow Democratic majority placed a great premium upon reliability in attendance and joint efforts and voting on the part of the moderate and liberal Democrats. It also convinced some of the liaison agents that they needed to induce a number of Republicans to support their bills. The unknowns implicit in each of these conditions may have acutely sharpened the degree of uncertainty with which departmental liaison officers viewed the House.

Only subsequent research in another period with some differences in these variables can confirm whether perceptions of uncertainty and irrationality for the Congress as a whole will be concurred in by other executive lobbyists. At this point it seems reasonable to hypothesize that the extent of the party division in the Congress contributed significantly to Democratic executive lobbyists' stress on uncertainty. While the liaison agents in the Kennedy Administration acknowledged that the precarious position of their party in the House of Representatives might have affected their perceptions and behavior, they maintained that in the

---

[6] To the extent that the Republican liaison agents in the Eisenhower Administration stressed uncertainty and irrationality, they tended to confirm the prediction of the Democratic lobbyists. However, the Republicans were so preoccupied with the fact that they had faced a Democratic Congress that it was difficult to discern from their comments whether they felt that these were inherent characteristics of the Congress or merely a function of the domination of Congress by the opposition party. On one point they did clearly agree with the Kennedy lobbyists—uncertainty and irrationality in the Congress had caused them problems.

elements of uncertainty and irrationality they were identifying what was *intrinsic* to the legislative system. Party division in the House, with all the problems that it raised for them, may after all have only accented what was in fact a basic characteristic.

Uncertainty Is Deliberately Built In by Legislative Actors

It was generally agreed that much of the uncertainty and irrationality of congressional behavior was *deliberate*. Members of the legislative system sometimes purposefully introduced confusion—deliberately violated expected patterns of behavior—*so that executive leaders would pay attention to them.* "Many congressmen assume a posture of uncertainty," explained an exasperated but understanding liaison officer from a small department. "It's done so that they can ask for and get things from the executive. One way to do this is to vote irregularly." In a large department that sponsored a wide range of bills, the executive lobbyist made the same point in assessing the erratic behavior—deliberate in his opinion and frustrating for his department and the administration—of a key subcommittee chairman:

The communications process is very important. If they always vote for the administration, they feel that they tend to get nothing; and they're largely right. But if they're in and out, that is important, and X is perfectly aware of this. It is a signal to us and the administration that we can't rely on his vote and that we'd better do something about it.

Such deliberate behavior on the part of congressmen was most disconcerting. Especially was this so in the face of close votes and when even the mustering of a quorum in committee presented a problem. Nevertheless, liaison agents accepted unpredictable behavior as implicit in the system. Since congressmen realized that it paid off, they could be expected to resort to such behavior.

Uncertainty Is Magnified by the Unexpected

Uncertainty in the legislative process stemmed also from the impact of unexpected events upon the mood and behavior of legislators. "Part of the problem is the unexpected. It can kill us or it can help us" was the way one liaison agent expressed it. The sudden shift of a major interest group tilted the vote against his department's bill, contended another. An HEW lobbyist stated that the thalidamide scandal had favorably altered the climate in which drug-control legislation was being considered. In still another department, the liaison agent complained that a number of his bills, in a subject area that generally elicited bipartisan support, were being trapped in an atmosphere of partisanship as Republican lines tightened in a clash with the Democratic leadership.

Liaison agents acknowledged that actions by their own superiors, which they could not always control, could adversely affect the chances of their legislation. One liaison agent reported that an unexpected decision of his secretary in the extremely delicate area of civil rights had completely undermined the chances of an important piece of legislation. The civil rights issue was an aggravating one for still another executive lobbyist, whose department's bills were basically unrelated to that issue. It was now inappropriate to push his bills in the House of Representatives, he contended, because the Attorney General's trip into the South had so irritated the southern contingent in the House that they were refusing to cooperate on his department's legislation.

Both the executive lobbyists and Milbrath's sample of private lobbyists judged timing to be extremely important in the legislative system. But the executive lobbyists stated that it contributed to the uncertainty and irrationality of the Congress. "You can get murdered one week and three weeks later win big—so much is visceral with them [the legislators]." This imposed a tremendous burden, explained the liaison agents, upon their efforts to plan accurately. Timing was almost always difficult to control in a precise way. "You can get your peak of strength marshaled too soon or too late—it's damned difficult to know the right time and too easy to move at the wrong time."

Uncertainty was seen as arising out of the inevitable misunderstandings inherent in the relations between two massive systems. Communication between the Hill and the executive was often poor, it was maintained. Moreover, much of the information and signals between actors in the two systems filtered through secondary and tertiary sets of hands. All too frequently this affected adversely the relations between executive and legislative actors. "Not only is it easy to make gross misunderstandings regarding the Congress," exclaimed one exasperated liaison agent, "but so darn many misunderstandings are possible!" When actors from two different systems deal with each other, even from a sympathetic stance and with common interests, some degree of misunderstanding is inevitable, and behavior patterns emerge that exacerbate relations.

Irrationality Complicates the Degree of Uncertainty

A number of the liaison agents coupled irrationality with uncertainty in their perceptions of the legislative system. "One must have a real sense of the absurdity in the legislative process and the irrationality in it" was a typical comment. Their examples illustrated a number of facets of this phenomenon. Congressmen who may have been personally affronted by certain executive actors expressed their resentment, it was noted, by responding negatively or in a confusing manner to proposals by other actors in the executive system. "Congress is loaded with this kind of stuff," liaison agents declared. When one tried to ascertain why things were not proceeding as expected in the Congress, they reflected, it was always advisable to raise the question: "Who is rubbing against whom the wrong way?"

Relations among the legislators themselves in their dealings with others outside the Congress might lead to complications. Congressman X, chairman of an important committee, opposed a bill that a department was sponsoring. It was understood that he was anxious to have an unsightly public works project removed from his congressional district; he would pay any price. But such an action was dependent upon Subcommittee Chairman Y in another committee, who would not initiate the appropriate action. This congressman, it developed, was indebted financially to someone outside the legislature who had no interest in the bill in question, but who was vitally concerned with retaining the project in its district. Consequently, legislator Y could not be prevailed upon to act in a manner that would permit the executive leaders to consummate a bargain with legislator X. Initially the executive actors could not understand why a simple step could not be taken to resolve their problem. It was rarely if ever obvious, they observed. Only as they processed legislation through the Congress were they able to discover someone making noise, whereupon they would have to backtrack in order to run down and disentangle the complex personal relations of the members that underlay legislative stalemates.

Congressmen Engage in Self-Protective Behavior

Members of the Congress engaged, moreover, in a type of self-protective behavior vis-à-vis outsiders which complicated the job for liaison officers. This was a practice of the party leadership as well, they noted ruefully. Party leaders in the Congress made deals with the House Rules Committee chairman as to which bills would be permitted to move to the floor. These leaders never said to the executive actor: "I made a deal with X; that's all," but rather "We can't get the bill passed." When the liaison agent, his department's allied interest groups, and the administration put the heat on the leaders and committee members from their districts, they replied: "We're in favor of the bill, but the southerners are against it." "It's never because of a deal, but they protect themselves, because they've made the judgment," was the bitter conclusion of a departmental liaison agent whose investment of time, energy, and resources had come to nothing. Enough of the legislative system, claimed the executive actors, was loaded with what they referred to as "hidden agenda" to compound the normal problems they faced.

Executive Innovations in Policy Add to Uncertainty

The degree of uncertainty in the Congress was enlarged in proportion to the novelty of the executive system's proposals. Whenever their departments urged new types of proposals upon the Congress rather than the renewal of familiar programs, legislative liaison officers reported that they encountered additional trouble. Innovations in public policy were certain to generate much greater resistance among legislators than traditional ideas, even when proposed by members of the Congress. Undoubtedly this situation is characteristic of most if not all systems: the traditional is more palatable; the new is both strange and threatening to the actors involved. Executive lobbyists are handicapped, moreover, by virtue of the fact that they must help push something new through a system other than their own.

In the eyes of some liaison agents, the reaction of legislators to new ideas was also associated with irrational behavior. At times, they complained, proposals were rejected or accepted by legislators on grounds that had nothing to do with the inherent value of the proposals themselves. For example, many congressmen were disturbed by an innovative piece of legislation that included a provision for special enforcement machinery. When the same idea was repackaged in the form of an amendment to legislation already in existence, with identical if not greater discretionary power in the administrator, no one objected at all. "There was no sense to it," protested the liaison officer who was responsible. "It's just that anything new is much more difficult, even if the essence is the same as the old." Congress accepted the second approach, he observed, because its members were accustomed to it, even though they did not particularly like it; but they "fight like hell if it's new." On another bill, the Republicans on the substantive committee had raised a storm of protest against what they alleged to be an unconstitutional delegation of power. The department reexamined a bill of the previous year and discovered that the Republicans had at that time accepted both the principle and the procedures that the new bill embodied. When this was called to their attention, recounted the liaison officer, the Republicans immediately quieted down and the bill moved easily through the committee.

THE LEGISLATIVE SYSTEM IS ONE OF DIFFERENTIAL INFLUENCE AND POWER

From his concern with communications theory and with assessing the tactics lobbyists employ, Milbrath concluded that they did not aim their messages indiscriminately at legislators. Rather they directed their communications selectively. A particular individual or group was the key to each problem; others in the Congress looked to them for guidance. It was therefore upon these influential members that lobbyists focused their attention. Among those usually found in this category were the chairmen of the committees and often respected staff assistants. To them the lobbyists directed the heaviest flow of communications. "Lobbyists, then, must locate [and persuade] the key people. . . ."[7]

The executive lobbyists conceptualized the Congress in a manner congruent with Milbrath's findings. They, too, perceived it principally in terms of sets of key actors operating at different levels in the legislative process. This is not to say that these executive agents dismissed the remaining congressmen as insignificant or that the latter failed to generate problems for them. They recognized, however, that power and influence were distributed unevenly in the Congress, and that those who wielded power and exercised influence so dominated the legislative system that its operations could not be understood apart from them. Consequently, the fate of executive legislation and the relations between the two systems were intimately affected by the attitudes and behavior of these special legislative actors. Three sets of such actors were seen by legislative liaison agents as shaping the legislative process and as crucial to executive aspirations: committees and their chairmen, unofficial leaders in the House and Senate, and party leaders.

The Committees and Their Chairmen

All the legislative liaison officers regarded the standing committees as the most important loci of power in the Congress. It was to these special subsystems that their legislation was initially committed. Should the committees reject such proposals, any opportunity for their adoption by the Congress was to all practical purposes terminated. Affirmative action, on the other hand, provided a tremendous impetus to the subsequent progress of such bills, although most changes imposed in committee had to be accepted. While action deemed undesirable might be reversed, the legislative system was structured in favor of the decisions of

[7] Milbrath, *op. cit.,* p. 216.

its committees. Of course, not all favorable committee decisions guaranteed success for their bills in the Congress.

One legislative liaison agent in Treasury reported a relationship with the House Ways and Means Committee that was atypical and resulted in the committee's exercising a degree of control over executive proposals greater than that of other substantive committees. Tax legislation, he related, was never presented in the form of a finished bill to the Ways and Means Committee; rather the committee received from the executive a proposal containing policy positions and supporting arguments. The committee itself drafted the bill. With other committees, executive leaders followed a practice of submitting completed drafts of their bills.

Additional dimensions of the importance of committees were revealed in the *special* relations between each committee and certain sets of executive actors. First of all, committee members were considered to be much closer to the particular departments with which they dealt—in terms of interacting with and understanding their legislation and problems—than were most other legislators in the Congress. They were able to do more to help or hinder the departments. Secondly, such committee members were viewed as "wanting special things from us": imposing extra demands upon the departments most concerned with them and expecting special consideration over other members of the Congress. And, not least in importance, committees assumed a special relevance because in the allocation of responsibility between departmental and White House lobbyists the former were primarily responsible for legislation in the committees; the White House assumed a more active role when legislation came to the floor.

Sometimes the nature and composition of a committee imposed a severe set of restraints upon the behavior of executive actors and the chances of their legislation. Members of X Committee, for example, were pictured as badly split and engaging in backbiting and overtly contemptuous behavior toward each other. It was very difficult to work with this committee, admitted two liaison agents from different departments. The fact that the committee was not representative of the larger subsystem of which it was a part contributed to its ineffectiveness on the floor of the House. A liaison agent for another department complained that his principal committee was extremely partisan. If a few of his party defected or failed to attend its meetings, his department's bills were trapped within the committee. When bills were reported to the floor, they invariably were accompanied by so many warning flags as to guarantee their becoming once again the focus of intense party conflict.

A few liaison agents saw their principal committees as possessing virtually no influence with other legislators. Hence the problems facing such departments and executive lobbyists were magnified greatly. His Senate committee, asserted a deputy to the Assistant Secretary of State for Congressional Relations, was very strong in its senior ranks. But the "House committee does not carry influence on the floor." While he was not certain whether this was a cause or an effect, it was his contention that the committee did not draw its share of ambitious congressmen, which hurt the department. Many of its members were "up to the average of the House of Representatives, but the top people in the House simply are not on the committee. As a result we have a much harder job." The assistant secretary also categorized his key committee in the House as a problem—it was suspect among the other congressmen. The Republican leadership had not helped the situation by adding to the committee five very conservative members; this had made it more acrimonious than before. Since it was not a particularly strong committee in the first place, this move weakened it further. The traditional practice of the House members, to be guided by the recommendations of its standing committees, was breaking down, he charged, in the case of the committee principally identified with his department's legislation.

Within the committee it was the chairman who was singled out by the liaison agents as the key actor. Not only did a tremendous range of powers lie within his grasp, but by virtue of his great advantage over the other members—through his experience, knowledge, and established patterns of relationships—he could wield great influence in the committee and on the floor. "The chairman is very influential if he wants to help," explained an executive lobbyist whose department's major legislation was generally handled by two sets of committees and often by a third. "If he's indifferent, it means a loss of important support for us. And if he's opposed, he represents a tremendous obstacle and an extremely dangerous opponent." In some committees, chairmen deferred to their subcommittee chairmen but reserved certain major areas of legislation to themselves. Moreover, the subcommittee chairmen generally recognized that the decisions of their units must not conflict unduly with the strongly held views of their chairmen.

Uncertainty and irrationality in the Congress were greatly compounded when it was a chairman who was the source of the department's difficulties. The problems confronting a liaison agent in such circumstances are illustrated by a comparison of two chairmen—one who could be relied upon to react rationally, the other quixotic and absolutely unpredictable—drawn by an executive actor who had to deal with both. Would the chairman of the first committee buy his department's legislation? "That's the only problem," he insisted. In effect, Chairman X was the committee. The rest of its members, he contended, were intimidated by the chairman's knowledge and his mastery; unlike X, they were not experts. While this chairman might turn in one direction when the executive actors expected him to head in another, "his behavior always has something to do with getting necessary support somewhere." Referring to Chairman Y, the liaison agent said: "You can never tell what he will do and why. Nobody knows." Chairman Y's unpredictable behavior "grows out of the personality of the chairman, and you may never understand it." This unpredictability of Chairman Y was "our greatest problem. He creates so many uncertainties for us!" A liaison agent in another department characterized Chairman Y as probably the most ineffectual chairman on the floor of the House.

The problems caused by a very strong chairman were paradoxically both simple and difficult to resolve. If he cooperated with the executive actors, everything was virtually settled. Should he prove obstreperous, executive actors almost invariably found that the committee could not be budged; it would rarely repudiate its chairman.

In his House committee, reported one liaison agent, the chairman ran affairs with an iron hand; he made all the decisions. Although he rated the chairman in the comparable Senate committee not as strong, "little gets through unless Z supports it." Both the House and the Senate adopted virtually unchanged the authorization bills advanced by these committees. Although such acceptance stemmed, in part, from the subject matter involved, the competence of their chairmen and the general respect in which they were held by fellow legislators played a major role.

In contrast, another liaison agent spelled out a list of complaints against a weak chairman whose committee processed his department's legislation. First of all, the chairman tended to be lazy; he did not drive his committee as hard as he should. Secondly, he was temperamental and difficult to deal with, a prickly problem child for the department. Thirdly, he performed poorly, at times, as floor manager for the department's bills. One important bill had been defeated in good part as a result of the chairman's ineptness and his lack of sensitivity to the mood of the legislature. When the department and chairman had come to the floor they had been confident that they controlled the necessary votes. But these were lost on the floor. The chairman had accepted too many amendments and he had carried out his role as floor manager much too facetiously, alienating members by his attitude. Moreover, he had cavalierly dismissed the amendments of legislators who were favorably disposed toward the bill, but who had political problems in their districts which demanded some change in the legislation. That this was not mere sour grapes on the part of the liaison officer was attested to by the fact that legislators and lobbyists for interest groups concerned with the bill made the same assessment.

An observation made about a number of chairmen was their invulnerability to executive pressure. Referring especially to southern conservatives, an executive lobbyist said: "I have to depend on these chairmen to get what we want. They can't be intimidated by threats, and the administration knows it can't defeat them, and they know it too."

Unofficial Leaders

In some committees, members other than chairmen were perceived as exerting significant influence. Not all of these were the subcommittee chairmen; informal influentials also existed. Discussing the members of a committee, aside from the chairman, a liaison officer asserted that they were not all equal: "It's not just a question of seniority or power, but members exhibit different degrees of interest, concern, and willingness to work on the committee." A Republican liaison agent in the Eisenhower Administration reported that while each committee was different, in each a special relationship was developed between the chairman and the ranking minority member. This was critical, he contended, and had to be taken into account by the liaison officer. Similarly, a Democratic lobbyist in a Kennedy department noted that in one of his committees, the chairman always made special concessions to the senior Republican member, which practice facilitated the passage of bills.

The late Senator Robert S. Kerr of Oklahoma was cited by a number of liaison agents to illustrate the importance of informal leaders.[8] A senior member of the Finance Committee, the senator was a man of great competence, who worked hard and sought the proper briefings. He also possessed an enormous ego, a driving personality, and a particularly withering style of debate. Senator Kerr was feared and respected by other members of the Senate. If his aid could be enlisted in behalf of the department's cause, its chances were materially improved. Conversely, another liaison officer pointed out that if the wrong member sponsored the department's bill, the effect could be very bad. "It's a status problem," he admitted.

[8] It should be noted, however, that Senator Kerr was also chairman of the extremely important Rivers and Harbors Subcommittee of the Public Works Committee, a most favorable vantage point from which to allocate favors and collect debts.

Party Leadership in the Congress

Although the official party leaders were not considered to be as crucial to the roles of the legislative liaison agents as were committee chairmen and informal leaders, they were recognized as a separate set of key actors within the legislative system. Their importance was determined in part by the margin of their party's majority and also by the commitment of that majority to the particular program of a department. When that majority was overwhelming, as was characteristic of the Senate in 1962–63, and the legislation commanded wide support among its members, the importance of leadership was played down. "We don't need the leadership in the Senate for X," explained one executive actor. "We've got so much support that we can get almost anything through there." When legislative proposals tended to divide the majority party, the liaison officers relied much more upon the party leadership and pictured its actors as playing extremely important roles within the legislative process.

In general, the significance of the majority-party leadership was associated by departmental liaison agents with problems and processes of communications, influence, and scheduling in the legislative system. Uncertainty and irrationality in the legislative system elevated the Speaker and Majority Leader in the House and the Majority Leader in the Senate, together with their whips, to positions of great importance for the functioning of that system. "They must know in advance how the House or Senate are going to go. They must know reliably how it is going to vote." When the leadership did not exhibit a capacity for performing this role effectively, "everything really got mixed up."

With its whip mechanism and its constant probing of the intentions of members, the leadership was viewed as central to the communications system of the party. Because it was also in contact with the minority-party leadership, the majority-party leadership was seen as being in the business of monitoring the internal communications system of the whole House or Senate. Consequently, the leadership represented for the executive lobbyists a key set of actors for assessing the mood and the sense of direction of the houses of Congress and for ascertaining party decisions on bills or on parliamentary maneuvers. With timing considered so intimately related to success in the legislative system, the leadership was in a crucial position to know when to move or to delay on legislation. The official leadership of the majority party was responsible for the scheduling of debate and legislation and, in the House, for ruling on important parliamentary motions.

The liaison agents also credited the majority-party leaders with exercising considerable influence with individual legislators of their parties in the House and Senate. As party leaders they were in a position to appeal to both chairmen and individual party members to close ranks in support of themselves and their parties. And since they could help or hinder a member's future as well as his bills, party leaders were advantageously situated to exert influence over others to appear on the floor, to vote, or to change their votes. Consequently, if the bills of the departments encountered difficulties, the liaison officers had to do more than touch base with this leadership. They found that they had to work closely with the latter as allies and often as their assistants.

SOME OTHER ATTRIBUTES OF THE LEGISLATIVE PROCESS

Accommodation Is Essential in the Legislative Process

All the liaison agents concurred with the conclusion of the Assistant Secretary for Legislation (HEW) that "the legislative process is an accommodation process to find areas of agreement." Rarely, stated these executive actors, could major legislation move successfully through the Congress unless it reflected a number of adjustments to help assure it majorities at the key points in the process. Legislative norms of bargaining and accommodation shaped the behavior patterns of the legislative actors. The latter expected adherence to these norms by executive actors as well as by each other. Executive lobbyists had to anticipate, therefore, that they might often settle for less than what their principals requested. "I know I can't get the X bill out of the subcommittee," explained an executive lobbyist who exercised considerable discretion regarding the substance of certain bills. "The chairman called me and said they were tied four to four; what should they do? I have to decide how far I should go to get the bill out. And this means that I have to do things I do not like to do." What the chairman had said was that the bill "does not matter to me or my constituents; they couldn't care less. But if you want it, work out something with the Z industry people." This chairman was invulnerable to the political pressure that the department and the White House could generate. "Unless I am prepared to undertake an accommodation, I am not going to get *any* legislation," the executive lobbyist asserted.

The Legislative Process Is a Complicated One

A number of the liaison agents, although not all, offered additional observations regarding the legislative process: (1) It was highly complicated. Complications arose not merely out of the number and variety of actors who were involved, but out of the rules and procedures that characterized the House and Senate. The rules afforded legislative actors opportunities to tie up the process, to force or avoid certain procedural steps, and to expedite or impede action. (2) Its pace was leisurely. "Largely a waste of time!" exclaimed an exasperated liaison agent. An executive impulse to move swiftly had to be accommodated to the legislative system, whose members wanted consultation from the executive system, a chance to hear what the folks back home were thinking, and an opportunity to touch base with others in and out of the Congress. Congressmen, it was contended, looked at each issue carefully to ascertain how it would affect them and their constituencies as well as their relations with other key legislators, and how it would tie into party politics. Mutual deference for other legislative actors, one of the norms of the House and the Senate, inevitably imposed further delays.

Congress Improves Executive Proposals

Some liaison agents concluded that Congress frequently improved the executive product. This judgment was totally unexpected, considering the problems liaison agents faced in the Congress and their frequent expressions of frustration. Their thesis was that the alterations demanded by members of the legislature or required to win the necessary majorities to move executive proposals along often resulted in improvements in such proposals. As a result of the compulsions of the legislative system, the legislation that emerged was better than what had been originally proposed by the executive leaders. Of course, not all the liaison agents expressed this view. The representative from one department was noncommittal, and those from three departments, including State and its agency AID, asserted a contrary feeling. Nevertheless, such a perception on the part of a number of executive lobbyists predisposed them to view positively the role of congressmen in the development of official policy.

CONGRESS IS TWO SEPARATE SYSTEMS

Despite their generalizations about the legislative system, executive lobbyists distinguished sharply between the House of Representatives and the Senate. They perceived them as diverse subsystems of the Congress, each of which presented its own unique problems and opportunities for these executive actors.

Size and Numbers Are Different

The liaison officers maintained that size made a substantial difference in the problems they faced in the House and Senate. To conduct a proper nose count, an action upon which important decisions rested, opponents, proponents, and uncertains had to be spotted correctly. An accurate assessment of strength and weakness was much more difficult to obtain with a larger number of legislators than with a smaller number. "Sheer weight of numbers in the House complicates our problems. It's a lot easier to count a hundred than four hundred and thirty-five" was a refrain echoed by the liaison agents.[9] Moreover, members of the Senate tended to work with one or two key legislators on different issues, which simplified the liaison officers' job. "One key to understanding and working with the Senate on anything is the value of one or two persons. If we can get them, then the others will tend to go along."

The Constituency Makes a Difference

The nature of House and Senate constituencies affected the attitudes and behavior of their members, contended the departmental lobbyists. Since House members represented narrow congressional-district interests, it was harder to sway them. Senators represented a greater diversity of interests: "They can afford to be more statesmanlike."

The assessments of a Department of Agriculture lobbyist and his chief assistant were particularly appropriate. Many House members, both asserted, did not have agricultural constituencies. Their only interest in Agriculture centered on recreation, forestry, and food for consumers. Hence, it was harder to win such congressmen to their department's legislation, and these executive lobbyists and their associates had to expend considerable time and effort in explaining their bills to House members. In the Senate practically every member had some kind of rural constituency. Consequently senators were more understanding and sympathetic, which simplified the job of the executive lobbyists. As for those House members who represented agricultural constituencies, the two liaison agents felt that these responded more to the pressure of a special interest. Many of their districts tended to encompass primarily one type of agricultural product. Senatorial constituencies included a multiplicity of agricultural interests; a senator would find that the impact of any one of

[9] A former Deputy Assistant Secretary for Congressional Relations (State) pointed out: "It's a hell of a job to talk with and assess the House; size is important. You may know that seventy are OK and eighty are wrong and still need to talk to the rest—that's the institutional difference."

them tended to be diffused by the others. Interestingly enough, executive lobbyists concerned with urban problems expressed the same sort of assessment from a different perspective: many House members represented specific agricultural interests, whereas most senators had both urban and rural constituencies.

Dissimilar types of constituencies may also affect the ability of the liaison officer to direct his resources into the legislative system. As will be noted in the next chapter, liaison agents considered special executive favors, i.e., administrative decisions, one type of resource they could employ in dealing with legislators. An executive lobbyist in a very large department claimed that the nature of the constituency made a difference in the favors he could do for congressmen. "If I want to do favors for House members, the number and kind are restricted. We run out of them after a while. There are relatively more favors we can do in our department for senators."

Terms of Office Affect the Distribution of Executive Resources

The disparate terms of office for House and Senate members imposed different demands upon them to play special roles in the Congress. Everyone in the House came up for renomination and election every two years, whereas the terms of only one-third of the Senate expired every two years.

In the House, it's dog eat dog. Congressmen on the committee fight among themselves as to who gets to sponsor X bills. They all need exposure unless they come from safe districts. Senators only come up once every six years. So there is no equal need for exposure regarding the sponsorship of a bill.

The special need for exposure on the part of senators facing impending election battles was much more sympathetically viewed by their colleagues. This made it easier for the liaison officer to aid these particular senators without causing the resentment that might be the case if he dispensed such privileges among House members.

Staff Makes a Difference

The liaison agents all agreed that a different emphasis upon staff in the House and the Senate significantly affected their own behavior in the two subsystems of the Congress. Staff was not stressed in the House, in contrast with the Senate, where it constituted a tremendous source of strength to the senators and provided invaluable aid to the liaison agents. House members were characterized as lacking the necessary staff to study legislation and to keep themselves informed. Many House committee staffs were considered weak as well. In the Senate, individual members and committees were respected for the strong staffs with which they equipped themselves. "Take Congressman X [a senior southern Democrat on a House committee]. He has no one on his staff higher than a stenographer! But Senator Y [a senior Democrat from the same state on the parallel committee] has three guys with major responsibility on [the subject matter]."

Most administrative assistants employed in the House were not considered to be very close to their bosses; such staff aides often did not even work on legislation. "In most cases, the House member is his own legman." Often, maintained the liaison officers, there was no point in bothering senators on certain items, since "we can do an awful lot with their staff." Or as one executive lobbyist phrased it: "The pressure to do my homework is greater in working in the House. In the Senate I can rely on their staff." A few of the liaison agents even claimed that the senators who dealt with their departments' bills tended to dominate the conference committees with the House because their staffwork was that much better.

The Two Sets of Congressmen Operate Differently

Liaison officers pointed out that in certain respects representatives operated differently from senators. The House was more susceptible to change. House members changed their minds quickly on the floor; senators did not alter their votes easily. The five-minute rule in the Committee of the Whole House was considered disadvantageous from the executive lobbyists' point of view. Their opponents might make highly misleading remarks on the floor, but each ally had only one opportunity and a very few minutes to undo the damage. "Everything moves very fast, and you have to be ready to move quickly with it." On the other hand, the tradition of unlimited debate in the Senate meant that issues could be discussed at length and what was misleading could be exposed to a detailed rebuttal. "You can relax and listen, knowing your guy can sit back and then talk ten to thirty minutes or more to rebut those arguments made against our bill or in favor of amendments that would hurt its chances."

The availability of staff in the Senate was also seen to affect both floor debate and opportunities for executive actors to play a role in what was occurring. House members were precluded from taking staff to the floor with them; but senatorial offices invariably contained two to three top staff aides on legislation who worked closely with their senators and accompanied them to the floor. "If something comes up, he alerts his

senator, who says, 'Write it out,' which he may do in the cloakroom."
This procedure afforded executive lobbyists tremendous advantages.

I can rely on the staff. Not only is there a strong staff on the committee, but
the senators come with their own staff to committee meetings and on the floor
for debate. Since the senators have this right to bring their staff with them,
we've got a direct line to the floor. We are also able to get technically competent persons from the department to aid the X committee, and to sit on the
floor with the senators.

None of the Kennedy or Eisenhower departmental lobbyists referred to the Senate's "inner circle," but this term was employed by a
liaison agent from State who had served during an earlier administration.[10] The Senate, he concluded, was much more sophisticated than the
House. It was a club run by a small group that was bipartisan in composition. A key to expediting measures in the Senate, therefore, was to solicit the cooperation of the influentials who comprised this inner circle.
Liaison officers faced different situations in the House and Senate
because of the nature of legislative rules. Those whose departments' bills
went through the House Ways and Means Committee encountered special advantages. A closed rule, which meant a committee's bill could not
be amended on the floor of the House, was requested for much of their
legislation. Since the Rules Committee generally acceded to such requests from this committee, the main focus of the department remained
the Ways and Means Committee rather than the Rules Committee or the
House as a whole, although careful work went into guaranteeing majorities in the latter. White House liaison played a major role in the latter
two, especially if difficulties were anticipated. No closed-rule procedure
existed in the Senate. Bills were open to amendments from the floor that
could weaken what the executive actors and the committee had agreed
upon and could fragment the support that had been built up. Nonger-
mane, controversial amendments could be offered, moreover, that complicated the business of getting the bills adopted in the Senate and
through a subsequent conference committee.

[10] The conception of the Senate as a club with a dominant inner circle is a highly
controversial one. The journalist William S. White has argued this thesis in
The Citadel: The Story of the U.S. Senate (New York: Harper, 1957), chap. 7, "The
Senate and the Club." See also Dean Acheson, *Sketches from Life of Men I Have
Known,* 1st ed. (New York: Harper, 1959), pp. 131–32. Note, however, Nelson W.
Polsby's skeptical assessment of this concept in his *Congress and the Presidency*
(Englewood Cliffs, N.J.: Prentice-Hall, 1964), pp. 32–41. In the present study no
specific questions on the validity of the inner-club concept were asked of liaison
agents. On the other hand, the fact that none of the Kennedy or Eisenhower lobbyists, including three assistant secretaries of State, mentioned it raises some doubt
about its usefulness at the present time in understanding the Senate.

Access

The degree of access—an essential concomitant to any successful relationship between lobbyists and legislators—was differentially affected, said the departmental liaison officers, by the nature of the principal actors in the House and the Senate. Regardless of the department or the partisan nature of their administration, the executive actors found that House members were, on the whole, more accessible than senators. One explanation stemmed from the level in prestige that liaison agents associated with membership in the House and Senate. The senators were considered much more prestigous actors than House members. At the same time, senators clearly demonstrated their own sense of importance. Comments by liaison officers from various departments illustrated this phenomenon and its impact upon their own operations. From an executive actor representing an agency within the State Department: "They have a view of themselves as the equal of any department or agency head. They want to talk only to the Secretary of State, although they do talk with my boss, and some of them talk with me." In another department an executive lobbyist and his deputy agreed that "senators have greater prestige. They want to deal directly with the secretary. And they always get mad at a higher level than do House members." A Republican former Assistant Secretary of State for Congressional Relations charged that "the average guy in the Senate is not at all impressed unless the secretary himself calls. Many times I've had to cool my heels in a senator's office. But I could walk into any House office and almost immediately see the congressman."

The difference in the prestige of senators and representatives affected other aspects of the liaison agent–legislator relationship. "I can deal with House members on a first-name basis more easily," confided one liaison agent. "I never use first names with the senators, even though I used to talk intimately with them when I was in the Senate." And the remarks of a Republican liaison officer from the same department during the Eisenhower Administration indicated that he too sensed a difference in importance and prestige between the two sets of legislative actors. "It was a lot easier to hit it off with House members. They were around more, they weren't as busy, and they were younger. The senators were older men and you could feel that they demanded more respect."

The relative accessibility of House members and inaccessibility of senators were attributed also to their differences in staff and to the degree of pressure upon their time and attention. The very fact that House members lacked highly qualified staff assistants meant that they were not so easily screened from outsiders. Moreover, House members acted more as their own legmen on legislation, which inevitably meant they were more accessible to liaison agents. Senators were pictured as extremely busy. Their constituencies were wider and more complex, as were their policy problems. They carried a burden of service on a larger number of committees than did House members, and they were concerned with more legislative issues. "They're considerably more inaccessible, unless you're working with them on some particular issue or problem," declared the departmental liaison officers. An agency lobbyist complained, "The senators are harder to see. When you do see them, you can't see them for long. So you don't have the time to reason with them." But the valuable staff aides in the Senate were not only knowledgeable on the policy and politics of legislation; they had more time to spend with the executive actors. In addition, they were seen as having much more authority to speak and act for their senators than the assistants in the House.

Executive and Private Lobbyists Contact Legislative Actors

It is appropriate to compare some of the foregoing findings with Lester W. Milbrath's, which were based upon a sample of Washington lobbyists for private interest groups. In some respects the data coincide, especially in the lobbyists' common appreciation of the importance of congressional staff in the communications process. They agree also upon the difficulty in establishing personal contacts with senators and the relative ease in contacting their staffs directly.

The two sets of lobbyists contrast sharply on three points. Most of Milbrath's private lobbyists clearly preferred contacting staff assistants rather than the legislators.[11] Aside from one liaison officer, the preference of the executive lobbyists was for direct relations with the official decision-makers themselves, although they were perfectly willing to approach legislative staff assistants. Staff members were worth contacting when they saved liaison officers time and other resources, and when the staff assistants were close enough to their principals so that the latter turned to them for advice. Milbrath's lobbyists made no distinction between House and Senate staffs, whereas the liaison agents were convinced that, with few exceptions, staff aides to individual legislators were significant only in the Senate, not in the House. In general, the same attitudes held for the committees, although there was greater respect among executive lobbyists for House committee staffs than for House member staffs. Finally, executive lobbyists apparently found it easier than did their private counterparts to approach House members directly.

[11] See Milbrath, *op. cit.*, pp. 266, 267, 269. He refers to such attitudes in the context of tactics employed by private lobbyists in attempts to establish and maintain contacts with legislative actors, and of the lobbyists' important sources of inside information.

SPECIAL PROBLEMS: STATE AND DEFENSE

Executive actors in each department were inclined to feel that their own department stood in a special relationship with the Congress, that the problems they encountered there were unique. There was sufficient validity to such a contention that it could not be dismissed entirely. After all, each major group of chairmen and substantive committees created a set of special relations between the departments and the Congress. From the point of view of the Congress as a whole, however, these differences shrank in significance except in the case of two departments: Defense and State. The intrinsic nature of each of these departments affected the orientation and behavior of their legislative liaison officers.

Only in Defense and State did a department's identification with a policy area appear to be in any way a significant variable affecting the problems and therefore the compensatory behavior of the liaison agents. This was certainly not the case in the remaining departments, where executive lobbyists stressed almost entirely[12] the nonpolicy variables. Of course, these variables loomed exceedingly important for Defense and State as well.

Both State and Defense are concerned with the United States' involvement outside its own boundaries, Defense to a much lesser degree than State. Both make demands upon the Congress for substantial sums of money, although State's requests are dwarfed by those of Defense. Their relations with the Congress, however, are radically different. The legislative program of Defense benefits immeasurably from the most sympathetic, permissive attitude on the part of congressmen; Defense's liaison officers encounter few problems regarding their legislation. State's congressional relations represent the worst possible interaction between executive and legislative systems. Lobbyists for State confront tremendous obstacles in attempting to advance their department's position and program in the Congress.

Defense's relations with the Congress are epitomized in the following assessment by one of its liaison officers: "You have to start with the premise that Congress treats Defense relatively like motherhood." This did not mean, he added, that strains did not develop in the relations between the two. The TFX controversy during the Kennedy Administration and the perennial clashes over policy pertaining to the National Guard and the Reserves prove otherwise. And, as was noted in a discussion of liaison agents and their own bureaucracies, the service depart-

---

[12] For specific reference to congressional concerns of departmental liaison officers in the policy areas of agriculture and taxation, see pp. 154, 161–62, 177, 203.

ments have a tradition of going independently to Congress, bypassing and undercutting the Secretary of Defense, a practice not unappreciated by the legislators.

Defense benefits from two extremely powerful forces in the legislative system: a combination of patriotism and nationalism, on the one hand, and a direct, positive link between the department's activities and the well-being of the legislative constituency, on the other. The politics of the United States and its major role in international relations are inextricably related, in the eyes of the legislators and their constituents, to a strong military establishment. Moreover, a national awareness that powerful enemies, overt and covert, endanger the position of the country and its allies in the world environment enhances Defense's appeal for legislators. Most of them have not the slightest doubt that the interests of the United States coincide with those of the Department of Defense. In terms of internal, domestic considerations, the programs of the Defense Department are tangibly and directly linked to the individual legislator's concern with the well-being of his own constituency. Defense contracts offer employment opportunities and affect economic conditions. Military installations inject tremendous amounts of purchasing power into local communities. And not insignificantly, constituents expect the best in equipment and conditions for their sons, daughters, and relatives who serve in the armed services.

"We will have cuts imposed on us; that is to be expected. But nothing in the order of what is done to the domestic program," maintained a liaison officer for the Secretary of Defense. In fact, he noted, in both the Kennedy and the Eisenhower Administrations, Defense had sought to dissuade the Congress "from giving more money for certain things than the department wished!" With such an advantageous set of special relations existing between his department and the Congress, a liaison officer in Defense confronts a totally different Congress than does his counterpart in State.

If Congress responds to Defense as to motherhood, its relations with State more nearly resemble cold war.[13] And the chronic tensions between State and Congress occasionally erupt in open hostilities. The two approach each other with suspicion, antagonism, and distrust; no other part of the executive system has such appalling relations with the legislature.

[13] The assessment that follows is based primarily upon interviews with Frederick G. Dutton, Assistant Secretary of State for Congressional Relations in the Kennedy Administration, who subsequently publicized some of his remarks in " 'Cold War' Between the Hill and Foggy Bottom," *New York Times Magazine,* September 15, 1963, pp. 36, 94–95. Members of State's liaison staff and others in the department confirmed this analysis.

The peculiar relations between the two were ascribed by Frederick G. Dutton, Assistant Secretary for Congressional Relations, primarily to the fact that State and Congress "are sharply different creatures," an assessment concurred in by others outside the department. Congress was pictured as looking inward to the United States, "politically glandular," preeminently concerned with reelection, assertive in its approach to the world, and in favor of making everything in the foreign policy field most explicit. State looked outward, contended Dutton. It was intellectual, tentative, and cautious about coming to conclusions about the meaning of what occurred in foreign affairs. "Its recommendations often recognize that only part of a problem can be influenced, and decisions are sometimes deliberately left implicit." As a result of developments since World War II, Dutton concluded, contacts between the two diverse systems had widened and become complicated, making tolerable accommodations between them "vastly more difficult."

State, moreover, was pictured by its liaison staff as being different from other departments in ways that significantly set it apart from the Congress. Large sectors in the Congress had some interest in the Departments of Agriculture, Interior, and Labor, as did many powerful private groups. Defense tied into the economies of many congressional districts and states. State, on the other hand, possessed no large social or economic constituency upon which it could depend for sympathy or support.[14] It had neither patronage nor defense contracts.[15] Moreover, foreign policy lent itself less readily to comfortable congressional relations: confidential information could not be fully or publicly released without a risk of undermining the country's foreign policy. Hence Congress was often "in the dark, operating in a vacuum." Leaders in State felt they could disclose little to legislators that would not leak out. "This lack of information and lack of close cooperation and support" aggravated the tensions between members of the two systems.

Members of the Congress and the Department of State referred to each other in the most uncomplimentary terms. Congressmen described State's officers and personnel in such terms as "cookie pushers," "weak-

[14] A former Assistant Secretary of State for Congressional Relations who was elected to the U.S. Senate remarked with some bitterness about his fellow congressmen: "If I am on the Senate floor and attack Agriculture's or Labor's programs, a lot of people will rise up to answer me. If I attack State's, almost all will agree. It has no constituency."

[15] A two-term House member, sympathetic toward State's problems in foreign affairs and with the Congress, contended that State had only ideas, policies, and irritations to offer the Congress. Other departments controlled tangible assets with considerable political impact in congressional districts and each department had a potent constituency as well.

169

kneed," "dupes of foreigners"; they depicted them as being more concerned with the interests of foreign countries than with those of the United States. "We are vulnerable to the argument that we talk for foreigners," reflected an Assistant Secretary for Congressional Relations. At the same time, State was pictured as historically antagonistic toward the Hill, its officers as hostile to Congress as congressmen were to them. As experts in the business of foreign affairs they "saw no reason why they should be guided by people whose chief claim to fame was that they had gotten themselves elected from some gerrymandered district somewhere in the country." Foreign policy experts dismissed congressmen as "uninformed," "opportunistic," "special-interest oriented."[16]

Such rhetoric and stereotypes tended to sharpen the differences and antagonisms between the two systems. Foreign Service officers considered politics contemptible; legislators considered State to be unrealistic. Congressmen were inclined to discount what State said, to assume that "we misjudge world politics." Some congressmen were driven by their anticommunist phobia, it was argued in State, to place self-defeating limitations upon U.S. policy. Moreover, Congress often wanted more than a reduction in executive discretion on policy. The legislators themselves wanted to determine policy, country by country, and to impose detailed specifications upon such policy. Even in their written communications with each other, the two systems started from different premises that led to misunderstandings and ill feelings. State tried to keep everything conditional and equivocal so that its options were not foreclosed. Congress was characterized as trying to "jazz things up" to satisfy political needs. It wanted responses that were simple, quick, well digested.

While we are concerned with the perceptions of liaison agents, it is significant that others, both in and outside the Congress and the department, share in these assessments. A member of the House of Representatives who worked assiduously to help State in its congressional relations listed a number of problems inherent in the flow of communication between State and the Congress. Even if these could be improved, he asserted, the chief cause of the tension between the two lay in "the profound differences in style, psychology, and role between the two institutions." In a critical study of the department, a long-time Foreign Service officer has argued the same thesis.[17] Politically and psychologically, State

[16] A House member who was friendly toward State and understood its problems with the Congress reported the following, which he admitted was an overstatement: "I once heard a top State Department official say, 'There are three great enemies in the eyes of the typical Foreign Service officer: the Soviet Union, the American press, and members of Congress.'"

[17] Smith Simpson, *Anatomy of the State Department* (Boston: Houghton Mifflin, 1967), pp. 152–83.

and Congress constitute different worlds that foster different perspectives, interests and judgments. As a result, suspicion and misunderstanding pervade State-congressional relations, and communication between the two systems becomes extremely difficult. "It is often easier," an Assistant Secretary for Congressional Relations said, "to communicate U.S. intentions to a tribal chief in central Africa through a Swahili interpreter, or to Kuala Lumpur across ten thousand miles of cable and radio . . . than across the two miles from Foggy Bottom to the Capitol."[18]

A similar set of assessments was offered by three social scientists who studied the politics involved in one particular policy area, the extensions of the Reciprocal Trade Agreements Act during the Eisenhower Administration. Raymond A. Bauer, Ithiel de Sola Pool, and Lewis A. Dexter conclude that much of the conflict between the Congress and the State Department arose from a difference between two personality types that were identified with each.[19] The favorite phrase of State's people was said to be: "You've got to think in the overall." They perceived Congress as selfish or against the national interest. Congressmen viewed State's personnel as cold, failing to provide them with usable answers to the complaints of their constituents, and unwilling to do anything for Americans who suffered from the adverse effects of foreign competition. As a result, note the three authors, there existed a "fuming anger on both sides." In fact, the hostility of Congress toward State was a central factor in President John F. Kennedy's decision in 1961 against permitting the Department of State to assume the responsibility for his major trade expansion bill.[20]

[18] *Ibid.*, p. 154.
[19] Bauer, Pool, and Dexter, *op. cit.*, p. 446.
[20] See chap. 9.

CHAPTER VII

Strategies and Tactics I:
Direct Lobbying

STRATEGIES AND TACTICS take shape as a result of the goals actors pursue and the roles they must play. The strategies and tactics are affected by the rules of the game, which are determined in large measure by what other actors expect and permit. And they are fashioned in terms of the actors' perceptions of those with whom they must relate in order to achieve their ends. At the same time, the strategies and tactics employed by actors are determined by the resources they bring to the game. In a complicated set of intersystem relationships involving many actors on both sides, the actions and attitudes of one's associates must also be considered an important element affecting strategies and tactics. An examination of liaison agents within their own system (Chapter V) has revealed some of the advantages that accrue to them as well as the constraints imposed upon them as a consequence of others in the departments.

The strategies and tactics of actors in all games invariably reflect their past experiences and their personalities. With due recognition of the self-confirming elements inherent in any research design, the conclusions of this study indicate that in the case of the liaison officers—who, it must be reiterated, are not independent actors—strategies and tactics were primarily related to factors other than the personalities of those filling the positions.

Since liaison officers shared common roles and more or less common perceptions regarding executive actors and legislators, they resorted to similar strategies and tactics. Nevertheless, differences in emphasis emerged as a consequence of special relations between subdivisions of the executive system and of the Congress. The dissimilar types of resources that liaison agents could marshal introduced additional variations, as did the style in which these individual actors carried out their strategies and tactics. Patently, personality was reflected in style.

LIAISON AGENTS AND THE ANTILOBBYING LAW

In view of an explicit legislative prohibition against executive lobbying, it is in order to inquire whether the law inhibited the liaison agents in developing or implementing strategy and tactics. Congressmen, it has been noted in an earlier chapter, ignore their own formal rules in responding to their personal needs as legislators and their recognition that executive leadership in the legislature is legitimate and necessary.

Some of the Republican liaison agents who served during the Eisenhower Administration regarded the antilobbying law as a decided restraint upon their behavior.[1] One ascribed his reluctance to engage in active lobbying to the law itself. "I did worry about the U.S. Code. It was one reason why I stayed away from the substantive wheeling and dealing in the Congress." He and his staff confined themselves to the task of making their department's position known to legislators. On the other hand, a fellow Republican attributed his hesitancy to the partisan division between the administration and the Congress:

It's one thing when your own party controls the Congress. There are severe limitations if the other party is in power. If Republicans had been in power in the Congress, we'd have lobbied with public funds. But we weren't going to violate the law with the Democrats in control.

Democratic legislative liaison officers also expressed some misgivings about lobbying because of the law, despite the bipartisan permissiveness exhibited during the Democratic-controlled Eighty-seventh and Eighty-eighth Congresses. As in the case of the other Republicans who refused to be intimidated by the law, the Democratic liaison agents accommodated themselves to it without much trouble. Nevertheless, they were sensitive to the fact that the law did embody a prohibition against what they were doing.

Such a sensitivity manifested itself in the expressed understanding of the law by a number of the liaison agents and in their compensatory behavior patterns. Some of these executive actors asserted that under

[1] Two of the five departmental liaison officers who were interviewed responded in this manner. The restrictive approach of another Republican liaison agent is reported by Michael K. O'Leary, *The Politics of Foreign Aid* (New York: Atherton Press, 1967), p. 106. A former liaison agent in AID believed that the AID liaison operation during the Kennedy Administration was clearly in violation of the law.

this law they were officially precluded from assuming the initiative in the Congress on behalf of their departmental clients. Consequently, they engaged in subterfuge that they felt legitimized their efforts. This attitude is epitomized by the statement of one of them.

I interpret the law that I can answer any requests from a member. So I send out a blanket form stating that I hope I can be of assistance to them and their offices, and, if so, would they please call on us. I've gotten replies from every congressman on the Hill. So I'm fully protected.

In other words, even if the request for assistance were stimulated by the liaison agent, and regardless of the type of assistance requested, if the initiative were ostensibly taken by legislative actors, the liaison agent felt free under the law to play the role of lobbyist.

Two within this group of liaison agents signaled their concern with the law by interpreting it to preclude their soliciting votes from congressmen. When pressed in subsequent interviews to reconcile such an interpretation with their own conception of their roles, they conceded that they did, in fact, solicit votes. This was accomplished either in the manner in which they explained their legislation or somewhat more directly by the statement "We hope you can come along with us on it." Or it might be in the form of a specific request for the legislator's vote. One of these two agents apparently compartmentalized lobbying as the solicitation of votes, as distinguished from selling bills to congressmen. "I really don't regard myself as a lobbyist. I don't do much in the way of soliciting votes, but I do sell things on their merits." Now and then, he admitted, he did seek out a legislator in order to ask for his vote.

Almost all the liaison agents, however, clearly regarded themselves as lobbyists. One who acknowledged that he worked actively in Congress to advance his department's legislation, which also involved him in soliciting for votes, noted that he and his staff stayed away from the Congress on legislation until his secretary had testified. Another remarked that, while the law did not limit her, she was well aware that she and the other liaison agents obviously violated it often.[2] Contrasting attitudes were expressed in one department by the deputy to the secretary's liaison officer and by the deputy to the liaison agent for an agency. The former

[2] This liaison agent, Jim Akin of HEW, broke an apparently unofficial rule for departmental liaison agents below the level of assistant secretary: Keep out of the news and avoid public reference to yourself as a lobbyist. In Chicago in 1963 a newsman published an interview with Mrs. Akin in which she was quoted as saying: "I'm really just a lobbyist." See *Congressional Record*, 88th Cong., 1st sess., May 6, 1963, p. A2764. Only one congressman, a Republican, raised the issue of her possible dismissal. No serious concern appears to have been expressed by anyone else in the Congress. Legislators' comments to me merely revealed a wry amusement that Mrs. Akin's lapse of judgment had momentarily proved embarrassing to her and her department.

stated: "We do everything you do . . . if you are a hired lobbyist outside, except we don't have a slush fund." The other deputy observed that their legal counsel had interpreted an amendment to their legislation, which prohibited the agency from engaging in propaganda in the United States unless authorized to do so by the Congress, as limiting both the congressional relations and public relations staffs: "Selling in the Congress is sticky, since the X [agency] lobbying operation is a very difficult one. There is wide opposition to X in Congress and to anything smacking of propaganda or lobbying on our part." The agency had become so vulnerable on other matters that in the face of legislative hostility, its congressional liaison staff and superiors felt strongly inhibited. Nevertheless, the deputy described meetings that had taken place with groups of congressmen and their assistants as "part of our selling the program."

All the departmental legislative liaison agents—Republican and Democratic—were agreed on one point: they were restricted in lobbying with appropriated funds. This they construed to be the spending of money on activities extending beyond the customary personal and informational relations between executive and legislative actors. An example of lobbying with appropriated funds was the dispatch of telegrams to all members of the House of Representatives by HEW Secretary Anthony J. Celebrezze on behalf of an education bill in 1963 (see Chapter III). Criticism in the House over the spending of money for these telegrams quickly died down, but it did prove embarrassing; the secretary felt that he had burned his fingers. This departmental action had occurred in the absence of the Assistant Secretary for Legislation, who asserted that he would have vetoed the idea of a telegram—"too blatant and obviously expensive"—but that he might have agreed to the sending of a letter to each legislator.[3] The concern of other departments, especially State, with avoiding the use of appropriated funds for food and liquor in any effort to "educate" congressmen exemplifies further the type of lobbying considered to be affected by this law.

DIRECT LOBBYING

In direct lobbying, lobbyists endeavor to interact personally with those whom they wish to influence. An alternative or rather supplemental approach is indirect lobbying, which is discussed in the next chapter.

[3] As HEW'S secretary in 1968, in the Johnson Administration, this assistant secretary was embarrassed when Republican senators revealed that HEW personnel were telephoning them that projects in their states would not be forthcoming should a $6 billion spending cut be included as part of the tax surcharge bill desired by the President. The Republicans insisted that this constituted lobbying, in violation of the law. See *Congressional Record,* 90th Cong., 2nd sess., May 22–23, 1968, pp. S6090–91, S6187–88, S6275–78.

Executive lobbyists relied upon both on the premise that each possessed particular advantages.

A Strategy of Exchange Focused on the Constituent Needs of Legislators

In meeting the enormous demands made upon them by their constituents, congressmen may transfer to the executive system part of the burden and responsibility for carrying out their own representational roles. In many cases they must do so, for the ultimate decisions are not theirs to make. Members of the executive system are in a favorable position to accommodate legislators in this respect. A strategy employed by all departmental legislative liaison agents centered upon exploiting this type of executive-legislative relations.

(A) ROUTINE SERVICES FOR ROUTINE NEEDS: CREATING GOOD-WILL. What is involved at this level is not high strategy, not issues of transcending importance, not even legislation per se. Rather it is a strategy of day-to-day attention to the ubiquitous political needs of the congressmen to service their constituents and to shore up their own images in their constituencies. On this basic level, each set of actors has something to exchange—resources that benefit the other, which are not too expensive, and which facilitate working relationships between them.

Resources that executive actors bring to this exchange may be conceptualized as routine services within the departments. These accommodate the representational needs and demands of legislators. In exchange, members of the Congress may provide goodwill, embodying varying degrees of favorable attitudes and actions that contribute to a more hospitable legislative environment.[4] Since the objectives of the departments are more easily pursued in a friendly environment, executive lobbyists work assiduously at effecting a good climate between legislators and their departments. And since congressmen are extremely sensitive about their constituency relations, the liaison officers do more than respond to congressional requests. They aggressively search them out and assume the initiative in devising new ways of contributing to a congressman's efforts at enhancing his representational image with his constituents.

Impressed with the uncertainty and irrationality of the legislative system, liaison officers are fully cognizant of the problems that improper attention to constituency considerations can engender for their depart-

---

[4] Raymond A. Bauer, Ithiel de Sola Pool, and Lewis A. Dexter point out that goodwill is "one of the resources that affect the outcome of issues." See their interesting discussion in *American Business and Foreign Policy: The Politics of Foreign Trade* (New York: Atherton Press, 1963), p. 481.

ments. It is inevitable, therefore, that a major part of the time and effort of a department's liaison staff will center on the multitude of minor items that can aggravate or improve relations between the legislators and their departments. While a vote is rarely if ever gained by service, one may be lost by *poor* service. Many congressmen vote on issues that are of great concern to a particular department, but of little immediate importance to themselves or their constituents. At a minimum, proper executive action can avoid the generation of unfavorable legislative attitudes that reflect resentment because congressmen feel a department has ignored or rejected their legitimate needs as representative actors.

Before considering the services and favors that liaison officers can dispense, two institutional factors must be considered: the differential in resources that each department commands and the organizational advantages that some departments possess over others in processing congressional requests. In two of the eight departments that were studied, liaison staffs felt they were at some disadvantage in not possessing the range of services available to their fellow departments.

Treasury's Assistant to the Secretary for Congressional Relations maintained that his department had nothing to "give away." Other departmental liaison staffs had the job of straightening out the administrative details and personnel problems of congressmen and constituents, but his department handled almost none of this; whatever there was, the bureaus handled, while the liaison staff concerned itself strictly with the movement of legislation. As for the Internal Revenue Service, an obvious focus of constituent complaints, the secretary insisted that it be kept free from politics. The liaison staff operated under a rule never to discuss income tax matters. Only when a major controversial issue arose, or one loaded with political dynamite, was the liaison agent dragged in. Nonetheless, the chief liaison officer, himself a former congressman, conceded that he did have some patronage to disperse.

State's liaison staff also lamented that it had nothing substantial to offer. "We have no services or administrative alterations, as does Agriculture, and no expensive programs in the congressional districts, as does HEW," regretfully noted an Assistant Secretary for Congressional Relations. Both he and one of his deputies reported that they could perform services that helped congressmen function better, but none that could bestow immediate, visible benefits to their districts.

While it is true that State is not endowed with the resources of a domestically oriented department, it is not devoid of services that have some relevancy to congressional constituents. Indeed, James A. Robinson's study of Congress in the making of foreign policy examines in great detail relations between the staff of the Assistant Secretary for

Congressional Relations and congressmen during the Eisenhower Administration in terms of the servicing of constituents' requests.[5] Moreover, he refers to Assistant Secretary Breckinridge Long's having communicated with Secretary Cordell Hull during the Franklin D. Roosevelt Administration regarding patronage requests from senators. In one case this liaison officer talked with his secretary about his efforts to bolster a Georgia senator's position among his constituents by securing favorable publicity for him in his state.[6] A Kennedy Assistant Secretary for Congressional Relations might have claimed that he had no patronage at his disposal, but a predecessor during an earlier Democratic administration reported that he had possessed a considerable reservoir of favors for disposal in congressional relations, since no American citizen could go abroad without the department's approval.

I got authority from the secretary to pass on all congressional requests. It's quite as important to refuse as to agree. All the requests came to the secretary, but of course they really came to me. It soon penetrated to them [the congressmen] that I was important, and they needed to be on the good side of me.

In a letter sent to all members of the Congress in 1962, the Assistant Secretary for Congressional Relations described the following new services undertaken by his office, which he hoped congressmen would find useful.[7] (1) *Newsletter possibilities.* Twice a month a compilation of items on foreign policy developments would be available to congressmen who prepared newsletters for their constituents. Legislators were assured that such reports would be objective and nonpartisan, and that they would not duplicate regular news sources. (2) *Briefings for special visitors.* At the request of individual congressmen, the department would institute foreign policy briefings for visitors in Washington, D.C. Held three mornings a week, these briefings were to be followed by early-morning tours of the White House. (3) *Radio and television taping.* State Department officials were to be available for brief TV and radio interviews with individual congressmen. For legislators who were to appear on regular radio or TV programs, the department offered to furnish up-to-date background material on current foreign policy matters. (4)

---

[5] James A. Robinson, *Congress and Foreign Policy-Making: A Study in Legislative Influence and Initiative,* rev. ed. (Homewood, Ill.: Dorsey Press, 1967). See also Joseph C. Rigert, "The Office of the Assistant Secretary of State for Congressional Relations: A Study of An Aspect of Executive-Legislative Relations in the Formulation of Foreign Policy" (unpublished master's thesis, Georgetown University, 1959).

[6] Robinson, *op. cit.,* p. 103.

[7] Letter from Frederick G. Dutton, Assistant Secretary of State for Congressional Relations, to all congressmen, dated March 7, 1962.

Notice of appearance of State Department officers in congressional constituencies. The liaison office promised to inform congressmen when State officials would accept speaking engagements throughout the country so that the legislators could schedule speeches by these officials in their constituencies. (5) *Congressional correspondence.* Congressmen were assured that the department was engaged in a stepped-up drive to guarantee that its replies were prompt, responsive, and accurate. Criticism of such correspondence was solicited. (6) *Telephone inquiries.* For matters too urgent for a letter, congressional offices were informed that they could telephone a special number for action.

"The steps listed above," the assistant secretary wrote to the Congress "are being taken to encourage better service for members of Congress and to facilitate better public understanding of United States foreign policy objectives." Undoubtedly, public understanding was one goal, but it was clear that a primary aim was to improve relations with the Congress. The letter concluded with a request for suggestions on how the liaison office could be of greater assistance to the legislators.

Organizationally some departments are better structured than others to elicit as well as respond to constituent complaints and inquiries. Defense was outstanding in this respect. To say Defense, however, is to mislead, for the Office of the Secretary of Defense (OSD) did not station a legislative liaison office permanently on the Hill, whereas each of its service departments did. The service departments had their own quarters, staffed with uniformed personnel, in close proximity to the congressmen in the Senate and House office buildings. Not only could the legislators communicate by phone or letter with the services' liaison staffs inside the Pentagon, but enlisted men and officers were immediately available for personal consultation on constituent problems and inquiries. To the extent that the OSD's own liaison staff became involved in providing services and favors for legislators, it was much more adequately staffed than other comparable departmental legislative liaison offices.

Two additional departments among the eight that were studied maintained part of their liaison personnel permanently on the Hill, but their presence constituted only an infinitesimal fraction of that of Defense. Commerce in 1962–63 kept two of its staff members from the office of the Deputy to the Secretary for Congressional Relations permanently assigned to desks with the committees on Commerce. In 1963 the liaison officer in Agriculture assigned one assistant to spend his entire time on the Hill, walking from office to office picking up information on legislators' needs. If he could not respond to a request himself, he was to route it to his liaison office or to the proper bureau. "The House of Representatives is so damned busy," declared Agriculture's liaison officer, "that I need someone to stop in unannounced at the different offices. At any office, he comes out with one or two items that need to be done."

The other departments did not ignore the servicing of Congress. A major responsibility of the staffs of their liaison officers was to devote themselves to such service. The categories of services that they commanded were analogous to those referred to in State's letter.

(B) SCARCER EXECUTIVE SERVICES FOR LESS DIFFUSE GOODWILL. Domestic departments control not only more resources, but resources that are somewhat different from pure services, for they are endowed with the quality of special favors. They tend to be scarce resources that may or may not be offered equally to all legislators. Liaison officers can exercise more discretion in exchanging them with legislators and expect a more positive degree of goodwill in return.

Keeping legislators informed of departmental actions and decisions, unfavorable as well as favorable, is one important service liaison officers can provide. These include decisions on grants, contracts, appointments, laboratories, and surveys. "Every action that the department takes regarding their district or state, good or bad, we let them know," reported one liaison officer. Congressmen prefer advance notice because it offers them an opportunity, if they wish, to associate their names with a concrete benefit to their constituency. This helps build up credit with their constituents. In one department the liaison officer had personally opposed all advance notification of contract awards. When he sought "to cut off this information, such a howl arose in the Congress that we didn't dare fool with it." Advance notice proves functional to the congressmen from another perspective: it protects them from public embarrassment when the press questions them regarding departmental actions. Being forewarned, legislators can comment intelligently rather than reveal a lack of knowledge on a matter directly affecting their constituencies. Even if the news is negative, the legislators are accorded a breathing spell during which to prepare a proper rationale to concerned citizens or to the press. "I've had some of them [congressmen] say: 'You're killing me, but at least we know about it, so we're not embarrassed by hearing it first from the press!'" However, their bureaucracies, reported the liaison agents, were not happy to inform a congressman of a negative decision.

Patronage—obtaining jobs, promotions, or transfers for candidates recommended by members of the Congress—constitutes another category of resources. "We have over a hundred thousand people working for us," disclosed the liaison officer for a large department, "and there is such a turnover that we can place about twenty-five per cent of the job requests that we get." One department was so richly endowed with job resources, and legislators turned to it in such numbers, that the liaison agent assigned to an assistant—an individual professionally experienced in personnel work—the full-time responsibility of placing congressionally sponsored applicants. While not all liaison officers are directly responsible for patronage, it is so important a point of contact with Congress that it is frequently linked closely with them. In a small department, the liaison officer noted that patronage did not come directly to him; it was handled by an assistant to an assistant secretary, but the assistant "might as well be on my staff, he coordinates so much with me."

The liaison officer can also help the legislator cut through bureaucratic resistance or political stumbling blocks in order to expedite his requests or to compel a reconsideration of departmental decisions. The nature of requests that came to him from his roving assistant on the Hill, explained the lobbyist for a larger department, might include the following: "A loan rejected—we look at it again; a friend in trouble with one of our agencies—we arrange for him to see the administrator; a project in a congressional district that's gotten fouled up—we help him disentangle it from the red tape."

One valuable service that can be provided a legislator is personally satisfying a constituent who strongly presses a grievance against someone or some act of the department. Should a senator wish to assist a constituent without regard to the merits of his case, a meeting can be arranged at a policy level which brings together the constituent, the legislator, and senior administrators. Whatever the outcome, it was pointed out in one department, the legislator had clearly demonstrated to his constituent both his concern and his influence in the department. The liaison officer and one of his aides attended such meetings so the legislator could state that a personal representative of the secretary had been present. In most cases, observed this liaison staff aide, the government was correct in its actions; no mistake had been made. But this service was a courtesy they could accord legislators.

A recent action that his office had secured for a congressman, reported the liaison officer in a large department, was obtaining $5,000 for a special survey in a legislator's district. Not only was this considered good politically for the congressman, but it was a worthwhile project; the proposed survey had merely become lost in the administrative shuffle. Suppose such a request seemed to him improper, he was asked. He replied that his secretary had firmly laid down the rule against undertaking anything that was improper. Nevertheless, there was always a gray area, he noted, between the proper and the improper, which afforded him some discretion because of its ambiguity. "Anyway, I have never been asked to do things I shouldn't do. When they ask, I can easily stop things by saying, 'Put your views down on paper and send them to us.' "

Undoubtedly, improper requests have from time to time been initiated by legislators. Those considered blatantly improper are fielded or nullified more or less easily, but in the gray area of ambiguity, political necessities lead at times to some accommodation to legislative desires.

One category of favors or services reported by some departmental liaison agents and their staffs differs radically from the others. It is related neither to the constituent nor to the legislator playing representational roles, and it has nothing to do with strategy regarding bills or the legislative process. It touches upon style more than anything else. This is the highly personal expression of concern for the congressman as an individual. One example will suffice. "If we learn that a member is sick, we send him a note over the secretary's signature. It's surprising how much this means to a person." Goodwill cannot be left to chance; it must be cultivated.

Only one departmental liaison officer insisted that he never resorted to the *quid pro quo* in dealing with legislators; the others were quite frank about its use. Involved were resources at the most significant level of services and favors, as well as others to be discussed later, which enhanced the internal legislative roles of such congressmen. Legislators who already exercised power and influence as well as those judged to be moving toward such positions were especially cultivated in this manner by executive actors. When Congressmen X and Y [a committee chairman and a subcommittee chairman] called him and wanted something, explained the lobbyist in a large domestic department, "I go out of my way to do something. I want them to be indebted to me, to ask me for favors."

I was interviewing a departmental lobbyist when an associate called to find out whether a decision had been reached on the site for a highly desirable laboratory. Apparently the chairman of a committee was joining his state's advocates. "He isn't going to get the lab," the liaison agent replied, "unless he gives us something on X [a departmental bill bottled up in that committee]." Sometimes it is the legislator who places his chips on the table. A senator called the liaison officer in another department, requesting employment for someone, "just because he took over our appropriations subcommittee." The liaison officer suggested that the department had better give the request serious consideration. Robinson cites a memorandum from an Assistant Secretary for Congressional Relations (State) noting that the chairman of the Senate Foreign Relations Committee had requested an exchange of resources.[8] Since the chairman was taking up in committee two of the department's bills on foreign claims, upon which he expected favorable action, he felt that he was

[8] Robinson, *op. cit.*, p. 102.

entitled to some consideration in naming the chairman of the claims commission.

More likely the *quid pro quo* is simply understood between actors who know the unofficial rules of the game. "The understanding is all that's important," declared one liaison officer. "An overt act is unnecessary when the political climate is such that we all know what it's all about. Nothing is said, but it's understood." Each understands that an obligation has been created, that the executive actor may subsequently capitalize upon it. "We can say yes or no with regard to grants and facilities," elaborated another liaison officer. "If the requests have equal merit, we employ a political factor." He had recently intervened in his department to secure a grant for the congressional district of a senior committee staffman who was also a good friend of the Democratic senator from that state. As it happened, the senator was a supporter of the President and therefore entitled to the service. Nevertheless, the liaison officer remarked, "We create banks of blue chips this way. They know that's what we're doing, and they expect it."

One of the most amusing exchanges was reported by an Assistant Secretary of State for Congressional Relations in an earlier Democratic administration. It had occurred between himself and "a reactionary Illinois congresswoman who was trying to louse up our bill" in a House committee. He had invited the legislator to lunch and had made her the following proposition:

You're not doing any good for yourself or any real harm to me. You're mixing things up and we'll unscramble them anyway, but we'll both waste a lot of energy. I'll write a speech against the bill. You deliver it for the record. Then why don't you absent yourself. Go to Chicago and campaign or something. You're not going to defeat the bill anyway.

An agreement was reached and both parties kept their bargain.

(C) The Pattern of Resource Allocation and the Results. Up to this point we have considered the *kinds* of constituent-oriented resources, called services and favors, which departmental liaison officers have at their disposal when they wish to pursue a strategy of exchange. It is also in order to inquire into the *pattern of dispersion*. Are these resources afforded all legislators? If services and favors are not offered equally to all legislators, who takes precedence and why?

The liaison officers agreed that members of their substantive committees and appropriations subcommittees took precedence in time and attention as well as services and favors over other members of the legislative system. Majority-party leaders in the House and Senate, of course, were also given special consideration. In view of the importance assigned by liaison officers to committees in the legislative process, no further comments are necessary. But some liaison agents and their staffs further distinguished between Democrats and Republicans on their committees. The consequences of a strategy of exchange with this type of resource must be assessed.

Both for the committees and for the general membership, partisanship entered significantly into the willingness of a number of legislative liaison agents to offer certain services and favors. In affording legislators advance notification of departmental actions that affected their districts or states, the liaison officers in the Kennedy Administration favored the Democrats. Either they notified the Democrats and not the Republicans, or they communicated with the Democratic legislators first, thereby furnishing them an advantage over their Republican colleagues who were also concerned with this information. This, it was asserted, was what members of their own party in the Congress expected; it was not just the result of White House pressure. In the opinion of the liaison agents, it was understood within the Congress, as an informal rule of the game, that legislators whose party controlled the executive system would benefit as party members. One departmental officer noted that such a practice had preceded his coming into the department in 1961; it had been engaged in by his Republican predecessors.

Interviews with Republican departmental liaison agents from the Eisenhower Administration disclosed that some of them had followed the same principle of partisanship. Nevertheless, the situation in which they had found themselves was very different and somewhat more difficult, for while their party had controlled the administration for eight years, it had been the minority party in Congress for six of these years. When some of the liaison agents had pursued a partisan role in distributing favors to their Republican legislators, they had discovered that the boundaries of that system were jealously guarded by the majority party. "We handled releases on a partisan basis," explained a liaison officer for a very large confederate department. "I pursued this policy until Senator [Hubert H.] Humphrey threatened to call me before the Government Operations Committee and so scared Secretary X that we were asked to stop it thereafter."

Another Republican liaison agent in a more unified department argued that partisanship was inherently dysfunctional. "We played both sides, Republicans and Democrats. Today the Kennedy Administration is all partisan in its approach. It does things only for the Democrats and it pays the price in terms of the unwillingness of our congressmen today to cooperate." Republican congressmen during the Kennedy Administration did complain about partisan advantages accruing to their Democratic colleagues and about discrimination against members of their party.

Whether Republicans would have cooperated more than they did during this period if the Kennedy Administration had not been so partisan cannot be ascertained. I doubt it.

Whatever the Republican image of the Kennedy Administration, it was obvious that State did not employ partisan tactics. Rather, its leaders maintained a careful bipartisan approach toward the Congress. On the other hand, its liaison staff complained that their department had no special favors to dispose of anyway. While Defense conceded that announcements of contract awards were relayed first to Democratic legislators, its legislative liaison officers insisted that no contracts were directed to businesses and areas for political purposes. In a third department, however, the liaison officer stated flatly that its services were directed toward helping Democrats, not Republicans. Referring to the Republicans on his substantive committee in the House, he said: "We contact them with regard to little favors, but if we helped them in terms of contracts and patronage and other things, the local Democratic party [in the constituency] would squawk."

With regard to job patronage, a Democratic liaison officer in a department with many jobs available for legislators to fill maintained that Republicans and Democrats were serviced alike, those voting against as well as those voting for his department's bills. He claimed—and this lends some credence to the argument of the Republican liaison agent that partisanship was dysfunctional—that "the Republicans appreciate it [his nonpartisanship] and therefore help me out." Yet he acknowledged that if there were a job opening that in the normal course of events both a Republican and a Democrat wanted to fill, he would give it to the Democrat. In contrast, a liaison agent in still another department, who claimed that he did not have enough to give away, perceived patronage as part of an exchange that involved more than mere goodwill. He would not furnish jobs that were at his department's disposal to any and all legislators, whether or not they voted for his department. Of course, their voting records would count, he asserted. But even being a Democrat would not guarantee the congressman as much preference as would his personal relations with the liaison officer or the extent to which he could subsequently prove useful.

I'd say to a congressman: "Jobs are awfully scarce. How much do you need it?" And if he said, "A lot," then I've got it. If it's "Not that much" and he can live with it, well, he may or may not get it. It all depends, of course, in both cases: if I go to him for something, if I have a personal relationship with him that's important, or if I want to use this [job] later with him as a blue chip.

It was obvious that in his eyes, departmental resources were to be disposed of for the maximum range of exchange resources that he could extract from legislators. He was employing such resources for more than the establishment of a nonhostile atmosphere—for goodwill and for legislative behavior on a *quid pro quo* basis.

One last variation should be cited, if only to illustrate further that not all Democrats were treated similarly even if they were on a department's major committees. The following observations about providing services and favors to members of a Senate committee were made by a staff assistant to a liaison officer: (1) Not all were "friends"; therefore, the same services and favors were not provided everyone. (2) It depended on their importance on the committee as well as their friendliness to the administration. (3) The liaison staff initiated offers of aid to some committee members, but worked with others only if they asked for such assistance.

Does a strategy of exchange oriented to the representational roles of legislators pay off? The evidence, at least in terms of assessments by the legislative liaison officers themselves, was somewhat contradictory. It was obvious that it did pay off, although not all the departments saw themselves benefiting in the same way. For most of the liaison officers, it was a minimal, albeit an essential, strategy for helping to shape a favorable congressional climate in which other strategies could be undertaken.

From his interviews with staff members of State's Assistant Secretary for Congressional Relations during the Eisenhower Administration, James C. Robinson reports that they did assume that nonpolicy service to Congress generated goodwill that was transferred to and reinforced the foreign policy positions of the department.[9] However, Robinson concludes from his interviews with congressmen that support for State's foreign policy was *not* affected by the degree of their satisfaction with State's handling of their constituent requests. He could find no significant statistical relationship between the two variables: satisfaction with services and political support. Nonetheless, this did not necessarily mean that the department's attention to congressional constituent services failed to affect its position in the Congress. Should State discontinue its services, predicts Robinson, or perform them unsatisfactorily, such behavior would certainly lead to increased criticism of the department within the Congress.

How do Robinson's findings and conclusions conform to those in the present study? This study covered eight departments including State, but the interviews did not focus upon the legislators' satisfaction or lack of satisfaction with constituent services or with policy preferences. No statistical approach is attempted, therefore, to refute or confirm Robinson's data or conclusions. However, it is possible to suggest a hypothesis that

[9] *Ibid.,* pp. 162–63.

reconciles Robinson's conclusions (pertaining to State) with those advanced by liaison officers in other departments regarding this strategy.

Apropos of State during the Kennedy Administration, interviews with executive actors conducting legislative liaison revealed some disparity in attitude from that recorded by Robinson in the Republican Administration. Two who served as the Assistant Secretary for Congressional Relations were interviewed for the present study, as were three members of their staffs. The latter type of actors constituted the population from which Robinson drew his conclusions on executive attitudes. Only one of the interviewees in 1962–63, a deputy assistant secretary, envisaged a very positive payoff from constituent-oriented services: "We can handle the mail expeditiously and keep the congressmen's constituents happy, and therefore keep the Congress happy, which has a surprising affect on foreign policy." Two others—assistant liaison agents—felt that furnishing such services made little if any contribution toward developing or strengthening positive congressional attitudes toward U.S. foreign policy. The two assistant secretaries, who were the senior aides to their secretary on Congress, also rejected the thesis. It was their contention that such services as State could furnish were simply expected by congressmen; to perform them poorly was to risk incurring the ire of legislators. State's services were viewed primarily as reducing the amount of tension between the two systems rather than affecting positively legislative attitudes regarding the administration's foreign policy. Only one positive bonus was envisaged. The good services provided by their staffs enhanced their ability to approach legislators on other matters; i.e., the communications channel between executive and legislative actors was kept open and could be exploited. Four of the five who were interviewed in 1962–63 did *not* accept the assumption adhered to by the staff assistants in State's liaison office in the Eisenhower Administration.

One explanation for Robinson's failure to find any meaningful correlation between congressional satisfaction with constituent services and positive congressional attitudes toward foreign policy may be traced in part to the limited nature of services that State can provide. It may be hypothesized that the nature of the resources that State has available for disposal handicaps the department in affecting congressional attitudes, and that there is a substantive difference between answering constituent mail or nonpolicy inquiries and the type of services and favors that directly and concretely impinge upon the congressman's renomination and reelection image in his constituency. Included in the latter category would be those services and favors that cover grants and contracts and which point up a congressman's ability to induce executive leaders to reverse unfavorable administrative decisions affecting his constituency. It should be recognized, however, that the basic attitudinal pattern among congressmen in 1961-63 toward State was already negative and hostile. Whether different types of services and favors would have materially affected attitudes toward State's foreign policy is questionable. But the department itself could have benefited from a more favorable climate, which itself might have improved State's chances to sell its policies.

On the whole, executive lobbyists in domestically oriented departments (including Defense) expressed the opinion that much more positive results accrued to them and to their departments as a result of their employing the strategy of services and favors. In discussing this strategy, all attributed greater political efficacy to projects, grants, contracts, patronage, and other administrative decisions than to informational services and promptness in replies to constituent requests. Only one flatly rejected, as had the assistant secretaries in State and two of their three assistants, any relationship between constituent-oriented services performed by executive actors and congressional support for legislation. "We can do a lot of things for congressmen which may affect their attitudes, but this does not affect results for us in terms of legislation," he said. "Some of them might have felt better, but they wouldn't have voted any differently." Even he, however, was ready to trade a project in a congressional district for a more favorable disposition on the part of a committee chairman toward processing certain departmental bills. On the other hand, two other departmental liaison officers were convinced that such a strategy could and did, at times, affect the votes of congressmen. Still others believed that it was effective in orienting congressmen favorably to their departments and themselves; they could not afford to neglect it because of these reasons and because of the possibility that it had some impact on votes. All expressed the opinion that this was one strategy that, in conjunction with other strategies, helped hold together their friends in the Congress.

According to a liaison agent from a confederate department, the success of his bills in the House of Representatives was based on a grand strategy of welding together three groups of legislators. The largest group, which constituted the core of the department's supporters, approximated 150 in number. In the second group were fifty or so congressmen whose votes the department stood a chance to capture through the merits of its bills or through legislative accommodations to suit the needs or wishes of these House members. As for the third and smallest group, the department had to rely upon the party leadership in the House to swing them on the basis of its own resources and relationships. As long as the first group adhered to the department, he asserted, "we have a fighting chance to get fifty or more on the basis of the legislation." A number of factors contributed to the willingness of members in the largest group to stick with the department through the quorum calls, the debates, the votes, the amendments in the Committee of the Whole House, and the final votes. Among these factors, he declared, was "keeping them feeling you are interested in them and their needs, keeping fully informed about them and their constituents, trying to help them on matters about which they are concerned." Although they were Democrats, not everyone in the initial group, he explained, had to vote with the department. A particular bill might mean very little to some of them personally, and have no direct impact upon their congressional districts. But they would "cooperate easier if we've protected them all along from being embarrassed in the press and with their constituents, if we've been concerned enough to shore them up in both places."

A staff assistant to a liaison officer in another department asserted that even opponents on legislation could prove useful at times, and that services and favors helped with them as well. At the request of a Republican member on his major House committee, he had spent an entire morning with the congressman and representatives of four industries from the latter's district on their problems. "He opposes us on all our legislation, and I could have refused to cooperate, but I didn't. I interpreted the law for them and even recommended, unofficially, what I'd do under the circumstances when they went to the Defense Department, where their questions were eventually referred." Why had he cooperated in this manner? "Keeping channels open is a real problem in the Congress. We can't afford to stop working on it and improving it. He sees we're fair and helpful, and since he's not a bad guy, he'll see no reason why he shouldn't be fair and helpful to us in some ways when we ask." It wasn't policy satisfaction that concerned this assistant liaison officer; he recognized that this congressman would never agree with the basic policies of the department under the Kennedy Administration. However, he might cooperate by passing on information about other Republicans on the committee or in other ways.

In still another department, those engaged in liaison work contended that they benefited directly by helping members on their Senate committee resolve their problems with the department. A strategy of services and favors aided the executive actors in establishing and reinforcing a close relationship with the senators and their staff. The latter two considered the liaison agent a friend who would guard their interests in the department and fight the bureaucracy for them in order to obtain favorable action. As a result the department was better protected, for these legislative actors were more likely to withdraw some of their own demands upon the department if the liaison agent appealed to them. "After all, I am an employee and must protect its interests as well as theirs. If I feel that they are making unreasonable demands on the department, I'll reason with them and urge them to get off of our backs." This could more easily be accomplished with legislators and staff aides whom the lobbyists knew well: "If we've done things to help them, it works both ways."

In 1966 a memorandum on strategy from the liaison agent for the Office of Economic Opportunity to its director was publicized in the press.[10] Its stress upon certain services and favors is highly relevant at this point, although it occurred during the Johnson and not the Kennedy Administration. The memorandum recommended "drastic improvement in service to Congress to consolidate friendships and, wherever possible, to ameliorate enemies." The liaison officer warned that "leaks of grant awards, etc. . . . cannot be tolerated—the loss of announcement priority in one case can cost one or more votes on OEO legislation. All announcements will be made by CR [Congressional Relations], with no exceptions tolerated." To improve relations with Congress further, regional OEO offices were instructed to proceed immediately to appoint a staff member to handle inquiries from the legislative liaison officer for members of the Congress.

An important congressman who is antagonized because he has lost the publicity advantage of a grant can, if he wishes, greatly complicate the job of a liaison officer. A traditional stalwart of the administration, on a committee closely linked with one department, had somehow—through an error on the part of his own secretary—missed an announcement that the liaison officer had relayed via telephone. As a consequence he forfeited an opportunity to associate himself with a sizable grant from the department to his district, which error he blamed upon the liaison officer. "He telephoned to inform me that I was an s.o.b," related the embarrassed liaison officer, "and that he would demand that I be fired. I was also warned, 'Don't ever come into my office again.' " So enraged was this legislator that he called the chief lobbyist for President Kennedy to complain about this departmental lobbyist. That the legislator was a subcommittee chairman made the loss of access all the more serious.

A Strategy of Exchange Focused on the Legislative Needs and Roles of Congressmen

Constituent-oriented services and favors can help engender the goodwill of legislative actors toward liaison officers and their depart-

[10] See "Inside Report . . . The Poverty Lobby" by Rowland Evans and Robert Novak in the *Washington Post,* February 1, 1966. The OEO was not among the departments and agencies covered by the present study. Indeed, it did not exist at the time the interviews were being conducted, and its liaison officer was serving in 1962–63 as a congressional staff assistant and chief staff aide to the Democratic Study Group in the House.

ments. But the extent to which such goodwill contributes positively to the legislation of the departments is uncertain. The types of services and favors that enhance the congressman's role as legislator affecting policy and process within his own system, that cater to his status and his influence among his colleagues, and that, at the same time, benefit his district are considered by executive actors to pay off more immediately in their legislative campaigns.[11] These services and favors will be referred to as legislative-oriented resources.

Just as the administration proposes legislation and solicits the support of congressmen, so too do the latter want executive actors to cooperate with them as allies and assistants in legislative politics (see Chapter III). Hence the liaison officers are in a favorable position to exploit this situation also by allocating legislative-oriented resources. Nevertheless, the extent of the needs and the dependencies of the two sets of actors varies with what is being sought.

In the area of constituent services and favors, the legislative actor is the more vulnerable one. It is he who feels it imperative to demonstrate concretely to his constituency that he has its interests at heart, and it is he who almost invariably assumes the initiative in contacting the executive system. Although the executive actor pursues a strategy of exchanging such services and favors, the legislative actor is the dependent one, the one who requires but does not control these resources. Conversely, in the area of legislation, the congressman controls the votes, dominates the process, determines in large measure the outcome. The executive actor is compelled to come to the legislative actor for his resources. On the whole, the latter has much less at stake than does the executive actor, who *must* help implement the legislative leadership of his secretary and the White House.

Legislative-oriented resources are used by liaison agents to achieve a close, personal relationship with legislative actors—based upon respect, trust, and mutual advantage—in order that the congressmen and their staffs will cooperate with them as allies, and will permit them to inter-

[11] The value of collaboration between lobbyists and legislators on policy and on process as it affects policy is well documented in the literature on interest groups, congressmen, and lobbying. Lester W. Milbrath, for example, reports that congressmen and their overworked offices welcomed the services offered by lobbyists: providing speeches, preparing reports, drafting bills, etc. (*The Washington Lobbyists* [Chicago: Rand McNally, 1963], pp. 232–34). His sample of lobbyists felt that this afforded them an excellent opportunity—"no better way"—to affect policy. Robinson reports a statistically significant relationship between the satisfaction of congressmen concerned with foreign policy roles (basically committee members) and policy aspects of the communications network involving State and the Congress (*op. cit.*, pp. 164–65). When Robinson divided his congressional respondents according to political party, his findings held true only for the out (of the executive) party and not for members of the in party (*ibid.*, pp. 166–67).

vene advantageously in the legislative process. Such a relationship contributes to the maintenance of open communications channels. It fosters a congenial climate in which legislators and liaison agents can interact, and it brings the two together so that they can exchange valuable information relating directly to prospects for legislation. Liaison officers can more easily secure thereby the services of legislators to act as intermediaries in lobbying their fellow congressmen for executive ends. The departments are afforded a voice in shaping the substance of bills initiated within the congressional system as well as those originating within the executive system. And, finally, liaison officers capitalize upon such relations to facilitate their personal approach to congressmen in order to sell legislation and to appeal directly for their support and votes.

Individual liaison officers differed at times in their approaches, but all stressed the importance of cultivating relations with senior legislators on their committees. Legislators were seen as changing their positions in their committees, some leaving, others moving up. Consequently it was absolutely necessary, one departmental lobbyist asserted, to establish proper relations with those moving into positions of influence and power. Senator X was now third in seniority on a committee that handled the department's bills; the chairman took him along to the House-Senate conference committees. "I want to know him on a face-to-face, personal basis and share legislative experiences with him." The liaison agent could then approach the senator on a first-name basis, "level with him," and have the senator "level with me." This relationship could not be achieved at their first meeting or only "when the chips are down"; it had, rather, to be cultivated to the point where the executive actor could use it effectively.

The liaison officer had recently arranged for Senator X to introduce two bills in a certain policy area, although the senator was no liberal and had opposed one of the department's most important proposals. Not only did the department stand to benefit, since it needed both bills, he reported, but the senator improved his own reputation by sponsoring them. What had the liaison officer gained from this move? "I've needed a line to him—entrée—so I can find out what's happening in the committee and among the conservatives when I need to." This was already producing results, for the senator was calling him about such matters. The senator had proved very helpful on other problems. At the request of this executive actor, the senator's chief assistant had asked a favor from the senior senator from the same state, who presided over an appropriations subcommittee. As a result, an amendment had been eliminated in that subcommittee which in effect restored $1.5 million to one of the department's newer programs. "I've got the senator to the point where I can go to him for such special problems and where he takes the initiative and calls me."

A limitation on a strategy of collaboration was embodied in the maxim subscribed to by all the liaison agents: "Don't overuse the congressmen." Requests made upon legislators for assistance could not be excessive. Moreover, a separate evaluation had to be made of each congressman: "Some congressmen like to be talked with, others don't. This is a delicate area of decision and action." In addition, liaison officers recognized that legislators and their assistants were extremely busy and were preoccupied with much that extended beyond the concern of any one department. Proposals for cooperation and collaboration were to be broached with many legislative actors only when action was impending. "Senators work on what they are concerned with *now*."

(A) COLLABORATIVE PATTERNS AND PROBLEMS. By briefing particular legislators and consulting with them, liaison officers and their associates engage in tactics that are beneficial to both sets of actors. Such tactics cater to the egos of legislators, provide them with privileged, valuable information that other legislators do not or cannot obtain until a later date, and involve them with executive actors in common problems of policy and strategy on items coming up in the Congress. Such tactics are addressed principally to the chairmen and to members of the departments' committees, for committee decisions are critical in the legislative system.

In some instances—when the chairman is extremely influential and when the executive has assigned a high priority to the legislation—the liaison officer may actually travel with his superiors to the congressman's district in order to consult with him. One liaison officer reported that not only had he and his undersecretary called upon the chairman of the House committee in this manner, but all three subsequently flew to the home of the second-ranking Democrat on the Senate committee. In this way the executive actors conveyed to these legislators the importance they attached to their proposals and their recognition of the congressmen's significance. At the same time they sought through these meetings to familiarize these legislators with the department's thinking, to clarify any questions, and to elicit from the congressmen their ideas on policy and process. "We try to make absolutely sure that we brief X and Y prior to taking any official action." After the President's State of the Union message and before a special message on the topic was sent to the Congress, the undersecretary, the secretary, and this liaison officer divided among themselves the Senate committee members in order to talk personally with each about the proposed legislation. House committee members were also briefed, although not so thoroughly.

Legislative liaison officers and executive actors in all the departments and agencies made it a practice to consult with their committee chairmen almost every time their departments proposed major, and sometimes even minor, legislation. Nevertheless, there were exceptions. In one committee, lobbyists from two departments worked principally with the subcommittee chairmen and members rather than with the chairmen of the full committee. These liaison officers disclosed that they did not discuss their legislation with this chairman beforehand, although they always made a *pro forma* presentation to him or to his staff prior to sending up their bills; he was not interested in discussing the substance of the legislation.

Liaison officers were careful to keep in constant contact with chairmen while executive proposals were in their committees and when they were on the floor. One liaison officer reported that normally he met with the chairman three times a week, but when legislation was before the committee, the rate of personal interaction between them increased to at least three times a day and many more times daily over the phone. An agency liaison officer noted that he stopped by every morning before mark-up sessions to ascertain the chairman's plans, after the meeting to discover what had transpired, and later to learn the chairman's thinking about the next day.

In one case the liaison officer complained that the chairman demanded more consultation than the department could afford; in fact, the chairman posed a problem "because he wanted to be consulted on everything the department did." Even though they had consistently consulted with him, he remained petulant and angry with the department. "On the X bill of 1962, the secretary, others, and I went to the Hill from October on for untold hours, discussing it with congressmen and with Y [the chairman]." They had even met at the chairman's house for more intimate discussions. "I think we have done a fairly good job in keeping him advised as to our plans and projects. But some decisions we have to make and not discuss with anyone."

As a tactic, consultation with committee members proved rewarding in eliciting from them useful information, suggestions, and help with strategy and tactics in the committee. Sometimes committee members could be induced thereby to vote for the department and against their chairman. One departmental liaison officer dealt with a committee over whom its chairman presided "like an absolute autocrat." This executive actor reported that the department was finally able to detach a few legislators from this chairman's previously unanimous committee through careful consultation with and briefings of key members. He and his staff painstakingly kept in contact with these members, ascertaining what they were thinking and doing and seeking their counsel on policy matters. In general, however, legislative liaison officers can scarcely hope for such spectacular results.

State has probably systematized the consultative process more than any other department. In the 1940s an Assistant Secretary for Congressional Relations instituted a "series of conversations" from time to time with members of the Senate Foreign Relations Committee "to take them more into our confidence from the point of view of general policy" and to enable them to understand the current situation.[12] To a lesser degree, the same policy was pursued with the comparable House committee. A deputy liaison officer in the department during the Kennedy Administration, who had served with its legislative liaison office for many years, disclosed that State had found it impossible to brief the entire House committee as frequently as it desired. Consequently, an Assistant Secretary for Congressional Relations had developed the idea of having the two committees create subcommittees for foreign policy areas. The liaison officers then encouraged the secretary and his substantive assistant secretaries to establish close relations with the chairman of these subcommittees. They met from time to time with subcommittee members to keep them abreast of developments and used the subcommittees for consultation "where problems are known to be arising which might turn out badly or on which we felt it important or expedient or both to inform Congress before we actually made the policy decisions."[13] Within the office of the Assistant Secretary for Congressional Relations in the Kennedy Administration, the assistants who worked in Congress for him were also assigned areas corresponding with those of the subcommittees to facilitate their day-to-day relations.

More than briefing and consultation may be provided by executive actors. One liaison officer for a domestic department based his strategy for his committee upon the premise that he could accomplish more with its members if he made himself subservient to its wishes. Within two days after assuming the position of departmental liaison agent, he had contacted the chairman and subcommittee chairmen to inform them of this sentiment. With each of his department's bills he had extended an offer of help to the chairman, placing himself at the chairman's disposal. When the latter had presented bills to the Rules Committee, the liaison officer had stood by for instructions. "If he had asked me, I would have talked

---

[12] See Robinson, *op. cit.,* p. 120.
[13] From transcript of address by the Deputy Assistant Secretary for Congressional Relations before a seminar at Harvard University, 1961. There was some dispute in the seminar with the professor over whether the department had actually conceived of the idea of subcommittees for the House committee or whether it had originated within the committee.

with X and Y on Rules and worked with them to help get the others to give us the rule we wanted." Once a rule was proposed, the liaison officer together with his senior assistant solicited support in the House to ensure the rule's adoption.

In the process, committee members and the liaison officer aided each other. He had conducted negotiations with them that had led to concessions and hence an agreement on one bill, he pointed out. However, before the House voted on it, changes had been incorporated which threatened trouble for some of his committee members. "So I made a few calls to senators to guarantee that we could fix it there. And when everyone was reasonably protected, we went ahead and had a roll call." In return, committee members helped him. They warned him whenever trouble materialized in the committee or when problems were likely to arise on the floor. On his last bill, when two undesirable amendments had been offered on the floor, he had been notified in time so that he could take proper counteraction.

So closely was this liaison officer identified with his collaborators in the committee that he clearly intimated that, if the department pushed legislation that the committee strongly opposed, he would not campaign as aggressively or persuasively for such bills as he might for others. In part, his reluctance stemmed from a realization that such action would impair his special rapport with the committee. This liaison officer was actually torn between his obligations to two sets of clients: his committee and his departmental superiors. His close ties with the legislators on his committee, legislators with whom he had been associated for over a decade, manifested themselves in the following assertion: "I am not going to sell my friends in the Congress a bill I do not agree on."

Committee and subcommittee chairmen frequently request departmental liaison officers to help them bring together a quorum of their members. These executive actors, together with the technicians whom they bring from the departments, serve also as staff assistants to the chairmen in clarifying political and technical points when committee members consider the bills and when legislation comes to the floor of the House or Senate. In the latter case liaison officers and their assistants operate from the galleries or from out of the Speaker's or Vice President's office. From these locations they can be called upon for help with the debate or in ascertaining the secretary's position on some proposed change. When they consider it necessary that certain points be clarified, the liaison officers may themselves call congressmen off the floor.

The importance to the department of the legislative history of its bill requires liaison officers to devote special attention to floor debate. Should a bill pass with certain questions still unanswered, they pointed out, the legislative intent may be unclear. They could prevent this by alerting the bill's manager to the problem or by arranging for another congressman to ask the appropriate questions; the proper definition or interpretation could then be definitively placed on record. In this manner they protected the guidelines or interpretations that the department desired for administering the law.

It was necessary to be close to several senators, noted one executive actor, so as to elicit quickly special favors in dealing with the legislative process: placing a statement in the *Congressional Record* or getting word to a senator to continue talking so that another senator could arrive on the floor and have his colleague yield to him. "It is very important to have a way to get to and control the floor." In the midst of fast-moving floor action, explained this liaison officer, senators did not always know what a proposed amendment would do, whether it was good, bad, or indifferent.

To intervene and avoid trouble when his bills came to the floor, he needed to know senators well, reported another liaison officer. When they knew and trusted him, he could speak frankly with them and rely upon them for cooperation. With a legislator whom he did not know well, he was at a distinct disadvantage. In the interest of improving an important bill that the department was sponsoring, a Democratic senator had recently offered an amendment that actually complicated the politics surrounding the bill.

I don't know Senator X well. So I can't talk with him as I would with the other Democrats or Republicans who are pro. I'd say to them: "Please, leave us alone. We have enough trouble without your amendment." And they would come along. But I don't know this Democratic senator, and I can't lay it on the line that frankly.

Should a chairman or subcommittee chairman not prove helpful or particularly competent, liaison officers may address themselves to less senior members who are friendly to the department and who have invested the time and effort in their committee work to make themselves highly knowledgeable. Actually executive lobbyists and legislators seek each other out, for it is to their mutual advantage to collaborate in sharing intelligence and in planning action. "I work closely back and forth with X," disclosed a departmental lobbyist. "While he's not high in seniority, he's very good on strategy and on thinking through the problem of whom to talk to and how best to accomplish a goal." A number of liaison officers made it a practice of lunching with legislators in the House when they first joined their committees. They used these occasions to discuss the policy and programs of the departments as a means of laying the foundations for more fruitful relations with these congressmen.

Nevertheless, collaboration with junior congressmen, while useful, has its dangers, since such action runs counter to prevailing legislative norms of seniority and specialization. An executive lobbyist who complained about the ineffectiveness of his House committee noted that the department could count on bright young supporters from both parties outside the committee. "But they are junior and are not representative of the House. We try to avoid offending the seniority system. If we work with them too openly, we lose X and the others."

Collaboration with committee members is absolutely essential, but it is not without its costs. A major problem for one liaison officer arose out of a conflict between demands from his allied interest groups and his own need to collaborate closely with a moderately conservative senator moving up in seniority on his key committee. To develop special entrée with that senator and to seek his aid with legislation, the liaison officer assisted him in many ways, permitting the legislator to gain credit within his constituency and within the Senate. Such action irritated the liberal interest groups and some liberal congressmen who usually cooperated with this liaison officer. For a while his relations with these allies became extremely awkward. Some of them, in fact, displayed considerable disillusionment with this liaison officer and expressed a loss of confidence in him. "The trouble is," he protested, "that they simply don't comprehend my problems. They have a cops-and-robbers mentality while my basic rule is 'You must always keep your avenues of communications open.' " The liaison officer had the most impeccable credentials as a liberal. However, the dictates of winning, he claimed, demanded that the department bring along on key votes a number of legislators to the right of the administration.

The conflict surrounding this liaison officer as a result of his collaborating with committee conservatives pointed up a widespread discontent among liberals during the Kennedy Administration. Time and again liberal congressmen and their staffs, together with their collaborators among the interest groups, charged that the Kennedy Administration ignored its friends and cooperated with its enemies. Liberal congressmen complained that special advantages were provided those who refused to stand up and vote with the administration, whereas, when the chips were down, the liberals could be relied upon to vote the right way.

The realities of politics in the Congress convinced the liaison officers that they could not afford to ignore conservatives if the latter were senior legislators and held positions of power as committee and subcommittee chairmen. Not to cultivate them or those moving up toward such positions would seriously handicap their departments' legislative programs, argued the liaison officers. The knowledge that the liberals' votes were virtually guaranteed and that such votes did not in themselves suffice impelled the liaison agents to take these legislators for granted and to cater to the others. The ill will generated among the liberals was directed principally against the White House lobbyists, but some spilled over to the departments as well. Some liberal congressmen began deliberately behaving in an inconsistent manner so that the departments and the White House could not afford to assume they were safely locked in.

Collaborative efforts benefited the Kennedy departmental liaison officers in one way that I had not anticipated, one not shared by lobbyists from private interest groups. A number of legislative committees permitted departmental liaison officers to work with them in their executive sessions, even in the mark-up sessions on bills. This constituted a tremendous advantage for these executive actors. By sitting in during these closed sessions where legislators spoke more frankly with each other, the executive lobbyists were afforded a marvelous opportunity to garner intelligence firsthand, to pinpoint for their senior leaders those committee members who needed reassurance or additional clarification, and to orient their allied interest groups to bring pressure to bear on specific legislators. When liaison officers did not attend, their senior executive actors or technicians from the bureaucracy were often asked to aid the committees; these executive actors could be queried by the liaison officers to ascertain the attitudes of different committee members.

None of the lobbyists for the private interest groups interviewed during the course of the present study were granted such privileges. In fact, a few of them, whose groups were at odds with the administration, expressed indignation at the advantages made available to the executive lobbyists.

Not all committees are willing to permit executive lobbyists such access, and some committees extend this advantage to only some departmental representatives. The House Ways and Means Committee is renown throughout the Congress and the executive system as a committee that always invites the departments to have their representatives attend its sessions. Senate Finance during the Kennedy Administration did not like having executive actors participate in its closed sessions, although some did. While a number of committees allowed the Kennedy lobbyists to sit in on their closed meetings, others merely invited them in to respond to certain questions; they were then expected to wait outside until the committee requested their presence again.

Despite this apparently invaluable advantage, at least three departmental liaison agents did not find such arrangements satisfactory. Two felt ill at ease sitting with all the members of the committee or subcommittee in executive session. "I feel awkward to be in their executive sessions," explained one liaison officer. "And anyway, it restrains my freedom of movement." His colleague from another department claimed that he did not attend a committee's executive sessions unless he was requested to speak on a matter that concerned the committee. He was fearful that otherwise the legislators would call him out of order. Moreover, as a staff assistant in the House, he had become convinced that the presence of executive actors stimulated some members to charge that the executive was trying to dominate the legislature. The third liaison officer agreed that it was better for executive lobbyists not to sit in regularly. The chairman of his House committee had invited him a number of times but he was inclined to refuse. His experience had been that, when he attended such sessions, the chairman invariably pushed aside the item under consideration and the members proceeded to make speeches to the administration and the secretary via the liaison officer. His preference and his practice, therefore, was to wait in the outer office of the committee while it met in closed session and to participate only when they called him in to ascertain what he thought the secretary's or the administration's views would be should the committee move in one direction or another.

(B) WORKING WITH COMMITTEE STAFF. Liaison officers and their assistants spend a considerable amount of time with committee staffs, since "so much of the program goes through them." Committee staffs want a wide range of aid from the departments. They need information on when proposed legislation will be sent to their committees, the current position of the secretary and his associates on policy, and the meaning and intent of specific provisions of executive bills. They require assistance in expediting departmental reports on bills, scheduling their committee hearings, and preparing committee reports. In turn, liaison officers seek information from them about the disposition of committee members toward executive bills and the intentions of the chairman as well as the others. Committee staffs are asked at times to poll their members in order "to call their attention to our bills which have been languishing there." The liaison officers reported that they concerned themselves principally with the chiefs of staff or chief clerks for the committees and with the staff aides closest to the chairman and subcommittee chairmen.

Robinson notes that State's liaison officer made a special effort to cultivate the staffs of its two primary committees.[14] These executive and legislative actors were more in contact with each other than were the liaison personnel with the personal staffs of legislators on the committees. It was not unusual, for example, for the Assistant Secretary for Congressional Relations to invite the committee staffs to a Christmas party with his own staff. Yet Robinson found that on the whole key committee aides

[14] Robinson, *op. cit.*, pp. 130–36.

were averse to cooperating with the executive staff when the latter requested information on the political thinking and intentions of committee members. It is possible, of course, that this reaction stemmed from the fact that at the time the committee majority belonged to one party while the executive system was controlled by the other party. The present study of liaison agents and congressmen during the Kennedy Administration, with one party controlling both the Congress and the departments, uncovered no hesitation among committee staff members to cooperate on such matters. It was obvious, however, that in the Senate Foreign Relations Committee as well as in one or two other committees, staff members did not always afford the legislative liaison staffs the respect and importance they exhibited toward actors from the more substantive areas of the departments.

Selling Legislation in the Search for Votes

(A) THE RELATIVE ADVANTAGES OF MERIT, ARM-TWISTING, AND FRIENDSHIP IN SELLING LEGISLATION. Regardless of the other resources at their disposal in soliciting legislative cooperation, departmental liaison officers, with two exceptions, were adamant in their conviction that the merit of their legislative proposals was their most effective asset for obtaining votes from congressmen. This was the position of even those whose departments commanded a rich supply of jobs, favors, and services. An Assistant Secretary of State for Congressional Relations in the Kennedy Administration disagreed. It was his contention that the great majority of congressmen were simply uninterested in the merits of his department's legislation; what counted with them was the extent to which the President committed himself to such legislation and mobilized public opinion behind it in their constituencies. His department's largest group of supporters, pointed out another liaison officer, was cultivated more by constituent-oriented services and favors than by the merit of its bills; as good Democrats, they were already disposed to support the department.

All agreed that the soft sell was their only effective approach. Acknowledging that the White House achieved results at times by arm-twisting, the departmental lobbyists repudiated this approach as inappropriate at their level. They recognized that congressmen could not be pushed around by departmental personnel, and with two exceptions they strongly affirmed that departmental liaison officers should make no such attempts. Two conceded somewhat uncertainly that they might engage in such tactics if they could, but that they controlled nothing of sufficient value to deny or deprive legislators.

Friendship was not judged a particularly useful exchange commodity for votes, although it was deemed a valuable asset in executive-legislative relations for obtaining information and other types of assistance. While all of the liaison officers stressed the importance of developing good personal relations with congressmen and their staffs, most of the departmental actors contended that congressmen would not vote for their legislation on this basis alone. An assistant to one liaison officer offered the following assessment of a friend:

> I am very close to Congressman X. We come from the same state and I was the state party chairman. He's on the Appropriations Committee, which is important for us, and he does a lot of favors for me personally and for the department, including influencing other congressmen. But he wouldn't give me a vote if he were opposed to our legislation or if it hurt his district.

Similar doubts about the effectiveness of friendship as a source of votes were expressed by one of State's chief liaison officers in the Kennedy Administration: "Friendship is a very weak reed if we want to rely on it for votes." If a particular vote were a test of friendship, he believed that it would not last long: "For the congressmen, a new vote comes along every day." A former lobbyist in the Eisenhower Administration entered a demurrer: had it not been for his friendship with his former employer in the Senate, the latter would probably have voted against the department's legislation. "But even here I had to persuade him," he added. Friendship alone was insufficient.

One liaison officer in a Kennedy department emphasized friendship more than his colleagues. He had recently aided a fellow liaison agent whose legislation, a priority item in the administration's program, had encountered considerable resistance in the Congress. Two or three legislators who resented all contacts from the department sponsoring the legislation had intended to cast negative votes. "I asked them to vote for the X bill, and they did—as a favor to me. They did this even though they said that this would hurt them somewhat in their congressional districts; and it did." Nevertheless, he too concurred in the general consensus that not more than a handful of such votes at the most could be obtained for any piece of legislation.

(B) EXPLICATION AND ADVOCACY. In selling their legislation, liaison officers resort primarily to explication as their principal tactic. Legislation is almost always complicated. By clarifying uncertainties and explaining how the legislation will work and what benefits it will produce, they provide a valuable service to the overburdened legislator who must vote on innumerable amendments and bills. All the liaison officers seek opportunities to explain their legislation to congressmen and their staffs. They utilize, at times, the straightforward approach employed by the

Treasury liaison officer who telephoned every senator's office to inquire whether the senator wished to be briefed on his department's bill. Or a legislator might be asked, in the course of a conversation about a bill, whether it presented any particular problems for him.

Liaison officers believe that clarification and explanation influence those legislators who are uncertain and on the fence. A number of executive lobbyists reported occasions when votes were secured in this manner or when someone who had previously voted in opposition switched to a live pair. And, of course, all of them claimed that they had to counteract their opponents, who presented their own interpretations. Complexities in both tax and agriculture bills and the unfamiliarity of urban legislators with agricultural policies placed an even greater burden on executive actors from these departments to explain and clarify their proposals.[15] A liaison officer in another domestic department reported that 99 per cent of the congressmen never asked questions about the details of his department's bills; nevertheless, he prepared intensively so that he knew in detail the bills he was peddling. He and the others felt that they had to be always prepared to explain the substance or effects of their bills.

Subtle interjections of advocacy in the course of explanation is considered proper and helpful by both executive and legislative actors. Even in indirect explanatory contacts, advocacy may be introduced. After his secretary had testified before a congressional committee on a bill, one liaison officer wrote to all the congressmen offering to send fact sheets, at their request, explaining the technicalities of the proposed legislation. A strong case of advocacy was built into such fact sheets, the liaison officer confessed.

Despite their conviction that the most effective tool for obtaining votes from a legislator is his personal opinion that a bill represents the best, most desirable solution to a problem, liaison officers recognize that a collateral approach may be necessary. If it can be demonstrated to legislators that a bill benefits their constituencies, they will be influenced favorably. On the other hand, to solicit their support for bills that congressmen consider incompatible with the politics or interests of their constituencies is to ask the congressmen to risk generating trouble for themselves, perhaps even endangering their prospects for reelection. Providing a legislator with a reason why he can afford to vote for a department's bill constitutes, therefore, another important tactic. "We recognize that a congressman

---

[15] The Treasury liaison officer during the Kennedy Administration reported that on the Kennedy tax bill he had contacted ninety-six senators face to face in an effort to explain the bill satisfactorily to them and to clear up misconceptions. In the House he had gotten as far as he could—150 members.

must work with his district and that he needs to win reelection. This means we have to know his congressional district and its problems. It also means that we have to help give him a rationale for voting for us."

One liaison officer discussed this tactic in terms of his problems in inducing conservative southern Democrats to support his bills. A number of these southerners wished to go along with the party, he reported, but they wanted to explain their vote in a manner consistent with their previously expressed philosophy. "If we can show them how they can do this by explaining that it is really the conservative thing to vote pro—that it would cost less in the long run—then we can enable them to come along." When this tactic did not work, liaison officers resorted to other actors to influence the legislators or they deferred to the political imperatives that congressmen faced. "If a member says that he cannot, that it will hurt him in his district when I ask for a vote, I say OK. If I have enough votes, I call the member and say, 'Vote against us, it's OK.' " Selling a bill—substantively and politically—demands great skill and perception from executive actors. They must at all times be sympathetic to the political problems of the legislators.

(C) LEGISLATIVE ACCOMMODATION. Another tactic used in virtually all departments, State claiming to be the exception, is altering bills to make them more acceptable to legislators. A liaison officer has earlier been described as dividing his potential supporters in the House of Representatives into three groups. The initial, pro-administration group was cultivated with services and favors. For the second set of legislators, more concerned with the nature of the legislation, adjustments were made in the bills. "Legislation is the art of the possible," he explained, "and the department is not omniscient or omnipotent. Lots of changes are made in bills which we propose, most of them to accommodate enough people to get a majority."

(D) DIRECT REQUESTS FOR VOTES. In soliciting support, executive lobbyists directly request votes from three groups of congressmen: supporters of the legislation, the undecided, and personal friends. It must be remembered that in most cases liaison officers rely upon other executive actors as well as upon legislative actors, professional lobbyists, and leaders of interest groups to approach congressmen directly for votes. Only one agency liaison officer and an assistant to a departmental liaison agent indicated that they did not directly solicit votes. The first asserted that it was not in accordance with the law, while the other believed that congressmen were not influenced by anyone at his level of importance in the department. A number of the assistants to the liaison officers sought votes from legislators only if they were personal friends.

In their study of the politics surrounding the extension of reciprocal trade agreements legislation during the Eisenhower Administration, Bauer and his associates express great surprise at the failure of private lobbyists to contact those legislators believed to oppose their bills. They conclude that, as a result of a reluctance to approach those designated as opponents, lobbyists miss important opportunities to pick up votes.[16] Milbrath, too, emphasizes the psychological barrier that inhibits lobbyists from communicating with known opponents in the legislature: it is painful for the lobbyists and they also consider such efforts a waste of time.[17] Robinson's study of the relation between State and Congress notes a similar reluctance on the part of the staff members of the Assistant Secretary for Congressional Relations.

On the whole the departmental lobbyists conformed to this pattern. If they knew a congressman had decided to oppose their legislation, they did not personally endeavor to dissuade him.[18] Whether such a tactic led to a failure on their part to communicate with those who might have been convinced or who might have agreed to a compromise could not be ascertained in this study. But since the liaison agents are part of a larger intelligence network, mistakes in assessing the intent of congressmen tended to be minimal.

(E) SEEKING VOTES FROM THE OPPOSITE PARTY. One aspect of liaison officer–legislator relations is not characteristic of the private lobbyist–legislator pattern. As distinct from the other Washington lobbyists, who, according to Milbrath, avoided being too closely identified with any political party,[19] there was never any question about the partisan identification of executive lobbyists in the Kennedy Administration. Executive lobbyists were extensions of their secretaries, who were, despite the previous Republican identification of two of them, active members of the Democratic administration. Moreover, departmental liaison officers were considered by White House liaison officers to be a subordinate element

---

[16] Bauer, Pool, and Dexter, *op. cit.*, p. 350.

[17] Milbrath, *op. cit.*, p. 217.

[18] A Republican Assistant Secretary for Congressional Relations contended that, while liaison agents rarely tried to convince their legislative opponents, opponents could sometimes be counteracted by other means. In one case he had deliberately played poker until late in the morning with a Texas Democratic congressman—a friend and former colleague—to ensure that this opponent would be asleep when the department's bill came to the floor. Another time he promised the floor manager of the bill that he would arrange for the withdrawal of a Republican friend— also an opponent—from the floor. The legislator did leave at the critical moment; he had been informed that the assistant secretary had information for him regarding one of his most important constituents. It must be understood, however, that such examples are definitely atypical of the behavior of liaison officers.

[19] Milbrath, *op. cit.*, pp. 207–8.

in their own operation. Except for State and Defense, legislative liaison agents and their assistants in the eight departments had all been Democratic partisans. State maintained a bipartisan staff below the level of the Assistant Secretary for Congressional Relations, whereas half of the staff commanded by the Assistant to the Secretary (DOD) for Legislative Affairs were uniformed personnel with no party identification.

Private lobbyists felt that partisanship was dysfunctional. How did it affect the liaison officers of the Kennedy Administration in carrying out their roles in the Congress? To what extent did they attempt to secure Republican as well as Democratic votes? And what strategy did they employ? Were they successful?

When Republican congressional leaders made a partisan issue out of a bill or when a particular issue had traditionally been entangled in partisan congressional politics, departmental liaison officers encountered extreme difficulty in cutting into Republican ranks. On minor bills or on those around which party lines had not rigidified, Republican votes were more easily obtained. In accordance with the pattern of liaison officer–congressional committee relations, departmental lobbyists worked, on the whole, more closely with Republicans on their committees than with those in the entire House or Senate. That the liaison officers were Democrats and represented a Democratic administration did not deter them from making the attempt. At the same time it was clear that, excluding State, Defense, and perhaps one other department, the liaison officers would have preferred to work with their own party colleagues in the Congress if they could have afforded to do so. The nature of the division within the Democratic party, in relation to the size of the Democratic contingent, often dictated a strategy of searching for Republicans in the House, whereas with a few exceptions these factors permitted the liaison officers to ignore Republicans in the Senate if they wished.

Liaison officers in two domestic departments complained that Republican votes in the House were almost impossible to obtain for their bills. One noted that minority party legislators had cooperated much more in 1961 than in 1962 or 1963. "Within the last year, they've become very partisan. I almost never get Republicans any more. So we've had to carry our legislation on a party basis, although this is much truer of the House than the Senate." He and his staff worked with the Republican side of his House committee, but not with other Republicans in any manner comparable with their approach to Democrats off the committee, almost all of whom were canvassed. On much of their legislation, both executive lobbyists reported that they went into the House with the feeling that they could not depend on the Republicans for assistance.

The second liaison officer was responsible for legislation upon which the parties had taken conflicting stands in their national platforms. This legislation had also sharply divided the Congress along partisan lines during the Eisenhower Administration. Discussing his House committee, he characterized it as extremely partisan: the Republicans were almost solidly opposed to the department's bills. Although he was friendly with a number of them, he worked personally with only two Republicans on the committee. "I don't bother with the rest—it's an absolute waste of time." With two or three Democrats "off the reservation," committee votes were extremely tight, and the bills were bitterly contested on the floor, the department winning or losing by very small margins. The House committee chairman had pressured the secretary and his aides to draft bills that would elicit broader support. "But this may mean surrender, not just compromise!" exclaimed the liaison officer. The department had proved willing to compromise on one bill long identified as a Democratic product, but the Republicans had insisted on moving the program involved to a different department where its very nature would have been altered. "Even then," he remarked, "a couple of them admitted to me that they would still vote against the bill." He reported considerable evidence that the House Republican leadership cracked the whip when his department's bills came up for a vote. One bill was just right for a Republican committee member, he said, and he had almost induced this member to vote favorably. "It's not a bad bill," the Republican had confessed to him. "If I were free I'd vote for the bill, but I can't. Halleck [the Republican floor leader] wouldn't accept it."

On the Senate side the liaison officer and his aides pointed to only three Republicans on the committee "who are reasonable and with whom we can reach some agreement." However, the preponderance of Democratic votes in the Senate negated the effect of Republican partisanship, and there was little if any need to seek Republican votes outside this committee.

In two other domestic departments where legislation also evoked a partisan division in presidential and congressional politics, the executive lobbyists reported a flexibility within Republican ranks that permitted a more rewarding emphasis upon a strategy of cooperation. These liaison officers and their superiors were prepared, in differing degrees in the two departments, to cooperate with the Republicans in shaping legislation. Again, this strategy was directed primarily toward the House, there being no problem about the Senate's passing their departmental bills in view of the size of its Democratic majority. Even in the Senate, however, the departments felt they had to seek Republican support as the race question intruded more and more into the administration of their programs in 1963 and as defections among southern Democrats increased.

"We work harder among the Republicans in the Senate than we might have done because of the segregation question," reported one of these officers. In the House he engaged in a special strategy aimed at the Republicans on his principal committee. It was dictated in part by the nature of the Democratic majority on that committee and by the chance to use committee Republicans to attract votes from other Republicans in the House. He spent much more time with the Republicans on his House committee than with the Democrats, principally because the latter were so predictable in their voting. Through the Republicans on his committee he felt that he was able to pick up the votes of other Republicans in the House: "I work with those who are really working on our legislation. My relationship with them is of great importance in bridging the gap to get the possible." His legislation, he explained, depended upon 150–160 certain Democratic votes, 30–35 southern Democratic votes, and 30–40 Republican votes. "The difference between getting twelve Republicans, those invariably voting with us, and forty to fifty is the amount of time and effort I spend with the Republicans on the committee." He worked with them on possible compromises. "They know I am testing Republican opinion beyond them this way." Three moderate Republicans on the committee, who were respected by their partisan colleagues in the House, represented the link to the additional votes from the opposition party. "It is always worth tailoring the legislation to their desires," he observed. He was proud of his relationship with the committee Republicans; they trusted and respected him and he spoke frankly with them.[20] Except for those on the committee, however, he had very little contact with Republican congressmen in general.

For cooperating with the Republicans on his House committee, the liaison officer was severely criticized by several lobbyists whose interest groups were allied with both the department and the administration. Nevertheless, he acknowledged only one possible liability: he had been trapped in a case of bill stealing while acting as the go-between for a Democratic subcommittee chairman and an ambitious Republican in working out a compromise on a bill. Since the Senate had already passed the bill, securing an agreement on the amendments that should be introduced was all that was involved. When negotiations between the two legislators collapsed, the Republican unexpectedly introduced a substitute bill embodying many provisions that Democratic senators had proposed. The liaison officer and the subcommittee chairman were both

---

[20] This assessment by the liaison officer was confirmed by the three Republicans on the committee who were interviewed.

embarrassed, the former being blamed by private lobbyists and others for permitting the Republicans to steal Democratic legislation. The subcommittee chairman subsequently introduced his own bill, which the House accepted, but the incident made the liaison agent wary of being caught in the middle between Democratic and Republican committee members. "Someone in my job has to play it carefully, even just to protect himself."

In another department the executive lobbyist operated on the following maxim in cooperating with Republicans as well as Democrats who often opposed the department's legislation: "It's always better to be on the inside looking out than on the outside looking in." This way, he contended, the department knew what such individuals were thinking, the latter trusted and cooperated more with the executive lobbyists, and compromises could more easily be worked out. "Our principle," said his deputy, "is never to close lines of communication with the minority for information or technical assistance on bills." Republican votes were considered worth cultivating, especially if the essence of the department's legislation were not compromised. This deputy had met with a House subcommittee considering a major departmental bill and succeeded in satisfying Republican objections to it. In this manner the department was able to redraft the bill so that the Republican subcommittee members could vote for it on the floor. In the Senate his superior labored to attract Republican votes behind one of the most important bills of the Kennedy Administration. The bill could not be moved in the House, and White House strategy called for a vote in the Senate, both to pressure the House and to provide an issue for the election campaign that year. The executive lobbyist had collaborated principally with one Republican and with a small group of his associates who were prepared to negotiate an acceptable compromise. Unfortunately, the Republican senator who was supposed to be the key for opening up enough Republican votes to compensate for Democratic defections was too atypical a member of his own party to deliver the others, and the strategy failed.

Only one liaison officer from a domestic department assumed a completely bipartisan posture. He was a loyal Democrat, he insisted, but he was bipartisan in his congressional relations, which fact was widely recognized in the Congress. "I have strong bipartisan relationships—honestly and on as well as off the record." He judged none of the bills in his department to be partisan.

For the most part those liaison officers in the domestic departments of the Kennedy Administration who tailored their bills and engaged in other collaborative endeavors with Republican legislators did so principally because their bills could not command legislative majorities among the Democrats alone. Two of their counterparts in the Eisenhower Administration expressed the same reason for having sought Democratic support. They and their associates did approach Democratic as well as Republican legislators; but "if we had had the votes," said one, "there would have been no need to work with the Democrats." Another, an assistant to a Republican senator in 1962–63, noted that: "They [the Democratic departmental liaison officers] are in a much better position than we were in, since on most items they don't have to come to the Republicans to make a majority in the Senate."

When I returned to Washington, D.C., after the Democratic majority in the House of Representatives had ballooned as a result of the 1964 election, the situation had been totally altered. House Republicans who had been cooperating with Democratic liaison officers from the domestic departments complained ruefully that, except in the case of the bipartisan agent, they were not being contacted as in the previous Congress. There were Democratic votes in abundance, they explained, and the administration could win despite sizable southern defections. Since Republican votes had sharply depreciated in value, the liaison officers had lost much of their incentive to seek out and compromise with Republican members. Both liaison officers and Republican congressmen were well aware that when the Democratic liaison officers had sought their help, it had not been granted without some modifications in the legislation.

CHAPTER VIII

Strategies and Tactics II: Indirect Lobbying

TWO RECENT STUDIES of lobbying in Washington, D.C., are relevant to initiate a consideration of indirect lobbying by the liaison agents. Lester W. Milbrath's sample of Washington lobbyists expressed the belief that a direct presentation of their own case to decision-makers was much more effective than any indirect approach, i.e., the use of others or through the communications media.[1] But although 80 per cent of his respondents preferred the direct personal approach and rated it the most effective, they relied increasingly upon intermediaries who were presumed to have better access to decision-makers. This shift away from the direct approach had occurred despite its being considered less complicated, less risky, and less expensive than the indirect method. Milbrath advances this explanation for the change: The competition for the attention of legislators has become so great and the communications overload on the legislators so heavy that lobbyists resort to alternative routes to ensure that their messages will get to the legislators. "The high competition of lobbyists trying to deliver direct messages to officials encourages lobbyists to seek alternative transmission routes which have better access."[2]

The authors of the second study, concerning the politics surrounding reciprocal trade agreements legislation in 1953–55, stress the point that when lobbyists shifted from acting as auxiliaries (to allied legis-

[1] Lester W. Milbrath, *The Washington Lobbyists* (Chicago: Rand McNally, 1963), pp. 211–15.
[2] *Ibid.*, pp. 231, 234. Officials in this study included not only legislators but also executive actors, although Milbrath's primary emphasis seems to have been upon congressmen and their staffs.

lators) to acting as agents of persuasion, they were more likely to resort to stimulating and involving other actors. The other actors were "generally congressmen, businessmen, public figures, and the like whose application of pressure usually is regarded as more legitimate than is the same activity if carried out by a paid representative of some special interest."[3]

In effect, Bauer, Pool, and Dexter are contending that lobbyists believe they can more effectively present a case if they utilize intermediaries rather than approach congressmen directly themselves. From their common emphasis upon communications theory, the authors of this study agree with Milbrath that congressmen were exposed to demands from many directions and that their communications networks with their constituents and committees, etc., were generally overloaded. But Bauer and his associates also discovered that the congressmen were in actuality not overloaded in their communications from lobbyists, which finding clashes with Milbrath's point regarding the high competition among lobbyists to deliver direct messages. Bauer, Pool, and Dexter note with great surprise something they had not anticipated: "how few were the congressmen who had heard anything from the major pressure groups."[4] Many congressmen not only were puzzled as to how they should vote, but would have appreciated some clearer indication of what the issues were. This does not sound as if the attention of the legislators was being besieged by lobbyists from a great variety of interest groups. While it is true that the second study was devoted to one special issue only, its authors seem inclined to extend their conclusions to lobbyists and issues in general.

Strategy of the Proper Mix: Indirect and Direct Approaches

Legislative liaison officers for the departments deviated from and yet coincided in some respects with this pattern of lobbyists for private groups. It must be kept in mind that one important role of executive lobbyists was to help focus the intervention of their senior leaders in the Congress. Liaison officers *did not,* in contrast with Milbrath's sample of lobbyists, rate direct presentation on their own part as the most effective way of carrying their departments' case to legislators. Rather they recognized, with perhaps one exception, that their senior political officers were

[3] Raymond A. Bauer, Ithiel de Sola Pool, and Lewis Anthony Dexter, *American Business and Public Policy: The Politics of Foreign Trade* (New York: Atherton Press, 1963), p. 357.
[4] *Ibid.,* p. 351. Bauer and his co-authors conclude at one point that the following axiom lies at the heart of effective lobbying: "The job is to approach the right congressman at the right time and in the right way" (*ibid.,* p. 432). Ignoring at this moment the critical question of time, the concept "right congressman" and "right way" are in large part components in the strategy of the proper mix.

more important than they in the eyes of the congressmen. Consequently these other executive actors engaged in most of the selling and a good deal of the vote-getting. They constituted an extremely valuable resource around which strategy was designed. The liaison officers did see themselves, however, as playing a direct and effective role with Congress as bargainers and as agents of persuasion, which contrasts with the findings of Bauer, Pool, and Dexter. The central proposition for the executive lobbyists was that their approach was basically that of a mix of senior executive actors and themselves; one that was most congruent with the mix of legislators with whom they had to deal. In some departments it was slanted much more to the senior executive leaders; in others the liaison agent played a larger direct role himself.

This strategy reflected what lobbyists referred to as the "rifle" rather than the "shotgun" approach. It was based upon the theory that each legislator had to be treated as a unique actor who responded better with some actors, worse with others, and indifferently with still others. To succeed, an approach to the Congress had to be tailored to particular executive actors who possessed the best access to the legislators. For lobbyists in general, it was not, as Bauer, Pool, and Dexter imply, a strategy based upon fear or reluctance, nor was it essentially, as Milbrath suggests, derivative from the intensity of competition among lobbyists and others to communicate directly with legislators. The individual legislator—the target—was the determining factor; the executive actor with the best access to him, the dependent variable. Affecting this strategy, of course, was the amount of time senior executive leaders could devote to Congress, their willingness to engage in such politics, and their personal temperaments. Two other primary considerations in the employment of particular executive actors in this mix were the nature of their personal relations with the legislators and the level of policy and politics involved. Nevertheless, at certain times and with certain legislators these considerations were ignored or carried less weight than was usually the case.

The pattern that developed in one large confederate department illustrates the complexity of the proper mix as a strategy. Its liaison officer reported that he dealt with the Senate primarily through other executive actors, whereas in the House of Representatives he assumed greater responsibility for dealing personally with its members. In each case there were exceptions to this overall pattern.

Since the chairman of the substantive Senate committee liked the secretary very much, it was the department head who was his chief contact; the liaison officer met with the chairman approximately once a week. The liaison agent worked with most members on that committee from time to time, but he relied principally upon others in the department, including one member of his own staff, to handle them. The principal executive actor to work with the chairman of the department's subcommittee on appropriations in the Senate was an assistant secretary who came from the senator's state and knew him well. In his capacity as adviser, the liaison officer discussed with the secretary and the assistant secretary the political nuances of the business to be transacted before they visited the two chairmen. These senior executive leaders always kept him informed on what had occurred at such meetings. With the chairman of another Senate committee, whose jurisdiction covered part of the department's program, it was the liaison officer, as an old friend, who was the principal executive actor.

The pattern of relations with members of the main House committee was less precise. The liaison officer saw the chairman at least three times a week. When legislation was pending in the committee, the rate of their direct personal contact rose to three or more times a day, plus considerable communication over the telephone. The rule determining which executive actors would deal directly with the chairman depended on the issue. On questions of major policy the secretary was brought in. Apropos of legislation or departmental action affecting the chairman's state, the undersecretary or an administrator from one of the agencies, both from that state, met with the chairman. On more routine matters of legislation and on the politics of processing the legislation through the committee or the House, the liaison officer acted as the principal contact with the chairman. Nevertheless, he noted, these general rules pertaining to the House committee chairman were violated more often than not, depending upon who was available and how busy the various executive actors were.

With the rest of the House committee, the liaison officer ordinarily spent approximately ten to fifteen hours a week. Legislation pending in the committee greatly multiplied his contacts with its members. On such occasions, except for the time he spent in his secretary's office, he would occupy himself, from 9:30 A.M. until 6 P.M. every day, with individual members or with the committee as a whole when he was called into its executive sessions. A number of the active senior members on the committee, Democrats and Republicans, he handled personally. The second-ranking Democrat was depicted by this executive actor as working harder on the committee's business than the chairman. The liaison officer worked with this influential legislator on the political aspects of the committee, while the assistant administrator in an agency dealt with him on the program part of the legislation. The liaison agent observed, however, that he too discussed policy with this congressman. In addition, he assumed primary responsibility for working with those having the least amount of seniority, although his contacts with such members were more with Democrats than with Republicans.

How and why did he use intermediaries to approach others on this committee? He reported that the ranking Republican and he maintained a very formal relationship. Consequently he utilized the department head with this congressman as much as possible. In the case of another congressman, a Democrat, the liaison officer worked almost entirely through the legislator's assistant, who was a close friend of his. When necessary, the liaison officer relied also upon an official in an interest group from the congressman's state. A senior southern Democrat, who frequently opposed the department, was handled entirely by a senior executive leader from his state who was familiar with its politics. The liaison officer had personally approached this congressman not more than three times during his service with the department, and then only in a formal manner.[5] On the Senate committee he worked with a number of Democrats and a few Republicans, but he relied heavily upon others in the department for their contacts with particular senators.

It was his job, asserted this liaison officer, to know who in the department and its agencies were the proper individuals to work with each legislator. With some legislators, it was a question of their desiring to deal with high-ranking officials; with others, it was a matter of personal friendship. A few preferred executive actors who were political allies from their states, while still other legislators were satisfied with someone with expertise who had collaborated with them on previous occasions. One element in this pattern of relationships was clear. Aside from senior leaders who were requested for status reasons, executive actors were useful as intermediaries by virtue of their being known and trusted by the legislators. They could be relied upon not to mislead the latter into taking a position that might prove disadvantageous to them in their roles within the legislative system or that might harm their chances for renomination and reelection in their constituencies. To the extent that the liaison officer established a relationship of confidence or usefulness with these legislators, he too was able to work with them. Where he had not, he was aware that he had to be much more cautious in personally approaching them: "You can wear out your welcome pretty quick with some of these guys."

This was only one department, of course, and it represented a unified team effort on the part of the liaison officer and his political superiors and associates. His department contained not only a large number

[5] This senior Democrat found it difficult to remember the name of the secretary's liaison agent, so infrequently had the two been in contact. In contrast, all the others on the committee, Republicans and Democrats, immediately responded correctly when asked to identify him.

of senior leaders but the type who were politically oriented and willing to engage in selective lobbying. To the extent that the other departments approximated this one in their use of strategy, the considerations that determined the mix in this department prevailed in the others.

In only one case was I aware of a departmental lobbyist condemning the use of a particular class of senior political actors. A U.S. ambassador to a communist country had returned to assist in persuading Congress to adopt a more flexible approach to that country in an AID bill. The Assistant Secretary for Congressional Relations considered his involvement a serious political mistake, an opinion concurred in by a predecessor from another administration. It was their position that an ambassador should be completely detached from congressional politics and never appear to legislators as an advocate for a foreign country in the Congress.

Bringing Legislative and Executive Actors Closer Together: Creating Better Understanding

State, in particular, has employed a broad-gauged approach of bringing together legislative and executive actors as one strategy for coping with its environment. Its legislative liaison agents and friendly critics agree that friction between the department principally responsible for foreign affairs and the Congress is inevitable. Distrust and misunderstanding characterize the relations between both sets of actors. Although the authorization committees themselves are sympathetic, the larger legislative system is hostile. Consequently, one strategy is to encourage favorable contacts between members of the two systems on the assumption that the attitudes and semantics that mar their relations will be altered.

The Kennedy Administration did not initiate this strategy. When the office of Assistant Secretary for Congressional Relations was established in the Truman Administration, one of the first steps its occupant took, according to a long-time staff member with this office, was "to bring people together so that those on the Hill and those in the department would see each other as real people. There is a difference between people and bureaucrats, and we wanted to show that these were people." The assistant secretary's principal tactic was to invite all House members to the Forrestal House in groups of twenty-five to thirty to meet with leaders of the department. Separate meetings were held with senators, who attended in smaller groups. "It was pretty useful" was the conclusion of an immediate subordinate to the assistant secretary at the time. The entire leadership of the department attended, each of whom spoke. Congressmen were afforded an opportunity to address questions on any subject to the secretary, undersecretary, and assistant secretaries. At the same time individual legislators were able to meet socially with the senior leadership of the department in an informal atmosphere, with food and liquor available to help expedite the process. Those who organized these get-togethers were obviously very sensitive that they might be criticized for employing appropriated funds to lobby, for the costs of such entertainment were borne personally by the undersecretary and all the assistant secretaries. "It was very important work and not one drop of booze was paid for by government funds for this project. We even paid for the lights in the place so there would not be any criticism."

In the Kennedy Administration, Assistant Secretary for Congressional Relations Frederick G. Dutton also devoted himself to "narrowing the gap," as he phrased it, between State and the Congress. Weekly off-the-record briefings were organized in the House of Representatives at which key State Department people spoke to congressmen. This was an attempt to make the department functional to the general membership of the House and to afford the congressmen some guidance on foreign policy issues. It was felt in the department that many House members were no longer looking to the Foreign Affairs Committee for guidance. In the Senate, however, the department continued to concentrate upon the prestigious Foreign Relations Committee.

When the effectiveness of this particular tactic was judged solely in terms of the number of legislators responding, the results were not spectacular. This assistant secretary himself admitted the department was fortunate if fifty or more attended a briefing; many told him that they simply did not have the time. In an article Dutton also pointed out that "some who stay away claim they don't get the unequivocal answers they want."[6] As expressed to me, however, the reaction of such congressmen was much harsher: They were being fed pap; they could learn more by reading the *New York Times;* and the answers to their questions never reflected a dialogue between foreign policy experts and legislators but a restatement of the official line.

To establish better contact with other actors in the legislative system, briefing sessions were organized for the staffs of senators and representatives. According to Dutton, four such briefings evoked a sensational turnout. He estimated that between four and five hundred staff aides attended, together with an undersecretary and assistant secretaries, for one-and-one-half-hour sessions. Another tactic employed was the distribution to all congressional offices of speeches by executive leaders on background papers. This elicited a very favorable comment from the Hill.

Dutton's key innovation, however, was his effort "to do missionary work for Congress inside the department." One of his major responsibilities, he contended, was that of acting as a bridge between the department

<hr>

[6] Frederick G. Dutton, " 'Cold War' Between the Hill and Foggy Bottom," *New York Times Magazine,* September 15, 1963, p. 95.

and the Congress, extending better understanding both ways—to the members of each system. As he saw the situation, if the two were fumbling for communication, each contemptuous of the other, then out of necessity part of his strategy had to be oriented toward his own department. Executive attitudes of hostility and contempt for legislators were dysfunctional for the department. It depended on the legislature for authorization and appropriation legislation, and it required a permissive atmosphere for discretion and innovation in administrative organization as well as in foreign policy. Consequently, he developed a number of devices to help educate foreign policy personnel to the thinking, environment, and needs of the legislators.

A number of senators were invited by the Assistant Secretary for Congressional Relations to meet with Foreign Service officers. Perceptive assistants to legislators were also brought in to meet with senior departmental officials so the latter could pick their brains on congressional criticism and on their suggestions for dealing more effectively with the Congress. Against considerable resistance in his own department, Dutton inaugurated a program whereby junior Foreign Service officers spent a two-week internship in a congressman's office. Conceding that this brief period was inadequate, he maintained that it was at least a step in the right direction: career officers could begin to appreciate the problems of the Congress, and legislators could see bureaucrats as human beings and realize that State was interested in their problems. Career officers scheduled to go overseas and those returning were also encouraged to visit their congressmen and to return to their congressional districts while on leave.

Agriculture is another department whose legislative liaison staff during the Kennedy Administration sought to educate congressional actors on its workings and services. Its approach was more narrowly focused than State's. One of the assistants to the chief liaison officer made it a practice, in 1961 (but not in 1962, "because it was an election year"), of taking staff members of legislators on "educational" trips. Groups of twelve or more administrative and legislative assistants from the Agriculture Committees in the House and Senate were invited to observe various parts of the department in operation. One visit was to an agricultural experiment station "to improve their understanding of the appropriations angle." Another visit stemmed from the fact that the Soil Conservation Service, an agency within the department, had informed her that congressmen did not understand the Watershed Act and what it was accomplishing. A number of staff aides to Agriculture Committee members accompanied her and an SCS representative to a nearby watershed project. The local mayor and banker lunched with them and explained how the act affected their community. Not only did the trip educate staff members of legislators who were significant to the department, reported the liaison agent, but it afforded her an opportunity to become acquainted with those whom she did not know, and under very favorable conditions. She made no attempt during the trip to sell the department's program.

While the initiative in this strategy of bringing legislative and executive actors together for better understanding originated with the liaison officers, the resources used to carry it out were provided by the senior political leaders of the departments and the bureaucracy. To the extent that the latter two were sympathetic to the need for improved relations with the Congress and understood the problems of the liaison officers, the job of these executive lobbyists was greatly facilitated. Where this was not the case and the other executive actors were indifferent or uncooperative, liaison officers operated under a considerable handicap in employing such a strategy.

Outside Interest Groups: A Resource for the Indirect Approach

In addition to employing other executive actors, legislative liaison officers may utilize another resource outside of the legislature to communicate with and influence legislators—the support that interest groups and their lobbyists can provide. In four of the eight departments covered in the study, liaison officers worked actively with and enlisted the aid of outside lobbyists; in the other four departments, they had little or no contact with these lobbyists or their interest groups. When interest groups did become active in the Congress in behalf of the latter departments, it was frequently on their own initiative and in persuance of their own goals. On the other hand, bureau chiefs maintained close relations with their own clientele groups, and senior leaders associated with the secretaries had access to such groups as well as to others that concerned themselves with a range of issues, and therefore a number of departments. While close collaboration between executive actors and lobbyists from interest groups existed, the liaison officers in these departments played virtually no role in it.

The liaison officers in four departments solicited the cooperation of such outside lobbyists and their interest groups, crediting them with facilitating their jobs and with contributing materially to the cause of their departments' legislation in the Congress. These liaison officers worked carefully at maintaining good relations with clientele groups and cooperated with the more general interest groups. They shared with them ideas and information regarding policy and legislators, and they collaborated in canvassing the Congress. In providing intelligence regarding the Congress, cooperative groups and their lobbyists served as one important means for reducing the uncertainty inherent in executive-legislative relations. The liaison officers sought to ensure that these lobbyists and the communications they generated in their own interest groups focused properly upon those congressmen with whom they were most influential. In two departments the liaison officers helped organize ad hoc coalitions of interest groups behind specific pieces of legislation and served as the principal day-to-day departmental representatives with such coalitions.

Even within these departments, there were issue areas where the executive actors expressed doubt that certain interest groups could furnish significant help. Such groups might occasionally transmit important information on congressmen, and some might prove useful in conducting an accurate head count in the legislature—both valuable adjuncts to the intelligence roles of the liaison officers—but their impact upon the congressmen in securing support for the department was considered negligible.

On the other hand, the executive agents were very much aware that some of these same interest groups could hurt the departments' legislation in the Congress by opposing it. The liaison agents sought the cooperation of these groups on the assumption that legislators were more likely to take affirmative action in the absence of controversy among the concerned parties.

Liaison officers in two departments worked with the interest groups and their lobbyists, but primarily as subordinates to their senior political leaders. With respect to one major piece of legislation, the undersecretary in one department played the principal role in establishing a broad citizens' committee of various groups to exert pressure upon the Congress. In lining up interest-group support for their bills, the secretary, undersecretary, and liaison officer were all active. The former two concerned themselves with the major general groups—NAM, AFL-CIO, U.S. Chamber of Commerce. The legislative liaison officer worked primarily with the smaller business associations, religious organizations, and other minor groups. The three endeavored to explain and to sell the proposed legislation to such groups. Subsequently they also worked closely with many of them in contacting legislators. With some groups their concern was to neutralize them so as to eliminate their active opposition in the Congress.

In the other two departments, the liaison officers themselves assumed the major responsibility for lining up the interest groups. One of these liaison agents reported that he had recently carried out the difficult assignment of setting up a wide coalition behind a departmental bill, which was also an administration item. The important but uncommitted groups were especially cultivated: "You try to get them aboard. You use your ingenuity and good sense to help them get aboard." He had invited their representatives to his strategy meetings, arranged for others to "connect them into the coalition," and persuaded their leaders to deliver speeches in behalf of the legislation. After considerable tugging and pulling among the groups, an ad hoc committee was established with a full-time secretary whom he helped choose. He worked very closely with her to coordinate the various groups in the coalition. According to the two of them, the coalition legitimized what was essentially an innovative policy, and its constituent groups were important in alerting their people in the field to the merits of the legislation. Their system of communications with people in the constituencies became, in effect, that of the department. "The mail that they can generate in support of legislation is terribly important—they can pull out the stops if they want to." The liaison officer's experience as a staff assistant in the Congress had taught him how influential such concerted efforts were with legislators.

Such coalitions of interest groups can pose troublesome problems for liaison officers. Aside from the initial problem of activating disparate groups to join together, attempting to keep them working in tandem can prove difficult. His legislation, observed one liaison officer, was supported by a number of groups, each of whom was interested in a different provision. "One critical part of my function is to keep both types of groups in harmony. Each thinks the other's provision is not a suitable device. Each has to feel, therefore, that we're a hundred and eighty degrees behind its proposal." Fully one-third of his time was spent with the interest groups: making certain they remained active, coordinating their efforts, and smoothing the relations among them. One could say that the interest groups constituted a separate set of clients for some liaison officers. In fact, one liaison agent used a term analogous to "clients": "I think that by and large my customers are satisfied with my job."

The attitude among liaison officers in the other four departments toward mobilizing and using the resources of interest groups ranged from a flat denial of any such responsibility to a realization that whatever groups were associated with their departments had no political muscle. The most negative position was that espoused by an executive lobbyist in a domestic department who insisted that he maintained no contact with interest groups; in fact, he denied that it was incumbent upon him to do so. Such a responsibility, he asserted, lay with the public relations officer and the substantive agencies within his department. Since his Republican counterpart in the previous administration had maintained liaison with a number of interest groups, it may be surmised that a matter of style as well as role orientation was at issue.

That style may be a factor was evident from the remarks of a liaison agent for another domestic department in this group: "I just don't use the tactics of marshaling letters and telegrams." He was suspicious of such tactics and reluctant to utilize interest groups for fear of building up antagonism against himself and his department. He reported having sat in on some conferences with outside lobbyists and having attended a few of their luncheons, but he boasted that so far he had been able to avoid using them.[7] He could recall having coordinated with two groups that were interested in one of his bills, but he simply preferred not to work with interest groups and their lobbyists in approaching the Congress. His Republican counterpart in the Eisenhower Administration disclosed a different pattern. He had established close relations with certain groups, and he and others in the department had worked "at pulling them along for our position." They had been utilized, he said, "as troops on the Hill."

In State, the nondomestic department among the four, liaison officers expressed considerable regret that their department did not have the natural or influential constituency that was the fortune of the other departments. One Assistant Secretary for Congressional Relations characterized the many volunteer organizations that sought to help the department in the Congress as very ineffective, having little impact upon legislative process or policy. Had State the backing of the Kiwanis and Rotary clubs in the country, he maintained, his department would be supported by groups strategically distributed throughout congressional districts and highly respected by the legislators. The liaison staff in AID agreed with the staff of State that the interest groups supporting their policies were basically ineffective in terms of the needs of the foreign policy agencies in the Congress.[8] In both State and AID, however, responsibility for liaison with such groups was assigned to other executive actors.

[7] Interviews with lobbyists from a number of interest groups closely concerned with legislation and policy in his department revealed that some either knew very little about this liaison agent, confirming his lack of contact with them, or felt that in certain policy areas he was simply not part of the department's inner group on strategy and tactics of politics.

[8] An interview in 1967 conducted by Professor Richard F. Fenno, Jr., with the AID liaison officer elicited the same general conclusions. However, this liaison officer claimed that the program was in trouble not because of the absence of a constituency but because many people had grave doubts about the program. "Any program which can't claim success will have the same trouble. Look at the poverty program and the troubles it's getting into. They can't bring it out because they haven't the votes . . . because of its lack of success." Nevertheless, the results of the Office of Economic Opportunity's campaign to secure its legislation that year demonstrated that a strong lobbying effort had ultimately been marshaled in its behalf by some of its friends, and by Republican as well as Democratic mayors whose personal solicitation of their congressmen did pay off for OEO's bill. See the *New York Times,* December 25, 1967.

Eliciting the Resources of the Majority Party Leadership in the Congress

In the Congress, legislative liaison officers are outsiders. They are accepted, permitted, even encouraged to carry out their roles by members of the legislature, but they remain representatives from another competitive system. Legislators interact more frequently and intimately with members of their own system, particularly in those specialized formal and informal subsystems to which they belong in the Congress. A subsystem of great importance to the operation in each house of the Congress is the official majority party leadership. The majority leaders, the whips, and the Speaker in the House comprise this group of actors. In a system where pieces of power must be carefully fitted together into majorities and where timing is a crucial factor, such general party leaders are on the whole better attuned than are outsiders to the nuances of mood among their party members. As insiders, they exercise a significant degree of control over the legislative process on the floor and wield considerable influence among members of their party. It is imperative, therefore, that executive agents adopt a strategy designed to utilize such partisan leaders.

Such a strategy clearly works best when both sets of actors have a common partisan identification. Since during the Kennedy Administration both the executive and legislative systems were officially led by Democrats, the liaison officers called upon the official leaders of the House and Senate as fellow partisans. It was these general party leaders, as distinct from committee chairmen, who were invited to the Monday-morning leadership conferences in the White House with the President—the ultimate superior in the executive system and the recognized leader of both sets of partisan actors. Both sets of actors, consequently, had in common not only party identification, but a common legislative program. On a working level, both had something to gain by cooperating with each other: the legislators could more effectively exercise their leadership, and the executive lobbyists could improve the prospects for their legislation.

Legislative liaison officers and their superiors made it a practice at least to touch base with the leadership on all of their bills. Close work between them occurred only on the major pieces of legislation and on the tough ones, the two almost invariably coinciding. When the departments encountered no trouble with their bills on the floor of the House or Senate, liaison officers maintained only minimal contact with the leadership. Such was invariably the case with Defense. Liaison officers were inclined to defer to the White House in dealing with the Speaker of the House of Representatives; they worked much more with the majority leaders in the

House and the Senate as well as with their whips. Nevertheless, some did work closely with the Speaker.

One leadership resource that the liaison officers sought to employ was their influence in the scheduling of legislation. Only two types of aid in scheduling bills were mentioned by departmental liaison officers: help with the House Rules Committee and delaying the announcement of votes so that additional politicking could alter the outcome. Although one or two of the departmental lobbyists tended to rely on the White House for obtaining a rule from the House Rules Committee, most worked through their secretaries or their committee chairmen; a few personally solicited the assistance of the Speaker. Even those whose legislation rarely encountered difficulties in the Rules Committee contacted their allies among its members to obtain advice and information regarding its intentions. This committee always had to be handled carefully, since the type of rule as well as the timing of the debate and vote could vitally affect the chances of legislation. Therefore, it was essential on controversial bills to hold strategy sessions regarding the committee with the majority leader, key members of the Rules Committee, and/or the Speaker.

"The leadership becomes especially important on major bills such as ours that barely get through the House," explained one liaison officer. "They can help us by stalling the vote, and they are then in a position to switch votes for us on the floor." On one bill, his department was behind 192 to 200 when the leadership employed a delaying tactic and held up the announcement so that congressmen could come to the well of the House to inquire how they were recorded. In the interval the leadership "engaged in some trading, saying: 'Go with us on X and we'll let you off on the Y bill.' " With others, "they appealed and pleaded with members: 'Damn it, come along, we need just one or two more votes.' " On this occasion, sufficient votes were changed so that the final tally stood at 202 to 197. Another liaison officer disclosed that, when departmental and White House solicitation had still left a number of legislators undecided and the necessary majority had not been reached, the party leadership was asked to engage in a final effort for votes. "They have the ability to marshal extra votes, to work on the undecided in a manner we can't." The leadership was "focused in" by the departmental and White House lobbyists so that "they would not scatter their shots, but concentrate them where they could do the most good. We help direct their attention to where the marginal members are—the ones in doubt."

Since with one exception departmental liaison officers in the Kennedy Administration experienced little trouble in the Senate, fewer demands were made upon its majority leader for direct aid in procuring votes and scheduling action. An Assistant Secretary for Congressional

Relations (State) from a previous Democratic administration described an approach to the Senate which none of the Kennedy departmental liaison agents emulated. The Senate, he observed, was run like a club, with an inner circle of members from both parties who made the decisions. Its members lunched frequently with Leslie Biffle, the Senate parliamentarian. The assistant secretary had requested Biffle to arrange such a luncheon for him and permit him to handle the conversation. "They ate and then sat around and drank bourbon," he recalled. "This way we worked out much of the X legislation." If the department wanted to bring debate to an end in the Senate, all that was necessary was "to get them to agree and somehow it always happened. The Vice President would say very fast, 'Unanimous consent to end debate on Friday. Any objections? None.' Senators would look around and mutter, 'What happened?' only to be answered by others, 'It's OK, this has all been arranged.' "

The Democratic leaders also permitted the departmental agents the use of their offices immediately off the floor in order for them to campaign among the members. In the House it was the Speaker's office; in the Senate, that of the majority leader. Such close proximity facilitated last-minute lobbying. Since, moreover, Democratic congressmen talked with the executive agents and their principals in the quarters of their own legislative leaders, this lobbying was legitimized and the arrangements were conducive to more satisfactory results. All but three of the departmental lobbyists reported having worked with their secretaries in the legislative leaders' offices to convince undecided or wavering legislators and to work out compromises. Sometimes they were aided in the Senate by the chief assistants of senators who were their allies. Defense, on the other hand, indicated that it had never found it necessary to employ such tactics, and the new legislative liaison officer in Commerce had not been engaged in a major legislative battle in the Senate at the time of his interviews. Only one liaison officer, who represented a domestic department, repudiated such tactics, asserting that he was opposed to working out of the Speaker's chambers. This was the liaison agent who contended that he was known throughout the House as being bipartisan in his orientation and whose bills were primarily bipartisan.

The most frequent occasion for liaison officer–party leadership interactions arose out of the need of the former for advice and intelligence and the reciprocal need of the legislators for information to help them function effectively as leaders of their party in the Congress. The initiative for this exchange of important resources stemmed primarily from the executive actors. In the process both sets of actors, together with White House liaison officers on administration legislation, comprised, in effect, a joint legislative-executive partisan team. On each major bill a different set of executive actors combined with the majority party leadership to pool their common knowledge, to plan together, and to ensure proper coverage of those legislators who remained to be contacted. Private lobbyists were also at times brought directly into this combined type of operation. Departmental lobbyists were eager to obtain information from the Democratic leadership as to when their bills would be scheduled, what problems could be anticipated, and what the prospects were for their enactment. "I ask the majority leader for advice. He's a good sounding board since he's there all the time and talks with the members. Will there be trouble on the bill next week? What are its chances?" Executive actors need to know and to advise their own superiors when to move legislation and when to delay in order to pick up votes, who is undecided, and which actor can most effectively approach these legislators. What better source for such information than the leaders of the legislature who share their partisan identification?

In their search for information, liaison officers must try to gauge the voting intentions of members of the legislative system. All liaison officers and their staffs are constantly operating as intelligence agents in their own right. However, the party leadership possesses its own formal communications network through the party whip system. The whip count is an instrument of the leadership for canvassing its partisans to ascertain how they are disposed toward bills. The executive lobbyists sought to activate the whip system to learn how the leadership assessed the chances of their bills. "They should be able to tell exactly where we stand at the moment, who is undecided. And that way we should know better how hard we have to work." Another stated: "The whip count helps show us where the problems are. So we have to depend on them. But a lot of this intelligence we try to do ourselves."

In effect, two communications networks are integrated at this point —that of the executive party and that of its comparable legislative party —in an effort to obtain the best intelligence assessment possible on the voting intentions of each legislator. Whereas the legislative whip system is a formal, systematized process, that of the liaison agents is considerably less so.

According to the departmental lobbyists, the congressional leadership wanted from them a clear idea of the problems that would confront these legislative actors when executive bills came to the floor: the amount of strength upon which executive leaders could count, the areas in which the bill might be subjected to damaging amendments, the counteraction envisaged by executive actors in such cases, the degree of support that was expected for specific provisions of a bill, what changes the executive sponsors would themselves propose. "We exchange information," noted

226

one liaison officer, "about strategy, congressional opinion, the voting intentions of congressmen, amendments—anything that will affect our bill's chances on the floor."

Despite the fact that they were partisan allies, an element of tension and conflict characterized the relations between the Kennedy departmental liaison agents and the House leadership. In all probability some tension was inevitable between allies who had their own frames of reference and priorities despite their common interests. A major contributing factor was the abrupt shift in the Democratic House leadership upon the death of Speaker Sam Rayburn during the first year of the Kennedy Administration. A less experienced team took over, led by Speaker John S. McCormack, who had associated with him a new majority leader and a new whip. From a different perspective, one could also say there was some professional jealousy between the two sets of intelligence agents. However, a number of the departmental agents and their associates alleged that the congressional whip system in the House was itself inherently flawed, no matter who managed it.

Two liaison officers underscored the weakness of the new Speaker. An able, perceptive Speaker was crucial to their dealing with the House. In addition to his use of the whip system, the Speaker had to establish his own informal relations with individual members so that he could adequately sense the mood of the House. "The only way the leadership can operate effectively is to know in advance what the House is going to do. When the leadership doesn't have the capacity to ascertain this reliably, everything really gets mixed up." No criticism was voiced about the Senate's majority leader or his whip.

One point of irritation for some departmental liaison officers was the tendency of their House leaders to be more concerned at times with priorities of their own than with those of the executive leadership. This meant, related one executive lobbyist, that they could not always automatically depend upon the party leadership in the House: unless executive priorities were fully impressed upon the legislative leaders, the latter would devote neither the attention nor the time necessary to help these bills through. Proper signals had to be sent with sufficient energy behind them to catch the full attention of the House leadership. "I learned early," reported one liaison officer, "that it's vital to get them to see that the bill is very important to us. The one bill I lost, I had not apparently explained its importance to the leadership." From another department came the criticism that the new Speaker had completely misread the signals from the White House; the department's bill had been bargained away by the leadership, in part because the latter did not clearly recognize the priority assigned to the bill.

The leadership is weak and it doesn't even grasp the priorities from the White House. Legislation piles up in the Rules Committee, including our bill, and Chairman Smith smiles and says to McCormack: "You can't have all this legislation. What ones do you want?" I'm certain that McCormack says: "Give us X and Y, and it'll be OK." But McCormack didn't even realize that the White House wanted the Z bill.

Only one liaison agent offered any criticism of the House leadership's ability to marshal votes on the floor. His major bill had just been defeated by a very close vote, part of the blame for which he attributed to the inability of the leadership to secure three live pairs. Both the leadership and the executive actors were at fault. Three congressmen who had promised to vote affirmatively had been absent. Since the closeness of the vote had been predicted, their absence reflected on the poor planning of the partisan executive-legislative team. Had the three been present, he contended, the majority against the bill would have been small enough at one point for the leadership to have swung over the few legislators necessary to save the bill. The wider the margin against a bill in a tightly fought battle, the more difficult it is to persuade congressmen to alter their votes so as to reverse the results.

Lobbyists from four of the eight departments were extremely critical of the effectiveness of the leadership's whip system: it was often unreliable and tended to mislead the combined executive-legislative team. The legislative part of that team, they claimed, was prone to underassessment. This stimulated the legislative actors to send danger signals that misled executive actors into engaging in unnecessary negotiations and concessions in order to make up the necessary votes. It also meant, contended the executive lobbyists, that they had to check and double-check their own information to ensure that they had an accurate nose count. In all fairness to the leadership, most of these grievances concerned whip counts in 1962, although one or two pointed to examples in 1963.

Sentiment ranged from such moderate statements as: "The leadership has the necessary intelligence, but it's not complete and we need to check it out ourselves," to "They just don't know how to count," or "I consistently find the whip count wrong." One complaint was that many legislators did not answer the whip count. "They can't get more than one-third of the people to do so" was an extreme version of the criticism. Noting that he had participated in four major votes during the previous year, one liaison officer asserted that the leadership had listed congressmen as undecided when he knew personally this was not the case. Liaison officers complained also that not all the regional whips were reliable; some were unenthusiastic or even opposed to particular legislation and therefore unwilling to help the proponents. Apropos of one regional whip, a laison officer commented: "There's no way to get through or under him to find out—unless we and our allies check these guys out ourselves."

Not surprisingly, the House whip and his immediate assistant were equally distrustful of the intelligence count of the departmental liaison officers.[9] According to the assistant to the whip, they relied too much on other actors to put together their information. As a result, they were always overconfident and their figures were inflated. Clearly the legislative leadership in most cases tended to a much more cautious count than the departmental liaison agents. However, as with all intelligence networks, when a great many independent actors must be monitored there is bound to be some inaccuracy in the count by any one set of intelligence agents.

The overlap of executive-legislative networks, while requiring each set of actors to duplicate much of the work of the others, was decidedly functional. It improved the statistical chances that they would not over-look valuable information, for each was bound to have better contacts with some legislators than with others. It afforded them a perception in depth of the thinking of House members on any particular piece of legis-lation, and it allowed them to challenge each other's more dubious or uncertain data. In view of the needs of each set of actors for intelligence, it afforded each a sense of greater certainty and independence. At the same time it is obvious that a certain amount of jealousy was engendered by this arrangement, especially on the part of the legislative whips, who seemed to feel that this was really their province and prerogative. They tended to view the executive actors as outsiders, amateurs who meddled inefficiently and produced soft rather than hard data.

[9] Randall B. Ripley, who studied the whip system in the House during this period, concludes that the whip was correct and that the liaison officers were the ones with the more faulty information. "During 1962–63 the White House or depart-ment concerned rarely had information as accurate as that which the whip organi-zation had collected" (*Party Leaders in the House of Representatives* [Washing-ton, D.C.: Brookings Institution, 1967], p. 68, n. 19). It is Ripley's contention that the executive outsiders "know less about the peculiarities of individual members and are likely to arouse resentment among them" in their efforts to obtain infor-mation.

CHAPTER IX

White House and Departmental
Legislative Liaison

THE PREEMINENCE of the White House liaison staff in executive-legislative relations was one of the outstanding attributes of the Kennedy Administration. The formalization and institutionalization of the legislative liaison begun under President Harry S. Truman and considerably upgraded by his Republican successor were continued, emphasis being placed upon integrating legislative relations within the entire executive system under the leadership of the President.

Liaison with the Congress—in the formal sense that special political actors assumed responsibility for roles that were differentiated from other aspects of leadership—was conducted therefore at two levels, the White House and the departments. President John F. Kennedy attempted to systematize his personal legislative liaison and that of the administration by establishing a separate unit at the highest policy level in the White House. His immediate assistant for legislative liaison spoke authoritatively for the President and his administration, both in the executive system and in the Congress, and, together with a staff of his own, this assistant assumed primary responsibility for advancing the relations of the President with the Congress and the legislation that the administration sponsored.

As subordinate units the departments are an integral element of an administration. While not all departmental legislation is necessarily accorded an administration label, the leaders of the departments comprise the Cabinet; their goals are primarily determined by White House priorities and their resources may be tapped for administration purposes by the President's liaison agents. Departmental legislative liaison is, consequently, subordinate to that of the White House in terms of strategy, tactics, priority of bills, and also political significance in the eyes of the Congress. Moreover, the resources that the White House commands are ultimately superior to those commanded by departmental actors.

Depending upon the nature of the White House leadership, the departments may be welded into a highly integrated administration team at all levels of political leadership, including that of legislative liaison. Or the reverse may be true: they may be left on their own while the White House conducts its own operation in the Congress. Departments may also be permitted to campaign for their own bills but with some White House cooperation or supervision. A more aggressive, integrated pattern was pursued by the Kennedy White House and continued under President Lyndon B. Johnson; a more restrictive one prevailed during the Eisenhower Administration. Once a President assigns major responsibilities to his own liaison unit, some type of relationship must be developed between the White House and departmental liaison officers.

The research for this study focused primarily upon the departmental liaison officers and their relations with the White House liaison unit. While White House liaison staffs were interviewed and the White House liaison unit per se was studied, no effort was made to examine the relations of its actors with the substantive staff assistants to the President, such as Theodore C. Sorensen, Meyer Feldman, and Lee C. White in the Kennedy White House. Nor was the linkage between the chief lobbyist for the Kennedy White House and the Democratic National Committee pursued through interviews with the chairman of that committee. And, unfortunately, I did not have the opportunity to talk with the late President Kennedy, or for that matter with President Harry S. Truman or President Dwight D. Eisenhower, to ascertain how each chief executive assessed his own legislative liaison officers.

UPGRADING LEGISLATIVE LIAISON IN THE WHITE HOUSE: THE ACTORS[1]

Officially designated agents for legislative liaison first appeared in the White House during the Truman Administration.[2] The entire operation was subsequently expanded and upgraded under Presidents Eisen-

[1] Interviews were conducted with Bryce N. Harlow and Edward A. McCabe, two members of the Eisenhower White House liaison staff; Joseph G. Feeney, one of President Truman's two liaison officers; and all the members of the Kennedy White House liaison unit: Lawrence F. O'Brien, Henry Hall Wilson, Mike N. Manatos, Richard K. Donahue, Charles U. Daly, and Claude J. Desautels.
[2] A brief but colorful history of the use of presidential aides for legislative liaison assignments, starting with the Wilson Administration and extending through the second year of President John F. Kennedy's term, may be found in Neil MacNeil, *Forge of Democracy: The House of Representatives* (New York: McKay, 1963), chap. 10, "The Chief Executive."

hower[3] and Kennedy. In analyzing the three liaison units, I attempt initially to demonstrate how and why they differed from each other. A hypothesis is advanced that, regardless of the personality and style of the incumbent President, no chief executive will hereafter feel that he can afford to deal with Congress without a special liaison unit or to staff it with other than highly sophisticated political actors.

The Size of the Liaison Unit

Compared with the total number of departmental and agency personnel officially conducting legislative liaison, the White House has consistently maintained a small unit. In fact, White House liaison actors have insisted that their numbers should remain limited in order to cope with the acute problem of coordination at their level. It should be noted that during the Kennedy Administration the liaison officers and staffs for the Secretary of Defense and the Secretary of State numbered in each case more than those working for the President. Yet at some point size *does* enter into the effectiveness of a White House liaison unit and serves as one index of the importance assigned to it. Not only must White House liaison officers deal with the administration's program as it cuts across all the departments, but they must contend with both the House and the Senate and with departmental lobbyists and those representing a variety of interest groups.

No official liaison officer served in the Truman White House unit until after the 1948 election. Two were appointed around the middle of 1949, one being assigned to the Senate, the other to the House. In view of the ill health of the latter (he died in 1951), his associate carried a major portion of their liaison work with both houses of the Congress. In 1952 he was the only one officially responsible for liaison.

A much larger number of political actors was officially involved in legislative liaison for the Eisenhower White House. Initially, in 1953, a staff of four was assigned this responsibility. While the personnel changed, and additional persons occasionally served part time, the regular liaison unit remained at four or five throughout the Republican administration. According to Bryce N. Harlow, who served as chief lobbyist from late 1958 through 1960, he had a full-time staff of three working with him plus two others who devoted a considerable amount of time to assisting regular staff members.

The size of the Kennedy liaison unit did not increase too much be-

[3] Eisenhower makes some reference to the importance of his liaison unit in *Mandate for Change, 1953–1956: The White House Years* (Garden City, N.Y.: Doubleday, 1963), pp. 116, 194. See also Sherman Adams, *Firsthand Report: The Story of the Eisenhower Administration* (New York: Harper & Row, 1961), pp. 10ff.

yond that of its Republican predecessor. Initially five staff members were employed, two of whom were not engaged in immediate contact with congressmen. It was soon enlarged to five full-time liaison officers who worked directly on the Hill, plus one who served as the inside personal assistant to the chief lobbyist, but who was in communication with departmental liaison officers and congressmen over the telephone. In total, six full-time professionals were concerned with legislative liaison, although only five went to the Hill.

Relationship to the Chief Executive

The importance of the legislative liaison unit is attested to also by the proximity of the actors to the President, the degree of respect accorded them by other political actors, and their discretion and involvement in decision-making at the White House and in the Congress. Judged by these criteria, the two liaison officers of the Truman Administration did not measure up to their successors. In fact, the contrast is so great as to suggest that a completely different level of operation was conducted under Eisenhower and Kennedy. Organizationally, moreover, these Presidents placed responsibility for their legislative liaison on one officer—of a senior White House rank—who engaged in relations with the Congress, acted as a principal adviser to the President, and supervised a staff of subordinate liaison officials.

Not only did President Truman conduct a good part of his own relations with the Congress, but he relied principally upon other associates in the White House—Clark Clifford and Charles S. Murphy—for major liaison with the Congress. The President's two legislative assistants, as his liaison officers were officially titled, were employed at a much lower level of relations with the Congress. Although official titles are often misleading, it is evident that the administrative assistants and the counsel to the President ranked higher in importance and status than the legislative assistants. Moreover, neither of the two liaison officers had been a long-time associate, a political ally and collaborator, or a close personal friend of the President when he was appointed.

Two members of the Truman White House, one of whom held a very high position, characterized the liaison unit as understaffed and relatively ineffectual. The legislative assistants attended the President's staff meetings, but they rarely spoke up. In the Congress they had little discretion to commit the President or to speak authoritatively for him so as to influence votes, strategy, or tactics. In the eyes of the two White House staff men, the legislative assistants were primarily messengers rather than responsible political agents. The failure of the national press to

note their behavior and the absence of any reference to them in the books
dealing with the Truman presidency reinforce the conclusion that they
were indeed minor actors in the White House.[4] Further confirmation of
this assessment comes from another political actor, Bryce N. Harlow,
who had served as liaison agent for the Army during the Roosevelt
Administration and as a key staff member on an important standing
committee in the House of Representatives during the Truman Administration. In this latter capacity, he was for a time the committee's staff
director and consequently worked closely with the Democratic chairman.
He concluded that "legislative liaison from the White House, during the
Truman Administration, was virtually non-existent. The President had a
couple of runners and relied principally upon Murphy and Clifford."
From his own background and his relations with his chairman, maintained Harlow, "I would have known of any White House liaison operation. I had been sensitized to the White House. Yet I never saw any
significant operation or knew that any existed."

President Eisenhower selected as his initial chief liaison officer one
of his closest personal friends and a long-time military associate.[5] Not
only had the President known Major General Wilton B. Persons in the
Army, but Persons had returned from retirement to serve him as an aide
in his NATO assignment. He had been an intimate associate of Eisenhower during the latter's campaign for the presidency, and in the White
House he was considered by his associates to be one of the three most
important aides to the President.[6] The President's respect for his chief
lobbyist is attested to also by the fact that he promoted Persons during
his first year in office to the position of deputy assistant to the President.
When Sherman Adams resigned as the assistant to the President, Persons
was appointed in his place.

Bryce N. Harlow, another member of the original liaison team, had
also been known to the President since World War II, when Harlow had

---

[4] Neil MacNeil, who served as a Washington correspondent for the United Press
in 1949 and subsequently became *Time Magazine's* chief congressional correspondent, makes no reference to either of the two, although he does refer to Murphy
and Clifford as engaging in congressional liaison (*op. cit.,* p. 253). The *New York
Times* contains only two brief references to the legislative assistants: one in 1949,
when the first was appointed, and the second in 1950, when the other agent was
raised in military rank. See the *New York Times,* July 13, 1949, and August 17,
1950. *Facts on File* also contains only two brief notices of the appointment of each
to the White House. See *Facts on File Yearbook, 1949,* pp. 228D, 253G.
[5] Persons "had long been one of my admired and respected associates" (Eisenhower,
op. cit., p. 116).
[6] Emmet John Hughes, *The Ordeal of Power: A Political Memoir of the Eisenhower
Years* (New York: Atheneum, 1963), p. 64. Other books by Eisenhower associates
testify to the closeness of General Persons to the President (Adams, *op. cit.,* pp.
10ff).

conducted legislative liaison for General George C. Marshall and Secretary of War Henry L. Stimson. Their relationship continued when Harlow served on the staff of the House Armed Services Committee as chief staff officer for Chairman Carl Vinson during the latter part of the Truman Administration. In the White House, Harlow subsequently became the President's chief speech writer for a period and eventually Deputy Assistant to the President for Congressional Affairs, the chief lobbyist. While the subordinate officers in the White House were on the whole not previously known to the President, one, Homer Gruenther, was the brother of Eisenhower's former chief of staff and had served with the President during the 1952 campaign.

The chief liaison agents for the President acted as his advisers and also represented him in his relations with the Congress. In some ways their relations with the President and the Congress were more limited than those of the liaison chief for the Kennedy Administration. For the major part of the Eisenhower Administration, the principal staff member in the White House was the assistant to the President, Sherman Adams; no one else on the staff equaled him in stature or in importance. Access to the President, moreover, was largely controlled by Adams, who was the President's chief adviser and who had been delegated wide discretion to act in many areas, some of which cut across the concerns of congressmen. When Harlow became chief lobbyist, he was responsible to Adam's successor, although no one ever equaled Adams in preeminence. A further restriction on the liaison unit was the partisan composition of the Congress. From 1955 through 1960 it was a Democratic Congress, which imposed constraints upon the roles that the legislative liaison staff could play.

Legislative liaison was elevated to the highest level of importance in the Kennedy Administration. There was no one comparable to Adams in the White House, and the chief liaison officer held a rank equal with that of the other principal assistants to the President. Lawrence F. O'Brien, as chief lobbyist, did not have to approach the President through anyone else; he reported that he had direct, frequent, and intimate contact with the President. The latter made it absolutely clear to his staff, to the Cabinet, and to the Congress that O'Brien was his personal representative, one with whom others had to clear their requests and proposals and their suggestions for strategy and tactics on legislation.[7] "I speak directly and authoritatively for the President," O'Brien told me.

[7] See MacNeil, *op. cit.*, p. 257, for corroboration on this point. It was also apparent in the interviews I conducted with congressmen from both parties, lobbyists for private interest groups, and Cabinet members as well as departmental liaison officers. All recognized the preeminent position of the President's chief lobbyist on matters affecting the Congress.

I have a very close relation with the President and he leaves me a great deal of leeway. I have full responsibility and am free to decide on strategy and tactics regarding legislation. I can at the spur of the moment, if necessary, make changes in substance or process without checking with anyone.

Of course, he added, in making such decisions he tried to work very closely with the Cabinet officer whose legislation was being considered and with the Democratic leaders in the Congress.

In appointing O'Brien his chief for congressional liaison, President Kennedy chose a close political collaborator. O'Brien had managed Kennedy's Senate campaigns in 1952 and 1958, and he had directed the campaigns for his nomination and election to the presidency in 1960. Richard K. Donahue, a subordinate member of the liaison staff, was another political associate and friend from Massachusetts politics. The President had also been acquainted with two others: Mike N. Manatos had been a Democratic administrative assistant in the Senate and Charles U. Daly had worked under Sorensen in Senator Kennedy's office in 1959.

Political and Congressional Backgrounds

The occupants of the legislative liaison positions in the three White Houses represented three different sets of political backgrounds. The two Truman liaison agents had never been employed in the Congress in any capacity, nor had they any previous background in partisan politics. Before joining the Navy in World War II, Joseph G. Feeney had worked for years in the field of adult education in Pennsylvania. As a uniformed liaison officer for the Navy, he was principally responsible for helping senators handle their constituent mail. It was, he insisted, a job that had nothing to do with politics. "The President recognized that I could get along with opposition party members." His associate, Charles Maylon, had been a career officer in the U.S. Air Force and had worked in Air Force and Army legislative liaison during his later years in Washington. He, too, had no partisan identification or experience.

While the political and congressional background of the Eisenhower legislative liaison agents is impressive, it is characterized by one feature that distinguishes them sharply from comparable actors in the preceding and subsequent administrations: a number of the Eisenhower lobbyists had bipartisan backgrounds. General Persons had the least partisan experience, approximating that of the career officer in the Truman Administration. He had served in liaison for the military under two Democratic administrations, yet he had been active with Eisenhower in the 1952 nomination and election campaigns. Two of the other lobbyists had, in fact, worked for Democratic Congresses. Gerald D. Morgan, a member of the original staff in 1953, had served as assistant legislative counsel for the House of Representatives from 1937 to 1945. After leaving the Congress, he had been employed by the Republican National Committee to help draft the House version of the Taft-Hartley Act. Bryce N. Harlow had come to the House of Representatives in 1938 as a patronage appointee of a Democratic congressman. He subsequently served as secretary to this Democratic congressman, and during the war he worked in Army liaison with the Congress. From 1947 to 1951 he was a professional staff member of the House Armed Services Committee under Republican and Democratic majorities; in fact, he served as assistant to the chairman and as chief clerk under a Democrat, but Armed Services is not recognized as a partisan committee. Harlow's acceptability to Democrats is attested to by the fact that Lyndon B. Johnson, who had served on the Armed Services Committee, twice offered Harlow a position on his staff.[8] In 1949, when Johnson became a senator, he offered to make Harlow his administrative assistant. Four years later, upon becoming Democratic majority leader, Johnson proposed appointing him director of the Democratic Policy Committee. Both offers were rejected. Harlow reported that he was only a minor participant at the local level in Oklahoma in Eisenhower's 1952 campaign. An additional member of the White House liaison staff, Edward A. McCabe, had served as chief assistant first to a Republican and then to a southern Democratic chairman of the House Committee on Education and Labor.

Among the other political actors who held liaison posts in the Eisenhower White House, strong Republican partisanship was the rule. From 1944 to 1953 Jack Martin worked with Senator Robert A. Taft, serving as Taft's administrative assistant from 1946 on and participating in his campaigns for the Republican presidential nomination in 1948 and 1952. Homer Gruenther had for many years been an executive secretary to Republican legislators in the House and Senate and had been an active member of the President's campaign staff in 1952. Jack Z. Anderson had served for seven terms as a Republican congressman from California. Clyde Wheeler had been a leader in Oklahoma and national Young Republican politics; he had subsequently served as administrative assistant to a Republican congressman. Both Wheeler and Anderson had lobbied for the Republican Secretary of Agriculture before coming to the White House. And Earle D. Chesney had once served on the White House staff of President Herbert Hoover.

It is evident from the above résumé that the Eisenhower liaison staff had an exceptionally strong background of association with the legislative

---

[8] Rowland Evans and Robert Novak, *Lyndon B. Johnson: The Exercise of Power* (New York: New American Library, 1966), pp. 20, 62.

system. Every one of its members either had served as an elected or staff member of the Congress or had worked with legislators from both parties in legislative liaison for nonpartisan divisions of the executive system. Chesney came to the Eisenhower White House after three decades of handling congressional problems for the Veterans' Administration on the Hill. The accumulated experience of these members in working with the Congress far exceeded that of the Kennedy liaison staff.

The Kennedy White House liaison staff differed from the Eisenhower lobbyists in their strong partisan backgrounds and in their more limited experience with the Congress. With one exception, all had a background of intense involvement in state and/or national Democratic party politics. Before assuming his position in the White House, O'Brien had been director of organization for the Democratic National Committee, handling Kennedy's presidential campaign. Previously he had served as organizational chief for Kennedy's campaign to obtain the nomination. His reputation was made earlier as a political operator, a strong partisan from the tough party politics of Massachusetts, where he had directed Kennedy's two Senate campaigns. His original assignment in the White House called for him to handle personnel as well as legislative liaison, which placed him squarely in party patronage politics. Harlow, in the Republican White House, had avoided being involved in patronage; he contended that it was too closely identified with partisanship and it made too many enemies. Although O'Brien soon disengaged himself officially from the personnel side of his job, unofficially he remained a key patronage link between the Congress and the White House and between the latter and the National Committee.

His principal lieutenants were also active Democrats. Henry Hall Wilson, who represented O'Brien in dealing with the House of Representatives, had been president of the Young Democratic Clubs of North Carolina; he had been an active Democratic legislator in that state and in charge of the state headquarters of the winning Democratic candidate for governor in 1960. He had also served as a Democratic national committeeman in 1960 and had participated on the Kennedy campaign team. Mike N. Manatos, O'Brien's special representative for the Senate, had been associated with four Wyoming Democratic senators from 1937 to 1961. Richard K. Donahue had been active in Massachusetts politics, serving as a member and a vice-chairman of the State Democratic Committee. He had been a political assistant to Kennedy in his Senate campaigns and deputy director of organization for the Democratic National Committee in the 1960 campaign. Claude J. Desautels, O'Brien's personal assistant in the White House, had served on the staff of a Democratic congressman from 1949 to 1961. He had also been active on the local level in Maryland in the Kennedy campaign of 1960. Only Charles U. Daly, the most junior member of the staff, did not come from a background of intensive involvement in Democratic party politics. While he was an active party member, he was principally a newspaperman. Under the auspices of a fellowship, he had worked briefly in 1959 for Democratic Congressman Stuart L. Udall and Senator John F. Kennedy. In 1960 he had edited a campaign handbook for the Democratic Study Group, an organization of liberal Democrats in the House.

The Kennedy lobbyists contrasted also with the Eisenhower actors in their comparative inexperience with the Congress. O'Brien had been associated with the House of Representatives for a two-year period only as administrative assistant to a Massachusetts legislator. Neither Wilson nor Donahue had ever been associated with the Congress. Daly had worked in the Congress for one year. Only two members of the White House liaison staff were congressional types. Manatos had served twenty-three years in the Senate and Desautels twelve years in the House, both of them as administrative assistants to members.

In addition, the two White House liaison units differed markedly in the age of the actors involved. The Republican liaison staff was older than the Kennedy staff, the latter approximating more their departmental counterparts. In the Eisenhower White House four were over fifty years of age when they assumed their positions; the others were in their forties, except for Harlow, who was thirty-six. Among Kennedy's assistants, two were in their early and middle forties, four were in their thirties. It is noteworthy that the two units did approximate each other in one respect: half of the Democrats and a little less than half of the Republicans were lawyers.

The combination of youthfulness, lack of congressional experience, and highly partisan background of President Kennedy's officers was the focus of certain critical remarks by congressmen and their staffs. Some White House lobbyists were charged with displaying a lack of respect for their elders in the Congress and with using crude tactics more appropriate to the rough-and-tumble of party conventions than to the political process in a coequal branch of the national government. There is no doubt that the deference congressmen expected and received from interest-group lobbyists was not always duplicated by White House lobbyists, especially when the latter were desperately trying to save an administration priority bill. Such criticism was not voiced about departmental lobbyists, nor for that matter was it ever directed against Wilson or Manatos within the White House liaison unit.

Attitudes Toward Partisanship
and Congressional Experience

In view of their disparate backgrounds, how did the Eisenhower and the Kennedy liaison agents compare in their attitudes toward partisanship and congressional experience? The extent of the divergencies in their attitudes regarding partisanship was considerable. They stemmed from differences both in style and in the partisan situation confronting their respective administrations.

Despite the strong Republican identification of most subordinates in the Eisenhower liaison unit, the two principal officers and one of their colleagues had not been active partisan types. They were known to Democrats as nonpartisans and they were liked by members of both parties. "We three had worked with the Congress for years, as had Eisenhower, and none of us had been particularly partisan. We had a tremendous number of friends on both sides of the aisle," reported Harlow. Two situational factors supported the avoidance of strong partisanship in their dealings with the Congress: the incumbent President and the executive-legislative party division. President Eisenhower was definitely not a partisan type, and he did not encourage an aggressive partisan style. Moreover, the opposition party controlled both houses of Congress for six years during the Republican administration. Executive leaders had to deal with a Democratic Speaker, Democratic majority leaders and chairmen, and Democratic majorities on all committees. In fact, Democratic votes were often needed to rescue administration-sponsored legislation when Republican support in the Congress fell away.

Harlow advanced the thesis, as a generalization for all White House liaison regardless of situational factors, that legislative liaison from the departments and the White House should not be overly partisan in nature. In his opinion, partisanship was dysfunctional, whereas bipartisanship had distinct advantages. Liaison agents should be actors who could cross party lines without too much tension. This was more true for the White House than for the departments. "It is important for the White House. It has to go back continually and reestablish lines of communication with the other side. Party lines get clogged up so easily and quickly." If White House lobbyists were too partisan, they would hesitate, he suggested, to approach members of the opposite party, and the latter would in turn be reluctant to approach them and would resent them. It was vital to maintain good relations with the opposition party because the understanding and cooperation of its leaders were often required in the legislative process, as were votes from its members. Harlow had specifically warned O'Brien, when O'Brien had discussed legislative liaison with him, to avoid assuming public positions if he and his assistants expected to be able to work with the Republicans. "But O'Brien has made political speeches. It is tough enough already, but this makes it even tougher for him to go up there and ask Halleck [the Republican floor leader in the House] for cooperation."

Partisanship was more intense in the Kennedy White House than it was among the departmental liaison officers, most of whom also emphasized Democratic party identification in their dealings with the Congress. The strong partisan spirit in the White House arose in part, of course, from the backgrounds of the actors in Democratic politics. It stemmed as well from other factors, three of which stand out. First, John F. Kennedy was a much more aggressive political type than was Eisenhower. Secondly, President Kennedy proposed a program, conceptualized under the rubric of the New Frontier, which incorporated an ambitious set of legislative proposals with far-reaching effects—socially, economically, politically. Whereas congressional Democrats could cooperate with the somewhat moderate Republicanism of the Eisenhower Administration, Republican lines stiffened against the Democratic administration. Finally, Kennedy came to power with a bare plurality of the popular vote and an actual loss of Democratic strength in the Eighty-seventh Congress over the Eighty-sixth. The margin of the Democratic majority in the House was such that Republicans could anticipate prevailing over the administration if enough southern Democrats defected and their own ranks remained intact.

The extremely partisan leadership of the Republicans in the House of Representatives was repeatedly mentioned by White House lobbyists as inhibiting any cooperation between the administration and the opposition party.[9] O'Brien reported that, although he tried, he found it impossible to work cooperatively with the Republican floor leader, Charles A. Halleck.

When we have off-the-record meetings, it's all on top of the table. I can't get really confidential and open the books or it will be in the press and out in the party immediately. Halleck is totally partisan. I spent an hour and a half with him the other day; after all, we still have to maintain relations and can't ignore the Republicans, but it was completely unproductive.

It was not that the Democrats were overly partisan, contended O'Brien, but rather that the House Republicans could not forgo a parti-

[9] MacNeil, whose book was published early in 1963, reports that the President "and his White House aides scarcely bothered to try to win their [Republican] votes" in the House of Representatives. After some initial cooperation from the opposition party in 1961, "Kennedy could hardly count even a single Republican for any of his bills" (MacNeil, *op. cit.,* p. 265).

san posture on anything. It was the President's desire, he pointed out, "to work out lines of communication and accommodations that can hold and be productive." Efforts had been made on a number of issues to pass bills with bipartisan support. He had promised the Republican leaders that the President would credit their party as well as the Democrats for these achievements. "I feel that we have tried, but its no use," he concluded.

Everett M. Dirksen, the Republican leader in the Senate, was a different type, declared OBrien. He was much less dogmatic and partisan. It was easier to deal with him, for Dirksen was a man with whom one could bargain, even in terms of ordinary patronage and favors. If Halleck had approached politics more as a traditional politician, claimed O'Brien, they might have worked out mutually satisfactory arrangements. "Halleck won't even ask the administration for anything. After all, with a *quid pro quo* we'd be ready to move."

On most issues O'Brien admitted that the administration never sought bipartisan support, for the Republicans were overwhelmingly opposed to much of the New Frontier program. "They're totally dedicated to obstructiveness, to 'How can we gut them?' " His aides in the House were equally if not more adamant in their insistence that the Republican opposition to the Kennedy program compelled the administration to be even more partisan in its approach. "Of course we are partisan; it's the only way we can win," argued Donahue.

Wilson, who was directly in charge of liaison with the House, expressed the feeling in these colorful terms: "Our attitude is that you pass nothing with Republican help. It's like a bank loan with them—you get it only when you don't need it." The administration did try often to obtain Republican votes, but it received very few. And most of those, he contended, came because some congressmen could not afford to have it known in their districts that they had opposed a particular issue; but they really wanted to defeat the administration! Halleck attempted to tie southern Democrats and Republicans together, and often demanded that the latter follow their party leaders on the final votes as well as on recommittal motions.

Even the liaison officer with the Senate, whose political problems were not comparable because of the huge Democratic majority and the close cooperation between Democratic and Republican floor leaders, admitted, "I operate on the thesis that I have to win or lose with Democratic votes. What we get from the Republicans is extra." A few Republicans generally supported the administration on "gut issues," and others delivered their votes if they could be persuaded on the basis of merit. But most were opposed. Manatos voiced a reluctance to tackle the Republicans for votes, preferring that the departments and agency people work with them. In the event a close vote promised to materialize, however, he, too, would approach them.

President Kennedy's senior lobbyist expressed an attitude toward the employment of congressional types in the White House which contrasted with that of the Eisenhower liaison officers. The latter had pointed with pride to the fact that their congressional experience had aided them in working for the White House. O'Brien had deliberately sought out nonlegislative types. "My inclination was against placing any emphasis on Hill experience. My two years as administrative assistant in the House led me to conclude that it was really not that important." Donahue reported that O'Brien's decision to avoid congressional types stemmed from a belief that they came with attachments to different power centers in the Congress and also brought with them other liabilities.[10] This last point was strongly supported by Wilson. It was his contention that Congress was analogous to a pecking order: its staff members came with the disadvantage that congressmen continued to look upon them as subordinates while they themselves retained inhibitions about dealing aggressively with the chairmen and others to whom they had traditionally deferred.

Both Wilson and Donahue conceded that they were personally handicapped in assuming their positions because of their lack of familiarity with the particular indivduals and special procedures in the House. Donahue claimed that he compensated for this lack of experience by his extensive contacts among Democratic members and state party leaders and organizations as a result of his participation in the 1960 campaign. In discussing his relations with the substantive officers in the White House, Wilson acknowledged that he and O'Brien had not found the time to become involved in the substance of legislation during their first year, although their participation had been solicited by others in the White House. The two liaison officers had been too busy familiarizing themselves with the Congress and dealing with the immediate problems that continually impinged upon them.

To a certain extent the White House liaison officers who worked with the House were helped in compensating for their inexperience by the

---

[10] The *Congressional Quarterly* reports O'Brien as saying that he was "not particularly looking for men with Hill experience, because I did not want individuals whose ties might be binding" to any faction in the Congress. "I was more interested in the public relations aspect of the job. My concern was to put together a team representing New Frontier vigor, a group with political acumen or political savvy" ("White House 'Lobby' Operates on Capitol Hill," *Congressional Quarterly Note to Editors: C.Q. Fact Sheet on White House–Congress Relations,* May 30, 1961, p. 3). This "fact sheet" was sent to newspaper editors only. It was not published in the usual weekly issue of this journal, although an extremely abbreviated version of this seven-page issue did appear in the *Congressional Quarterly,* June 1961, pp. 1–2, but failed to include this quotation.

cooperation of fellow party members in the Congress. Neil MacNeil reports that a few weeks after the new Democratic President assumed office, O'Brien, Wilson, and Donahue caucused with three liberal Democrats who were well versed in House politics and knowledgeable about their fellow members.[11] While the three White House liaison agents took notes, Richard Bolling (Missouri), Carl Elliott (Alabama), and Frank Thompson, Jr. (New Jersey), systematically canvassed every member of the House. Despite such assistance, it was clear that in their first year the liaison officers learned principally by doing.

The President and White House Lobbyists:
A Hypothesis

A White House liaison unit has been institutionalized now under five Presidents. Lyndon B. Johnson employed a liaison unit throughout his administration and Richard M. Nixon has appointed Eisenhower's former chief liaison officer, Bryce N. Harlow, to serve him in that capacity. Although the pattern in which subsequent Presidents will organize their personal staffs remains to be seen, a hypothesis may be advanced that future chief executives, regardless of their particular styles, will continue to depend upon a special staff of White House officers for liaison with the Congress. The role of chief legislator imposes tremendous demands upon Presidents. At the same time an effective instrument for helping the President carry out this role has already been institutionalized under Republican as well as Democratic administrations. The personality and style of a President undoubtedly shape his own relations with the Congress and with his immediate assistants, but it is questionable whether future chief executives can forgo relying upon a special staff for congressional relations or fail to appoint such actors to a major rank in the White House.

This study did not cover the administration of President Johnson. By continuing to utilize his liaison agents as important actors in dealing with the Congress, even after he had been elected on his own program and record in 1964, Johnson demonstrated that the needs of the President for such instruments to carry out his leadership in the Congress remain significant despite the style and personality of the incumbent.

President Truman was a congressional type who enjoyed the battles of politics and involved himself actively in his legislative campaigns. His special liaison staff, though, was ineffective and insignificant compared with those of his successors. It has been suggested that President Eisenhower was less interested in domestic politics than in national security

[11] MacNeil, *op. cit.,* p. 258.

problems and foreign policy, and that he did not relish the bargaining of presidential-congressional relations. Hence his congressional liaison unit became very important in the White House.[12] Arthur M. Schlesinger, Jr., an intimate associate of President Kennedy in the White House and a historian of the Kennedy Administration, observes that working with the Congress did not afford Kennedy the "greatest pleasure or satisfaction. This made his congressional liaison staff all the more important. . . ."[13] It is unwarranted, however, to conclude from these three cases that a White House liaison unit will be utilized in an important manner only if a President is less concerned with domestic legislation or is by temperament detached from congressional politics.

Lyndon B. Johnson did enjoy congressional politics. He was an expert in the area of congressional relations and legislative maneuvering. His personality disposed him to personal, direct involvement in the Congress on a massive scale to ensure the adoption of his program. Clearly Johnson was a different type than his predecessor, and his arrangements with his staff reflected his unique style and personality. He retained O'Brien as chief liaison officer even after elevating him to be Postmaster General, and he built Vice President Hubert H. Humphrey into the President's liaison team in a manner unique in American politics. Yet he continued to employ the principal members in the Kennedy liaison unit as an essential set of staff officers up to 1967, when he eventually replaced them with others. The importance of a liaison unit in the White House was fully recognized by a President who pursued a personal, aggressive role in offering leadership to the Congress.

WHITE HOUSE LOBBYISTS:
STRATEGIES, TACTICS, AND RESOURCES

Strategy and tactics are closely associated with the resources of actors. The White House controls a greater amount and a wider range of potent resources than any of the departments. And the White House has the priority in strategy and tactics as well as the broad responsibility for the program of the administration which cuts across the departments.

The President: The Most Important Resource

The awesome office of the presidency endows its occupant with prestige and power that no comparable individual in the national govern-

[12] Alex B. Lacy, Jr., "The Development of the White House Office, 1939–1967" (a paper delivered at the 1967 annual meeting of the American Political Science Association), p. 25.
[13] Arthur M. Schlesinger, Jr., *A Thousand Days: John F. Kennedy in the White House* (Boston: Houghton Mifflin, 1965), p. 711.

ment or the country possesses. He is party leader, chief executive, chief legislator, and chief of state, all in one. Decisions made at his level are final for most of the executive system and extend deeply into national-state-city relations. From the point of view of the legislators, the interest groups, his Cabinet, and his lobbyists, the President is therefore the most significant executive actor in congressional relations. The President can be used to influence the Congress indirectly via his press conferences or through more immediate appeals to the general public.[14] The messages that accompany his bills are carefully designed to affect both congressional response and public opinion.

President Kennedy and his chief lobbyists believed, however, in the personal approach as the most effective one for establishing good relations with the Congress. Direct contact between the Chief Executive and the legislators was pursued in a variety of ways. Congressmen in groups of fifteen or so were invited to the White House to socialize with the President, and at such occasions each legislator was afforded an opportunity for an informal chat with him.[15] Appointments with the President were arranged for individual legislators, and the President's liaison staff brought congressmen into the White House for off-the-record sessions. Committee chairmen were accorded much more deferential treatment, each being invited for a personal conference with the President. And the Democratic party leaders in the Congress met regularly with the President. Congressmen were invited among others to the social evenings in the White House. When the President wished to offer a grand gesture to someone of consequence in the Congress, he went personally to that legislator. Such occasions were rare, but one example was President Kennedy's unexpected trip by helicopter to a gathering in Virginia honoring the chairman of the Senate Finance Committee. While the Kennedy White House probably systematized these contacts with the Congress more than had the preceding administration, one of Eisenhower's chief lobbyists, Bryce N. Harlow, contended that Eisenhower had similarly been involved in congressional action.

He was a heavy participant in it, infinitely more than he has been publicly given credit for. A lot of it was off the record. He phoned, had meetings with congressmen at breakfast and dinner and in private sessions in the evenings. A great part of this the press was unaware of.

---

[14] MacNeil (*op. cit.*, p. 267) writes that O'Brien and President Kennedy had little confidence in a successful appeal to the people over the heads of Congress. They felt that such action ran the risk of engendering additional antagonism toward the administration.

[15] "Twice this week," noted O'Brien in an interview with the author in 1963, "we've invited congressmen to the Executive Mansion, in the President's living quarters. It's called coffee hours but it's really cocktails, and they let their hair down."

President John F. Kennedy recognized fully the importance of cultivating the Congress, and he was willing to assume this responsibility.
Nevertheless, O'Brien expressed the theory that the President should be
protected from being involved too much. "I'm cautious about overextend-
ing him." As chief assistant to the President for congressional relations,
he felt responsible for making as many decisions as possible by himself.
"I try to avoid using him with congressmen; there are too many demands
already on his time." The two conferred frequently over strategy, O'Brien
having easy access at all times to his political superior and the President
calling him in for discussions three or more times a day. Only if a problem were totally out of control did the liaison officer turn to the President
for his personal intervention. "I say: 'Here is the situation. I've tried and
failed. Either we have to try something else or you have to get involved.' "
On priority legislation, O'Brien did not hesitate to employ the President
to shore up the administration's position with a committee chairman. "If
I get nervous regarding Wilbur Mills and the timetable on the tax bill, I
can reach a point where I want Mills to restate to the President what his
position is. He is put on record with the President and this relieves me."

The White House staff reported that it avoided using the President
to call congressmen for their votes. President Kennedy did call frequently
during the crucial Rules Committee fight of 1961, but on the whole the
White House resisted employing this tactic. "We discovered that we have
to keep him off the phone when things get tough," explained Wilson.
There were actually very few such phone calls by the President because
his staff concluded that if he started using the phone for votes, all the
members would expect to be asked by the President personally. His staff
and the whips would then begin to accumulate a tremendous number of
"uncertains" in replies from congressmen who wished to exploit the situation. Consequently it was rare that the President called to round up
votes. More often, he would call after a victory to congratulate a legislator, or to seek someone's advice.

The President was also the source of O'Brien's mandate. The liaison
officer required from the President a type of intervention that legitimized
his own authority to act decisively within the Congress and the executive
system. When O'Brien took over White House–congressional liaison,
Harlow warned him that the President himself would pose a major problem for him, one that would have to be solved. Inevitably, the President
would become personally engaged in relations with congressmen on his
own initiative or in response to direct calls from them. The danger lay
in the President's becoming so busy that he overlooked the necessity of
"filling you in on what he's done. You have to plead with your President
never to call over your head without telling you and always to keep you

informed of what he has done." It was a problem that departmental lob-byists also faced with their superiors. Secondly, Harlow advised O'Brien that as chief lobbyist he would have to make certain that Cabinet mem-bers as well as congressmen knew that he spoke for the President, that their relations were very close. Unless he was established as the Presi-dent's man in the eyes of legislative and executive leaders, they would bypass him, downgrade his opinions and decisions, and doubt his capac-ity to commit the President. "You have to establish yourself. Make cer-tain that you ask the President to address questions to you in their presence so that they see he relies upon you."

According to O'Brien, he encountered no trouble in either respect. "There is very little slip-up between the President and me," he reported. While occasionally the President would talk on the phone with someone on the spur of the moment, the President's secretary always forwarded to O'Brien memos of the President's calls. But it was rare that the Presi-dent and he had not coordinated their approaches to the Congress well in advance. As for representing the President in the eyes of executive leaders and legislators, O'Brien was satisfied that no problem existed. "The key to my spot is that I do speak authoritatively for the President, and the others know it." He participated in Cabinet meetings as the President's liaison officer and also in the President's Tuesday breakfasts with the Democratic leaders of the Congress, where strategy and tactics were discussed. O'Brien reported that he and his staff were also involved in policy-making in the White House. "We have a voice in the prepara-tion of legislation and the President's messages. Not a veto, but a strong voice regarding the political and legislative possibilities." In the fall of each year, when the substantive assistants to the President were prepar-ing the legislative program for the next session of Congress, a member of the liaison staff represented the chief lobbyist in their discussions. O'Brien himself spent a week at the Palm Beach White House while the State of the Union and other major messages were being hammered out.

The Personal Approach of the Liaison Staff

The chief lobbyist for President Kennedy emphasized the value of a personal approach to Congress, and he patterned the entire approach of his office upon that premise. This meant that the White House liaison staff had to know the Democratic congressmen as individuals and to be prepared to deal directly with them. The President had made mention of the fact that when he was a congressman, no one from the White House staff had ever contacted him. " 'I recall my fourteen years on the Hill, and

I cannot recall during that . . . period having any direct or meaningful contact with a member of the White House staff.' "[16]

On both an informal and a formal basis, Kennedy's chief liaison officer attempted to establish personal links between himself, his staff, and the Congress. On assuming his post, he had sought to become personally acquainted with as many congressmen as possible. MacNeil reports that O'Brien requested a Massachusetts congressman to serve as his host for a series of cocktail parties with legislators.[17] He met separately with the liberals in the House who composed the Democratic Study Group. And throughout each congressional session, the O'Briens entertained important members of the Congress at their home for Sunday brunch.

In the formal day-to-day work with the Congress, each liaison officer was responsible for a specific group, thereby reinforcing the personal relations he had established with the legislators. In general, O'Brien as chief lobbyist worked primarily with Democratic party leaders, with committee chairmen, and with Republican leaders. Congressional Democratic leaders met with and called the President directly, but in the main it was the President's principal liaison officer to whom they addressed themselves and who sought them out. As has been pointed out, O'Brien participated with them in the leadership meetings at the White House. In the Congress he collaborated with them on strategy, nose counting, and the persuasion of legislators.[18] His staff was instructed to deal with the rest of the Congress, although he was available to resolve difficult problems.

His two principal assistants, titled administrative assistants to the President, also worked with committee chairmen and the Democratic leadership. One, Mike N. Manatos, was assigned solely to the Senate, although O'Brien continued to consider the Senate his special responsibility in view of the status of the senators and their insistence in many cases upon dealing personally with the most responsible executive leaders. His lieutenant for the House of Representatives, Henry Hall Wilson, was assisted by other liaison agents since the House was considered too large to be assigned to any one liaison officer, and it posed the greatest challenge to the Kennedy program.

[16] The quote may be found in National Education Television, "A Complete Transcript of Interview with Lawrence F. O'Brien . . ." (prepared for the NET series *The Changing Congress*, pt. 8, "From the White House to the Hill," 1956, mimeographed), p. 3.

[17] MacNeil, *op. cit.*, p. 260.

[18] References to O'Brien and others in his unit participating in such common endeavors may be found in a number of sources. See in particular Randall B. Ripley, *Party Leaders in the House of Representatives* (Washington, D.C.: Brookings Institution, 1967), pp. 128–31.

The White House recognized, moreover, that the Democratic membership in the House was divided into discernible segments, each of which required special attention. The most important of these groups was the southern contingent. Defection among these congressmen—unless contained within manageable limits—threatened every major Kennedy proposal. The careful cultivation of southern Democrats to retain them as administration supporters was a basic component of White House strategy. Hence the principal assistant for the White House was a southerner. As past state president of the Young Democratic Clubs of North Carolina and as a former state legislator, Wilson was a southern type in all but ideological orientation; he had long been associated with the liberal wing of his state party. As the chief liaison officer for the House, he worked with the Speaker, majority leader, and whip, and with the committee chairmen, but the southern and border congressmen were his special assignment.

The nonsouthern Democrats in the House were assigned to two subordinate legislative liaison officers. Initially, Richard K. Donahue, the senior of the two, had not been engaged in direct contact with congressmen; he had represented O'Brien in the development of substantive policy at the White House and he had concentrated upon patronage problems. With Wilson devoting himself to southern and border congressmen as well as to the leadership and committee chairmen, complaints had arisen from other Democrats who wanted personal attention from the White House. As a result Donahue was assigned the big-city delegations from the northeast and midwest. Subsequently an additional liaison agent was appointed to collaborate with Democrats from the West and the few noncity party members from the northeast and midwest. The responsibility of these two liaison officers was defined as affording "those who will automatically vote for us a direct link with the White House. They touch base with them, hold their hands, and in general worry with them." The two were responsible as well for making certain that these congressmen appeared for important votes, knew the White House position on legislation and amendments, and voted the correct way. "O'Brien and I have no time for the saved," explained Wilson. "Most of our work is in lining up the critical votes. Donahue and Daly are employed to cover the liberal Democrats who complain that 'we're taken for granted.' "

Patronage and Special Favors

Just as departmental liaison agents capitalized upon the needs and desires of legislators for special favors affecting their constituents, so did the White House laison staff devote itself assiduously to this task. During his three years in the White House, reported O'Brien in 1963, he and his staff had developed a tremendous service operation. "We could never have survived unless we had had and had used patronage. We get the vote, but not just by an appeal on the basis of merit or substantive discussion with members." He and his staff were not moral crusaders, he pointed out; their job was to get the legislation through.

O'Brien had been responsible for patronage on the Democratic National Committee between the November 1960 election and the inauguration of the President. His title in the White House had originally called for him to be concerned also with personnel, a recognition that patronage and legislation were linked together. Although he was officially divested of his personnel assignment, he continued to serve as a patronage boss in the White House. The departments were alerted to keep the White House informed of important patronage opportunities and to furnish data on major contracts, projects, and services.[19] Similarly, the White House demanded that departments give preferential treatment to Democrats so that they could capitalize upon projects directly affecting their constituencies. "It is not in the best interest of legislative harmony," counseled the White House, "to have Republican Senators announce projects directly affecting Districts with sitting Democratic Congressmen. . . . An orderly, considered treatment of the Congress will result in an expedited Administration Program."[20]

It was O'Brien's contention that by integrating and exploiting the resources of the departments, the White House could provide much more extensive service than had the comparable unit in the Eisenhower Administration. The President's more ambitious program of legislation could therefore be more effectively advanced. Such services were considered to contribute to a favorable climate in which White House lobbyists and legislators could interact. The White House could also more readily affect votes, both indirectly and directly. One of O'Brien's assistants disclosed that the White House sought to "jockey into a position where they [those Democrats who did not usually support the administration] call

[19] A weekly publication of the Republican National Committee, *Battle Line,* no. 27 (May 1, 1961), p. 2, reprinted a letter from the Assistant to the Secretary of the Interior in the Kennedy Administration, criticizing the department's officers for not performing satisfactorily in providing advance notice to the White House, particularly on important contracts. "It is mandatory that we give the White House forty-eight hours notice before we announce contracts of this sort. We must also notify Lawrence O'Brien. On the Florida matter . . . O'Brien's office was not notified, when considerable mileage could have been made by giving the White House a chance before the weekend of notifying interested members of Congress."

[20] See "Memorandum to All Cabinet Officials and Agency Heads," April 21, 1961, from Lawrence F. O'Brien, Special Assistant to the President, reprinted in Republican National Committee, *Battle Line,* no. 28 (May 7, 1961).

us" in order to create a sense of obligation on their part. When such congressmen sought special favors from the departments, the latter were alerted to cue in the White House so that its officers could suggest to a member that "he can't get it unless he goes along with us." Donahue, who worked with the big-city delegations, maintained that patronage for their party organization was often much more important to these legislators than the substance of bills. At times, he told a *Congressional Quarterly* reporter, "our hearing is better than at other times," and it was more sensitive during legislative showdowns, when "we expect their hearing to be more sensitive at the other end of the line, too."[21]

On the whole, the Kennedy liaison unit did not employ constituent-oriented resources to deny legislators their requests or to deprive them of what they had. Rather the principal approach was positive—finding ways to provide grants, expedite contracts, and fill positions. Nevertheless, the White House could turn a deaf ear to requests or refuse to expedite matters in which congressmen were interested. According to the liaison officers, the knowledge that the White House controlled such resources in itself constituted an inducement to legislators to be cooperative.

"Muscle"

Merit, compromise, and political rationalization were major tools employed by the White House liaison officers, as they were for their departmental counterparts. However, by the time the White House unit entered into most legislative battles, positions had tended to become hardened on substance and along party lines. Consequently White House lobbyists had to fall back upon a tougher approach to congressmen.

Both congressmen and departmental liaison officers agreed that "muscle" resided in the White House. It was this group of political actors who got tough when it was necessary. That the Kennedy White House got tough at times was not denied by anyone, although recourse to such tactics occurred only when the administration felt that there was a great deal at stake on a vote and that the results were uncertain. Under such circumstances the White House employed both direct and indirect pressure. Of course the very uncertainty associated with the disposition of favors and services constituted a type of pressure. Hence the resources themselves added to the muscle available to the White House lobbyists. But when the liaison officers referred to muscle or pressure, they often emphasized other means for influencing legislators.

One direct type of pressure applied by the White House was insistence that it needed the member's vote and that he had to comply. "When we're down to a handful of votes, we call members and say 'We need your

[21] *Congressional Quarterly Note to Editors*, pp. 2–3.

vote to make it.' They say, 'We're staked out already,' or 'Our constituents oppose it.' You draw it cold for them: 'This is it. You've got to
take the heat.' "

The liaison officers acknowledged that they were applying pressure
simply by calling to assert a White House interest in an item or to ascertain how the congressman stood on the issue. Wilson explained:

When I call a member of a committee it's because he's on the line or undecided. The fact that I call him on a committee matter is more than just a substantive argument pro or con; it's the White House calling. They go on the
defensive and we proceed from there. They know we wouldn't call unless we
know they're reluctant to vote or attend.

O'Brien suggested that by invoking the name of the President in a
direct appeal ("The President wants you and this is the key to his program") he made it difficult for a congressman to beg off. Common party
ties helped, he contended, since in most cases Democratic congressmen
started with a basic loyalty to their party and to the President as party
leader. Unless special problems arose for them in their districts, appeals
in the name of party loyalty and to support their party's leader tended to
evoke cooperative responses from such congressmen.

The White House used other congressmen, especially legislative
party leaders, to obtain or reverse votes. So, too, did it collaborate with
the Washington lobbyists from allied interest groups. It reached into the
state and local parties as well as to other influential groups and individuals in the legislators' constituencies. In the case of big-city congressmen,
the White House was not averse to asking their local party leaders to
swing them into line. The press publicized one such incident: A Roman
Catholic congressman threatened to offer a parochial school amendment
to a public school measure, thereby endangering the bill's chances. In response from an appeal by O'Brien, the legislator's district party leader
telephoned him to ask, "Who sent you there, me or the Bishop? And
who's going to keep you there, me or the Bishop?"[22] Nevertheless, when
a city congressman was himself a local leader, such as James J. Delaney
of New York, "there is no way we can keep him in line if he goes off; he's
as independent as hell in his district."

The liaison staff also appealed to state party leaders to marshal support within their delegations for the administration. During the House
Rules Committee fights of 1961 and 1963, when the White House and
the House Democratic leadership strove to ensure that they could control the decisions of that committee, calls were placed to party leaders in

[22] *Time Magazine*, September 1, 1961, p. 14. See also Richard F. Fenno, Jr., "The
House of Representatives and Federal Aid to Education," in *New Perspectives on
the House of Representatives*, ed. Robert L. Peabody and Nelson W. Polsby (Chicago: Rand McNally, 1963), p. 241, n. 10.

southern states. The 1961 contest occurred too early in the year for the new administration to generate maximum pressure from state party leaders. But for the 1963 fight the White House started working on sympathetic party leaders early in November 1962. By the time Congress convened in 1963, asserted a senior White House liaison officer with reference to one state, "there was an incredible amount of pressure from the state, generated by the state party." One Washington observer reported that, in seeking to defeat an amendment to a bill expanding unemployment compensation, O'Brien had telephoned governors whose states stood to benefit from the bill, urging them to contact their senators for their votes.[23]

As a last resort the White House would in desperation reach into the constituency of Republican congressmen as well. In the 1963 fight on the Rules Committee, the White House reported that it "got to some Republicans" by contacting their sources of contributions in their districts. "We tried to find where these lines were and we made them responsive to us on this vote." It was a tortuous path, tracing the relations between the Republicans and their financial supporters and then persuading the latter to pressure their congressmen to support the Democratic position. Knowing that the businessmen were vitally concerned with the impending tax bill, which was the top-priority White House bill for 1963, the White House lobbyists and their associates employed the following logic: "We know the Congress. If you don't let us decide strategy and handle this fight, we can lose it. If we lose on the Rules fight, we'll lose labor support for the tax cut, and thus lose the tax cut itself."

Another resource that the White House mobilized was support from business executives whose companies held contracts with the national government. On the extremely tight fight in 1962 to extend the debt limit, an important bill in itself but linked closely to the politics of the Trade Expansion Act of 1962, calls were placed by certain political officials outside the White House to defense contractors. It was indicated to them that, should the debt limit not be raised, defense contracts faced a cutback. The businessmen called their congressmen, Republican and Democratic, to express their concern. "We wanted it and needed it," stated a senior White House liaison officer. "I don't consider this undue pressure. Anyway, our position was that we had never heard of it. X [an actor placed in Defense by the White House] took the rap." Criticism for such action came entirely from the opposition party.[24]

---

[23] Helen Fuller, *Year of Trial: Kennedy's Crucial Decisions* (New York: Harcourt, Brace & World, 1962), p. 162.
[24] See *Congressional Record,* 87th Cong., 2nd sess., June 13, 1962, pp. 10408–10, 10414, 10490, for such Republican criticism. However, a few Democrats did ob-

With one group of Democratic congressmen, the White House liaison officers conceded that their muscle had not provided much leverage: the southerners, particularly in the House of Representatives, who were the Democrats most likely to defect. The Kennedy White House liaison unit recognized that there was little that could be done to force the southerners into line. Other tactics were more effective, although on the whole most southern congressmen remained impervious to the strategies and tactics of the White House.

Southern Democrats were not comparable to northern city congressmen, Wilson contended. City bosses—the kind found in Chicago, Philadelphia, and New York—simply did not exist in the South. In most southern constituencies, organized labor possessed no influence; if anything, its support was often a liability. Southern Democrats looked for financial assistance neither to labor unions nor to the national party, but to local businessmen whose national interest groups opposed the administration's program. Moreover, many southern congressmen were much more concerned with winning the nomination in their primary elections than they were with the November elections. The President could offer little or no help in the first and, as head of the ticket, he wasn't a great asset in the final election either; in contrast, his name at the head of the ticket could mean votes for many northern Democrats. There was little, therefore, that southern Democrats could gain from the administration except a smile and a pat on the head.

It was clear, however, that more than a smile and a pat were available for dealing with southerners. They too could be approached through their concern with winning government contracts for their new industries and securing nationally supported projects and laboratories for their districts. Another tactic of the White House liaison staff was to reduce the political liability at home for those asked to support administration measures. "They do not want to get stuck out in left field in their states as Kennedy men." One tactic was to persuade more senior members of southern delegations to identify with an administration measure, thereby making it easier for the others to do so. "They can then feel that they can afford to vote with us." In many cases, Wilson asserted, southern Democrats wanted to be friendly. It was a matter of discovering how they could be permitted to take advantage of their common party identification and other links with the administration without hurting themselves in their districts. Often this was merely a question of helping them conclude that

---

ject publicly to administration tactics in the Rules fight of 1961 and on an agriculture bill in 1962. See *Congressional Record,* 87th Cong., 1st sess., January 31, 1961, pp. 1515–16; February 28, 1961, pp. 2615–18; 87th Cong., 2nd sess., June 21, 1962, pp. 11342–43.

a supporting vote was politically feasible. Of course, southern Democrats could be prevailed upon to cooperate more easily on voice votes, standing or teller votes, or by providing bodies for a quorum—this participation was not publicly recorded. But even on roll-call votes, where they were committed on the record, some of them responded to "A vote this one time and we'll let you off the hook on the next one."

Additional Aspects of White House–Legislative Liaison

White House lobbyists, like their counterparts in the departments, engaged in the role of intelligence agent. The White House lobbyists covered a broader area of congressional relations and served as a center for integrating the entire executive system. Although they too tended to concentrate upon authorization legislation, they were much more actively involved in appropriation politics than were departmental liaison officers. And of course they also worked very closely with lobbyists from the interest groups that supported administration legislation. However, only the senior White House lobbyists reported that they sometimes tried to nullify the efforts of groups that opposed them by frightening off their lobbyists.

In contrast with the departmental lobbyists, the President's assistants did become engaged, on rare occasions, in altering the composition of standing committees in the Congress. Only two cases of such intervention by the executive leadership have been brought to my attention, one of which I have already mentioned. The Rules Committee fight of 1961 was initiated before the Kennedy Administration took office. A number of Cabinet officers, including the Attorney General and the Secretary of the Interior, joined O'Brien and the House Democratic leadership in a campaign to increase the Democratic majority on that committee.[25] According to O'Brien, his liaison unit became engaged only after the second head count by the House Democratic leadership showed that they would lose. The liaison unit participated much earlier and more extensively in the 1963 controversy over the Rules Committee.

The other case of intervention by President Kennedy to enlarge a committee so as to enhance the chances of his legislative program occurred in the Senate in 1963. The President's tax bill was the top-priority item that year, which explained the White House effort to expand the size

[25]For some references to their involvement see also Fuller, *op. cit.,* pp. 85–89; Robert L. Peabody, "The Enlarged Rules Committee," in *New Perspectives on the House of Representatives,* ed. Peabody and Polsby, p. 158; Milton C. Cummings, Jr., and Robert L. Peabody, "The Decision to Enlarge the Committee on Rules: An Analysis of the 1961 Vote," in *ibid.,* pp. 176, 185.

of the Committee on Finance. One of the liaison officers admitted to me that he and others in the White House unit had called upon Democratic senators for their support for such action.[26] However, the committee's membership was not increased. The White House had either failed in this tactic or abandoned it; I was never able to ascertain which.

On the whole, the President's chief lobbyist was aware of the danger of excessive executive intervention in the Congress. The White House, he maintained, did not usually become involved in determining the membership of committees. It did pass on suggestions to the party leaders and the Democrats on the Ways and Means Committee (who served as their party's "committee on committees" in the House), "but we do *not* try to run it from here." The White House had to beware of charges that executive leaders interfered unduly in the Congress: "That can weaken us terrifically." When he first undertook to lobby for the President, he had moved somewhat cautiously; he had been uncertain whether he and his staff would be accepted and whether they would have the freedom to maneuver with the Democratic leadership and the members. "I think I was always filled with a certain degree of concern, trepidation, if you will. . . . At the outset I don't know how the Speaker felt about us, but I do know that we were very, very careful not to cross that barrier that we felt existed Constitutionally."[27] He claimed that the White House had never crossed it, but they had discovered "you can talk across it."

The legislative liaison agents had only minimal contact with the Bureau of the Budget, a major staff unit to the President. The Bureau was engaged in its own relations with the Congress; it was not closely tied on a day-to-day basis with the liaison unit. According to one senior officer in the Bureau as well as the liaison agents, the latter did check with the Bureau occasionally to ascertain whether some transaction in which they were involved with legislators coincided with the program of the President. More often the senior members of the liaison unit went with their problems directly to their substantive counterparts—Theodore C. Sorensen, Meyer Feldman, Lee C. White—in the White House office. The liaison officers said that they respected the Bureau of the Budget as another source of political intelligence and as "very responsive and savvy." "We try to use them without totally using them." One criticism of the Bureau was its tendency to say that Congressman X or Y "won't give. We find that we need to knock their heads a couple of times and we're in business."

In the Kennedy Administration the Vice President apparently did not participate in the politics of advancing the administration's program in the Senate. None of the liaison officers reported that they had dealt with

---

[26] See also *Washington Post,* February 1, 1963.
[27] National Educational Television, *op. cit.,* p. 9.

him or that he was a resource—as far as important executive leaders were concerned—whom they involved in the Congress. Rowland Evans and Robert Novak contend that President Kennedy had decided to use Vice President Lyndon B. Johnson on the Hill, but that the Vice President did little to help the administration's program and seldom offered a suggestion at the weekly leadership meetings.[28]

Although this study did not extend into the administration of President Johnson, it should be noted that his vice president, Hubert H. Humphrey, was perfectly willing to lobby the Congress. An interview in 1965 with one of his assistants revealed that the President had assigned to Vice President Humphrey the movement of legislation as his major task. At this time O'Brien was still a full-time lobbyist in the White House.

The assistant to the Vice President was responsible for helping his superior advance the President's program. "I pick up and pass on information; am in constant contact with all the committee staffs; help with the nose counts." He also carried on some discussions with senators, although this was primarily Vice President Humphrey's assignment, to which he devoted three to four hours a day. The Vice President and his assistant supplemented the White House liaison unit and coordinated very closely with it, the assistant representing the Vice President at the general meetings of legislative liaison agents convened by O'Brien at the White House. It was the assistant's contention that for the departmental liaison officers the Vice President represented a much higher level of political strength than before: "They can go so far, then they have to go one level up in the Senate to the Vice President."

Vice President Humphrey continued to serve as a special liaison actor with the Congress. It was reported by the press during 1965–67 that the administration owed certain gains in the House and the Senate to the lobbying efforts of the Vice President.[29] In April 1967 the President designated Vice President Humphrey as his chief troubleshooter on Capitol Hill. No official announcement was made, but the press stated that the Vice President's role was spelled out by the President at a Cabinet meeting. Humphrey was to help map legislative strategy, persuade dissident southerners to vote for the administration, and "restore enthusiasm to discouraged Democratic liberals." Among the factors allegedly responsible for the Vice President's being handed this assignment were the difficulties O'Brien faced in continuing as the chief legislative liaison officer while serving as Postmaster General and the impending departure of Henry Hall Wilson.

[28] Evans and Novak, *op. cit.,* pp. 311, 313.
[29] *New York Times,* August 13, 1965; May 11, 1965; May 20, 1965; October 16, 1966; April 23, 1967.

BUILDING DEPARTMENTAL LIAISON INTO THE WHITE HOUSE TEAM: A SPECIAL STRATEGY

The Truman White House made no use of the departmental liaison officers. The two legislative assistants on the White House staff of President Harry S. Truman did not themselves play the major role in congressional relations for the chief executive. And according to Joseph G. Feeney, one of the President's legislative assistants, the White House did not endeavor to utilize the departmental liaison officers that existed at the time.

Alex B. Lacy, Jr., writes that General Persons, President Eisenhower's first chief lobbyist, made a careful effort to coordinate all executive legislative liaison from within the White House.[30] A member of the White House liaison staff presided over a meeting of all the departmental liaison agents every Saturday morning. On the basis of their discussion, the White House staff prepared a detailed agenda for the President's Tuesday-morning conferences with his congressional leaders. However, while the two chief lobbyists for President Dwight D. Eisenhower did use departmental personnel occasionally, their basically negative attitude toward identifying the White House with the departments in the Congress precluded their building departmental liaison officers into an integrated operation in the Congress. State's Assistant Secretary for Congressional Relations during the first three years of the Eisenhower Administration claimed that initially there was no integration among the departmental agents in the Congress until he suggested it to Persons.[31] And Edward B. McCabe reports that some common White House departmental meetings were held in the early days of the administration, but that none took place during his tenure with the liaison unit in the White House during Eisenhower's second term. On occasion, departmental people were called in for conferences when their particular bills were of major consequence in the eyes of the White House: "We tended to keep a tighter rein on them then," said Bryce N. Harlow.

Both McCabe and Harlow argued that the White House should never be involved in more than one or two major issues during any one

---

[30] Lacy, *op. cit.*, p. 25.
[31] State's first Assistant Secretary for Congressional Relations in the Republican administration reported that when he had assumed his position there was no cooperation among the departments or coordination by the White House. "I'd go to the cloakroom of the House and if I heard them cussing out Secretary Benson, I'd say 'OK, it's not my boss.' " But he soon discovered that this practice of indifference to the other departments was hurting his own superior and department. "I went to Persons and said: 'We're killing each other this way.' So we started to meet every Saturday, a number of us congressional guys. State was senior and took the lead. We started to work as a team. I worked on the Hill for two weeks on a tax bill." When Secretary Dulles complained, State's lobbyist answered: "I work for Secretary Humphrey these two weeks. Wait, next time he'll work for us."

year and that the departments should carry the rest of the legislation on their own in the Congress. Their primary rationale was that overinvolvement in legislative campaigns would weaken the White House in the Congress. McCabe quoted General Persons, the first chief lobbyist for Eisenhower, on this point: "Each department sees its own legislation as looming large in importance, and it wants to go to the White House for support. But if you fire a rifle often enough, you make a smooth bore out of it." The White House, observed McCabe, was a center of tremendous power and influence. "Trot it out too often and many people get to the point where they don't know what is important." This was what had occurred with the Kennedy Administration, he charged; so many proposals had come from the White House with a priority rating that the label "crucial" or "important" had lost its meaning; the really important items did not stand out from the others. Interestingly enough, the same criticism was raised by two Democratic liaison agents at the department level.

Departments tended to push their bills up to the White House for its support, McCabe maintained. This the White House had to resist. The departments should only "surface the White House" on the most important items. Moreover, he claimed, White House relations with the Congress would be impaired if the departments involved the White House in lost causes. Departments should invoke White House intervention only when their bills stood a good chance of winning. This, too, had its disadvantages as a strategy, he conceded, but it was his firm conviction that the White House should intervene only sparingly in the Congress.

The Kennedy White House disagreed with this policy and developed a pattern of close relations with the departments.[32] O'Brien's thesis was that the White House and departments were integral elements of a common effort—a Kennedy team proposing and supporting a Kennedy program. "Our entire approach from the beginning, regardless of department or bill, was that this was a Kennedy program." To accomplish this purpose the White House had to unify departmental activity in the Congress and centralize intelligence, resources, and efforts.

In part this too was a matter of style. "My background is in political organization," explained O'Brien, "and how to utilize the potential of other political figures." In part the team concept was determined by the need to maximize the resources of the executive system in view of the ambitious legislative program that the President proposed and which he wanted identified—in the eyes of the Congress and the country at large—with the image of the Kennedy Administration.

---

[32] Most of what follows is based upon interviews for this study, but some of O'Brien's comments on the team concept may be found in National Education Television, *op. cit.,* pp. 4–6. The *New York Times,* July 12, 1965, carried a story on the NET program.

On one level the team concept was developed with the heads of the departments themselves. "The Secretary of Agriculture had better be involved in the tax bill and vice versa," O'Brien said. Kennedy's chief lobbyist attended Cabinet meetings and made certain that he restated this point from time to time to the heads of the departments.[33] Unifying the Cabinet behind the major legislation that each department sponsored was a major advance for the Kennedy Administration, considering the traditional indifference and rivalry found among Cabinet members in the past.[34]

O'Brien also established close relationships with the secretaries' legislative liaison officers. Utilizing the resources of these departmental actors, the White House unit prepared for the President a weekly assessment of the status of the legislative program in the Congress. Each week the departmental liaison officers forwarded to the White House a report of their activities in the Congress and projections of what they expected for the coming week. A review of a number of these reports and discussions with Desautels, whose job it was to collate and integrate the material, revealed that they covered a range of items. One report, for example, indicated what the department was proposing and how it anticipated members of the opposition party would respond. Another, from Treasury, on expanding the debt limit, contained an intelligence assessment with data on the number of legislators considered to be doubtful, approving, and disapproving. One from Agriculture spelled out the latest developments on the feed-grain bill of 1963 and urged that the President take certain action in its behalf.

Some liaison officers were said to be more successful than others in keeping the White House fully advised on developments. Desautels judged the reports to be reliable, but tending to be more accurate when bills were in the committee stage. Thereafter the situation became so fluid, and so many congressional actors were involved, that departmental officers en-

---

[33] Kennedy's Cabinet members played a very active role in behalf of administration legislation sponsored by other departments. Nevertheless, some subcabinet leaders were careful in affording aid to such bills. An interview with a Secretary of the Army in the Kennedy Administration revealed a disposition to help the top political leadership with its legislative problems, but not to the point of endangering the Army's long-range relations with the Congress. The Secretary of Defense had called him to ask that his legislative liaison staff "be as helpful as we reasonably can" on a bill to expand the debt limit. The Secretary of the Army instructed his general in charge of legislative liaison to provide all the help he could to the Secretary of Defense's Assistant for Legislative Affairs, "but to play it in low key." He did not want the Army "to lose with the Congress" on any one issue outside its own jurisdiction, since "the Army will be here a long, long time." The same secretary reported that, at the request of his political superior and as a result of another White House campaign, he had called fifteen to twenty congressmen on a foreign aid bill to explain its importance to the national interest from the Army's point of view.

[34] See Richard F. Fenno, Jr., *The President's Cabinet* (Cambridge: Harvard University Press, 1949).

countered greater difficulty. On the basis of these weekly reports, the White House liaison unit prepared a working paper, incorporating its own analysis, for the President to examine the night before his Tuesday-morning conferences with the Democratic legislative leaders. His liaison unit also provided him with a prepared agenda for the meeting.

The White House liaison shop institutionalized another technique for maintaining and exploiting the team concept. Frequent conferences were scheduled in the White House at two- or three-week intervals in 1961–62 with all the liaison officers for the departments and agencies. In 1963, however, White House and departmental lobbyists reported that these conferences were not being scheduled so regularly. The President's chief lobbyist viewed these joint meetings in the White House as a means of keeping departmental personnel in touch with the problems and situations confronting important administration bills. It was a must, he was convinced, if the White House was to proceed in accordance with its team concept. Constant emphasis was placed on the fact that it was the President's program that they were supporting, that in the final analysis each department's bills were a part of a single program. Legislative problems on particular pieces of legislation were discussed and occasional head counts taken, individual liaison officers being assigned lists of congressmen to contact on behalf of the legislation. In August 1963, O'Brien reported, President Kennedy had appeared at one of these meetings, to "give a pep talk on the civil rights and tax bills." A representative from Justice had also explained several sections of the civil rights bill and had answered questions. In addition the Under Secretary of the Treasury and his liaison officer had discussed with fellow liaison officers what progress had been made on the tax bill.

A subordinate member on the White House liaison staff questioned the effectiveness of these conferences in contributing substantive knowledge on legislation to departmental personnel. Discussions on the bills were generally superficial, he concluded. But the meetings did serve a useful function in that they reinforced the team concept. He also agreed that the sessions on political intelligence were useful.

By establishing a team and maintaining close working relations with the other liaison officers in the executive system, the White House gained tremendous advantages in dealing with the Congress. The White House was not restricted to the use of its limited staff on the Hill: on major issues it was supplemented by a considerable increase in manpower. The team concept ensured that the activities of the administration would be properly channeled for maximum results. And it reduced tremendously the problems that arose when individuals moved in different directions in the Congress, with the consequent confusion in executive effort and irritation among legislators. These were among the benefits specifically attributed by O'Brien to the team concept and procedure.

He also felt that when the departments were tied closer to the White House, the resource base of the latter was expanded so that it could assume a broader service function for the Congress and could more immediately relate to individual legislators than had the Eisenhower White House. "Most congressmen do not come to us first with requests," pointed out one of O'Brien's principal assistants. "If a congressman does come, he's already been to the department; he doesn't come to us if he can get it on his own. Freshmen do, but they quickly discover they're cashing in chips with us, and they back off fast." Consequently, when White House liaison officers turned to their associates in the departments for assistance in providing services and favors, the President's lobbyists expected results. "I do not send over to get a refusal," said one of them. Otherwise, it was contended, congressmen would become "frustrated and contemptuous of our effectiveness, especially if they feel they have a legitimate request and we can't get it for them."

O'Brien and his staff maintained close contact with departmental personnel on an informal basis as well. There was a constant flow of telephone conversations, frequent meetings in the White House with specific departmental liaison officers and also with them and their superiors on particular bills, and occasional meetings with departmental liaison officers on the Hill or with lobbyists from interest groups associated with them in their legislative endeavors.

White House lobbyists expected departmental lobbyists to occupy themselves principally with their committees, while the President's own unit assumed the greater role on the floor of the Congress. Nevertheless, the White House intervened in committees and expected departmental liaison agents to help on floor action. It was evident also that the Kennedy White House lobbyists were much more tolerant of departmental requests for assistance than those in the Eisenhower White House had been. Such an attitude was consonant with the stress on a team concept. If departments cooperated on each other's legislation that had White House priority, the White House was prepared to intervene when departmental officers requested help.

"Scream when you're in trouble," was the White House policy toward departmental liaison officers, explained Wilson. He and O'Brien wanted them to come to the White House for aid before it was too late for corrective action to be taken. On the other hand, the President's lobbyists did not appreciate hearing their departmental colleagues cry wolf at every minor difficulty. The White House group was heavily engaged in the Congress; it could not enter into every fight without overtaxing its facilities and endangering its highest priorities. And, added Wilson, there were various levels of bills in the eyes of the administration; with regard to some, the administration simply did not intend to become involved. It was up to the departmental liaison officers and their superiors to see such legislation through on their own.

DEPARTMENTAL LOBBYISTS ASSESS THE WHITE HOUSE LEGISLATIVE LIAISON UNIT

To the departmental liaison officers in the Kennedy Administration, the President's liaison unit represented a welcome collaborator as well as a demanding superior in exploiting the resources of the executive system and conducting its legislative campaigns. The White House unit afforded them, moreover, an integrating center for involving the lobbyists of the other departments and agencies in behalf of their legislation. Each of these relational patterns—collaboration, superior authority, integration— posed problems for some of the departmental liaison officers.

Division of Lobbying Responsibilities[35]

In the day-to-day operation of the departments and the White House in the Congress, the dominant characteristic was a division of responsibility between the two sets of actors. Three corollary attributes of this relationship stood out: the cooperation between the two sets of lobbyists, the recognition by departmental actors that they needed to fall back upon the White House because of its greater potency in the Congress, and their awareness that the White House could assume control over a department's legislation and displace its liaison unit in the lobbying with Congress.

On many of their bills departmental liaison officers stated that they and their immediate superiors were the only executive actors involved. The White House did not participate and the departmental officers made no effort to involve the White House in the absence of any problems. And on some, the department went to the White House for only one facet of a bill. The liaison officers recognized that the White House could not afford to concern itself with minor bills. Nevertheless, a department occasionally sponsored a bill that it wished the White House would support but to which the White House refused to assign any importance.

Processing legislation through the committees was considered the primary responsibility of the departments, not the White House. "The

[35] Republican liaison officers reported a somewhat similar division within the Eisenhower Administration in terms of committee-floor assignments and the use of the White House for assistance in Congress.

White House helps in committee," a departmental lobbyist explained, "but they do not look for an opportunity to intervene." In most cases departmental officers brought White House lobbyists into committee politics only when they encountered problems. "Trouble" was the key word in their use of the White House, "plus one's sense of being part of a team proposition." Departmental lobbyists sought to carry their legislation as far as they could in dealing with members of their committees. When trouble developed and they had exhausted their possibilities for resolving the problem, the White House "expects us to call them in." On the other hand, three departmental liaison officers declared that the White House lobbyists "call themselves in," without waiting for a departmental request. If the White House was too busy or its senior officers assessed the situation differently from the departmental lobbyists, they refused to enter into committee politics despite departmental requests for assistance.

When the bill moved to the floor of the House or Senate, the White House assumed a greater degree of responsibility. "Two weeks before, they ask us, 'What have you done?' " reported a lobbyist for State, "and they start to move in." Never in a formal sense did responsibility shift; the White House simply began playing an increasingly larger role. Because there was never a definite cutoff time in the transition from departmental to White House control, he observed, some confusion and fumbling occurred among the liaison officers.[36] By the time of the vote itself, however, O'Brien and his staff had been in control for at least two or three days. According to the senior lobbyist for HEW, "At the point where we are enlisting votes on the floor, the White House is more of the coordinating agency than we are." Aside from one departmental liaison officer, whose department had no pressing legislation at the moment, and a second who feared that he might endanger his bipartisan image, the others reported that they were in constant and close relations with the White House liaison unit. The rate and intensity of their interactions rose sharply when the White House was helping them overcome a committee problem or when their legislation was scheduled for floor action. In such circumstances a liaison officer might be in contact with the White House unit— by phone or in person—up to ten times in one day.

[36] An incident during the Johnson Administration demonstrated some of the penalties accruing to departmental lobbyists by such confusion. Because of the confusion and irritation their lobbying caused, the lobbyists for Defense and AID were ordered by the majority leader to stay away from the Senate. Senator Mike Mansfield charged that those lobbyists were contacting the same senators already covered by himself or by White House aides, and thereby losing, rather than winning, votes for the AID bill. "Senators," he pointed out, "don't want to be seen again and again"; the lobbying by these departmental-agency representatives undermined his own efforts and those of the White House liaison officer (*New York Times,* September 2, 1967).

When their bills were in committee, on the way to the floor, or being debated and voted upon, departmental lobbyists engaged in a constant exchange of information with the White House unit.[37] Departmental lobbyists needed to know White House decisions on strategy, tactics, and substance. White House lobbyists needed to know what the departmental liaison officers were doing regarding their bills, any substantive changes the departments were considering, where problems were arising in the Congress. Both were interested in political intelligence about legislative actors. "The White House has been in on our legislation from the start," said a Treasury lobbyist, "so that when the moment of truth arises, there's no need to fill them in or suddenly call for help."

Recognizing that the White House was much more effective in the Congress than they, the departmental lobbyists turned to the President's lobbyists for muscle. They pointed to the prestige and influence of the President, the fact that O'Brien spoke directly for the President, the close ties between the White House and the Democratic National Committee, the linkage between the White House and state and local party leaders, and the control exercised by the White House over patronage, contracts, and projects. Explained one liaison officer:

The X committee is just not shoveable; they are too important and powerful. And yet some areas of legislation are so important for us that someone has to push them away from their convictions and make them stick to a party position. The White House can do that; we can't.

The White House was also credited with being very effective with those congressmen classified among the "maybe's" and the "anti's" on legislation.

In turn, departmental lobbyists declared that the White House insisted upon being kept informed about and exercising a close check over the special resources that departments commanded: patronage, grants or projects, defense contracts, the opening or closing of military installations, etc. "O'Brien uses them to build and keep congressional support." The liaison officers reported that the White House kept a record on every congressman which included not only his personal and political background and his voting record, but also the various contracts in his district as well as the projects asked for and those received.

[37] Every week, of course, they forwarded to the White House an assessment of their bills' standings in the Congress and an estimate of what would happen the following week. One liaison officer reported to me, however, that he felt certain information should not be put down in writing, even to the White House. Another indicated that he did not use the weekly reports to alert the White House; he felt that his material was buried there. If anything important arose, he wanted to talk immediately with a senior White House lobbyist.

On a few bills the White House departed from the usual departmental–White House division of responsibility and assumed complete charge, preempting the roles of department or agency actors. According to the lobbyist for HEW, the White House had intervened in 1961 to take a major education bill out from the control of the department. "They thought that they knew how to do it better, and anyway it was such a touchy issue." An important State Department bill was taken over in a similar fashion. Reported an aide to the Assistant Secretary for Congressional Relations: "Previously they had only asserted themselves at crucial points, not determined in advance, and generally when we ran into a tight squeeze." Both White House and State lobbyists agreed that the liaison unit for the Agency for International Development was displaced by State's Assistant Secretary for Congressional Relations at the insistence of President Kennedy in 1962. When AID encountered congressional problems, "I got a call from the President: 'What the hell's going on?' " recounted the assistant secretary. Thereafter it was he, not AID's lobbyist, who played a major role with the AID administrator in working out tactics, influencing votes, and mobilizing personnel from both agencies.

The departmental lobbyists dealt also with the substantive members of the White House staff, although not to the extent of their contacts with the liaison unit. The only one heavily involved in this manner was the Assistant Secretary for Legislation (HEW), Wilbur J. Cohen, who was responsible for developing the legislative program of his department.

Integrating the Lobbying Activities of Executive Actors

As the center of the administration's lobbying activities, the liaison unit in the White House is in a strategic position to integrate the efforts and resources of the departments behind items of high priority. In this manner any one bill becomes the concern of a number of departments, and their manpower is focused upon the politics of its passage. The department whose bill is afforded this support operates on a much broader scale in the Congress than if it had been left to itself. It is evident, however, that only the White House can undertake such an integrating function. Without its intervention, the departments tend to operate on their own, no matter how much the team concept is articulated and implemented on other legislation.

On the whole the departmental lobbyists assessed as valuable to themselves and to the administration the conferences that were convened by the President's lobbyists in the White House. Some stressed the fact that the meetings kept them up to date on what the others were doing. They could perceive the broader picture of the executive effort in the Congress, and they felt that they benefited by being alerted to problems that might possibly confront their own departments. Most of the liaison officers were pleased that a larger group was available to help them, that their colleagues were watching out for problems and opportunities affecting the legislation under consideration, and that their fellow liaison officers assumed part of the burden of canvassing the Congress as well as that of selling the legislation. In addition, liaison officers emphasized the benefit accruing to the administration from their being exposed to the overall administration program. The meetings impressed departmental personnel with the fact that there was more to the President's program than the proposals of their own departments. They realized that it was their obligation, as one of them pointed out, "to sell the whole program, not just our own," and they brought this message back to their departments. It was also asserted that the meetings afforded the departmental officers a better sense of the priorities of the President. All in all, they rated the meetings high in stimulating a sense of unity and participation in an administration team.

Two departmental lobbyists expressed some reservations. The meetings never plumbed the depths of the legislation, it was alleged; the real gut problems facing the bills were rarely analyzed. It was also claimed that departmental liaison agents were frequently too busy with their own affairs to become concerned with those of their colleagues.

A significant consequence of these meetings was the personal involvement by departmental liaison officers on behalf of legislation sponsored by other parts of the executive system. In most cases these liaison officers were asked to work with the members of committees with whom their departments traditionally conducted business. But they were also often asked to contact others in the Congress with whom they were personally acquainted. Not all the departments were urged by the White House to work on other legislation. State, for example, was exempt from campaigning for the rest of the Kennedy program. Only in the case of the Trade Expansion Act of 1962, which was a White House rather than a departmental bill and for which State had a traditional commitment, was its liaison staff involved. Defense was also not asked as much as the other departments, but its liaison officers disclosed that they and some of their superiors were asked to support bills on foreign aid and debt-limit expansion.

All the liaison officers for the domestic departments were asked to campaign for the major legislative proposals of the administration. "The White House feeling is that legislative liaison officers are working for the administration," declared a departmental lobbyist from within this group. "What's good for the administration is good for all of us. We are in such battles with both feet." These liaison officers reported that they diligently carried out their assignments on behalf of the other departments' legislation. My own limited observations as well as the assessment of those whose legislation was being supported confirmed this record of activity on the part of their fellow lobbyists. Primarily they gathered political intelligence on the leanings and intentions of legislators. In addition they were asked to explain the bills, answer questions raised by congressmen, relate the bills to the interests of the congressmen and their constituencies, and sell the legislation.

Some of them had reservations about their own effectiveness, or the effectiveness of others, in selling the legislation. "I can't sell legislation that's outside my department so well—I'm not as conversant with the details—but I can sell as hard," declared one departmental lobbyist. A few Democrats on his committee were even antagonized by his working for the bills of the other departments. But it was a price he had to pay, since he recognized the importance of the departments' cooperating with the White House in such campaigns. Another liaison agent indicated that, as a matter of principle, on bills outside her department she would request votes only from congressmen whom she knew well. Still another questioned how much aid, aside from intelligence data, his fellow liaison officers could actually provide for his legislation. "There's very little use for a liaison man to talk with a congressman regarding a bill about which the liaison agent knows very little. He is most effective in his own area of immediate concern, where he knows the legislation and the problems." A colleague who was not called upon by the White House as frequently as were the others said that he refused "to push other legislation if I feel that it'll hurt that of my department." On one occasion his secretary had admonished him to "get aboard" and become part of the team, but he had avoided identifying himself with the bill in the Congress. He was the exception to the rule, however. The others, whether they were called on frequently or only occasionally, were disposed to help the other departments when the White House organized the campaign.

In the absence of White House action, cooperation among the departments was minimal except when their self-interests were clearly interrelated. "We simply don't have the time to talk with each other," contended a liaison officer. Working on the Hill and "just keeping the pieces together here in the department" were as much as he could handle. Only if his department ran into trouble in the Congress did he ask the other liaison officers for help.

For the most part, then, unless a bill cut across their common interests, few departmental liaison officers directly sought cooperation from their colleagues in the other departments.[38] On his own volition, noted one liaison officer, he had called his counterpart in another department to place himself at the latter's service and to request a list of congressmen to contact. But this was because the bill in question affected what his own department was trying to accomplish. Another liaison officer stated that he never sought help from the other departments, although he was willing to aid them if they turned to him. At the time of his interview, he and the lobbyists from two other departments were cooperating on a bill for which one was primarily responsible. In this case the other two departments were officially committed to different provisions in the bill.

Criticism of White House Liaison by Departmental Lobbyists

The departmental legislative liaison officers were impressed with the operation of the White House unit. Almost all agreed that O'Brien ran a competent, hard-working shop. Its leading actors, especially O'Brien and Wilson, were characterized as able, sympathetic, realistic, and tough. Only one assistant to a departmental liaison officer voiced a criticism that coincided with a complaint heard in the Congress: some White House liaison agents approached the Congress with a disturbing lack of sensitivity, and behaved and expressed themselves crudely.

A heavy involvement of White House actors in the Congress was noted by all the liaison agents and served as a basis for complaints by two. These two declared that it was very difficult to contact the chief lobbyist when they needed him. As a consequence they sometimes encountered difficulties in acting effectively and with dispatch in their congressional relations. One liaison officer suggested that the White House liaison unit was too disorganized. He proposed that the chief lobbyist employ a senior deputy with his own assistants, each responsible for a number of subject areas and available in the White House for calls from departmental officers. The latter could thereby easily obtain guidance and advice on policy from individuals who would be conversant with their problems. O'Brien and Wilson were so heavily engaged on the Hill most of the time that they did not reach their telephones until the evening, when Congress was no longer in session. By this time, complained the departmental liaison agent, it was often too late to help him.

This liaison officer was the one who had insisted upon imposing tight control over his department's relations with the Congress. He was

[38] James A. Robinson reports that in 1961 the liaison officer for State did request assistance from the Postmaster General to secure congressional support for an AID bill (*Congress and Foreign Policy-Making: A Study in Influence and Initiative,* rev. ed. [Homewood, Ill.: Dorsey Press, 1967], p. 104).

also critical of the White House for failing to communicate with his department through him. "My main problem is the variety of people who try to call the shots." Some White House liaison officers were just as inclined to send their queries to others in the department as they were to him as the department's liaison officer. As a result, improper information was sometimes transmitted to the White House. He also expressed some irritation that his secretary and O'Brien failed to clear through him on common matters. The secretary had called O'Brien for advice on strategy and tactics. "Why call in the first place? I'm here. And why does O'Brien answer? He should say, 'I'll see,' and then check back with me." O'Brien had not been fully knowledgeable about the matter and as a result had offered what appeared to the liaison officer to be bad advice, compelling him to argue with his secretary about it. "I wish you people would get coordinated on whom you talk with in the department," he had told O'Brien.

Another liaison officer complained that there were too many short-notice emergencies that better planning and information could have prevented. White House spokesmen failed to consult adequately with congressmen on certain administration bills. And too large an administration program was being presented to the Congress: the White House was forcing too much, too quickly. The last criticism was concurred in by an assistant to the liaison officer in State. On the other hand, a deputy to a departmental lobbyist complained that O'Brien's approach to the Congress was too bland. It assumed that the carrot was always preferable to the stick, whereas with some congressmen only the stick would work—depriving them of patronage and diverting it to another faction in their party.

Much more serious objections were raised by two other liaison officers. One charged that the White House liaison agents had continually bypassed his secretary and himself in dealing with the Congress. "They wanted to run the whole show and I was to become an order taker and errand boy." They negotiated with congressmen on his department's bills without informing him or filling him in on what had occurred. He needed to know at least where the policy decisions were being made and what they were, and to have some voice in them. But the White House liaison unit often left him as well as his secretary out of the policy decisions. Consequently congressmen bypassed him as liaison officer, going directly to O'Brien on legislation and policy. His rapport with his own secretary was damaged as a result of the White House's undercutting and ignoring him. But according to White House liaison officers, this departmental representative had been completely ineffectual and they had maneuvered to ensure his departure.

Frederick G. Dutton, an Assistant Secretary for Congressional Relations in State, differed sharply with the White House liaison unit on strategy regarding his department. State was both too weak politically and too much disliked, he asserted, to deal effectively with the Congress. Only direct presidential intervention could help State's programs overcome these limitations. State could go only so far in working with the Congress, he said. "We can justify, but we appear to them as self-serving witnesses." The White House alone had the stature and ability to make the foreign policy program acceptable to the United States and to the Congress. The President, with his nationwide platform and his control over patronage, contracts, and other favors, was the most effective vote-getter in the Congress. Therefore he had to use his muscle and influence in domestic policy upon the area of foreign policy. Dutton reported that he could not sell this strategy to O'Brien, but that the President was interested "and sees it."

Three of the liaison officers who were critical recommended that White House–departmental relations be more tightly organized and controlled. A few of the agency and departmental liaison officers did not cooperate in the team efforts. Some "went off on their own, making commitments and taking steps that conceivably could harm our programs." In view of the fact that departments seldom kept in contact with each other except through the White House on high-priority legislation, they proposed that "the White House pull us together on the other legislation as well."

THE KENNEDY TRADE BILL:
A UNIQUE STUDY IN WHITE HOUSE
LOBBYING AND TEAM EFFORT[39]

The politics of moving the Kennedy trade bill of 1962 through the Congress represented such a sharp break with normal White House–

[39] Material for this section comes not only from interviews with the members of the White House lobbying unit but also from interviews with Thomas D. Finney, Jr., and Meyer Rashish, the two principal staff assistants to a new special assistant to the President who headed up a White House ad hoc unit on the trade bill; from Mrs. Rachel Bell of the Committee for a National Trade Policy; and from Peter T. Jones, Deputy Assistant Secretary for Trade Policy in the Department of Commerce, who also served on the interdepartmental work force set up for this bill. What follows is *not* a comprehensive study of the Trade Extension Act of 1962, but rather an examination of some of the elements involved in the relations among the regular liaison staff, the special White House unit, and the departments in their impact on the legislation. For a fine study of the politics surrounding the extension of the Reciprocal Trade Agreements Act during the Eisenhower Administration, see Raymond A. Bauer, Ithiel de Sola Pool, and Lewis A. Dexter, *American Business and Public Policy: The Politics of Foreign Trade* (New York: Atherton Press, 1963).

departmental liaison patterns as to warrant special attention. An ad hoc unit was established in the White House—distinct from the O'Brien liaison group—which assumed the traditional departmental sponsorship of an administration measure, its actors substituting in part for the roles that departmental liaison staff normally performed. It carried out as well some of the functions of the regular White House liaison unit. The latter kept a wary and suspicious eye on the new unit. The two coordinated their efforts, but the regular unit played its own special role with regard to the legislation, and in the end it displaced the ad hoc actors in the final stage of politics in the House of Representatives.

The President and his key advisers sought to integrate and involve all the resources of the White House and the departments behind an extra-special effort to secure the adoption of a controversial, innovative piece of legislation accorded the highest priority rating. For no bill that preceded or followed the trade bill of 1962 did the Kennedy Administration seek on a comparable scale to marshal the unified strength of the White House, the departments, outside groups, and public opinion. The tax bill of 1963, top-priority item for that year, approximated somewhat the efforts invested in the trade bill, but the scale of endeavor in the executive system was considerably reduced and no special unit of outside professionals was installed in the White House.

White House Control: The Ad Hoc Unit

The first and most important political aspect of the trade bill was the commitment of the President. Without his decision to grant the bill number-one priority, it is doubtful whether it would have evoked from the White House and the departments the intensive effort that was devoted to it. The second major decision was to bypass State and Commerce, which had assumed responsibility for legislation in this field in the past; none of the departments was permitted to sponsor the legislation. Instead the White House itself assumed full control from the outset.

O'Brien noted that the political consideration of the bill in the White House started with the assumption that Congress did not want State to be identified with the bill.[40] The chairman of the House Ways and Means Committee expressed grave concern to him about State's possible identification with the bill and any role that State would play in implementing its provisions. The rest of the White House liaison staff reported that State was intensely disliked in the Congress, and that the trade bill could not afford to be closely linked with this department. Senior staff members on the new special unit in the White House and

[40] See also *ibid.,* pp. 74, 447.

members of an interdepartmental coordinating group beneath the Cabinet level quickly became aware of State's poor congressional relations. According to Peter T. Jones from Commerce, who was a member of the latter group and who worked on the substantive selling of the bill in the Congress, he and Abram Chayes, legal adviser in State, were "flabbergasted at the extent of the hostility toward State on the Hill, its pervasiveness and depth." He quoted one southern senator to the effect that "what State needs more than anything else is an American desk." According to Jones, State's representatives did sit in on the executive sessions of the Ways and Means Committee, and they did deal with liberals in the Senate on the bill. "On the whole they did not have much of a selling job, as did the other departments, because as an institution they were not effective."

Organizationally the commitment of the administration to the Trade Expansion Act of 1962 was divided into a number of units, with key individuals acting as coordinating links between and among them. An ad hoc unit was organized in the White House around a new Special Assistant to the President for Foreign Trade, and a task force was established at the level of the secretaries and assistant secretaries of the departments. A working group of political staff assistants from the departments was also set up. The regular White House lobbying unit was involved, as were the regular substantive experts such as Meyer Feldman, deputy special counsel to the President. Among so many actors with diverse views and interests, conflict was inevitable on both substance and process; coordination was an absolute necessity.

In August 1961 Howard C. Petersen was appointed to the White House to serve as a special assistant to the President. Petersen was a banker and a prominent Republican leader in New Jersey. In effect, the administration had coopted a representative of the business community and of the Republican party in an effort to help nullify opposition among such groups. One element in the decision to establish the Petersen unit, according to White House sources, was an awareness that efforts to adopt even simple extensions of trade legislation had encountered great difficulty in the past. The possibility of marshaling a majority of votes in the House through the Democratic party alone was very difficult and growing more so. The Republican party in the House was strongly infected with the spirit of protectionism. Even when a Republican President had urged them to vote for such trade legislation, the majority of Republicans had stubbornly opposed it.[41]

Petersen established an organization that operated from within the White House. At its peak of activity, it employed a staff of fifteen to

[41] *Ibid.*, chap. 4, "Renewal 1954," and chap. 5, "Renewal 1955 and Since."

twenty professionals. Petersen acted as an adviser to the President and chaired the Cabinet-level task force as well as the working group that drafted a bill and prepared much of the presentation material for the Congress. He did not testify for the administration; this was the prerogative of the Cabinet members. However, he did participate in conferences with members of the Ways and Means Committee. Petersen may have been special assistant to the President on foreign trade, but he was not the sole adviser to the President in this matter. Bauer, Pool, and Dexter report that Petersen and State's Under Secretary George W. Ball had clashed in advising the President on the timing and the substance of a bill.[42] In 1961, Ball proposed that the President sponsor a major trade bill, but that it be deferred until 1963. Petersen preferred a more conservative bill, but favored immediate action in 1962.

The regular White House lobbying unit claimed that it had played a role in the President's decision to press for a major bill, but to secure its adoption in 1962. O'Brien and Wilson had disagreed with elements of both proposals: Ball's desire to delay until 1963, when the President would supposedly have stronger support in the Congress, and Petersen's plan to "go only for a simple one year's extension." The liaison officers opposed delaying until 1963 on the grounds that the odds were against the President's winning a more sympathetic Congress; Democratic strength in the House would in all probability decline. And they attacked Petersen's more limited proposal on the grounds that since the fight would be difficult anyway, "one in which we'll have to cash in a lot of our blue chips," the President might as well fight for a big bill. It is clear that major strategy differences arose at the outset and that the regular liaison staff was at odds with the others who sought to advise the President on the substance and timing of legislation as they affected congressional relations.

Petersen's unit carried on the major work in substance and intelligence. Work on the legislation itself was presided over by his deputy, Meyer Rashish. Rashish had been a staff assistant for the CNTP, the major business group favoring free trade. He had participated in the politics of the 1954 renewal of the Reciprocal Trade Agreements Act and subsequently had served as a staff member on the Ways and Means Committee, working with its Democratic chairman in the 1958 fight. Rashish and staff were responsible for helping Petersen draft a bill. They marshaled supporting data that the others in the White House and the Cabinet could employ, and they collaborated with the chairman and members of the Ways and Means Committee as well as with others off the committee on the substance of the legislation. When the bill was on the floor of the

[42] *Ibid.*, p. 74.

House, both Rashish and Petersen worked directly with the general membership of the House out of the Democratic whip's office. In the Senate, Rashish advised Senator Robert S. Kerr (D., Okla.), the floor manager for the bill, on its substantive points.[43]

An assistant to a Democratic senator was responsible for the other major functions performed by the Petersen unit: intelligence coordination and projection. Thomas D. Finney, who remained on his senator's payroll, headed a unit of five people who collated, assessed, and projected intelligence findings. Its members did not personally contact legislators. O'Brien and he had agreed that the special intelligence unit would not contact congressmen directly. What Finney and the White House feared was that too many White House actors would make the executive presence on the Hill too massive, aggressive, and conspicuous; congressmen might feel intimidated by the number of executive bodies.

Finney's intelligence unit worked from the raw data obtained by Petersen and Rashish, the departmental liaison officers, and other departmental leaders in the task force (State, Commerce, Treasury, Agriculture, Labor, and the Small Business Administration), sympathetic interest groups such as the CNTP and the CIO-AFL, and from data already accumulated in the *Congressional Quarterly*. Card files were kept on all congressmen in an effort to analyze the voting possibilities systematically. A fivefold classification was employed: for, probably for, undecided, probably against, and against. Not only did Finney's shop coordinate the data; it sought to project how the bill would be affected if certain congressmen defected as specific provisions were deleted. "Our hope was to make certain that we would not give away anything we did not need to on substance. Therefore we tried to provide a superior type of intelligence on where we stood in the Congress, and much earlier in the game than usual." They sought to substitute for the usual intuitive assessment of legislators, he asserted, a sound statistical basis for making strategic and tactical decisions.

Finney was one point of contact among the White House legislative liaison unit, the special interdepartmental working group, and the Petersen unit. He stated that he was as much a deputy to O'Brien as to Petersen; he fed intelligence data to both. A perusal of his file of memoranda shows a close contact with the O'Brien shop and with departmental liaison officers. Four memoranda will serve to indicate the nature of the

---

[43] Rashish reported that Kerr insisted he accompany the senator to the floor with him. "Any amendment that was proposed, he handed me for my opinion. If I said they hurt the bill, Kerr would fight them." According to Jones, he, Rashish, and Chayes worked closely with Senator Kerr as his advisers.

material forwarded and some of the problems encountered. One memorandum to O'Brien complained that some southern regional whips in the House were not providing the names and dates when members were contacted; they were reporting that support was mixed, or that all were for it, or that a tally showed five for and three against. The intelligence unit needed much more precise information to function effectively. A memorandum to Henry Hall Wilson informed him that an analysis of past voting records revealed a group of legislators from both parties who should be contacted "as soon as possible in an effort to head off their taking a firm position against the bill." O'Brien was also sent a detailed estimate of the support for the bill as of a specific date. And a departmental liaison officer was asked to confirm the data he had furnished on three congressmen: "You say they're pro; we feel they're anti."

The Petersen unit, contended Finney, provided additional personnel to supplement the regular White House operation. He and his associates were "able to take the load off of them" for a time, and his unit performed the function that O'Brien normally expected from a department when it "carried the ball on legislation in the early stages." With the in-depth intelligence data it had accumulated on each congressman, he claimed that his unit was able to do a better job of selling the legislation on its merits to legislators. Allied actors in the campaign, both within and outside of the government, were given specific assignments on whom to influence and on what basis. Finney and his group were also able to present an accurate estimate of the vote: "We missed by four votes in the House, and two of them were sick."

Rashish maintained that because of their ability to estimate accurately where they stood in the Congress at all times, they afforded Chairman Wilbur D. Mills of the Ways and Means Committee sufficient encouragement so that he did not follow his usual practice of compromising in advance with the senior Republican on his committee to ensure that his committee's bill would pass in the House. According to these two staff members, their operation also helped prevent panicky action and a weakening of the bill when legislative leaders became frightened a few days before the crucial votes in the House. "We fought off a lot of compromises by arguing with the administration and the House leaders till we were blue in the face," one of them said.

The departments participated in the initial policy decisions and in the drafting of the bill, and they also had a hand in working with the Ways and Means Committee. Their legislative liaison officers operated at two levels on the Kennedy Trade Expansion Act of 1962. They acted as part of the intelligence network that fed material into the White

House, and together with political associates from their departments they sought to influence the congressmen who usually acted on their legislation. One of the great advantages to this campaign over some of the others conducted by the White House–departmental team was that each department that was involved had a direct interest in the legislation, as did their major clientele groups. They could address themselves to the merits of the bill in general and to its affects on their own programs and clientele when talking with congressmen who were equally concerned with the programs of the departments and the constituents whom they served. "This is why the system worked on this bill. We used the departmental legislative liaison machinery, and they could still speak on the merits. No one was offended because the departments had a demonstrable interest in it."

Reaction to the Petersen operation in the regular White House liaison unit was mixed. The negative assessment, which predominated, ranged from annoyance and skepticism to outright condemnation and repudiation. Whether this was attributable to professional jealousy on the part of the White House regulars or whether it resulted from legitimate complaints is difficult to assess.

Finney was extremely generous in his evaluation of the O'Brien unit. It was, he said, "a major participant" in the campaign from the beginning. Its members were not a constant source of recommendation for surrender, as were other administration and congressional actors. Rather, O'Brien and his principal assistants were a considerable source of strength. "What we did was under their [O'Brien's unit] supervision, and we held periodic discussions together." Only in the later stages of the campaign did relations become strained, "primarily because tension over the bill was almost unbelievable." The Petersen unit had moved its operation to Chairman Mills's and the whip's offices, off the floor of the House, in order to supervise the count for O'Brien. Apparently this action triggered considerable resentment in the House and aroused antagonism on the part of some of O'Brien's staff.

Donahue, O'Brien's representative with the working group of interdepartmental representatives, in which Finney and Rashish participated, reported that Finney did a very good job. He was not complimentary about the rest of the Petersen operation. The Petersen group did perform well in certain areas, he conceded: collecting material for substantive presentation to the committees, "staying on top of the changes," and explaining the bill to congressmen. Since this was its primary assignment aside from the drafting of the bill itself, in which the Ways and Means Committee had a major hand, it would appear that on the whole the Petersen operation performed well in dealing with Congress on substance and in collating and assessing intelligence data.[44] Donahue's major criticism concerned two other areas that were clearly considered the special province of the regular White House lobbyists, and in which the Petersen unit apparently intruded. "They were too apt to say that they represented the President's views," he charged. And they presumed to determine strategy, an endeavor in which they were not competent.

It was the special unit's intervention in strategy and the involvement of its members in the House of Representatives before the key votes that called forth criticism from others in the O'Brien shop. In the final days before the vote in the House, contended Wilson, the staff of the Petersen unit became a decided liability for the administration. "They got underfoot, irritated the members, and the Congress began to feel that we were a lobbying outfit." Consequently they were ordered out of the politics of the floor fight and given a minor assignment.

White House Control: The Regular Liaison Unit

The assessment and actions of White House liaison officers in this campaign provide an insight into the approach of the President's lobbyists to legislative politics and a number of facets of their operations. From the point of view of the regular executive lobbyists, the success of the Trade Expansion Act was traceable in part to a number of strategic and tactical manuevers that they had devised. Interestingly enough, their strategy and tactics were not directed initially to the trade bill, but to other important pieces of legislation that they asserted were inextricably bound up in the politics of that bill.

The first problem facing the White House was making certain that the Ways and Means Committee was convinced that a bill of the magnitude desired by the President could be adopted. The background of the committee and its chairman for the past eight years, explained Wilson, predisposed them to compromise on a trade bill to pick up Republican votes as compensation for the loss of Democrats. "We tried to change them, to make the content meaner, and we argued, 'Forget the Republicans, and we will get the votes.'" This was difficult for this prestigious committee to accept, he elaborated, for it was more concerned with not being beaten on the floor than with the nature of the bill. Its prestige depended in part upon its commanding sufficient votes for its bills to win. All the Democrats were in favor of a trade bill, but the chairman was nervous as to whether the bill the committee could be persuaded to adopt

---

[44] Daley, another O'Brien aide who was also critical of the Petersen unit, complimented them on their education program in the Congress and for "improving the atmosphere" within which the bill was considered.

could pass the House. "We had a job to convince Mills that we could win."

In terms of this strategy, the White House liaison staff judged the tax bill of 1962, for which the same committee was responsible, to be crucial to the trade bill. On every contest on the bill, the administration won with no Republican votes and with minimum Democratic defection. The recommittal motion, which dealt with an extremely controversial withholding provision, was defeated by the administration, again with no Republican support. And on the final vote, only one Republican joined with the Democratic majority. "This sold the Ways and Means Committee that we could win."

It was still necessary, asserted Wilson, to demonstrate conclusively that the Republican–southern Democratic coalition, led by Rules Committee Chairman Howard W. Smith and Republican Floor Leader Charles A. Halleck, could be defeated. "Until the spring of 1962 the feeling prevailed in the House—a justified one—that Smith and Halleck had disciplined lines of communication and could move the votes, and that our side was disorganized and disunited." The Ways and Means Committee, which had already reported out the trade bill, also reported a bill to extend the debt limit. Two days before the latter bill went to the floor, the White House staff learned that Halleck and Smith had combined behind a recommittal motion to cut the permissible limit. This would have been a crushing administration defeat and the White House feared its effect upon the trade bill. "We fought—we had to win—and we got rough, but on the recommittal motion we obtained an almost unanimous Democratic vote."[45]

The key conflicts on the trade bill itself in the House of Representatives centered on the rule for the bill and the recommittal motion. In both, the White House liaison staff had to fight aggressively to block Halleck from so structuring the manner in which the House considered the bill that the opposition could split apart the coalition supporting it. Traditionally but not invariably, bills coming from the Ways and Means Committee, and especially trade bills, are granted a closed rule by the Committee on Rules. This prevents any amendments from the floor and permits only a recommittal motion to return the bill to its original com-

---

[45] Roughness involved, among other things, stimulating defense contractors to call their congressmen—Republicans as well as Democrats—to urge support for the debt-limit bill. Post Office representatives also lobbied members for the bill. "We were trying to exert pressure," reported another senior White House lobbyist. "The President would have expected this, and he would have been more angry if we had not done what we did and lost the fight." That there was resentment engendered among House members by tactics employed was conceded by the White House; the stakes were too high, however, to forgo any chance of winning.

mittee before the final vote. It is the recommittal motion that is critical. If it is defeated, the opposition leaders generally do not insist that their members vote as a unit, and many congressmen who vote for recommittal join those supporting the bill.

The Ways and Means Committee had bitterly contested the adoption of a provision in the trade bill for adjustment assistance to employees whose economic security might be impaired by increased competition from abroad. Labor unions had insisted upon this protection as their price for support; otherwise, they had warned the administration, they would fight to kill the bill.[46] The provision had narrowly escaped defeat in committee, being adopted 13 to 12. The Republican floor leader sought a modified rule from the Rules Committee, one that permitted one or two amendments so that an attempt could be made to kill the adjustment assistance feature. Such an amendment would have evoked the support of both southern Democrats and Republicans.

It was necessary, however, for Halleck to build bipartisan support for his rule: to persuade Democrats from the Ways and Means Committee who had voted against the provision to appear before the Rules Committee in behalf of a modified rule. Chairman Mills and Wilson agreed that these Democrats had to be persuaded not to appear and speak for the motion. As Wilson recalled:

We succeeded. Of course, you can't twist the arms of people like that—they're too important and independent. What we stressed was the importance of a closed rule to the trade bill itself, which they favored, although they were prepared to vote to strike the adjustment assistance feature. We couldn't have won if the Rules Committee had given a modified rule.

The White House staff also decided upon the tactic of allowing Halleck to think that he might prevail in the Rules Committee so that he would not devote himself to perfecting strategy on the recommittal motion itself. One Democrat on the Rules Committee who was wavering was "persuaded to go along with us, but to give the impression he would vote against us." In the end the committee voted 8 to 7 in favor of a closed rule. The White House had not only blocked the Republican leader, but cramped his schedule so that he no longer had the time to obtain the type of recommittal motion he wanted.

The precedents of the House now reduced even further Halleck's room for maneuver. A recommittal motion, by House practice, is drafted by the ranking minority member of the committee from which the bill originates. If he declines, the prerogative moves to the next senior minority member. In 1962 the senior Republican on Ways and Means was

[46] This point was confirmed in interviews with lobbyists from the AFL-CIO.

Noah M. Mason (Illinois), a traditional protectionist. "We were aware," Wilson reported, "that Halleck was having trouble with Mason, whose impulse was to prepare a simple recommittal or one extending the law for one year, without additional authority for the President to cut tariffs." A motion to recommit with instructions to kill the adjustment assistance feature would have unified the Republicans and divided the Democrats. Halleck, who had depended upon obtaining a modified rule for pulling the Democrats apart, had delayed too long. So short was the interval between the meeting of the Rules Committee and that of the Republican Policy Committee, which considered the issue, that he did not have sufficient time to generate support in his own party to head off Mason's recommittal motion.

On Mason's recommittal motion for a simple one-year extension of the law and no additional authority for the President, forty-four Republicans voted against their leadership and with the administration. Of this number, thirteen to sixteen were fully committed in advance to the bill. The balance, Wilson pointed out, "were never firm; they were prepared to leave us if we did not have enough Democratic votes." With its small number of committed Republican votes, the administration needed a minimum of 203 to 206 Democratic votes to reach 219 (the absolute majority in the House, there being 437 members at the time). Two hundred and ten Democrats opposed the motion. Had the Democratic vote been lower, down to 195 to 200, "we'd have lost on the recommittal; they would have scaled off the Republicans." Not until a few hours before the debate had the Republican leaders permitted their own members a free vote on recommittal; and only, contended Wilson, because it was evident that a sufficient number of Democrats would support the administration.

The forgoing analysis by the senior White House lobbyist for the House of Representatives indicates the strategy and tactics adopted by the regular liaison unit in the politics of this bill. Other factors also entered into the success of the bill. According to Bauer, Pool, and Dexter, there were major forces at work outside the Congress that affected the thinking of business, labor, agriculture, and politicians alike in favor of the bill.[47] The threat of the new European Common Market and the splitting of the traditional protectionist part of the business community, particularly the administration's winning over of the textile industry, with its pipelines into the ranks of southern Democrats, helped deliver many votes.

Bauer, Pool, and Dexter claim that "many congressmen, including Democrats, so resented the unusual intrusiveness of the Kennedy Admin-

[47] See Bauer, Pool, and Dexter, *op. cit.,* p. 427.

istration's tactics that they would have preferred to vote the President down."[48] Certainly the administration was massively committed to the bill in the Congress. The White House lobbyists admitted that they played a rough game on some of the legislation linked to the bill's success. It is also true, as Bauer, Pool, and Dexter point out, that on some other bills that year the administration was not so successful. Whether the same degree of strength could have been concentrated upon these other measures is questionable: the White House had exhausted its blue chips with many congressmen. The administration's top-priority item, a major advance in reciprocal trade agreements legislation, passed, however, and those involved did help ward off serious threats to its enactment. According to the White House liaison staff, the bill would have been decisively cut up but for their own efforts and those of their allies, regardless of the fear of the European Common Market or the substantive compromises made at the highest political level with certain industries. Moreover, in 1963, when I interviewed congressmen, and when the administration was still encountering difficulties with its legislative program, few congressmen expressed any resentment concerning the extent or type of White House lobbying for the Trade Expansion Act of 1962.

[48] *Ibid.*, p. 422.

CHAPTER X

Concluding Remarks

THIS STUDY has focused primarily on individual actors—liaison agents—as they related to two systems that must interact. It is in order now to shift emphasis, to consider the research in the broader context of executive leadership, lobbying, political parties, and policy outputs in the national government.

STRENGTHENING EXECUTIVE LEADERSHIP IN THE CONGRESS

It is clear that the organization and upgrading of special legislative liaison units represents a significant strengthening of the political executive in its relations with the Congress. In contrast to the deficiencies of this political leadership as late as the 1940s and early 1950s, the necessary staff and the ability to mount concerted, well-organized campaigns for legislation now exist in all the departments as well as the White House.

In the departments, legislative liaison has won increasing recognition as a key element in executive leadership. Its importance to the departmental secretaries is attested to by the fact that legislative liaison has been differentiated from other dimensions of leadership, that special groups of actors have been entrusted with this singular responsibility, and that they hold positions of influence at the highest echelons of the departments. And in the White House, recent Presidents have consistently relied upon legislative liaison agents so that they comprise today a vital unit in the President's personal staff.

Executive leadership is not merely a function of the policies, actions, and personality of the departmental secretary or the President. Those endowed with authority and responsible for leadership must have instruments for carrying out their policies. Leadership in large systems must be institutionalized at various levels if it is to prove effective. Neustadt has called attention to the fact that, while the President represents a tremendous source of power and influence, his leadership is dissipated and negated unless his decisions are carried through.[1] The same holds true for departmental secretaries.

Legislative liaison agents provide these political leaders with specialized staff, actors who are concerned almost entirely with implementing their policies; who are experienced in relationships involving bargaining, compromise, and the aggregation of votes; and who are acutely sensitive to the problems and nature of the congressional actors. By filling such roles as adviser, spokesman, coordinator, intelligence agent, lobbyist, administration team player, and service expediter, liaison officers strengthen and carry out the leadership functions of the President and the departmental heads vis-à-vis the Congress. Since, moreover, the chief leaders of the executive are freed from the burdens of day-to-day relations with the Congress and afforded a superior, reliable source of advice and information, they gain by being able to concentrate upon the policy, strategy, and difficult problems concerning congressional relations. It must be assumed that they are also freed to devote themselves to their multifaceted administrative responsibilities.

Although executive lobbyists are not principally experts on substance and are not expected to serve as policy advisers, they do contribute to the development of realistic policy proposals. Substance and process are intimately related, especially in the Congress, where power is extremely fragmented. There, executive proposals are dependent upon a number of groups of actors and must proceed through a series of steps over a period of time. By speaking up within the inner circles of the departments and the White House on the substance of legislation as it is affected by the problems of the legislative process, the peculiarities of individual congressmen, and timing, liaison officers contribute to the policy proposals of their superiors. Bills may be altered and compromises advanced or rejected as a result of their advice and activity. Because they must pay attention to internal administrative decisions that have an impact upon the constituencies of congressmen and consequently upon the attitudes and behavior of legislative actors, the liaison agents affect another type of executive policy-making.

[1] Richard E. Neustadt, *Presidential Power: The Politics of Leadership* (New York: Wiley, 1960), chap. 2, "Three Cases of Command." See also Joseph I. Coffey and Vincent P. Rock, *The Presidential Staff,* Planning Pamphlet no. 112 (Washington, D.C.: National Planning Association, 1961), pp. 76–77.

One danger is always present, of course, in allowing agents who process or sell policy to influence its nature. They may distort it by pressing too single-mindedly toward their own immediate goals of winning acceptance for the policy and keeping congressional relations from being exacerbated. Such a danger is inherent, however, in the design of all legislation, in packaging the proper mix of the desirable and the attainable. Moreover, any tendency on the part of liaison officers to overstress the practical side of winning can be resisted by other staff and senior members surrounding the executive leaders as well as by these leaders themselves.

The weakness of the Cabinet as a centripetal force in the executive system has long been recognized. Individual departments have traditionally made their own way in the Congress with little if any cooperation from the other departments or backup from the White House. To the extent that Presidents seek to shape a united administration behind policy and strategy determined at the highest political level, the liaison apparatus of the White House and of the departments are a great help. These actors have much in common so that cooperation is easy, White House and departmental resources supplement each other, and the departmental officers accept the superiority of White House priorities. The liaison apparatus contributes to the integration of the executive system in advancing its proposals to the Congress.

Effective executive leadership in shaping legislative policy is an absolute imperative for the proper functioning of the American national government. The President today has more effective means than ever before for mobilizing the leadership and resources of the executive system behind his program. How much further Presidents will proceed in this direction remains to be seen, but the structure has now been institutionalized and the practice established by which this can be accomplished.

STRENGTHENING EXECUTIVE LEADERSHIP IN RELATION TO THE BUREAUCRACY[2]

The institutionalization of legislative liaison at the top levels of the departments and the White House signifies also a greater domination by executive leaders over the bureaucracy. Ensuring that the bureaucracy acts

[2] Possible disadvantages of the emergence of legislative liaison officers for the bureaucracy, Congress, and the general public are outlined by G. Russell Pipe in "Congressional Liaison: The Executive Branch Consolidates Its Relations with Congress," *Public Administration Review,* 26 (March 1966): 14–22. Pipe suggests that the reduction of conflict within the executive system arising out of better integration from the top "may result in subsystem impotency as a counterforce to political or administrative expedience." In this he is correct, of course. He also warns that in acting as barriers to informal contacts between bureaucrats and congressmen, liaison agents may serve to suppress facts and independent judgment

under the leadership of elected and politically responsible executive actors is a major problem in the modern democratic state. Liaison officers work to ensure that career administrators do not operate independently in the Congress, pursuing interests of their own in disregard of or contrary to the goals or strategies of the political leaders. The resources that bureaucrats command are also marshaled by liaison agents for the purposes of the political leadership. And the performance of bureaucratic actors is monitored to reduce the possibilities of antagonism between members of the legislative and executive systems.

Legislative liaison agents make a clear distinction between political leaders with whom they identify and career executive actors, a distinction

---

needed by Congress and the public in order to achieve the best results in legislation. Undoubtedly, as the political leadership exerts more control over congressional relations in the executive system, the freedom of bureaucrats to play independent roles diminishes, as does the ability of legislative actors to penetrate the executive system for facts and independent judgments. Virtually all the legislative liaison agents, however, wanted their bureaucrats to interact—formally and informally—with congressmen, and a number of these executive lobbyists believed they could not possibly control all of such contacts. Moreover, congressmen are extremely sensitive to attempts by executive actors to cut off their personal access to others in the departments.

While Pipe calls attention to the need for additional research on the relations of liaison officers with executive and legislative actors, some of his conclusions unavoidably reflect the lack of data in this area. He believes that legislative liaison agents "help to kill . . . by neglect" congressionally initiated bills for improving executive efficiency and economy. Such an assumption is simply not valid. Liaison agents are not independent actors. It is not they, but their political superiors who decide which bills are to be promoted or neglected. This is too important a policy decision to be made by subordinates. When liaison agents participate in policy decisions, it is primarily as advisers to their principals on congressional relations and politics and not on the substance of policy per se.

Pipe's recommendation that liaison officers might fill the role of ombudsman, thereby nullifying the need for establishing an ombudsman as a separate arm of Congress, clashes directly with the highly political-partisan roles that such agents play. An ombudsman is supposed to be impartial, concerned solely with fairness and justice, and independent of the people he must investigate. Liaison officers fit none of these conditions. It is true that in their service-expediter role they help resolve problems that a congressman's constituents may have with their bureaucracies. But they do this solely for better congressional relations, utilizing the resources of their departments as a means of exchange with legislators. Departmental liaison officers are agents of their secretaries and they will seek to protect their political superiors and departments if political necessities demand such action. Good relations must be maintained with the bureaucracy, for the liaison agents must depend on cooperation from career actors to carry out a successful strategy of exchange with legislators. And it should be remembered that liaison officers allocate some of their services and favors on partisan grounds. One might just as well call for the liaison officers in the White House to serve as ombudsmen! On general principles it is unwise to entrust the ombudsman function to agents of any part of government that must be investigated and criticized. It is also highly unlikely that Congress would accept such a proposal.

that supports the thesis of those who suggest that the two represent different types. The interviews conducted with career administrators reinforce this conclusion. Patterns of cooperation and conflict appeared between both sets of actors in the Eisenhower and Kennedy Administrations. It is hypothesized that such patterns will continue in future administrations. Conflict should be minimal under a President and secretaries who sponsor ambitious legislative programs, since these are likely to coincide with the ambitions of the bureaucracy. Greater conflict may be expected when the executive leadership proposes extremely limited goals that it insists the bureaucracy support, and when the President and the majority of congressmen represent different parties.

The reaction of the Congress is always an uncertain and potentially dangerous restraint upon liaison officers' attempts to control bureaucrats in the interests of the departmental secretaries and the President. With regard to the Department of Defense, for example, congressmen have, through legislation as well as informal behavior, demanded that the services (bureaucrats) be free to pursue their own goals in relations with the Congress. Legislative actors insist, moreover, upon protecting their own pipelines into the bureaucracy. The instantaneous congressional reaction when State's Assistant Secretary for Congressional Relations sought to tap informal contacts between legislative and bureaucratic actors testifies to the congressional antagonisms that departmental political leaders face in attempting to maintain the boundaries of their own systems.

The close relationship that members of the House Appropriations Committee and the staffs of both Appropriations Committees maintain with special career officers in each department imposes another constraint upon the ability of the liaison officers to control the bureaucracy in its dealings with Congress. The extreme hostility of these legislative actors toward the departments' liaison officers reflects their reluctance to permit any interference in their special relations with the bureaucracy.

It is questionable, in view of the ambitions of bureaucratic actors and their support among congressmen and clientele groups, whether the political executive leadership could successfully displace bureaucrats in their special relations with the Congress, assuming it wished to do so. What is to be expected is that the liaison agents will constantly maneuver to place their superiors in the dominant position vis-à-vis the Congress and to enable them to take full advantage of ongoing bureau-congressional relations. The congressional response to these efforts needs to be studied further, as does the relationship between liaison and career actors and the means by which they solve their problems.

STRENGTHENING THE EXECUTIVE LEADERSHIP: OUTSIDE SUPPORT

The establishment of full-scale legislative liaison staffs has also strengthened the department heads by reorienting to their level the interests and activities of organized groups outside the national government. One of the principal defects in the department heads' relations with the Congress, according to Dr. John D. Millett of the 1949 Hoover Commission Task Force on Departmental Management, was the absence of any interest-group support in the Congress for the departmental position. As congressional relations within the departments have come increasingly under the control of the political head of the department, it is noteworthy that interest groups now find it to their advantage to work with and through this level of leadership. While the bureaucracy retains close ties with professional and clientele groups, political decisions of consequence that are made on programs and strategy are determined more and more at the level of the departmental secretary. To the extent that interest groups want to have a voice in departmental programs and relations with the Congress, they must address themselves to the levels where the decisions are ultimately made.

In a number of the departments the legislative liaison agent has become a focal point for rallying interest-group support for the departmental position and for marshaling the lobbying effort in which these groups can engage. And in the eyes of such groups, the liaison agent, who is one of the principal assistants to the secretary, becomes a very important channel to the secretary as well as to the rest of the department. The close relations between departmental and White House liaison units means, moreover, that the two sets of liaison agents afford interest groups extremely valuable access points for ascertaining executive decisions, for sharing in political intelligence, and for becoming involved in action patterns in the Congress. Interest groups now find it profitable to orient themselves to the departmental position in order to advance their own goals and operations in the legislative as well as the executive systems.

LOBBYISTS INSIDE AND OUTSIDE THE NATIONAL EXECUTIVE

Liaison agents for the departments and the White House may be compared to lobbyists for interest groups, public and private, that attempt to influence the policy outputs of the Congress. In many respects the two groups are similar: both represent political superiors and larger systems; both are employed to shape a favorable climate in which their leaders may interact with legislative actors; both are concerned with the legislative process and with policy output; both utilize somewhat similar stratagems and tactics.

Legislative actors consider both sets of lobbyists as representatives of groups whose interests have a legitimate right to be articulated in the legislative process. Congressmen and their staffs also perceive these lobbyists as functionally useful to themselves: service and collaboration are vital to legislative actors. Both lobbyists and legislative actors benefit, therefore, from an exchange of resources. At the same time, members of the legislature demand that lobbyists treat them with honesty and respect, and that they recognize the significance of the political situation in the legislators' constituencies and committees. Legislative actors can impose similar sanctions upon both sets of lobbyists: a withdrawal of trust and confidence and a denial of access. The legislators may also vote against their proposals and subject them to public attack. Both sets of lobbyists are keenly aware of the possibility of such sanctions, and shape their behavior accordingly.

The differences between the two sets of lobbyists and the differences in their relations with Congress are sufficient to suggest that executive lobbyists must be considered a distinct group. The two come from dissimilar backgrounds, liaison agents being much more partisan and more experienced in the Congress. In this respect the executive lobbyists are similar to the legislative actors, and the other lobbyists tend to be more like executive career administrators. Although both sets of lobbyists must also interact with executive actors, the liaison agents approach them as aides to the official leaders of the executive system, not as representatives of private groups. And, of course, as members of the official decision-making part of the executive system, the liaison agents are privy to matters not shared with lobbyists from groups outside the national government.

The relations that the two sets of lobbyists have with other actors within their own systems appear to differ markedly. Hence many of the opportunities, restraints, and problems that confront these lobbyists are dissimilar. However, these conclusions are advanced only provisionally. They need to be tested against data on liaison officers in future administrations. And before they can stand as valid, they must be supported by much more research than has yet been done on lobbyists for the private as well as public groups that seek to influence the decisions of the national government.

Liaison agents must cope with two sets of actors from within their own system—their political superiors and the bureaucrats whose attitudes and behavior have an important effect upon congressional relations. Congressmen are interested in and seek contacts with both sets of executive actors. Although this complicates tremendously the task of the executive lobbyists, it also affords them distinct advantages in dealing with the legislative system.

While the available research is meager and deals primarily with business groups and their lobbyists, it indicates that businessmen are more concerned with their businesses than with the politics of influencing government. They are involved only sporadically (and sometimes not at all) in trying to influence the Congress, and on the whole they find such politics distasteful. There is evidence, again scanty, that these leaders are somewhat contemptuous of the agents who lobby for them, and that the latter reciprocate this attitude. In other words, the close and cooperative relations that exist between most of the liaison officers and their superiors, their common recognition of the importance of dealing politically with the Congress (again with some exceptions), and the high degree of involvement of senior political executive actors in the Congress do not characterize the relations between the leaders of business and their lobbyists.

Secondly, the bureaucracy in the executive system at times constitutes a handicap for the legislative liaison officers with which other lobbyists, in all probability, do not have to contend. But this, too, calls for additional research. There has been virtually nothing published in this area. From what is known about institutional relations between subunits and their larger associations in agriculture, labor, and business, it is clear that the two differ often in their goals and politics. However, these associations are composed of more or less independent entities that may legitimately express their own self-interests politically, even if they diverge completely from those of their associations. The larger associations may be said to exist for their welfare and tend to be dependent upon the subunits for membership, funds, and support. These subunits are not bureaus, nor can they accurately be compared with them. Although bureaus and agencies—and even the service departments within Defense—have interests of their own, they are *supposed to subordinate themselves* to the broader general interest as defined by politically responsible leaders of the executive system. And of course they are not free to withdraw organically from the departments.

With regard to relations with Congress, the two sets of lobbyists differ on at least three major points. Congress specifically prohibits executive lobbying; it imposes only perfunctory regulations on lobbying by groups outside the boundaries of the national executive and legislative systems. True, the antilobbying law is honored only in the breach, and no prosecution of liaison officers has occurred or even appears likely as long as the leaders in one executive department, Justice, are responsible for prosecuting the leaders of other executive departments. Nevertheless, the liaison agents do feel somewhat inhibited in approaching Congress. Their counterparts in the outside interest groups may inundate Congress with their assistants, their allies, and their constituents; they may wine and dine the legislators. Executive lobbyists cannot directly employ such tactics. They recognize that Congress is jealous of its prerogatives as an independent and equal partner of the executive in the national government. Executive lobbyists are aware that the appearance in Congress of too many actors from their system is a source of irritation and resentment among legislators. The threshold of tolerance for executive intervention in the legislative process is much lower in this respect than for lobbyists representing outside groups. Nor do congressmen look favorably upon a massive lobbying effort by bureaucrats, whether they come from the capital or from the constituencies. On the other hand, constituents mobilized by outside interest groups are considered to be citizens and voters whom the legislators represent; the legitimacy of their appearance is unquestioned.

On another level, legislative liaison agents possess a tremendous advantage over the lobbyists for outside groups. As official members of the executive and representatives of its leaders, executive lobbyists, or their superiors or bureaucrats, are often permitted entrée into the executive sessions of the committees that work on legislation. Affording such access to private lobbyists is considered unethical and rarely occurs. Hence the liaison officers are in better position vis-à-vis the most important decision-making centers of the Congress to observe, obtain information, work out accommodations, and speak for their principals while a bill is still in the process of being shaped by the legislators.

Executive lobbyists and those from outside the national government differ also in their emphasis on and identification with partisanship. Since political party is treated separately, all that needs to be noted here is that outside lobbyists avoid partisan positions and identification. They want to work with all members regardless of party, and they represent groups that with one or two exceptions avoid an official identification with the campaigns or candidates of any of the political parties. These groups have members from both major parties. State and Defense are the departments that most closely approximate the nonpartisan approach of the other interest groups and lobbyists. Both of these departments seek bipartisan support and avoid playing partisan politics in committee. Nevertheless, some of the senior political leaders of Defense in the Kennedy Administration were utilized on partisan issues, and the tremendous resources of Defense were marshaled by White House lobbyists in support of their partisan politics.

POLITICAL PARTY AND THE
SEPARATION OF POWERS

Leon P. Epstein has pointed to the separation of powers in the American national government as "the crucial circumstance" in explaining noncohesive congressional parties.[3] The separation of executive and legislative actors into distinct systems also divides each of our major national political parties into two congressional parties, and it fragments one national party further by establishing in it an executive party. Assuming the Congress and the presidency are controlled by members from the same national party, the latter is composed of three different organizations with separate sets of leaders and intelligence apparatuses. Moreover, the separation of powers imposes a great strain upon cooperation between leaders and members of the legislative parties and the executive leaders of the same national party.

The President, as the official national leader of his party, is able to call upon his partisan legislative leaders for collaboration, a relationship functionally useful for both.[4] He can also depend, to a large extent, upon ties of common party identification and a sense of obligation on the part of congressional leaders from his party to support him as the head of their party. To a lesser extent the rank and file among his fellow partisans in the Congress also feel the tug of common party ties.

It is necessary to perceive the legislative liaison agents for the President and for the secretaries of his departments as additional links between executive and legislative partisans. Hence, at another level of executive-legislative relations, linkages between partisans are strengthened and institutionalized. In effect, therefore, the new executive lobbyists help ameliorate the divisive impact of the separation of powers upon a political party, and their partisan identification with congressional leaders and their followers facilitates executive involvement in the legislative system.

Congressmen from both national parties consider lobbying by the President and his representatives legitimate. Legislators recognize that executive intervention and leadership are necessary for themselves as well as for the chief executive and his associates. Nevertheless, partisanship on the part of executive lobbyists can be either dysfunctional or functional, depending upon whether both systems are controlled by actors from the same national party or whether one party dominates the

[3] Leon P. Epstein, "Political Parties in Western Democratic Systems," in *Essays in Political Science,* ed. Edward H. Buehrig (Bloomington: Indiana University Press, 1966), p. 114.
[4] For a perceptive analysis of this relationship see David B. Truman, *The Congressional Party: A Case Study* (New York: Wiley, 1959), pp. 289–308.

293

executive but not the Congress. In the latter case, liaison agents are handicapped, since they are identified by the leaders of the congressional majority party as representatives of the head of the opposite party and his colleagues. This does not mean that cooperation is impossible, but it does mean that the degree of entrée is restricted, a trust-confidence relationship is not fully developed, and collaborative endeavors are reduced to a minimum. While liaison agents in the White House and the departments (always with a few exceptions) feel closer to the members and leaders of their parties in the Congress, when the latter are in the minority they do not control the scheduling of legislation and they do not occupy the official leadership positions in the committees. Moreover, there is some evidence from the Eisenhower Administration, whose actors faced such a situation for six years, that with different parties in control of the Congress and the executive, the liaison agents felt more restrained in lobbying the Congress.

Criticism of executive lobbying emanates almost entirely from legislators whose party does not control the White House. When such members make up a majority in the Congress and control the Speaker, the majority leaders, and the committees, the dangers inherent in such criticism loom very large for the executive lobbyists. They need cooperation from the leaders of the majority party and a congenial atmosphere in which to deflect investigations and attacks. If it is the minority members who publicly complain about lobbying by executive actors whose administration their party does not control, the liaison agents may be temporarily embarrassed, but little else. The force of such accusations tends to be blurred by the fact that they come from members of the opposite party; legislators identified with the executive party tend to discount such charges as part of the normal course of partisan politics.

On the whole, legislative liaison agents in the White House and the departments have a strong background of political party activity and identification, as do legislative actors. The heads of the departments, unlike the official heads of private interest groups, either are experienced party leaders in their own right or are identified with the partisan administration of the President, who is the chief leader of his party in the nation. When their executive lobbyists approach the Speaker, the majority leaders, the whips, and the committee chairmen from the same party, they are contacting fellow partisans who share their attitudes and expectations. The legislative party leaders have already participated with the President in his weekly leadership meetings, at which program, strategy, and tactics are discussed.

The legislative liaison actors cooperate with these legislative leaders on strategy and tactics. The offices of the legislative leaders from their

party are made available to executive lobbyists for more immediate lobbying with members before votes are taken, and the two intelligence networks mesh into each other freely, for both represent common leaders
and both are actors in the same national party. In the case of the liaison
unit in the Kennedy White House, efforts were also made to utilize state
and local party leaders in lining up support for the President's legislation
among fellow partisans in the Congress.

ADDITIONAL ASPECTS OF THE FUNCTIONAL UTILITY OF LIAISON AGENTS FOR THE DEMOCRATIC SYSTEM

In an essay on the future of legislative systems, David B. Truman
raises the question whether, in the shift of legislation as a function away
from national legislative bodies to bureaucracies, something essential to
a system based upon universal suffrage may not be jeopardized.[5] He
suggests that administrators may be engaged in a different kind of political activity than are elected politicians, that the roles, skills, attitudes,
and perceptions of the two may be dissimilar. The contribution of the
elected politician to policy-making, assessing the proposals of substantive experts and reconciling them "with the feasibility that exists or can
be created in the electorate," may be lost to the system. "It is the primacy
of aggregate politics and its functionality for the system that may be at
stake."

The better the staff that the political leadership of the executive
system has at its disposal to direct bureaucratic actors on behalf of its
goals and priorities, the smaller the likelihood that the skills, attitudes,
and perceptions of elected politicians will be separated from the legislative function. The President himself is an elected politician, whose
elevation to and continuance in office is premised upon his success in
aggregate politics within the national electorate. His immediate staff
and his associate leaders, who preside over the bureaucracies in each of
the departments, are in many cases former elected politicians themselves
or have been actively engaged in the winning of nominations and elections for others. The legislative liaison officers in the White House and the
departments during the Kennedy Administration and many in the Eisenhower Administration represented this type of political actor. They
helped sensitize their leaders to the needs of the elected politician in the
legislature and they shared in mobilizing legislative majorities behind
executive bills. They recognized, moreover, the problems of aggregate
politics facing the President, both in marshaling public opinion behind

[5] David B. Truman, "The Representative Function in Western Systems," in *Essays
in Political Science,* ed. Buehrig, pp. 88–92.

his program and in assessing possibilities for the next election campaign.

While the legislative function may be shifting to the executive, it has not moved entirely to bureaucratic actors. The bureaucracy continues to be a source for many executive proposals to the Congress, but the goals and strategies are primarily those of the chief executive, his advisers, and his subleaders. Members of the White House staff think in the terms of the elected politician, and so do many Cabinet members and their assistants. As one group of assistants to the President and the secretaries of the departments, the liaison agents strengthen the number and influence of actors who are more similar to elected politicians in background and attitudes than to bureaucrats.

Political science must be concerned with the important question "Does it make any difference who governs?" Different ends are pursued and different groups represented when disparate groups of leaders contribute to the making of policy. By strengthening the senior political leadership of the executive system vis-à-vis both the Congress and the bureaucracy, the executive lobbyists contribute to a more unified central party. Thus they afford those groups—latent and organized—who associate their interests with the policy ends of the President and his leadership advantageous positions regarding policy. In other words, different groups are advantaged in the decision-making process of the national government and in its allocation of resources as a result of the strengthening of the President and his political associates.

Not only do the liaison officers deal directly in many cases with lobbyists from outside groups, but outside lobbyists seek them out as a point of access to the chiefs of the executive system and for collaborative endeavors in the Congress. The legislative liaison agents help also in reconciling the more parochial interests of the legislators and the narrow professionalism or clientele interests of the bureaucratic actors with the broader, more general set of interests represented by the elected leader of the executive system and his chief associates.

NAME INDEX

Adams, Sherman, 16, 232n, 234, 235
Acheson, Dean, 164n
Akin, Jim G., 90, 94, 99, 174n
Anderson, Jack Z., 237
Appleby, Paul H., 5n

Ball, George W., 275
Barr, Joseph W., 90, 94, 98
Bauer, Raymond A., 47n, 64n, 103n, 146n, 171, 176n, 205, 212, 213, 272n, 275, 282–83
Bell, Rachel, 272n
Benson, Ezra T., 259n
Bernstein, Marver H., 31, 122n, 124n
Binkley, Wilfred E., 5n
Birkhead, Kenneth M., viii, 90, 94, 98
Bolling, Richard, viii, 244
Buchanan, William, 47n, 146n
Buehrig, Edward H., 293n, 295n
Byrnes, John W., 65n

Carson, Rachel, 132
Celebrezze, Anthony J., 62, 175
Chamberlain, Lawrence H., 5n
Chayes, Abram, 274
Chesney, Earle D., 237, 238
Clapp, Charles L., 56
Clifford, Clark M., 10, 233, 234
Coffey, Joseph I., 285n
Cohen, Wilbur J., viii, 89, 90, 94, 99, 100n, 267
Corson, John J., ix, 122n
Corwin, Edward C., 5n
Cotton, Norris, 63n
Cummings, Milton C., Jr., 256n

Daly, Charles U., 40n, 231n, 236, 239, 250, 279n
Delaney, James J., 253
Desautels, Claude, 40n, 231n, 238–39, 261–62
Dexter, Lewis A., ix, 47, 64n, 103n, 146n, 171, 176n, 205n, 212, 213, 272n, 275, 282–83
Dirksen, Everett M., 242
Dodd, Thomas J., 68
Doig, Jameson W., 30n, 86, 91n, 92, 122n
Donahue, Richard K., 40n, 231n, 236, 238, 239, 243, 244, 250, 252, 278–79
Dulles, John Foster, 59, 87n, 106, 115, 259n
Dutton, Frederick G., 21, 68–70, 86–87, 89, 90, 94, 98, 141–43, 168n, 169, 178n, 217–18, 272

Egger, Rowland, 43
Eisenhower, Dwight D., 15–16, 59, 64, 139, 231–32, 234, 235, 236, 240, 244–45, 246, 259–60
Elliott, Carl, 244
Epstein, Leon P., 293
Eulau, Heinz, 47n, 146n
Evans, Rowland, 190n, 237n, 258

Feeney, Joseph G., 231n, 236, 259
Feldman, Meyer, 231, 257, 274
Fenno, Richard F., Jr., ix, 59, 71, 75n, 147n, 222n, 253n, 261n
Ferguson, LeRoy C., 47n, 146n
Finney, Thomas D., Jr., 272n, 276–78
Fowler, Henry H., 19

SUBJECT INDEX

Index

Treasury, Department of—*Cont.*
secretary, 61, 88
undersecretary, 19, 22n, 115, 262
Tax Bill of 1962, 203, 280
Trade Expansion Bill of 1962, 69, 108, 171, 254, 268, 272–83
Truman Administration, 7, 10, 18n, 133
liaison agents (department), vii, 216–17, 259
liaison agents (White House), 10, 15, 28, 230–34, 236, 244, 259
President (*see* Truman, Harry S in Name Index)

U.S. Chamber of Commerce, 220

Veterans' Bureau, 2
Vice President, 196, 225, 245, 257–58

War Production Board, 9
Washington Lobbyists (*see* Lobbyists, nonexecutive)
Water Pollution Act of 1956, 126
White House liaison unit (*see* Legislative Liaison Agents, White House and Department; also the different administrations)

Printed In U.S.A.